Medical Neuropsychology

The Impact of Disease on Behavior

Critical Issues in Neuropsychology

Series Editors:

Cecil R. Reynolds
Texas A&M University

Antonio E. Puente
University of North Carolina, Wilmington

Editorial Advisory Board:

Erin Bigler, *University of Texas, Austin*
Raymond S. Dean, *Ball State University*
Hans J. Eysenck, *University of London*
Charles J. Golden, *Drexel University*
John Gruzelier, *University of London*
Lawrence C. Hartlage, *Fairfax University*
Merril Hiscock, *University of Saskatchewan*
Lawrence Majovski, *Huntington Memorial Hospital*
Francis J. Pirozzolo, *Baylor University School of Medicine*
Karl Pribram, *Stanford University*

MEDICAL NEUROPSYCHOLOGY: The Impact of Disease on Behavior
Edited by Ralph E. Tarter, David H. Van Thiel, and Kathleen L. Edwards

Forthcoming:

ASSESSMENT ISSUES IN CHILD NEUROPSYCHOLOGY
Edited by Michael G. Tramontana and Stephen R. Hooper

HANDBOOK OF CLINICAL CHILD NEUROPSYCHOLOGY
Edited by Cecil R. Reynolds and Elaine Fletcher-Janzen

A Continuation Order Plan is available for this series. A continuation order will bring delivery of each new volume immediately upon publication. Volumes are billed only upon actual shipment. For further information please contact the publisher.

Medical Neuropsychology

The Impact of Disease on Behavior

Edited by

RALPH E. TARTER
DAVID H. VAN THIEL and
KATHLEEN L. EDWARDS

University of Pittsburgh
Pittsburgh, Pennsylvania

PLENUM PRESS · NEW YORK AND LONDON

Library of Congress Cataloging in Publication Data

Medical neuropsychology: the impact of disease on behavior / edited by Ralph E.
Tarter, David H. Van Thiel, and Kathleen L. Edwards.
    p.   cm.—(Critical issues in neuropsychology)
    Includes bibliographies and index.
    ISBN 0-306-42741-9
    1. Psychological manifestations of general diseases. 2. Clinical neuropsychology. 3.
Neuropsychological tests. I. Tarter, Ralph E. II. Van Thiel, David H. III. Edwards,
Kathleen Lou. IV. Series. [DNLM: 1. Behavior. 2. Disease. 3. Neuropsychology. WL
103 M489]
RC455.4.B5M44   1988
616.8—dc19   87-36138
                                                                            CIP

© 1988 Plenum Press, New York
A Division of Plenum Publishing Corporation
233 Spring Street, New York, N.Y. 10013

Printed in the United States of America

Contributors

BILL E. BECKWITH, Department of Psychology, University of North Dakota, Grand Forks, North Dakota

RICHARD A. BERG, Department of Behavioral Medicine and Psychiatry, West Virginia University Medical Center, Charleston, West Virginia

KATHLEEN L. EDWARDS, Department of Psychiatry, University of Pittsburgh School of Medicine, and Western Psychiatric Institute & Clinic, Pittsburgh, Pennsylvania

BRENDA ESKENAZI, School of Public Health, University of California at Berkeley, Berkeley, California

DIANA H. FISHBEIN, Addiction Research Center, National Institute on Drug Abuse, and the University of Baltimore, Baltimore, Maryland

HAROLD W. GORDON, Department of Psychiatry, University of Pittsburgh School of Medicine, and Western Psychiatric Institute & Clinic, Pittsburgh, Pennsylvania

ROBERT P. HART, Departments of Psychiatry and Neurology, and Division of Neurological Surgery, Medical College of Virginia, Virginia Commonwealth University, Richmond, Virginia

JEFFREY S. KREUTZER, Departments of Rehabilitation Medicine and Psychiatry, Medical College of Virginia, Virginia Commonwealth University, Richmond, Virginia

PETER A. LEE, Department of Pediatrics, University of Pittsburgh School of Medicine, and Children's Hospital of Pittsburgh, Pittsburgh, Pennsylvania

MICHAEL L. LESTER, Children's Medical Center, Department of Pediatrics, Tulsa, Oklahoma

DAVID C. LEVIN, Pulmonary Disease & Critical Care Section, Oklahoma University Health Sciences Center and Oklahoma City VA Medical Center, Oklahoma City, Oklahoma

NEIL A. MAIZLISH, California Occupational Health Program, California Department of Health Services, Berkeley, California

GEORGE P. PRIGATANO, Department of Neuropsychology, Barrow Neurologic Institute, and St. Joseph's Hospital & Medical Center, Phoenix, Arizona

CHRISTOPHER M. RYAN, Department of Psychiatry, University of Pittsburgh School of Medicine, and Western Psychiatric Institute & Clinic, Pittsburgh, Pennsylvania

BABETTE ANN STANTON, Department of Behavioral Epidemiology, Boston University School of Medicine, Boston, Massachusetts

LISA K. TAMRES, Department of Psychiatry, University of Pittsburgh School of Medicine, and Western Psychiatric Institute & Clinic, Pittsburgh, Pennsylvania

RALPH E. TARTER, Department of Psychiatry, University of Pittsburgh School of Medicine, and Western Psychiatric Institute & Clinic, Pittsburgh, Pennsylvania

DON M. TUCKER, Department of Psychology, University of Oregon, Eugene, Oregon

DAVID H. VAN THIEL, Department of Gastroenterology, University of Pittsburgh School of Medicine, Pittsburgh, Pennsylvania

Preface

Great strides have been made in the past several decades in clarifying brain–behavior relationships. Most of the research has focused on the direct effects of a brain injury on behavioral functioning. Only recently has attention been given to documenting the mechanisms by which the disruption of various organs and systems compromise cerebral integrity and ultimately how such disruption affects cognition and behavior. It is this relatively new topic of inquiry, medical neuropsychology, that comprises the subject of this book.

As will be noted, the chapters are organized on a system-by-system basis. Each of the organ systems contributes in a unique and specialized fashion to maintaining the integrity of brain functioning. Thus, the chapters by Prigatano and Levin, Stanton, and Ryan address the consequences of disturbed energy regulation and oxygen supply. Other chapters, specifically those by Tarter, Edwards, and Van Thiel and by Hart and Kreutzer examine the effects on the brain when the liver and kidney cannot efficiently catabolize or eliminate cerebrotoxic substances. The effects of metabolic disruption mediated through pituitary and thyroid gland mechanisms illustrate the complex and synergistic relationship among the various organs and systems and the brain. As discussed by Gordon, Lee, and Tamres, diverse intercorrelated processes regulate physical growth, cerebral specialization of function, and complex cognitive capacities. Beckwith and Tucker underscore the interrelationships among cognitive, affective, behavioral, and neurophysiological processes pertinent to thyroid functioning. The book concludes with discussions of three rather specialized topics of current interest. Eskenazi and Maizlish examine the issues and selected topics relevant to occupational exposure. Berg reviews the literature on cancer. Lester and Fishbein evaluate the effects of nutritional deficiency.

Although no attempt has been made to review all of the neuropsychological literature pertinent to each topic, the specific pathophysiologic mechanisms are discussed for the most researched diseases. It will be clearly evident that the field of medical neuropsychology is new, holds exciting prospects for neuropsychology and challenges the skills of both investigators and clinicians for contributing to comprehensive medical management and improved quality of life for medically ill individuals. It is to be hoped that this volume will additionally inspire a more formal and intensive integration of neuropsychological assessment and rehabilitation procedures with techniques employed by health psychologists, physiatrists, and consultation—liaison psychiatrists.

Appreciation is expressed to the authors for their efforts, and perhaps above all, in sharing with the editors the need to organize at this time the emerging literature on the topic of medical neuropsychology. The support of Cheryl Schmitt and her staff, Debbie Reichbaum, Michele Bevilacqua, Marty Levine, Theresa Cukanow, and Shari Paige, contributed greatly to expediting our task.

Ralph E. Tarter
David H. Van Thiel
Kathleen L. Edwards

Pittsburgh, Pennsylvania

Contents

Chapter 3

Neurological, Cognitive, and Psychiatric Sequelae Associated with the
        Surgical Management of Cardiac Disease

Babette Ann Stanton

Chapter 4

Neuropsychological Dysfunction Due to Liver Disease

Ralph E. Tarter, Kathleen L. Edwards, and David H. Van Thiel

Chapter 7

The Pituitary Axis: Behavioral Correlates

Harold W. Gordon, Peter A. Lee, and Lisa K. Tamres

Chapter 8

Thyroid Disorders

  Bill E. Beckwith and Don M. Tucker

Chapter 9

Effects of Occupational Exposure to Chemicals on Neurobehavioral
    Functioning

  Brenda Eskenazi and Neil A. Maizlish

Chapter 11

Nutrition and Childhood Neuropsychological Disorders

Michael L. Lester and Diana H. Fishbein

Perspective and Rationale for Neuropsychological Assessment of Medical Disease

RALPH E. TARTER, KATHLEEN L. EDWARDS, and DAVID H. VAN THIEL

INTRODUCTION

It is through the nervous system that animals interact with the environment. Unlike plant life, which reacts to the environment primarily through connective tissue, the nervous system evolved in animals to subserve information-processing functions and, through effector mechanisms, enables the organism to act on the environment. The capacity to receive, evaluate, store, and respond to information from the inner and external environments ultimately determines the adaptive potential of all higher organisms, particularly humans.

The evolution of vertebrates has been marked by a progressively larger cerebrum relative to total body size and, in humans, by a very large forebrain area relative to the whole cerebrum. In humans, the forebrain comprises approximately 30% of the brain mass, and it is from this substrate that the "executive functions" are subserved, namely the planning, self-monitoring, and termination of goal-directed behavior (Luria, 1966). Moreover, the greatly convoluted cortical mantle and large association areas compared to the area occupied by the primary sensorimotor cortex underlie the superior cognitive capacity and the greater regional specialization of cognitive processes in humans relative to other species.

The brain is almost totally dependent, however, on other organs and systems for maintaining its functional integrity. Oxygen, glucose, and nutrients, for example, need to be transported to the brain via the vascular system (and to a lesser extent, cerebrospinal system) because the brain has

RALPH E. TARTER and KATHLEEN L. EDWARDS • Department of Psychiatry, University of Pittsburgh School of Medicine, and Western Psychiatric Institute & Clinic, Pittsburgh, Pennsylvania 15213.   DAVID H. VAN THIEL • Department of Gastroenterology, University of Pittsburgh School of Medicine, Pittsburgh, Pennsylvania 15261.

virtually no capacity to manufacture or otherwise obtain these substances that are necessary for sustaining its viability. In addition, the brain also lacks any appreciable capacity to store energy, nutrients, or other necessary metabolic products. Hence, for optimal brain functioning to be sustained, there must be stable and efficient metabolic functioning of other organs and systems on an ongoing basis. Furthermore, compared to other organs, the brain's optimal requirements for life-sustaining substances are very high, thus necessitating the continuously efficient functioning of these other organs and systems. Considering the finely tuned relationship that exists between the brain and other organs and systems, it can be readily appreciated how certain medical diseases, even if transient, potentially have lasting adverse consequences on neurological functioning.

A neurological disorder emanating from systemic or organ disease can be expressed across multiple levels of biological organization. Histopathological abnormalities consisting of neuronal necrosis and glial cell disturbances have been found, for example, to occur following chronic liver disease. Gross brain morphology may also change to reflect the presence of atrophy or edema in certain medical conditions. Disturbances in neurotransmitter regulation typically occur subsequent to metabolic, biochemical, or endocrine diseases. Furthermore, neurophysiological functioning measured by cerebral blood flow, EEG, and event-related potentials may be disrupted as a consequence of numerous medical conditions. Thus anatomic, neurochemical, and physiologic disturbances of the brain may develop secondary to medical disease so as to compromise cognitive functioning and behavioral regulation.

The psychological concomitants and sequelae of disease have been receiving increasing attention by both clinicians and researchers. Two new specialty disciplines, *behavioral medicine* and *health psychology*, have recently emerged and have attracted a wide following. Much of this new interest is based on the revelation that many diseases are, in part, predisposed and sustained by psychological factors. For example, the relationship between the Type A personality and cardiovascular disease appears well established. Only limited research effort has been directed, however, to quantifying the association between cognitive functioning and disturbed biologic functioning due to disease (Tarter, Edwards, & Van Thiel, 1986), although there is a substantial literature documenting the emotional and psychiatric disturbances that are consequential to most common medical conditions (Jefferson & Marshall, 1981; Lishman, 1978).

RATIONALE FOR NEUROPSYCHOLOGICAL ASSESSMENT IN MEDICAL ILLNESS

Neuropsychological assessment procedures are among the most sensitive methods available for detecting the presence of cerebral pathology. Psychometric tests validated to detect cerebral pathology or dysfunction are superior to the EEG and neurological examination (Filskov & Goldstein,

1974; Goldstein, Deysach, & Kleinknecht, 1973) and are especially useful in cases where the lesion is either too small to be visually detected (e.g., early stages of dementia) or where the encephalopathy has a metabolic basis. In addition, neuropsychological tests can be employed to efficiently monitor the magnitude of any one of a variety of functional impairments over time and thus can be used to quantify disease severity and/or progression with respect to its neurologic sequelae. Moreover, the test scores can be utilized to document the extent of reversibility of cerebral impairment occurring as a consequence of medical treatment. And finally, neuropsychological test scores are predictive, to some degree, of social and vocational adjustment (Heaton, Chelune, & Lehman, 1978; Heaton & Pendleton, 1981). Hence the information accrued from a neuropsychological assessment of patients with medical disease is useful not only for diagnostic and medical management purposes but also for its prognostic value.

The prevalence of chronic diseases in the general population is climbing steadily, whereas the prevalence of acute diseases is declining. This trend is the result primarily of the advances in microbiology (e.g., antibiotics) for the treatment of acute infectious diseases and the application of preventative and public health measures. Technological innovations (e.g., hemodialysis) have made it possible to sustain or prolong biological viability for otherwise incurable conditions. Advances in neonatology have additionally resulted in an increased rate of live births; however, a high proportion of these additional surviving children suffer lifetime medical conditions. Furthermore, the medical diseases, particularly chronic illnesses, commonly associated with aging have increased in prevalence simply because the mean age of the population has increased.

Thus the changing pattern of the distribution of acute and chronic medical diseases in the population is producing an increasing number of individuals with cognitive and behavioral deficits that are consequential to disrupted cerebral functioning occurring as a result of an underlying chronic medical illness. In many cases, the functional deficits expressed are first manifest during the most productive period of the person's life. Inasmuch as it is cost-beneficial to society to maximize the educational and vocational successes of its constituents, maximize social adjustment, and create the conditions for an acceptable quality of life for its members, it can be seen that information obtained from a neuropsychological evaluation can contribute importantly to a program of comprehensive medical management and rehabilitation of the medically ill individual.

ETIOLOGY OF MEDICAL ILLNESS CAUSING CEREBRAL DYSFUNCTION

Numerous medical diseases are associated with disrupted cerebral functioning. Described next are the most common causes of medical diseases that can result in cerebral dysfunction or pathology.

Infection

Certain infectious diseases frequently produce cognitive impairments at least transiently. Fulminant hepatitis and subacute hepatic failure can produce a severe encephalopathy that, if not effectively managed, culminates eventually in coma and death (Conn & Lieberthal, 1979). Acquired immune deficiency syndrome (AIDS), especially in the late stages of the illness, is associated with significant neurologic pathology in many cases; however, systematic neuropsychologic studies have not been conducted. Neuropsychological deficits also have been found in persons with infections such as toxic shock syndrome (Rosene, Copass, Kastner, Nolan, & Eschenbach, 1982), and Sjogren's syndrome (Malinow *et al.*, 1985). Recently pancreatitis has been shown to be associated with transient neurological disturbances (Estrada *et al.*, 1979), although the evidence in this regard is not conclusive. Thus certain types of organ or systemic infections have neurological sequelae; however, the cognitive manifestations, as revealed by neuropsychological test performance, have not been systematically examined.

Toxin Exposure

Improvements in sanitation and statutes regulating food-processing standards have been largely responsible for the dramatic reduction in the prevalence of enteric diseases in this century. However, new and different public health dangers have emerged as the result of unchecked industrial development, particularly the increasing saturation of the atmosphere and water resources with potentially cerebrotoxic substances. This area of inquiry has substantial public health implications but has received only very limited attention by behavioral scientists. Also, chronic exposure to automobile exhaust, particularly lead, as well as a wide variety of herbicides and insecticides may have deleterious effects on the central nervous system of many people. Furthermore, occupational exposure to chemicals by industrial workers may have adverse neurological consequences at least in some cases. These latter toxic effects may result either from direct action on the nervous system or indirectly by disrupting normal physiologic functioning of other organs such as the lungs, liver, or kidneys.

Genetics

Inherited metabolic disorders underlie a variety of neurological disorders. Also, certain chromosome anomalies have been known for a long time to be associated with substantial cognitive impairments.

Life-Style

Tobacco consumption, particularly its chronic use, has been known to place the individual at risk for diseases of the cardiovascular and pulmonary systems. Excessive alcohol consumption is associated with an increased risk for a number of pathological conditions affecting the liver, heart, endocrine system, gastrointestinal tract, and nervous system. Diets that are high in sodium and fat augment the risk for hypertension, cardiovascular disease, and possibly also neoplastic disease. A sedentary life-style may also increase the risk for certain types of diseases. Indeed, approximately 50% of all chronic disease could be prevented if self-mitigating habits were avoided and life-styles could be modified (Lalonde, 1974).

Trauma

Traumatic injury to a vital organ, by impairing its functional efficiency, frequently results in impaired cognitive capacity. The traumatic injury can be caused externally (e.g., automobile accident) or be endogenous (e.g., myocardial infarction). For example, it has been found that myocardial infarction, even in the absence of an associated cardiac arrest, can cause major intellectual and cognitive impairments (Ergood & Tarter, 1983).

Several organ systems may interact synergistically to produce an identifiable impairment on neuropsychological test performance. For instance, individuals who do not suffer measurable cognitive disturbances following a mild craniocerebral trauma demonstrate deficits in cognitive functioning when tested at a simulated altitude of 3,000 m above sea level. Thus, the effects of mild hypoxia and a subclinical cerebral injury due to head trauma can summate to produce cognitive deficits at least in some individuals (Ewing, McCarthy, Gronwall, & Wrightson, 1980), illustrating the potential multifactorial basis of impaired performance on neuropsychologic tests.

DETERMINANTS OF NEUROPSYCHOLOGICAL TEST PERFORMANCE

Numerous factors influence the cognitive performance of medically ill patients. Although these factors are discussed in detail in the following chapters with respect to specific organs and systems, it is nonetheless useful at this juncture to describe the general factors that need to be considered for any medical disorder in which neurological functioning may be disrupted.

Stage of Illness

Acute biochemical, metabolic, or physiological disruption of normal organ system functioning, as noted before, can adversely affect neurologic integrity. Typically, many acute medical conditions are marked by a rapid onset that results in a florid neuropsychiatric syndrome (delerium) featured by disturbances in cognitive efficiency, consciousness, emotional regulation, and behavioral control. These neuropsychiatric disturbances are almost universally reversed following the institution of appropriate medical management.

In contrast, chronic illnesses typically do not produce a florid neuropsychiatric syndrome in affected individuals. The psychiatric manifestations of chronic illness are less marked, and, as a result, cognitive disturbances, when they occur, may not be detected without careful psychometric testing. Also, unlike acute medical illnesses, chronic diseases are more likely to be associated with lasting histopathologic and gross morphologic brain changes because of the long-term effects of the disease process. Within the domain of chronic illnesses, the manifest cognitive impairments are determined in large part by the duration or stage of the illness; however, systematic research has not been conducted as yet to ascertain whether there is a direct and close relationship between illness chronicity and recognizable and quantifiable cognitive and psychiatric impairments.

Treatment Effects

Neuropsychologic test performance to some extent may be determined, at least in part, by iatrogenic factors, that is, caused by the medical treatment used to correct an underlying medical problem. Certain types of medications, such as steroids and psychotropic drugs, frequently affect cognitive functioning adversely. Other drugs, including euphoriants and stimulants, may at least temporarily augment mental functioning. The effects of drugs on cognitive functioning that are used to treat most medical conditions have not, however, been studied systematically. Similarly, effects of radiation therapy on cognitive functioning also remain to be clarified. Thus, although there is a dearth of research on the mechanisms and effects of medical treatments on cognitive ability, it would appear that many standard medical interventions impact directly on cognitive functioning.

Age of Disease Onset

The age of the individual at the time he or she incurs a cerebral injury substantially influences the type of cognitive deficits that are manifest as well as the potential he or she has for recovery from the resultant cognitive deficits. Thus, for example, a lesion occurring in early life may prevent cognitive processes from developing optimally, whereas a similar lesion developing in an older person may only impair an already established cognitive process. The maturing cerebrum may be especially vulnerable to disruption. For example, there is some suggestive evidence to support the concept that an early age at onset is associated with more severe cognitive impairments for patients with diabetes than if the disease process had its onset after brain maturation has been completed (see Chapter 6).

Socioeconomic Status

Low socioeconomic status may contribute to impaired cognitive functioning in individuals with medical illness as well as mediate or sustain illnesses that are not otherwise related to social standing. For example, low-income neighborhoods are generally in the core of cities or in areas where there is excessive industrial pollution. The chronic exposure to atmospheric toxins occurring as a consequence of industrial pollution of the environment (e.g., lead from automobile emissions and industrial waste) has been shown to increase the risk for illness and thereby the neurologic sequelae of such illness. Poverty is associated also with poor nutrition as well as an increased susceptibility to infection, chronic stress, overcrowding, and substandard housing, to name but a few of the hazards of this condition. These latter factors also increase the individual's risk for illness. Thus socioeconomic factors both directly and indirectly influence disease formation and can exacerbate or sustain a disease state once it has developed.

ETIOLOGY OF THE COGNITIVE IMPAIRMENTS SEEN IN MEDICAL ILLNESSES

There are a number of mechanisms by which disturbed organ-system functioning can disrupt cerebral integrity. First, an organ system may be inefficient and thus not provide the brain with sufficient quantities of substances essential for its normal functioning. For example, there is some indication that asthmatic children perform deficiently on certain neuropsychological tests, presumably because the brain's need for oxygen is not being met adequately during exacerbations of their illness (Dunleavy & Baade, 1980). Nutritional deficiencies, due to either a reduced intake, storage, or absorption of vitamins, have been known to produce both neurological and cognitive disturbances (Grantham-McGregor, 1984). Neuropsychological deficits have been reported to occur in patients with anorexia nervosa (Hammsher, Halmi, & Benton, 1981), perhaps due at least in part to a chronic low-grade malnutrition that exists in such individuals. Second, an organ system may be overly active and thereby disrupt cerebral functioning. Overactivity of the thyroid, pituitary, and adrenal glands produces a plethora of cognitive and affective disturbances. Hyperventilation is another example of disrupted cerebral homeostasis caused by a metabolic change. Third, an organ system may not be able to fulfill its metabolic or physiologic functions. For example, the liver and kidneys are responsible for the detoxification and excretion of nonpolar and polar toxins, respectively. Fulminant hepatic disease and chronic liver disease (e.g., cirrhosis) typically induce an encephalopathy that can range in severity from mild cognitive impairment to deep coma. Renal failure similarly produces an encephalopathy that, if untreated, can result in coma and occasionally death.

Thus, there are three general biological pathways in which organ-system disease can disrupt brain functioning. It needs to be stressed, however, that there is a synergistic relationship among all organ systems in the living organism. Therefore, a disruption of any one organ system potentially can disturb any one or all of the others. With respect to neuropsychological research and clinical practice, this latter point has major ramifications, namely the organ-system that is disturbed may not be the only contributing factor, or even the major cause, of the manifest cerebral dysfunction. Recognizing the multifactorial etiology of the cerebral disturbance in medical illness necessitates a multivariate approach to delineating the neuropsychological sequelae. Moreover, it should be recognized that the manifest cerebral dysfunction, measured by neuropsychological tests, merely reflects the end point of an integral connected chain of biological events; hence, in any given individual, the demonstration of a deficit on neuropsychological testing reflects a unique interplay of manifold processes.

CLINICAL NEUROPSYCHOLOGIC ASSESSMENT OF MEDICALLY ILL PATIENTS

Cognitive functioning in medically ill patients can be difficult to evaluate. Not only must the multiple factors that potentially could influence test performance be taken into consideration, but, in addition, the results obtained may reflect a transient impairment that is only marginally related to the medical condition itself. Physical distress, restricted mobility, and medication regimens must each be considered prior to the decision to conduct a neuropsychologic assessment and selection of the test instruments to be used. Furthermore, in medical conditions where the metabolic status changes rapidly, it can be very difficult, if not impossible, to obtain an accurate picture of the person's optimal cognitive capacities and limitations.

Because of the uncertainty regarding the patient's amenability to testing, it is advisable to first evaluate general functional efficiency prior to committing extensive time and resources to a comprehensive neuropsychologic assessment. Brief screening tests can serve this purpose by determining the patient's overall general level of ability. A mental status evaluation can additionally provide useful information regarding the patient's capacity to participate in a lengthy neuropsychologic evaluation. Gross disturbances in attention, consciousness, orientation, and mental clarity can be easily documented in an objective manner as part of a mental status examination and provide the basis upon which a decision to conduct a formal neuropsychological examination can be made.

If initial findings indicate that there may be cerebral dysfunction despite a clear sensorium, then an evaluation that comprehensively documents cognitive strengths and weaknesses may be warranted. This evaluation could take one of two general forms: a standardized test battery such as the Halstead-Reitan Neuropsychological Test Battery or the Luria-Nebraska Battery or, alternatively, a special test battery can be composited that consists of selected standardized measures (Goldstein, Tarter, Shelly, & Hegedus, 1983). Regardless of whichever assessment strategy is employed, the main objective is to obtain a profile of the person's cognitive capacities and limitations. Even though the commonly used neuropsychological batteries differ substantially with respect to their theoretical focus, administration time, and specific types of tests, they have a substantial amount of variance in common and thus essentially measure the same cognitive processes (Kane, Parsons, & Goldstein, 1985).

Under special circumstances, highly detailed information about one modality or a particular category of cognitive functioning may be required. In such cases, the examiner must either devise a test protocol that evaluates a particular cognitive domain in depth or must select, from the few modalities or domains, specific batteries that have been developed to assess language or communication efficacy, perception, and motor capacity. These latter specialized batteries may be most useful for developing rehabilitation interventions. They also can assist in the overall medical management of patients. For instance, information about motor competency is especially important if the patient has a potentially dangerous job, operates power machinery, or drives a car. Thus, an assessment that proceeds from brief screening to a broad-based description of cognitive strengths and weaknesses to in-depth evaluation of specific cognitive domains or modalities is the most efficient and cost-effective strategy in conducting a neuropsychological evaluation of patients with medical illnesses.

SUMMARY

Traditionally, neuropsychologists have focused their attention on diseases of the central nervous system. Little consideration has been given to diseases of other organ systems that could compromise neurologic functioning. Within the past few years, there has been, however, a surge of interest in medical illnesses, partly as a result of recent developments in the fields of behavioral medicine and health psychology. In view of the increasing proportion of patients treated by physicians who have chronic diseases, this is becoming an increasingly important issue, especially because medical disease not only may be associated with physical disability but also because such diseases can militate against optimal adjustment by impairing those functional capacities (e.g., attention, memory, psychomotor efficiency) that are integrally required for meeting the demands of everyday living.

The following chapters examine the organ systems and disease processes for which neurologic and neuropsychologic sequelae have been researched. From these discussions, it will become apparent that manifold conditions are associated with impaired neuropsychologic capacity that, as noted previously, has substantial ramifications for comprehensive medical management and rehabilitation of afflicted patients.

REFERENCES

Conn, H., & Lieberthal, M. (1979). The hepatic coma syndrome and lactulose. Baltimore: Williams & Wilkins.

Dunleavy, R., & Baade, L. (1980). Neuropsychological correlates of severe asthma in children 9–14 years old. Journal of Consulting and Clinical Psychology, 48, 214–219.

Ergood, J., & Tarter, R. (1983). Neuropsychological measurement of encephalopathy after myocardial infarction. Journal of Cardiac Rehabilitation, 3, 368–370.

Estrada, R., Moreno, J., Martinez, E., Hernandez, M., Gilsanz, G., & Gilsanz, V. (1979). Pancreatic encephalopathy. Acta Neurologica Scandinavica, 59, 135–139.

Ewing, R., McCarthy, D., Gronwall, D., & Wrightson, P. (1980). Persisting effects of minor head injury observable during hyposix stress. Journal of Clinical Neuropsychology, 1980, 2, 147–155.

Filskov, S., & Goldstein, S. (1974). Diagnostic validity of the Halstead-Reitan neuropsychological battery. Journal of Consulting and Clinical Psychology, 42, 382–388.

Goldstein, G., Tarter, R., Shelly, C., & Hegedus, A. (1983). The Pittsburgh Initial Neuropsychological Testing System (PINTS): A neuropsychological screening battery for psychiatric patients. Journal of Behavioral Assessment, 5, 227–238.

Goldstein, S., Deysach, R., & Kleinknecht, R. (1973). Effect of experience and amount of information on identification of cerebral impairment. Journal of Consulting and Clinical Psychology, 41, 30–34.

Grantham-McGregor, S. (1984). Chronic undernutrition and cognitive abilities. Human Nutrition: Clinical Nutrition, 38, 83–94.

Hammsher, K. de, Halmi, K., & Benton, A. (1981). Prediction of outcome in anorexia nervosa from neuropsychological status. Psychiatry Research, 4, 79–88.

Heaton, R., Chelune, G., & Lehman, R. (1978). Using neuropsychological and personality tests to assess the likelihood of patient employment. Journal of Nervous and Mental Disease, 166, 408–416.

Heaton, R., & Pendleton, M. (1981). Use of neuropsychological tests to predict adult patients' everyday functioning. Journal of Consulting and Clinical Psychology, 49, 807–821.

Jefferson, J., & Marshall, J. (1981). Neuropsychiatric features of medical disease. New York: Plenum Medical.

Kane, R., Parsons, O., & Goldstein, G. (1985). Statistical relationships and discrimination accuracy of the Halstead-Reitan, Luria-Nebraska, and Wechsler IQ score in the identification of brain damage. Journal of Clinical and Experimental Neuropsychology, 7, 211–223.

Lalonde, M. (1974). A new perspective on the health of Canadians: A working document. Ottawa: Government of Canada.

Lishman, W. (1978). Organic psychiatry: The psychological consequences of cerebral disorder. London: Blackwell Scientific.

Luria, A. (1966). Higher cortical functions in man. New York: Basic Books.

Malinow, K., Molina, R., Gordon, B., Selnes, O., Provost, T., & Alexander, E. (1985). Neuropsychiatric dysfunction in primary Sjogren's Syndrome. Annals of Internal Medicine, 103, 344–349.

Rosene, K., Copass, M., Kastner, L., Nolan, C., & Eschenbach, D. (1982). Persistent neuropsychologic sequelae of toxic shock syndrome. Annals of Internal Medicine, 96, 865–870.

Tarter, R., Edwards, K., & Van Thiel, D. (1986). Cerebral dysfunction consequential to medical illness: Neuropsychological perspectives and findings. Annals of Behavioral Medicine, 8, 3–7.

2

Pulmonary System

GEORGE P. PRIGATANO and DAVID C. LEVIN

INTRODUCTION

The prefix *pulmo* is derived from the Latin term *pulmones*, which means organ of respiration or the lung (W. B. Saunders, 1981). Respiration refers to two processes: external respiration and internal respiration. The former is "the absorption of oxygen (O_2) and the removal of carbon dioxide (CO_2) from the body as a whole," and the latter refers to "the gaseous exchange between the cells and their fluid medium" (Ganong, 1981, p. 507). This chapter will focus on external respiration, particularly as it relates to lung–brain function and neuropsychologic disturbance.

OXYGEN REQUIREMENTS OF THE BRAIN

The O_2 consumption of the adult human brain averages about 3.5 ml per 100 g brain per minute, or 49 ml per minute for the whole brain. This suggests that 20% of the total resting oxygen consumption in the body is utilized by the brain. Various brain regions differ in their rate of oxygen consumption. The basal ganglia appear to utilize oxygen perhaps at the highest rate (Ganong, 1981).

The energy resources for the brain, under normal conditions, include oxygen and glucose. Thus, if lung function is impaired, the brain runs a risk of not receiving a vital energy source. Although a protective mechanism related to the blood–brain barrier allows the brain to receive oxygen when other organs may be partially deprived, this cannot continue indefinitely. Abrupt or gradual long-term oxygen depletion may, therefore, influence higher brain function, as is described next.

GEORGE P. PRIGATANO • Department of Neuropsychology, Barrow Neurologic Institute, and St. Joseph's Hospital & Medical Center, Phoenix, Arizona 85013.   DAVID C. LEVIN • Pulmonary Disease & Critical Care Section, Oklahoma University Health Sciences Center and Oklahoma City VA Medical Center, Oklahoma City, Oklahoma 73104.

BRAIN–LUNG ANATOMY AND PHYSIOLOGY

The primary homeostatic function of the lung is the addition of oxygen to the blood and the elimination of carbon dioxide, whereas other tissues (including the brain) utilize oxygen and produce carbon dioxide. Inspired air passes through the nasal passages and pharynx down the trachea to the lungs. The lung is a complex organ (Figure 1) with various subdivisions. The alveolar sacs and terminal bronchioles are the primary gas-exchange areas for O_2 in and CO_2 out of the blood. The pulmonary arteries from the right ventricle deliver the poorly oxygenated blood to the lungs, and the pulmonary veins carry the newly oxygenated blood to the left side of the heart for delivery to the rest of the body organs. Between the trachea and the alveolar sacs, the airways divide approximately 23 times, thus assuring a large surface area for O_2 and CO_2 exchange.

The arterial blood flow to the human brain is accomplished primarily by four arteries, the two internal carotids and the two vertebrals. The vertebral arteries unite to form the basilar artery. The Circle of Willis is formed by a juncture of both carotid arteries and both basilar arteries. This vascular ring is the origin of the six large vessels supplying the cerebral hemispheres (i.e.,

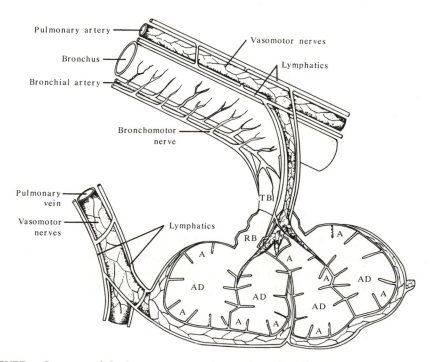

FIGURE 1. Structure of the lung. A—anatomic alveolus, AD—alveolar duct, RB—respiratory bronchiole, TB—terminal bronchiole. From N. C. Staub, The Pathophysiology of Pulmonary Edema. *Human Pathology*, 1970; 1, 419. Copyright 1970. Reprinted by permission.

the two anterior cerebral arteries, the two middle cerebral arteries, and the two posterior cerebral arteries).

Unlike other tissue, the brain is unique in what it accepts across the capillary walls.

> Over 70 years ago, it was first demonstrated that when acidic dyes such as trypan blue are injected into living animals, all the tissues are stained except most of the brain and spinal cord. To explain the failure of the neural tissue to stain, the existence of a *blood-brain barrier* was predicted. (Ganong, 1981, p. 479)

Subsequent research has shown that only water, CO_2 and O_2 easily cross the cerebral capillaries, and exchange of other substances is slow. It has been hypothesized that the purpose of this blood–brain barrier is to provide a very constant environment for neural tissue and ensure its full supply of energy sources (oxygen and glucose), even if the total amount of oxygen in the blood is reduced. There are, however, limits to the ability of the body to compensate for low blood oxygen (hypoxemia). Multiple factors influence cerebral blood flow and brain oxygen supply. The primary determinants of cerebral blood flow include intracranial pressure, the degree to which there is constriction or dilatation of cerebral arterials, the mean arterial pressure at brain level, the viscosity of the blood, and the mean venous pressure at brain level (Ganong, 1981).

For blood to be normally oxygenated, four important requirements of lung physiology must be met. First, for the lung to fulfill its gas-exchange role, there must be sufficient alveolar–capillary units to allow for adequate gas transfer. Normal alveoli, with pulmonary capillaries embedded in the walls, allow diffusion of oxygen in and carbon dioxide out during the time a given volume of blood traverses the pulmonary capillary bed. Second, not only must there be enough surface area to allow for gas exchange, but there must also be proper matching of ventilation and perfusion to allow gas exchange. The importance of ventilation–perfusion matching becomes obvious when one considers the fatal mismatch situation of all blood to the left lung (due to a large pulmonary embolus in the right pulmonary artery) and all air to the right lung (due to an aspirated foreign body in the left main bronchus). As will be described shortly, chronic airway obstruction (CAO) and asthma are main examples of lung diseases causing ventilation–perfusion mismatch.

Third, to provide adequate oxygen to the brain, there must be sufficient hemoglobin in the blood to carry the oxygen available to the alveoli to peripheral tissues. Fully oxygenated blood with a normal hemoglobin of 15 g per 100 ml of blood has an oxygen content of about 20 cc of oxygen per 100 ml. If the hemoglobin falls to 10 g, the full saturated oxygen content is only 14 cc per 100 ml. In severe anemia (hemoglobin $\leq$ 5 g per 100 ml), the maximum oxygen content would be $\leq$ 8 cc/100 ml, which is very nearly the amount of oxygen normally extracted by tissue. It is important to remember that, in anemia, the content is low in spite of a normal arterial PO_2.

Fourth, adequate cardiac output is necessary to circulate the oxygenated hemoglobin to all organs of the body. Thus, cardiogenic shock can be associated with significant tissue hypoxia in spite of normal blood gases. Conversely, in moderate anemia, a low O_2 content can be compensated for with a moderate tachycardia.

The lungs fulfill their role in gas exchange of oxygen by operating as a mechanical bellows, alternatingly inhaling ambient air (21% oxygen, no CO_2) and exhaling alveolar gases (17% oxygen, 5% CO_2). The lungs pause momentarily during this exchange, at full inspiration, to allow near equilibration of the pulmonary capillary oxygen and carbon dioxide with the same gases in the alveoli. This normally increases pulmonary arterial PO_2 of 40 mmHg to systemic arterial PO_2 near 100 mmHg and reduces pulmonary arterial pCO_2 from 46 mmHg to systemic arterial pCO_2 of 40 mmHg.

BRAIN HYPOXIA

The abrupt lack of oxygen to the brain is referred to as *brain hypoxia*. It is important to remember that the major cause of brain hypoxia is not low oxygen content of the delivered blood (whether due to lung disease or anemia). Rather, it is typically caused by local ischemic disturbance of the arteries. For example, in traumatic brain injury, notable ischemic damage occurs throughout the cerebral cortex, and particularly the basal ganglia and hippocampus (Graham, Adams, & Doyle, 1978). In these cases, one assumes that the lungs are adequately exchanging gases; but, because of cerebral circulatory disturbances, oxygen is not adequately delivered to the various brain regions. Questions arise as to whether there are also changes in the pulmonary system that can influence O_2–CO_2 exchange to a point the neuropsychologic function is adversely affected. In the next section, this will be discussed in some detail, particularly as it relates to diseases of chronic airflow obstruction (CAO) and asthma.

DISEASES OF THE PULMONARY SYSTEM AND NEUROPSYCHOLOGIC FUNCTION

Diseases of the pulmonary system that could potentially impact brain–behavior relationships can be categorized into four types: obstructive, infectious, parenchymal-autoimmune, and neoplastic. In this chapter, disturbances that produce airflow limitation and, therefore, gas-exchange abnormalities, will be emphasized. Certainly, diseases that are infectious in their nature (e.g., pneumonia) or involve the lung parenchyma and the autoimmune system (e.g., pulmonary fibrosis secondary to lupus erythematous or rheumatoid disease) potentially could directly influence brain–behavior function; but they will not be discussed because of an absence of neuropsychological literature on these topics. Metastatic lesions from lung carcinoma migrating to the brain obviously produce predictable neuropsychological and neurological impairment. Case examples of patients with CAO and brain tumors will be briefly described, as they emphasize a number of diagnostic issues important for the neuropsychologist working with this patient population.

CHRONIC AIRFLOW OBSTRUCTION (CAO)

Two diagnostic categories are typically placed under the label of chronic airflow obstruction (CAO), formerly called chronic obstructive pulmonary disease (COPD). One is chronic bronchitis, and the other is emphysema. Chronic bronchitis causes narrowing of the airways due to thickening of bronchiolar linings and the large amounts of retained purulent secretions. The narrowing increases the work of breathing as well as lowering flow to affected areas, thus disturbing the ventilation–perfusion matching. This can result in a drop in arterial oxygen content. In emphysema, the airways are better preserved, but there is a greater destruction of the supporting alveolar walls and the parenchyma, allowing narrowing or collapse of the terminal airways during expiration. The end result of emphysema is the same as bronchitis—arterial oxygen decreases due to the increased oxygen cost to breathing and the mismatching of ventilation and perfusion. Recent research has focused on the neuropsychological consequences of such permanent and progressive obstructive lung disease.

Asthma, or acute reversible airflow obstruction, has also received much psychological attention. Asthma is

> a disorder of the tracheo-bronchial tree in which there is a recurrent, at least partially reversible, generalized obstruction to air flow. It is commonly manifested by cough and respiratory distress and, classically, by expiratory wheezing. Overt wheezing does not have to occur, however, and the major manifestation may be cough. Asthma has been recognized for centuries. Until relatively recently, it was believed commonly to be neurotic or neurologic in origin (Pearlman, 1984, p. 439).

The potential neuropsychological consequences of asthma will also be considered.

CAO: NEUROPSYCHOLOGICAL AND PERSONALITY FINDINGS

A description of what comprises a neuropsychological evaluation, the variables that influence neuropsychologic test performance, the rationale for studying CAO patients with neuropsychological measures are presented elsewhere (Parsons & Prigatano, 1978; Prigatano & Grant, in press). In this section, the neuropsychological and personality findings of CAO patients will be summarized.

Three basic questions will be considered: (a) do CAO patients demonstrate neuropsychological and personality disturbances compared to appropriate controls? (b) If so, what are the typical deficits seen, and how do they relate to pulmonary and associated medical variables? (c) How do these disturbances relate to everyday functioning or quality of life in these patients?

Although neuropsychological impairment has been reported in CAO patients for some time (Krop, Block, & Cohen, 1973; Kass, Dyksterhuis, Rubin, & Patil, 1975; Fix, Golden, Daughton, Kass, & Bell, 1982), adequate control groups were frequently not included in these reports. Such variables as age, educational level, socioeconomic status, and the mere presence of chronic illness are obvious factors that need to be accounted for before interpreting neuropsychological test findings in this patient group (Parsons & Prigatano, 1978).

The first major studies on the neuropsychological functioning of CAO patients that included controls for age, education, and socioeconomic status were those sponsored by the National Heart, Lung, and Blood Institute during the years 1976–1982. These studies emanated from the Nocturnal Oxygen Therapy Trial (NOTT, 1980) and the Intermittent Positive Pressure Breathing Trial (IPPB, 1983). In both studies, large groups of CAO patients were studied using systematic neuropsychological measures. Reports by Grant, Heaton, McSweeny, Adams, and Timm (1982), Prigatano, Parsons, Wright, Levin, and Hawryluk (1983), and Grant, Prigatano, Heaton, McSweeny, Wright, and Adams (in press) summarize the neuropsychological findings obtained from these clinical trials.

Taken as a whole, these studies present evidence that neuropsychological impairments do exist in some CAO patients. The impairments are varied and can be related to age, education level and, to a modest degree, with certain pulmonary variables such as arterial PO_2 and FEV_1 (a measure of airflow obstruction). By combining the patients who were tested with neuropsychological measures in both the NOTT and IPPB studies, Grant et al. (in press) were able to systematically investigate how the degree of hypoxemia in CAO patients was related to neuropsychological test performance. A combined group of over 300 patients and nearly 100 age/education-matched controls were studied. The factor structure of their neuropsychological test performance was analyzed and related to the degree of hypoxemia.

CAO patients were classified into three groups: "mild" hypoxemia ($PaO_2 \geq 60$ mmHg; $N = 86$); "moderate" hypoxemia ($PaO_2 = 50$ to 59 mmHg; $N = 155$); or "severe" hypoxemia ($PaO_2 < 50$ mmHg; $N = 61$). Worsening hypoxemia was associated with a parallel increase in neuropsychological impairment. Controls ($N = 99$) obtained an Average Impairment Rating of 1.69. The mild hypoxemia group ($N = 86$) had an Average Impairment Rating of 1.81. The moderate ($N = 155$) and severe ($N = 61$) hypoxemia groups had Average Impairment ratings of 2.13 and 2.38 respectively. Controls differed from each of the three CAO groups. The mild group differed from controls as well as from the moderate and severe groups. However, the moderate and severe groups were statistically indistinguishable.

Considering specific areas of deficit, the following conclusions were drawn from that study: (a) Verbal Intellectual Abilities (Factor 1) generally were not influenced by CAO; (b) Perceptual-Motor Learning and Problem Solving (Factor 2) were impaired and seemed to be related to the degree of hypoxemia; (c) Alertness-Psychomotor Speed (Factor 3) seemed to be affected only in the more severe cases of CAO and was not substantially affected in the milder group; and (a) Motor Speed and Strength (Factor 4) were notably affected in the moderate and severe groups but not in the mild group.

Figure 2 compares controls and the three groups of CAO patients studied along these four factor structures. As Figure 2 also indicates, differences were highly significant in Factors 2, 3, and 4, although the pattern of findings differed across factors.

The predictors for each of these four neuropsychological factors were of special interest. They allowed for a more careful assessment of what variables seemed to predict these different factor scores. As Table 1 illustrates, education was a very important predictor for Factor 1 (i.e., accounts for 33% of the variance). In contrast, age and PaO_2 level predicted Factor 2 better than any other dimension. PaO_2 level accounted for only 7% of the variance of this factor score. Factor 3 was predicted best by educational level and respiratory rate. Respiratory rate accounted for only about 6% of the variance. Factor 4 was predicted by age and, to some degree, exercise level.

These factors are important because they suggest that age and education variables account for as much of the variance as do specific medical variables such as PaO_2 or respiratory rate. These findings suggest that the neuropsychologic deficits seen in CAO patients are a result of a complex interaction between their medical state and other nonmedical variables. It is clear

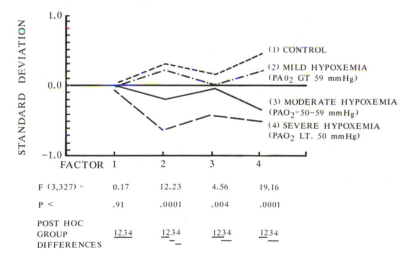

FIGURE 2. Factor analytically derived neuropsychological ability scores for COPD patients at three levels of hypoxemia, and controls. (From I. Grant, G. P. Prigatano, R. K. Heaton, A. J. McSweeny, E. C. Wright, and K. M. Adams. Progressive neuropsychological impairment in relation to hypoxemia in chronic obstructive pulmonary disease. *Archives of General Psychiatry*, in press. Reprinted by permission.)

TABLE 1. Results of Multiple Regressions Predicting Four
Factors from Medical and Demographic Variables[a]

Factor	Predictor variables	Cumulative R^2	p
Factor 1	Education	.33	.00
	$PaCO_2$	.34	.03
	$FEV_{1.0}$	.35	.06
Factor 2	Age	.14	.00
	PaO_2	.21	.00
	Education	.25	.00
	Resp. rate	.26	.03
	pH	.29	.01
	FEV_1	.30	.09
Factor 3	Education	.15	.00
	Resp. rate	.21	.00
	Age	.25	.00
	PaO_2	.26	.20
Factor 4	Age	.12	.00
	Exercise level	.18	.00
	Hemoglobin	.20	.01
	Education	.22	.03
	PaO_2	.23	.05

[a]Reproduced with permission from Grant, I., Prigatano, G. P., Heaton, R. K.,
McSweeny, A. J., Wright, E. C., and Adams, K. M. Progressive neuropsychological impairment in relation to hypoxemia in chronic obstructive pulmonary disease. *Archives of General Psychiatry*, in press.

from this table that the actual level of PaO_2, FEV_1, respiration rate, and
$PaCO_2$ account for a relatively small amount of neuropsychological test
variance.

Given these observations, what is the actual incidence of impaired neuropsychologic difficulties in CAO patients? Prigatano and Grant (in press)
and Grant *et al.* (in press) estimate that less than 10% of the mildly hypoxemic CAO patients have true neuropsychologic deficits. This is based on a
comparison of older, healthy normals' test performance versus this patient
groups' test performance. Using the same criteria, it was estimated that about
25% of the moderately hypoxemic CAO patients show neuropsychological
impairment on test results that cannot be accounted for by demographic
variables. Finally, approximately 40% of the severe hypoxemia group
showed deficits above and beyond what controls show.

How do these deficits actually impact on everyday functioning or quality of life? The answer seems to be that they impact somewhat, but again, the
relationship is not startling. McSweeny Grant, Heaton, Prigatano, and
Adams (1985) looked at a variety of neuropsychological variables and how
they correlate with several measures of psychosocial and physical functioning in this patient group. Their data showed that motor and psychomotor

speed tests did relate to physical mobility, self-care, home management, and socialization activities. As would be expected, language disturbances correlated with the ability to communicate. In general, however, the correlations between Sickness Impact Profile (SIP) scores and the Average Impairment Rating were moderate (correlation of Average Impairment Rating with SIP physical scores, $r = .43$; psychosocial scores, $r = .36$).

In a group of nearly 100 mildly hypoxemic CAO patients, Prigatano, Wright, and Levin (1984) demonstrated a modest relationship with neuropsychological impairment and these two dimensions, but the correlations were smaller ($r = .25$ and $.23$, respectively). What was quite significant, however, was that emotional or personality variables seemed to have a rather high correlation with quality of life as measured by the SIP. In a larger group of 985 patients, the POMS tension and anxiety measures correlated the highest with both SIP physical and psychosocial scores. These findings made it quite clear that personality variables are extremely important in understanding the quality-of-life problems of CAO patients.

Geddes (1984) has presented an interesting model showing that lung disease may produce a variety of symptoms that interact with emotional state to produce significant disability and reduction in quality of life. Figure 3 illustrates his model. As can be seen in this model, as patients experience a certain degree of dyspnea, they tend to become immobile. The immobility seems to increase their depression, and this adds to their sense of tiredness or lack of fitness. Then a vicious circle begins, where immobility produces more depression, which leads to less exercise, which produces more immobility. The question that many authors have attempted to address is: To what degree do CAO patients show signs of depression, anxiety, irritability, and other variables that could not be accounted for by chronic illness? This is a difficult question to answer, but some data exist in the field.

Prigatano, Wright, and Levin (1984) demonstrated that CAO patients show significant elevations on Scales 1, 2, 3, 7, and 8 of the MMPI compared to age-matched controls. This suggests that there is heightened concern about bodily function and a heightened degree of depression and anxiety. These individuals also tend to tire easily and, at times, may experience some degree of confusion in their thinking. Also, on the Profile of Mood States (POMS), these patients report a heightened degree of tension, anxiety, depression, anger, fatigue, and a lack of vigor. As noted before, these difficulties are clearly related to SIP values.

FIGURE 3. Lung disease and psychopathology: a model. From D. M. Geddes. Chronic airflow obstruction. *Postgraduate Medical Journal*, 1984, *60*, 197. Copyright 1984. Reprinted by permission.

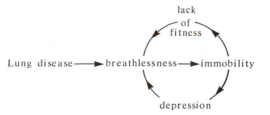

It is interesting that the level of emotional disturbance in these patients does not seem to be related to the degree of hypoxemia. Comparing the emotional disturbances of CAO patients reported in the NOTT study, which were clearly more hypoxemic than the CAO patients in the IPPB study, the following scores emerged: In the CAO patients with mild hypoxemia, the incidence of physical limitations is much less than in those who have severe hypoxemia (i.e., 12% versus 20%). However, both groups have comparable psychosocial limitations (that is, the mild group report 18% reduction in psychosocial activities versus 22% in the severe group). Prigatano, Wright, and Levin (1984) suggested that perhaps the single most clinically relevant finding from their study was that the degree of physical limitation in these CAO patients appears to be related to pulmonary disease, but the degree of psychosocial limitation was more related to variables other than pulmonary disease, namely personality disturbances.

In another review, Prigatano and Grant (in press) summarize a number of studies that looked at MMPI profiles of CAO patients and other chronic-illness patients. Generally, patients with any chronic illness show elevations on Scales 1, 2, and 3 on the MMPI (i.e., so-called hypochondriasis depression and hysteria). These findings simply suggest that, in chronic illness, these difficulties may be particularly present. The elevations on Scales 7 and 8 for the CAO patients, however, suggest that more may be going on in this patient group. These impairments may reflect subtle changes in their higher brain function that were captured by some of the neuropsychological measures. A major challenge for the field is to determine to what degree these affective problems are reversible in patients with CAO. Present data suggest that these affective disturbances are modestly related to neuropsychological impairment. For example, in the report by Prigatano, Parsons, Wright, Levin and Hawryluk (1983), depression, as measured by the MMPI, accounted for no more than 1 to 2% of the variance on neuropsychologic tests. This suggests that, at least as measured by this test, depression is a relatively independent factor. Also in the study by Prigatano, Wright, and Levin (1984), psychosocial limitations were generally not related to PaO_2, $PaCO_2$, or respiratory level. Although level of exercise did correlate with physical limitations, it did not correlate with psychosocial ones.

ASTHMA: NEUROPSYCHOLOGICAL AND PERSONALITY FINDINGS

As indicated before, asthma is a tracheobronchial-tree disorder in which there is recurrent, somewhat reversible, obstruction to airflow. To the degree that asthma produces hypoxia or hypoxemia secondary to ventilation–perfusion imbalance, it may produce subtle neuropsychological (i.e., brain–behavior) disturbances. The neuropsychological literature on asthma patients is relatively sparse. It is often assumed that the ventilation–perfusion imbalance is short lived, without any major consequences for the oxygen supply of the brain. The incidence of EEG abnormalities is reportedly no greater in children with severe asthma than in normal children (Nellhaus, Neuman, Ellis, & Pirnat, 1975). Yet, case reports of anoxic brain damage in children with asthma have been reported (Bierman, Pierson, Shapiro, & Simons, 1975). In past reviews of asthma, neuropsychological deficits are typically not discussed (Creer, 1982, Fritz, 1983; Friedman, 1984). In contrast, the role of nonneuropsychological factors contributing to asthmatic symptoms or in response to asthmatic episodes is amply reviewed. The review paper by Creer (1982) is especially helpful.

A study by Dunleavy and Baade (1980), however, specifically addresses the question of neuropsychologic disturbance in older children with *severe* asthma. Twenty asthmatic children between the ages of 9 and 14 were compared to matched nonasthmatic controls on the Halstead Neuropsychological Test Battery for Children. Severe asthma was defined clinically. Sixty-five children were screened before the sample of 20 patients was finally selected. It was reasoned that, in cases of severe asthma, there may be recurrent transient hypoxic episodes due to an acute bronchospasm leading to loss of consciousness and hemoglobin desaturation. Seven of the 20 severely asthmatic children (35% of the sample) showed neuropsychological impairment. These authors emphasize that the impairment involved "visualizing and remembering spatial configuration, incidental memory, and planning and executing visual and tactile motor tasks." Inspection of their data also reveals another finding—this subgroup of patients was slow in speed of finger tapping—a problem observed in older COPD patients who have moderate-to-severe hypoxemia (Grant *et al.*, in press). Given the high oxygen utilization of the basal ganglia, it is predictable that specific psychomotor disturbance as well as memory problems would be common in any group of patients deprived of O_2, either in a recurrent acute manner or in a slowly progressive way.

The work of Dunleavy and Baade (1980) emphasizes that, in their group of severely asthmatic children, the neuropsychological deficits were "very mild to mild" in nature. Clinically, this would be expected. Although a limited data set, their findings warrant replication and expansion.

Suess and Chai (1981) challenged the Dunleavy and Baade (1980) study on the grounds that certain antiasthmatic medications might account for their reported results. Corticosteroids have been suggested to negatively influence higher cerebral functions. Dunleavy's (1981) response emphasized that no relationship was found between pharmacological states of the children and their neuropsychological data. He emphasized that, of the 7 asthmatic children who exhibited neuropsychological deficits, only 3 were administered antiasthmatic medications. Furthermore, he points out that, of the 12 asthmatic children who showed no neuropsychological impairment, 7 were receiving such medications. This seems a reasonable response to the challenge of Suess and Chai (1981); however, further work needs to be done on this important question. Chai (personal communication, 1985) indicates that a 3-year project assessing the effects of various antiasthmatic medications on neuropsychological function will soon be reported.

Studying 95 asthmatic adults, Schraa, Dirks, Jones, and Kinsman (1981) reported a high incidence of memory difficulties in this population. However, only one test was given (Bender Gestalt), and no control group was used. Consequently, the interpretation of this study is difficult. At this point, however, the possibility of mild neuropsychological deficits in some asthmatic patients is a working hypothesis that should be further investigated.

A number of studies have tried to address the personality disturbances of asthmatic children. Perhaps the single major conclusion is that there is no personality syndrome associated with the asthmatic patient (Creer, 1982). A number of personality disturbances may emerge as precipitating an asthmatic attack. These disturbances seem to be as varied as the individuals themselves, and any simple behavioral or psychodynamic explanation does not seem to be appropriate for this heterogeneous group of patients. The reviews mentioned before concerning asthma amply describe these findings.

NEUROPSYCHOLOGICAL ASSESSMENT OF CAO PATIENTS WITH AND WITHOUT BRAIN TUMORS

The most obviously destructive disturbance of brain function by lung disease is metastatic lung cancer. Merritt (1979, p. 294) points out that "practically any malignant tumor may metastasize to the brain, but in approximately 60% of the cases the primary tumor is a carcinoma of the breast or lung."

In the IPPB clinical trial, 33 of the 985 patients (or 3.4%) who had CAO and mild hypoxemia developed bronchogenic carcinoma during the 3-year study. One of these patients was given neuropsychological testing prior to the detection of the carcinoma.

The patient was a 67-year-old male with 10 yr of formal education. His neuropsychological status was essentially within the normal range for a man of his education and age. The only exception was that there was some evidence of subtle memory difficulties and possible subtle difficulties in abstract reasoning. He obtained an Average Impairment Rating of 1.58, a Halstead Impairment Index score of .6, and a Brain Age Quotient of 97. His WAIS Verbal IQ was 95; Performance IQ was 90. Specific WAIS subtest scores were as follows: Information = 7; Comprehension = 7; Arithmetic = 13; Similarities = 5; Digit Symbol = 9; Vocabulary = 8; Digit Symbol = 8; Picture Completion = 9; Block Design = 9; Object Assembly = 8; and Picture Arrangement = 9.

On the Halstead Battery, this man made 66 errors on the Category Test; he made 5 errors on the Seashore Rhythm, and 7 errors on the Speech Perception Test. His total time on the TPT was 23.3 min. TPT Memory score was 6, and Location was 2. Speed of finger tapping was 46 taps in the dominant hand. On the Trails Test, Part A, his score was 36 sec; Part B was 97. On the Wechsler Memory Scale, he recalled a total of 18 bits on the short stories, and obtained a score of 4 on the geometric designs. Except for his nonverbal score on the geometric designs and his TPT Location score, his performance was generally within the normal range. His Category score of 66 errors and his Similarities score of 5 also suggested mild abstract-reasoning skills. However, in light of the overall profile and his age and education, it was assumed that the lung carcinoma has not metastasized to the brain, at least at this time. This man's profile was very compatible with other CAO patients who had no lung cancer as well as some controls. A later independent assessment of the patient records indicated no metastases to the brain at 1-year posttesting.

Another CAO patient had a carcinoma of the prostate and died from it. There was a brief time before his death in which he was extremely paranoid and confused. His neuropsychological examination was done in early 1979; he died in October of 1982. The carcinoma was limited to the bone; no metastases were found in the brain.

His 1979 test scores were as follows: Average Impairment Rating of 2; Halstead Impairment Index of .7; Brain Age Quotient of 83; Verbal IQ = 96; and Performance IQ = 96. Specific scale scores were: Information = 10; Comprehension = 6; Arithmetic = 10; Similarities = 8; Digit Span = 14; Vocabulary = 8; Digit Symbol = 6; Picture Completion = 8; Block Design = 7; Picture Arrangement = 5; and Object Assembly = 5. Total errors on the Category Test were 97, Seashore Rhythm, 5 errors, and Speech Perception, 5 errors. Total time with the TPT was 30 min. Memory score was 4; Location was 1. Speed of finger tapping was 53.9 taps in the right hand. Time to complete Trails Test, Part A, was 56 sec; Part B was 107 sec. On the Wechsler Memory Scale he obtained a short-term memory score of 10 and a nonverbal score of only 1. He was 66 yr of age and had 8 yr of education. In retrospect, his neuropsychological test scores do suggest the possibility of brain dysfunction prior to his rapid decline just preceding his death. Certainly his nonverbal recall on the Wechsler Memory Scale and his Location score of 1 suggest significant memory deficit. However, his scores were not different from those of other CAO patients with no carcinoma.

Perhaps the most interesting of all the cases, however, from a neurological assessment point of view, was a male CAO patient who developed a glioblastoma in the right frontoparietal area. He was tested in late 1978 and died of his malignancy in early April, 1979. His neuropsychological test scores were as follows: Average Impairment Rating = 1.17; Halstead Impairment Index = .7; Brain Age Quotient = 89; Verbal IQ = 96; and Performance IQ = 108. Specific test scores were as follows: Information = 8; Comprehension = 8; Arithmetic = 10; Similarities = 7; Digit Symbol = 10; Vocabulary = 9; Digit Symbol = 4; Picture Completion = 11; Block Design = 12; Picture Arrangement = 6; and Object Assembly = 10. He made 62 errors on the Category Test, 5 errors on the Seashore Rhythm Test, and 6 errors on Speech Perception. Total time on the TPT was 30 min. His Memory score was 8, and

Location score was 2. Speed of finger tapping in the dominant hand was only 33 taps. Trails Test, Part A, was 53 sec; Part B was 137 seconds. On the Wechsler Memory Scale he obtained a short-term verbal memory score of 18, and a nonverbal score of 4. When tested this man was 64 yr of age with 8 yr of formal education.

Just prior to his death, this man's neurologic examination revealed left-sided weakness with minor ocular-motor disturbance. The pathology report reflected significant brain damage, and this is quoted in some length to clarify the extent of the brain pathology:

> The cerebral hemispheres are grossly asymmetrical, with the right hemisphere somewhat larger than the left. The leptomeninges over the convexity and at the base of the brain are thin and delicate. The subarachnoid space is free of hemorrhage or exudate. There is a cortical defect in the right hemisphere approximately 6 cm from the occipital pole and 5 1/2 cm on the convex surface of the hemisphere. Elsewhere, the gyri of the right hemisphere are markedly flattened and sulci markedly narrowed, indicating a severe degree of cerebral edema. On the left hemisphere, the gyri are somewhat flattened and sulci narrowed, indicating a severe degree of cerebral edema, however, somewhat less than is evident in the right hemisphere. There is prominent subfascial herniation of the right cingulate gyrus. Both unci show grooving; however, these appear approximately symmetrical, and the grooves are located approximately 0.7 cm from the medial aspect of the unci. On the right, there is also parahippocampal herniation. The mammillary bodies are only mildly displaced caudally. The cerebellar tonsils are not abnormally located. The vessels at the base of the brain have thin, delicate walls, with only focal atheromatous changes. There are no significant anomalies (median artery of the corpus callosum) or aneurysms present. Cranial nerves examined in situ appear normal.

This man's neuropsychological test profile is significantly deviant only in a few ways. There is evidence of memory dysfunction on the TPT and the nonverbal memory section of the Wechsler Memory Scale. In light of other CAO patient reports, however, these findings are not especially deviant. It is somewhat sobering for neuropsychologists to observe a Block Design of 12 in this man who demonstrated a large frontoparietal lesion a few months after his testing. This reminds neuropsychologists of the potential shortcomings of neuropsychological measures in predicting the presence or absence of brain dysfunction.

In the combined data bank of the IPPB and Nighttime Oxygen Study that specifically investigated neuropsychological impairment (see Grant et al., in press), the cutoff score for the Average Impairment Rating, which correctly classified 79% of the controls as unimpaired, was an Average Impairment Rating of 2.10. This man's score of 2.17 provided some minor index of impairment above and beyond what we would normally see in CAO. Certainly the pattern of test findings was not especially indicative of right cerebral hemisphere dysfunction , and, in fact, a computer program utilized to diagnose lesions actually considered this protocol to be more indicative of a left hemisphere impairment versus a right hemisphere impairment. Clearly, the use of a purely psychometric approach and statistical methods for diagnosing brain dysfunction is inadequate in this patient population.

REHABILITATION WITH CAO PATIENTS

The observation that dysphoric mood is a major problem of CAO patients and is not related to degree of hypoxemia nor neuropsychologic impairment is an important observation for psychologists working with these patients. Educational activities and various forms of supportive psychotherapies potentially could reduce anxiety and depression and, thereby, enhance coping skills.

The fact that the degree of neuropsychological impairment is generally mild in patients except in the very severe forms of the illness and at higher age ranges should be noted. However, when patients show memory and abstract reasoning difficulties above and beyond what might normally be expected for this group, one should pursue other potential causes of the disturbance. Certainly this patient population is at high risk for other difficulties besides CAO, as noted in the previously mentioned cases. It is certainly important for clinicians and various rehabilitation specialists to document carefully the higher cerebral difficulties of this patient population and, when necessary, pursue further diagnostic techniques. Also, knowledge of this information, coupled with knowledge of their personality functioning, may allow for more humane and understanding treatment approaches in dealing with this patient population. The capacity of this treatment team to manage the neuropsychologic and personality deficits of these patients should enhance the overall cooperation of the patient in rehabilitation activities and allow for more informed family participation in patient care.

REFERENCES

Bierman, C., Pierson, W., Shapiro, G., & Simons, E. (1975). Brain damage from asthma in children. *Journal of Allergy and Clinical Immunology, 55,* 126.

Creer, T. L. (1982). Asthma. *Journal of Consulting and Clinical Psychology, 50,* 912–921.

W. B. Saunders. (1981). *Dorland's illustrated medical dictionary* (26th ed.) Philadelphia: W. B. Saunders.

Dunleavy, R. A. (1981). Neuropsychological correlates of asthma: Effect of hypoxemia or drugs? *Journal of Consulting and Clinical Psychology, 49,* 137.

Dunleavy, R. A., & Baade, L. E. (1980). Neuropsychological correlates of severe asthma in children 9–14 years old. *Journal of Consulting and Clinical Psychology, 48,* 214–219.

Fix, A. L., Golden, C. J., Daughton, D., Kass, I., & Bell, W. (1982). Neuropsychological deficits among patients with chronic obstructive pulmonary disease. *International Journal of Neuroscience, 16,* 99–105.

Friedman, M. S. (1984). Psychological factors associated with pediatric asthma death: A review. *Journal of Asthma, 21,* 97–117.

Fritz, G. K. (1983). Childhood asthma. *Psychosomatics, 24,* 959–967.

Ganong, W. F. (1981). *Review of Medical Physiology.* Los Altos, CA: Lange Medical Publications.

Geddes, D. M. (1984). Chronic airflow obstruction. *Postgraduate Medical Journal, 60d,* 194–200.

Graham, D. I., Adams, J. H., & Doyle, D. (1978). Ischemic brain damage in fatal nonmissile head injuries. *Journal of Neurological Sciences, 39,* 213–234.

Grant, I., Heaton, R. K., McSweeny, A. J., Adams, K. M., & Timms, R. M. (1982). Neuropsychologic findings in hypoxemic chronic obstructive pulmonary disease. *Archives of Internal Medicine, 142*, 1470–1476.

Grant, I., Prigatano, G. P., Heaton, R. K., McSweeny, A. J., Wright, E. C., & Adams, K. M. (in press). Progressive neuropsychological impairment in relation to hypoxemia in chronic obstructive pulmonary disease. *Archives of General Psychiatry.*

Intermittent positive pressure breathing (IPPB) therapy of chronic obstructive pulmonary disease: A clinical trial (participant). (1983). *Annals of Internal Medicine, 99*, 612–620.

Kass, I., Dyksterhuis, J. E., Rubin, H., & Patil, K. D. (1975). Correlation of psychophysiologic variables with vocational rehabilitation outcome in patients with chronic obstructive pulmonary disease. *Chest, 67*, 433–439.

Krop, H. D., Block, A. J., & Cohen, E. (1973). Neuropsychologic effects of continuous oxygen therapy in chronic obstructive pulmonary disease. *Chest, 64*, 317–322.

McSweeny, A. J., Grant, I., Heaton, R. K., Prigatano, G. P., & Adams, K. M. (1985). Relationship of neuropsychological status to everyday functioning in healthy and chronically ill persons. *Journal of Clinical and Experimental Neuropsychology, 7*, 281–289.

Merritt, H. H. (1979). *A textbook of neurology.* Philadelphia: Lea & Febiger.

Nellhaus, G., Neuman, I., Ellis, E., & Pirnat, M. (1975). Asthma and seizures in children. *Pediatric Clinics of North America, 22*, 89–100.

Nocturnal Oxygen Therapy Triad (NOTT) Group. (1980). Continuous or nocturnal oxygen therapy in hypoxemic chronic obstructive lung disease: A clinical trial. *Annals of Internal Medicine, 93*, 391–398.

Parsons, O. A., & Prigatano, G. P. (1978). Methodological considerations in clinical neuropsychological research. *Journal of Consulting and Clinical Psychology, 46*, 608–619.

Pearlman, D. S. (1984). Bronchial asthma. *American Journal of Diseases of Childhood, 138*, 459–465.

Prigatano, G. P., & Grant, I. (in press). Neuropsychological correlates of COPD. In A. J. McSweeny & I. Grant (Eds.), *Chronic obstructive pulmonary disease: A behavioral perspective.* New York: Marcel Dekker.

Prigatano, G. P., Parsons, O. A., Wright, E., Levin, D. C., & Hawryluk, G. (1983). Neuropsychological test performance in mildly hypoxemic patients with chronic obstructive pulmonary disease. *Journal of Consulting and Clinical Psychology, 51*, 108–116.

Prigatano, G. P., Wright, E., & Levin, D. (1984). Quality of life and its predictors in mildly hypoxemic COPD patients. *Archives of Internal Medicine, 144*, 1613–1619.

Schraa, J. D., Dirks, J. F., Jones, N. F., & Kinsman, R. A. (1981). Bender-Gestalt performance and recall in an asthmatic sample. *Journal of Asthma, 18*, 7–9.

Suess, W. M., & Chai, H. (1981). Neuropsychological correlates of asthma: Brain damage or drug effects? *Journal of Consulting and Clinical Psychology, 49*, 135–136.

3

Neurological, Cognitive, and Psychiatric Sequelae Associated with the Surgical Management of Cardiac Disease

BABETTE ANN STANTON

INTRODUCTION

In dramatic contrast to some areas of the world where cardiovascular disease is nearly nonexistent, as exemplified by the Massai tribe in Kenya, the incidence and prevalence of cardiovascular disease has, until very recently, experienced a spiraling increase in populations in the Western world. In the United States, about 650,000 persons succumb to death from coronary heart disease annually, and rates of new and recurrent myocardial infarctions per year have been estimated to be approximately 1 million based on data from the National Health Survey and the Framingham Heart Study. There currently appears to be a new trend toward a decline in mortality from cardiovascular disease that has probably resulted from a combination of factors, including an increased public awareness of risk factors that have been shown to result in the development of the disease; reduction of some or as many as possible of these risk factors with accompanying modification of life-style (e.g., cessation of smoking); earlier detection and improved treatment and control of hypertension, diabetes, hyperlipidemia, and obesity; rapid advances in pharmacology that have resulted in important new drugs that have drastically improved the efficacy and safety of medical management of coronary artery disease; rapid advancement and achievement in surgical techniques to palliatively correct the anatomical and physiological pathology; and scientific advances that have served to augment the overall

BABETTE ANN STANTON • Department of Behavioral Epidemiology, Boston University School of Medicine, Boston, Massachusetts 02118.

success of the surgery in terms of myocardial preservation, cerebral protection, and reduction in operative mortality and postoperative morbidity. The effects on survival of recent, encouraging short-term success with a less invasive new procedure—percutaneous transluminal coronary angioplasty—are as yet unknown.

In spite of the confluence of these medical, scientific, and technological advancements that have appeared to result in a new linear trend toward the reduction of death from coronary artery disease, the disease continues to pose a substantial and very serious threat to populations not only in the United States and the West, but also in underdeveloped countries that have attempted, or will attempt in the future, to emulate the habits of the West.

Improvements in the recognition and treatment of coronary artery disease evolved very slowly at first, but, in recent decades, progress in diagnosis and medical and surgical management of the disease has escalated dramatically.

The heart was the last remaining organ of the body to be subjected to operative procedures, and yet, of all fields of innovation in medical practice, no other has experienced more rapid advancement than cardiothoracic surgery. Open-chest thoracic surgery was first performed in 1933. The first repair of a congenital anomaly (patent ductus arteriosis) was accomplished in 1938 by Robert Gross in Boston. During 1944 and 1945, Dwight Harken successfully performed intracardiac surgery to remove fragments of shells from the hearts of surviving soldiers. The first successful surgical correction of stenosis of the mitral valve actually occurred in London in 1925 and was performed by Henry Sauttar; however, it was not reported, and this progress remained unrecognized until many years after 1948 when Charles Bailey in Boston, Dwight Harken in Boston, and Russel Brock in England independently performed their own first successful operations to relieve mitral stenosis by commissurotomy within days of each other. The heart–lung machine that allowed open-heart surgery was developed by John Gibbon and his wife in 1953, although it was not widely utilized until the 1960s. Successful use of hypothermic techniques to permit open-heart surgery in humans was first reported in 1955. Another major advance occurred in 1956 when Werner Forssmann shared the Nobel Prize in medicine with two others for developing the concept of cardiac catheterization. In 1929, he had placed a catheter in his own heart as an experiment and was, at that time, viewed as a lunatic. Replacement of the mitral valve was initiated in 1958. In 1963, Kirklin reconstructed a congenitally malformed heart. During 1967, Favalaro, in Cleveland, and Johnson, in Milwaukee, performed the first coronary artery bypass graft procedures in humans. Also in 1967, Christian Barnard, in South Africa, performed the first heart transplantation.

In the early stages of the evolution of cariothoracic surgery, much innovative experimentation and risk taking occurred. As it is probably obvious from this brief sketch of some of the major historical landmarks, it was initially necessary to perform cardiac surgery under very adverse circumstances. The heart was beating during the procedure. Under these conditions in closed-heart procedures, such as mitral commissurotomy, one major obstacle was that the surgeon utilized his sense of touch only, and he had no direct visualization of the defect or of the surgical site in the heart. Surgeons could only work intermittently on the heart at normal body temperatures for about a minute at a time because brain damage would result from the interruption of blood flow to the brain. The advance of total body hypothermia allowed surgery to be performed on a "bloodless heart" under direct visualization for a maximum duration of only 8 min. Development of the pump oxygenator has enabled cardiac surgeons to have up to several hours of operating time with direct visualization for surgery on heart valves, coronary arteries, the aortic arch, or congenital cardiac anomalies.

The technical advances and refinements in cardiac surgery have been accompanied by interest and research concerning the complications of the surgical procedure and postoperative period, assessment of hospital and long-term morbidity and mortality from the operations, and measurement of overall patient recovery and outcomes. Innovations in anesthesia, hypothermia, cardiopulmonary bypass, and drugs as well as the requirements for postoperative intensive care and invasive monitoring raised concerns from the beginning of cardiac surgery about neuropsychological changes of patients that result from all these factors.

ANATOMY AND PHYSIOLOGY

In order to discuss neuropsychologic aspects of cardiac surgery, one must understand the neurologic basis of consciousness and higher mental functions, expressed as emotions and intellectual activity, and the way in which cardiac disease can influence the central nervous system. Wakefulness or consciousness (Ropper & Martin, 1983) is maintained by an area of the brain stem, the reticular activating system, which activates both cerebral hemispheres by complex neuronal connections. Lack of consciousness or coma is produced by (a) mechanical damage to the brain stem or *both* cerebral hemispheres, or by (b) interruption of the metabolism in the brain from a lack of oxygen (hypoxia), glucose (hypoglycemia), or blood supply (ischemia), or from diffuse disruption of neuronal membranes from toxins or trauma.

Higher mental functions such as organized thought, learned behavior, and emotions are functions of the cerebral hemispheres. The left frontal lobe controls intellectual function, whereas the right frontal lobe controls emotional response such as mood, anger, and the like. The parietal lobes control perception of the position of the body in space and the location of bodily stimuli. The temporal lobes control and influence auditory and visual perception, learning, memory, and the emotions. The occipital lobes control and influence visual perception and sensation. All of these areas of the brain are interconnected by neuronal pathways. Particular mental functions can be affected by an insult to an area of one lobe of the brain, or all higher functions can be affected by generalized metabolic disturbances or trauma that affect the whole brain.

The heart affects the brain primarily through the brain's requirement for a steady flow of oxygenated (arterial) blood that also contains glucose. Arterial blood is carried to the frontal, temporal, and parietal lobes by the carotid arteries and to the brain stem, cerebellum, and occipital lobes by the vertebral and basilar arteries. In contrast to other tissues such as muscle or liver, the brain cannot convert other substrates such as amino acids or fats to sugar, and it is totally dependent on the glucose supplied to it in the arterial blood. Oxygen is consumed at 3.5 ml per 100 g of brain tissue per minute. Glucose stored in the brain lasts for only 2 min after arterial blood circulation stops. When lack of oxygen occurs along with lack of glucose, brain glucose stores last even less than 2 min (Ropper & Martin, 1983). An elevation in bodily temperature also increases the requirement for oxygen by all cells in the body, including brain cells.

In the reverse direction, parasympathetic and sympathetic nerve supply to the myocardial, coronary artery, and cardiac conduction system arise from the brain stem and spinal cord. There also are many polypeptides that are produced by the brain only a few of which are fully understood physiologically. For example, antidiuretic hormone (ADH) is produced by specialized neuronal fibers in the hypothalmic-neurohypophysial region of the brain. How many polypeptides produced by the brain have cardiac effects remains to be further investigated and defined.

Cardiac disease may affect the myocardium, causing decreased capacity for the heart to pump blood that may result in congestion, heart failure, and/or hypotension. Disease of the cardiac valves may cause obstruction to blood flow from narrowing or regurgitation of flow backward from valve dilation. Cardiac disease can affect the coronary arteries and cause narrowing from atherosclerosis that produces a decrease or total blockage of blood flow to the myocardium, thereby producing angina or myocardial infarction. Cardiac disease also can damage the specialized myocardial conduction fibers, thereby producing symptoms such as palpitations, decreased efficiency of the heart as a pump, syncope (if hypotension persists longer than 3 sec), and sudden death (if certain arrythmias are prolonged or if there is electrical standstill). All of these affect the brain by interrupting the continuous flow of arterial blood.

The flow of oxygenated blood to the brain is also affected if a congenital defect in the septum between the atria or ventricles permits the shunting of unoxygenated venous blood from the right side of the heart to the left side of the heart with oxygenated blood in the left atrial or ventricular chambers, thereby lowering the oxygen content of arterial blood in the left side of the heart. Surgery for congential heart defects, which occurs mainly in children, is excluded from this chapter.

To understand the potential side effects of open-heart surgery on the brain, a description of the operative technique and the means of providing extracorporeal circulation is helpful. The patient is premedicated with atropine and a barbiturate sedative and anesthetized with an endotracheal tube in place. Two peripheral venous catheters, a peripheral arterial catheter, and a central venous catheter are used to infuse fluids and medications intravenously and monitor venous/arterial pressures; a Foley bladder catheter measures urine output; and electrocardiographic leads monitor cardiac rhythm. The surgical incision is made through the middle of the sternum. Cardiopulmonary bypass, as represented schematically in Figure 1, is instituted by cannulating the superior and inferior vena cavae, right atrium, and ascending aorta after anticoagulation with heparin. All venous blood from the vena cavae and right atrium is rerouted by these cannulae to the pump oxygenator, where oxygen is taken up and carbon dioxide removed (in place of the lung's performing these functions), and then conducted by cannula into the patient's arterial system via a peripheral artery (usually the femoral artery). Because of the pump oxygenator, the heart and lung are able to be "bloodless" during the cardiac operation. The usual cardiopulmonary bypass time does not exceed 2 hr. At the end of bypass, all residual air must be evacuated from the cardiac chambers to prevent air emboli. As bypass is discontinued, circulatory volume is adjusted to maintain central venous and right ventricular filling pressures. Drugs may be needed to regulate blood pressure, cardiac rhythm, and blood acid–base balance. Transfusion of blood is only used if the hematocrit falls. Adequate urinary output is maintained throughout the procedure by maintaining blood pressure and intravascular fluid volume. After cardiopulmonary bypass is discontinued, heparin anticoagulation is reversed. A wire for cardiac pacing may be left in the tip of the right ventricle if necessary. Anterior mediastinal drainage tubes

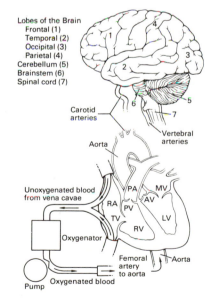

FIGURE 1. The technique of extracorporeal circulation.

are left in place after the chest is closed until there is a cessation of drainage containing blood. The patient is monitored in terms of cardiac rhythm, vital signs, respiratory status, urine output, acid–base balance, arterial blood oxygenation, and mental status in a surgical intensive care unit for 12 to 24 hr postoperatively, or longer if necessary.

The pump oxygenator, itself, has undergone considerable technical refinement. The bubble oxygenator uses oxygen bubbles in the venous blood pool to oxygenate the blood, but these bubbles can act as microscopic emboli if not totally removed before the oxygenated blood reperfuses the arterial system. Antifoaming agents to remove oxygen bubbles and turbulence of the blood can produce hemolysis and denaturation of plasma proteins. The disc oxygenator oxygenates a film of venous blood on discs as the discs rotate through a bath of venous blood. The disc oxygenator decreased the problems of air emboli and hemolysis but has been found to cause the formation of microaggregates that act as particulate emboli (Ashmore, Svitek, & Ambrose, 1968). The screen oxygenator allows venous blood to descend by gravity down a screen surrounded by oxygen. Flow over the screen produces oxygen–carbon dioxide exchange along with blood–oxygen interface without the formation of gaseous emboli and with minimum protein denaturation and decreased danger of particulate emboli. Prolonged pump-oxygenator infusions are least hazardous using the screen oxygenator.

The introduction of filters into the extracorporeal system along with improved blood volume management, which avoids intraoperative hypotensive episodes, decreased the incidence of neurologic damage in a retrospective study from 19.2% of 417 patients before these improvements in technique in 1970 to 7.4% afterward (Branthwaite, 1975). Aberg and Kihlgren (1977) reported a decrease in clinically detectable cerebral complications from 14.5% among patients from 1972 to 1974 to 3% in 1976 after the introduction of arterial blood filters, use of clear fluid as a solution to prime the pump, and other measures to remove microemboli. Perfusion time, units of blood given intraoperatively, and days in an intensive care unit also declined during this time. The patients in both time periods predominantly underwent cardiac-valve replacement procedures.

INCIDENCE AND PREVALENCE

In the early years of closed-heart repair of mitral valves with stenosis by performing a commissurotomy or the repair of atrial septal defects in adults, Priest, Zaks, Yacorzynski, and Boshes (1957) found that all of these surgical patients had severe anxiety levels preoperatively. They undertook a study to compare patients who had surgery with those for whom surgery had been planned but subsequently was canceled. They investigated a total of 60 patients of whom 47 had rheumatic heart disease which included mitral stenosis in 41 patients and aortic stenosis in 6 patients. One of the patients with aortic stenosis and 26 of the patients with mitral stenosis actually received cardiac operations. Nine other patients in the study had congenital lesions of whom 5 received cardiac operations. The remaining 4 patients had coronary artery disease, and 2 of these patients received an operation. Another 4 men had coronary artery disease. Psychiatric effects were observed in the first 2 to 3 postoperative weeks and were felt to be caused by the stress of the operation itself. Signs of organic brain damage as shown by Wechsler-Bellevue scores in mitral commissurotomy patients were found postoperatively and did not recover to preoperative levels for about 6 months. Organic brain damage in mitral commissurotomy patients seemed to result from the several periods of time, of 15 to 30 sec each, when the surgeon's finger occluded the mitral orifice, stopping left atrial to ventricular blood flow. Additionally, some surgeons had compressed the carotid arteries during parts of the cardiac surgery.

In another study undertaken by Zaks (1959), mitral commissurotomy patients were compared with patients who had nonrheumatic heart surgery. Preoperative visual-motor coordination involving abstraction and concept formation was assessed in this series of 75 patients. Commissurotomy patients did less well postoperatively, at 3 weeks, 6 months, and at the 1-year follow-up than the other patients. These findings were interpreted as "organic" neurologic changes attributed to the commissurotomy surgery. They persisted for as long as 3 years. Postoperative psychoses and delerium following closed mitral commissurotomy decreased as surgical techniques improved (Knox, 1963).

During this same time period, surgical experience showed that use of hypothermia down to 8 to 12°C commonly caused neurologic changes and/or delerium some of which could be permanent, whereas cooling to 24 to 30°C only rarely caused brain damage (Egerton, Egerton, & Kay, 1963). At 8 to 12°C hypothermia, 4 of 16 patients with a mean age of 56 years failed to regain consciousness or had gross neurologic disturbances, whereas 6 other patients with a mean age of 40 years were comatose for several hours postoperatively, convulsed as they were rewarmed, and showed focal neurologic signs or personality changes that persisted for several weeks. The focal brain-stem signs affected eye movements or caused facial palsies. Most of these more moderately affected patients exhibited hypotonia and loss of deep-tendon reflexes. These patients showed retrograde amnesia similar to patients with a concussion. Whereas focal signs resolved in 2 to 4 months in the group with moderate brain damage and intellectual function returned to normal, emotional regression and lability persisted. Autopsy of 1 of the patients who experienced severe brain damage and died as a result of hypothermia showed focal brain hemorrhages in the white matter, especially in the brain stem; microscopically there was neuronal degeneration. These findings were consistent with those in brains of animals cooled 0°C for 2 hr, which showed necrosis of nerves partly due to blood vessel damage. Duration of cardiopulmonary bypass and length of time under profound hypothermia (below 12°C) was critical. Severe brain damage resulted with hypothermia below 12°C for 135 min or more; moderate brain damage with durations about 130 min; mild damage with duration of 78 min, and slight damage with 73 min duration or less. At cooling temperatures of 24 to 30°C in another group of 24 patients, none had postoperative organic brain damage.

With optimal hypothermia levels established by the early 1960s, attention focused on cerebral injuries that resulted from emboli and hypotension. Findings of focal and geographic lesions in the absence of pathologic evidence of cerebral anoxia or edema correlated with severely decreased cerebral blood flow. In a series of 35 patients (Brierley, 1964), 22 of the 35 had focal or geographic lesions and 15 of the 22 had known hypotensive episodes with reduced blood flow as evidenced by low values for venous oxygen saturation. These episodes occurred either during bypass or within 60 hr of it. Solid emboli could not have caused geographic lesions, but hypotensive episodes could have done so.

During this same time period, Gilman (1965) studied 35 patients with different corrective operations (30 valvular, 4 atrialseptal defects, 1 ventricular aneurysm) to define the variety and causes of neurologic disorder following open-heart surgery. Deficits in intellectual function without significant disorders of motor or somatic sensory function on physical examination were found in 6 patients (17%). Hemiplegia occurred in 2 patients (6%), visual field defects were present in 2 patients (6%), and seizure disorders (during the first postoperative week) occurred in another 2 patients (6%). In total, neurologic disorders occurred in 12 patients (34%) among whom 5 died. Six other patients among these 35 died without a neurologic deficit or before neurologic evaluation took place postoperatively, resulting in a total mortality of 11/35 patients or 31%. In another small series of 10 valve-replacement patients (Sachdev, Carter, Swank & Blachly, 1967) who were normal from a neurological and psychiatric standpoint at 1 to 2 days preoperatively, all showed some clinical signs of focal cerebral deficit at some point in time postoperatively. Data were gathered by neurologic exams, daily interviews, and behavioral description provided by staff and relatives. Electroencephalograms were obtained 1 day before surgery and daily after surgery for 16 days. Focal signs observed in these patients were focal weakness, asymmetric deep-tendon reflexes, positive Babniski sign, cranial nerve deficit, and right/left confusion. Psychiatric abnormalities included confusion, decreased level of consciousness, hallucinations, abnormal dreams, agitation, and intellectual deficits. EEG abnormalities that were observed included slowing of frequencies instead of predominant rhythm and were maximal a few days postoperatively when neurologic abnormalities were most prominent. Psychiatric abnormalities usually followed the neurologic ones and persisted longer.

By the late 1960s, the incidence of neurologic complications in open-heart surgery patients was decreasing further. Gilberstadt and Sako (1967) investigated a series of 53 open-heart surgery patients. They were examined preoperatively and 3 weeks postoperatively to assess potential brain damage resulting from the surgery. The tests that were used included speed of perceptual-motor coordination, attention span, and rote memory. Only mild decreases in these measures were found, and these decreases did not impair postoperative adjustment or the performance of the patient's daily activities. However, the 3-week reexamination interval was insufficient to permit any conclusions regarding long-term follow-up. Results from another study demonstrated that, among 62 patients who required extracorporeal circulation, 8 patients (13%) had gross neurologic deficits, and 6 patients (10%) had psychosis or severe disturbances in emotions postoperatively, whereas none had deficits among 20 who did not have extracorporeal circulation (Lee, Miller, Rowe, Hairston, & Brody, 1969). In this study, neurologic and psychiatric examination and clinical testing were performed 1 to 2 days preoperatively, 10 to 21 days postoperatively, and 3 months postoperatively. However, five neuropsychological tests failed to confirm these clinical neurologic deficits in the open-heart surgery patients. These five neuropsychological tests were: the Wechsler Adult Intelligence Scale, the Trail-Making Test, the Tapping Test, the Graham-Kendall Memory-For-Designs Test, and the Minnesota Percepto-Diagnostic Test. The neurologic evidence of brain damage lasted for about 3 months. Again, Tufo, Ostfeld, and Shekell (1970) found cerebral dysfunction on the basis of neurologic examination in 15% of patients in a series of 100 open-heart surgery patients at discharge from the hospital, but they could not find evidence of these deficits with psychometric tests (i.e., the Stanford-Binet). In addition to increased age, intraoperative hypotension was a very important factor in the occurrence of postoperative cerebral dysfunction. Among those patients whose mean arterial pressure fell below 40 mm Hg, cerebral damage was three times more frequent than it was among those whose mean arterial pressure remained above 60 mm Hg during the postoperative period.

Overall, these studies have documented an immediate postoperative organic brain syndrome present when the patient awakens from anesthesia and a "postcardiotomy delerium" present several days postoperatively but preceded by a lucid interval of a few days in the immediate postoperative recovery period. Postcardiotomy delerium occurs with varying frequencies among different open-heart surgery operations. Blachly (1967), in the era before coronary artery bypass grafting procedures, found that it occurred more frequently among mitral or multiple cardiac-valve-surgery patients (85% of 34 patients) than aortic (pulmonary) valve patients (67% of 42 patients) and much less frequently among those patients undergoing atrial septal repair (25% of 16 patients) or mitral valve commissurotomy (33% of 21 patients).

Frequency of postoperative delerium decreased, as techniques improved (Blachly & Starr, 1964; Gilberstadt & Sako, 1967; Kornfeld, Zimberg, & Malm, 1965; Lee et al., 1969; Tufo & Ostfeld, 1968). Heller, Frank, Malm, Bowman, Harris, Charlton, and Kornfeld (1970) reexamined the phenomenon of postoperative delirium. They documented that a series of patients followed prospectively during 1967–1969 had an incidence of delirium preceded by a lucid interval of several days (mean 3.8 days) of 24% compared to a 38% incidence in 1965. However, the 1965 data were obtained by a retrospective medical record review that probably had underestimated the true incidence. Immediate organic brain syndrome based on prospectively collected data occurred in 8 of 100 patients in the 1967–1969 series and in 2 of 92 patients, based on retrospective chart review. This was felt to reflect the difference in study methodology rather than an actual increase in frequency.

Investigating postcardiotomy brain syndrome in the 1960s, Blachly (1967) noted that electroencephalographic (EEG) abnormalities often preceded its onset, that the delirium often coincided with normalization of body temperature after its usual postoperative elevation, and that cardiac arrythmias often occurred simultaneously. Hallucinosis occurred at a time several days postoperatively when cardiac output was rising as a result of successful replacement of the defective valve(s), whereas the acute brain syndrome occurred earlier in the postoperative course when cardiac output was still low (Engle & Romano, 1959). Patients who had atrial fibrillation or New York Heart Association (NYHA) functional class scores that were worse preoperatively were more likely to develop delirium postoperatively. Delirium has been demonstrated to be more common with increased age (Blachly, 1967; Egerton & Kay, 1964; Tufo et al., 1970); however, another research team (Kornfeld et al., 1965) was unable to document this in their series of cardiac valve surgery patients. Male patients were more likely to incur postoperative delirium than were female patients (Blachly, 1967; Gilman, 1965).

In 1972, Frank, Heller, Kornfeld, and Malm distinguished long-term task interference that was emotionally based and resulting from anxiety (functional) from that caused by structural or physiologic brain changes (organic). This was accomplished by administering an anxiety scale rated by a psychiatrist, an estimate of cardiac disease based on a 4-point version of the NYHA scale, and use of a 6-month retest interval to minimize practice effects that might be present in a shorter retest interval. Intellectual performance was measured by the Wechsler Intelligence Scale, Verbal IQ, information, similarities, and block design tests, and the Benton Visual Retention Test. Intellectual performance improved postoperatively mainly among those with highest anxiety levels preoperatively, and this was interpreted by the investigators as resulting from practice effects. It is also possible that it may have resulted from decreased anxiety in survivors. Improved intellectual performance was not related to improvements in NYHA functional class, implying that improved cerebral perfusion was not the reason for improved intellectual performance. Although the results did not quite reach statistical significance ($p = .05$), the data suggested that long pump times were associated with less intellectual improvement postoperatively. The latter is consistent with the earlier finding by this group (Heller et al., 1970) that pump times that exceeded 2.5 hr were related to postcardiotomy delirium and positive neurologic findings.

By the 1970s, coronary artery bypass surgery had become the major indication for cardiac surgery rather than cardiotomy for valve replacement. Sveinsson (cited in Kornfeld, 1978) found an incidence of delirium of only 12% among 77 coronary artery bypass graft (CABG) patients, even though transitory perceptual disturbances were included. Lumping together a variety of behavioral and transient neurologic effects, Rabiner and Willner (1980) reported that "psychiatric complications" occurred in 16% of a CABG patient group versus 41% of a postcardiotomy group. Kornfeld, Heller, Frank, Edie, and Barsa (1978) compared early postoperative brain syndrome and delirium among 38 cardiotomy patients and 50 coronary artery bypass graft patients operated on between the years of 1972–1975. Factors associated with increased likelihood of delirium in cardiotomy patients were preoperative organic disease, severity of heart disease, advanced age, increased bypass time, severity of recovery room (or intensive care unit) illness, unexpressed anxiety, active-dominant personality, sensory isolation, and sleep deprivation. Among these factors, only severity of recovery room or intensive care unit illness was associated with occurrence of delirium in coronary artery bypass graft patients. This confirmed Willner's previous finding that neuropsychological outcome among coronary artery bypass graft patients did not correlate with bypass time, age, or NYHA functional class. Unlike Willner, however, Kornfeld et al. did not find any difference in psychiatric outcomes among coronary artery bypass graft patients and cardiotomy patients, although Willner also included affective disturbances along with delirium. Among Kornfeld's cardiotomy patients, a fall in the cardiac index after aortic valve replacement or a failure of cardiac index to rise after mitral valve replacement was associated with delirium, but the same cardiac index data were not available for coronary artery bypass graft patients and the effect of cardiac output on occurrence of delirium could not be tested in coronary artery bypass graft patients.

By the late 1970s and early 1980s, the incidence of neurologic deficits had declined in major medical centers performing coronary artery bypass graft surgery when compared to the incidence in the 1960s. At the Cleveland Clinic, neurologic deficits occurred in 1.7% of 2,616 consecutive bypass patients (Zapolanski, Loop, Estafanous, & Sheldon, 1983). Mortality was 0.8% for men, 1.5% for women, and 0.9% overall. The most common causes of death were myocardial failure and stroke. Improved drug therapy had nearly eliminated, in all but the most serious cases, the need for a preoperative intraaortic balloon to assist cardiac output and control unstable angina until surgery. This incidence of neurologic deficits of 1 to 2%, about half of which have been permanent, did not change significantly from 1971 to 1981 in the Cleveland Clinic study population. Specifically, occurrence of perioperative stroke had not improved over that decade. However, by 1981, patients on average were older, had more severe coronary disease, had more impaired left ventricular dysfunction preoperatively, required a greater number of bypass grafts per patient, and had reoperations more frequently (7% in 1981 versus 5% in 1979). The fact that neurologic sequelae had not become more common as coronary heart disease patients became more ill is noteworthy.

In our own prospective study, conducted at four large medical centers in New England, which included patients who had elective open-heart operative procedures during 1979 and 1980, the incidence of moderate-to-severe neurological and psychiatric complications were examined. These included cerebrovascular accidents, seizures, hemiparesis, encephalopathy, phrenic nerve palsy, visual homonymous hemianopsia, and postoperative psychosis. A total of 2.4% of the first 334 patients who entered the study had documented moderate-to-severe neurological or psychiatric complications. An additional 12% of all patients experienced thrombo-embolic hemorrhagic complications. Differences were observed by the type of procedure in that none of the 47 cardiac valve replacement patients had documented moderate-to-severe neurological or psychiatric complications, whereas 5 of the 247 coronary artery bypass graft patients (2%) and 3 of the 38 patients who underwent multiple operative procedures (8%) suffered documented complications. Multiple procedures would be expected to prolong the duration of anesthesia and surgery, and it is understandable that they might impose additional risks for higher complication rates. Of those 10 patients who expired prior to hospital discharge, 2 had severe neurological complications. An additional 12% of all patients experienced thrombo-embolic hemorrhagic complications. Differences were observed by the type of procedure in that none of the 47 cardiac valve replacement patients had documented moderate-to-severe neurological or psychiatric complications, whereas 5 of the 247 coronary artery bypass graft patients (2%) and 3 of the 38 patients who underwent multiple operative procedures (8%) suffered documented complications. Multiple procedures would be expected to prolong the duration of anesthesia and surgery, and it is understandable that they might impose additional risks for higher complication rates. Of those 10 patients who expired prior to hospital discharge, 2 had severe neurological complications. Patients were seen and interviewed on the ninth postoperative day, or as soon thereafter as the patient could tolerate being interviewed. At this early follow-up assessment nearly one-fourth of the patients (23%) reported having experienced confusion and/or not knowing the names of family members or other familiar individuals. Disorientation was present with regard to the self 6%, the place 17%, and names 16%. Additionally, only 52% of these patients could recall both the current date and the date of admission to the hospital, and 12% of the patients did not know either the correct date or the correct admission date. A much smaller percentage (2.4%) did not even remember having seen or spoken with the same interviewer prior to surgery. Other disturbances included vivid dreams or nightmares for 16% of the patients, visual hallucinations for 7%, and both dreams and hallucinations for 6%. Marginal, new dysarthria was also observed during the interview in 3% of the patients.

Also as part of our more comprehensive longitudinal study of recovery and rehabilitation following major cardiac surgery, both short-term (Savageau, Stanton, Jenkins, & Klein, 1982) and long-term (Savageau, Stanton, Jenkins, & Frater, 1982) neuropsychological dysfunctions were investigated utilizing standard neuropsychological tests. The Trail-Making Test (Parts A and B) from the Halstead-Reitan Battery and the Visual Reproduction test from the Wechsler Memory Scale were administered preoperatively, 9 days postoperatively, and 6 months postoperatively. The Logical Memory subtest from the Wechsler Memory Scale was also administered on two occasions (preoperatively and 6 months postoperatively). All patients were alert, oriented, and medically stable during the preoperative testing, and patients who had documented neurological or psychiatric impairment were excluded. A total of 227 patients were included in the analyses: 172 coronary artery bypass graft patients, 29 mitral or aortic valve replacement patients, and 26 patients who received multiple procedures. Comparison of preoperative and 9-day postoperative test scores revealed that 70% of the patients remained within one standard deviation of the preoperative test score performance on all test scores. Nine-day postoperative decrements of greater than one standard deviation were observed in 11 to 17% of the patients on the test scores. Neither sex nor operative procedure was significantly related to test score differences. Patients with more precarious cardiac function, longer duration of surgery, and one or more metabolic disturbances were particularly prone to early neuropsychological dysfunction. Follow-up examination and testing at 6 months postoperatively documented the fact that only 5% of the patients who had early neuropsychological dysfunction continued to have residual impairment.

Intellectual dysfunction following CABG surgery was reported as being classified as mild and transient and without long-term sequelae when studied in yet another series of patients (Raymond et al., 1984). In this series, cardiac patients had a bypass time of 2 hr with an average hypothermia of 22°C, anesthesia time of 6 hr, and intensive care unit stays of an average of 76 hr. This is in contrast to a general surgical comparison group of patients who averaged 4 hr of anesthesia, required no hypothermia, and generally required 31 hr in an intensive care unit. Psychological tests included the Wechsler Adult Intelligence Scale (WAIS) score, simple digit, Buschke word list, Raven's Progressive Matrices Test, Benton's Visual Retention Test as well as the Zung Depression Scale, the Taylor Manifest Anxiety Scale. A mental status exam and a neurologic examination were also performed preoperatively. Age and educational level were similar in the two surgical groups. In the early postoperative period, there were abnormalities among coronary artery bypass graft patients that were not found among the general surgical group in nonlanguage measures of motor and visual/spatial performance, the WAIS IQ, attention span and concentration (digit symbol), and auditory memory (Bushke) that were gone at the later 6- to 8-week postoperative testing. Although many clinical observations have suggested that some coronary artery bypass graft patients are anxious preoperatively and depressed postoperatively, more anxious coronary artery bypass graft patients showed no differences in intellectual function than those who were less anxious, and anxiety and depression did not appear to influence these results. Whether these short-term effects on intellectual function are related to anesthesia, extracorporeal circulation, time in an intensive care unit, sleep deprivation medications, or a combination of these variables was not defined.

In another retrospective case-control study (Gonzalez-Scarano & Hurtig,

1981), a total of 18 of 1,427 patients (1.3%) who underwent coronary artery bypass graft surgery developed neurological complications within the first 14 days after the operation. Mortality from these complications occurred during the surgery, and 3 of the 5 patients who suffered a cerebral infarction during surgery expired as did 2 of the 3 patients who developed anoxic encephalopathy. Postoperative neurological complications consisted of cerebral infarction (6 patients), anoxic encephalopathy (2 patients), brain stem infarction (1 patient), and spinal cord infarction (1 patient). The patient with the spinal cord infarction was the only patient with a postoperative complication who expired as a result of renal failure. The patients who did survive their complications were discharged from the hospital either without or with very minimal residual neurological abnormality. When comparisons were made between these 18 patients who developed neurological complications and an age-matched control group of 18 patients who had the same surgery, no statistically significant differences were observed between the two groups with regard to the following preoperative risk factors: hypertension, hyperlipidemia, diabetes mellitus, cervical bruits, history of cardiovascular symptoms, history of cigarette smoking, and being a current cigarette smoker. No significant differences were observed between the two groups in terms of important intraoperative variables such as mean duration of bypass or the frequency with which difficulties were encountered in terminating bypass, nor were there significant differences between the groups in regard to postoperative hypotension. Although the mean arterial pressures were similar during operation for these patients, 2 of the patients who developed neurological complications did have a prolonged low mean arterial pressure, lasting at least 10 min, that had not been quickly reversible with vasopressor drugs.

In another study, Freeman et al. (1985) investigated whether or not decreased regional blood flow would result in cognitive impairment. Coronary artery bypass graft patients were assessed preoperatively and postoperatively utilizing the Mini-Mental State Examination. These investigators were unable to document any association between intraoperative decreased cerebral blood flow and scores on the Mini-Mental State Examination, a test commonly utilized to screen populations for cognitive impairment.

Nussmeier, Arlund, and Slogoff (1986), having observed that most neurological complications following open-heart surgery have focal manifestations that would implicate emboli as their source, conducted a study to attempt to reduce the manifestations of emboli. Based on previous knowledge that the barbiturate thiopental was an effective prophylactic agent against embolization and could lessen the size of cerebral infarcts that were caused by cerebral ischemia in animals, they sought to use the drug in humans to determine whether it would provide cerebral protection and reduce the incidence of neuropsychiatric complications. Patients selected for inclusion in the study were those believed to be at highest risk of embolization, namely those with intracardiac procedures (repair or replacement of a cardiac valve, resection of a ventricular aneurysm, or repair of a septal defect). Preoperatively, all patients received a thorough neurological examination and a psychiatric evaluation that consisted of an assessment of orientation, memory, affect, ideation, and any unusual behavior (e.g., hostility or withdrawal). Patients with known previous neurological or cerebrovascular disease or those with abnormal neurological or psychiatric evaluations were not included in the study. The Trail-Making Test was also administered to all patients both preoperatively and on the fifth postoperative day at which time the extensive neurological examination and psychiatric evaluation were repeated. A shortened version of the neurological and psychiatric evaluations were obtained the day after surgery. A total of 89 patients were randomly assigned to the control group. All patients received the customary dose of fentanyl, and patients in the treatment group received a dose of the barbiturate thiopental. At the time of the initial evaluation on the day after surgery, 5 of the patients in the treatment group and 8 of the control group patients were found to have neurological or psychiatric abnormalities. At the time of the more extensive evaluation 10 days postoperatively, all previous abnormalities had cleared in the treatment group but remained in the 7 patients who were in the control group. Variables that were significantly related to the development of complications included increased age, calcified valves, the procedure of aortic valve replacement, and longer duration of bypass. Hypotenstion was not significantly associated with the development of neurological or psychiatric complications. These investigators attribute embolization as the most probable cause of the type of sensorimotor dysfunction which is frequently observed following open-heart surgery. And their data offers promise for the use of thiopental in ameliorating some of the consequences of embolization.

STUDIES THAT CORRELATE NEUROLOGIC
AND ANATOMIC FINDINGS

Hypothermia to 8 to 12°C caused moderate-to-severe brain damage when its duration was over 130 min (Egerton et al., 1963). One autopsied case showed focal hemorrhagic lesions in white matter, especially the brain stem; neuronal degeneration was found microscopically. Animal studies at 0 °C for 2 hr have shown necrosis of nerves partly as the result of blood vessel damage; at temperatures about 0 °C for 1 hr, there was also damage to myelin in larger nerves.

When 35 cardiotomy patients who died were autopsied to examine brain lesions (Brierley, 1964), 22 showed focal and geographic lesions that correlate in 15 patients with known hypotensive episodes either during cardiopulmonary bypass or within 60 hours of it. No evidence of large emboli was found, and minor small emboli could not have caused such geographic lesions. When 215 patients were autopsied among whom 134 had cardiac surgery and 81 had nonoperative cardiac disease (mainly myocardial infarction), open-heart-surgery patients showed fat emboli among 80% and nonfat emboli in 31%. Surprisingly, fat emboli were also present in 48% of the brains of the myocardial infarction nonoperated patients whose main characteristic was advanced age (Hill, Aguilar, Baranco, Lanerolle, & Gerbode, 1969). In the Tufo et al. (1970) series of 100 cardiac surgery patients, 10 among the 15 who died in the first 2 weeks postoperative underwent autopsy examination. Nine of the 10 brains showed small, multiple lesions in both gray and white matter with anoxic damage to the hippocampus in 7 patients. Foci of infarction mainly in gray matter and perivascular damage in white matter were found in 6 brains. No particulate emboli were found.

Emboli were a hazard of open-heart operations that were decreased as technology and surgical technique (Longmore, 1982) were refined. Sources of air emboli included the extracorporeal pump oxygenator, trapped air in the left ventricle at the end of the surgery, poorly designed coronary suction devices, air-warmed fluids, accidental injection with cardioplegia solutions or placement of cannulae. Fat emboli could result from whole blood from unfasted donors, fat liberated in the blood from direct trauma to fatty tissues in the chest (and returned to the pump oxygenator via the coronary aspirator), direct exposure to gas in nonmembrane oxygenators, and from median sternotomy incisions more commonly than transverse ones. Particulate emboli could occur from silicone material in antifoam sprays, particles of fibrin or sponge, precipitates in prime and other fluids, or calcium emboli from calcified valves (Gilman, 1965). Microembolism of aggregated platelet or clots from whole blood as well as other forms of blood damage by the pump oxygenator (Allardyce et al., 1966) were lessened by improvements in the pump oxygenators and their filters as well as by the shift away from the use of blood as the solution to prime the pump.

Initial use of a normal electroencephalogram (EEG) pattern as a criterion for adequate perfusion was disappointing (Coons, Keats, & Cooley, 1959). Differing EEG patterns, in terms of early loss of rapid activity replaced by high-voltage slow delta waves or progression of early changes to a flat EEG intraoperatively, did not correlate directly with postoperative mental and neurologic status. The investigators felt that the variable EEG patterns reflected varying proportions of total perfused blood reaching the brain. EEG abnormalities are commonly recorded during occlusion of the vena cavae, at the initiation and conclusion of bypass and at the time of aortic clamping or during low arterial blood oxygen saturation, but these episodes correlate poorly with the subsequent clinical course. A normal EEG in the presence of a clinical deficit makes it likely that cerebral blood flow had not been decreased significantly. An abnormal EEG after surgery along with a clinical neurologic abnormality makes neurologic recovery more doubtful (Fischer-Williams & Cooper, 1964).

Utilizing computerized EEG recording for anatomic localization in open-heart surgery patients on the fifth day before and twenty-fifth day after surgery, Spehr and Götze (1982) have predicted postoperative psychiatric disturbances by comparing preoperative and postoperative EEGs within each of six behavioral (psychiatric) groups and by comparing five groups with behavioral disturbances to the normals. The six behavioral groups were normals, psychically disturbed, light (mild) organic brain syndrome, moderate organic brain syndrome with hallucinations, paranoid/hallucination brain syndrome with dysphoria, and delerium. Different types of wave slowing seemed to be associated with different degrees of symptoms. Discriminating EEG variables seemed to be provided by the left hemisphere, especially the posttemporal regions. Focal slowing of the left posttemporal area appeared predictive of disturbed orientation, whereas slowing on the right predicted both early and late (3 to 4 weeks) psychiatric disturbances. The investigators emphasized the need to define the other clinical factors that determine the predictive features of the electroencephalographic record in open-heart surgery patients.

PSYCHIATRIC AND PSYCHOLOGICAL COMPLICATIONS OF CARDIAC SURGERY

Operative procedures, in and of themselves, have been deemed an "insult to emotional equilibrium" (Greenspan, Bannett, & Pressman, 1960), and an extensive variety of psychiatric and psychological consequences have been reported to be associated with them (Abram, 1967). For more than four decades, the medical literature has been growing with regard to the psychological impact of operations upon nearly every organ of the body. Interest has grown in treating the patient as a whole human being in all subspecialities of medicine. Considerable evidence exists to support the fact that preoperative psychological state, long-standing personality traits, and patient attitudes and expectations with regard to the outcome of operative procedures do influence the early postoperative course as well as the potential for recovery and rehabilitation on a long-term basis.

Many clinicians and investigators, including Kimball (1969), have observed that psychological problems were not only different but appeared to be more common and frequently more severe following operative procedures on the heart. The fact that the heart is a critical organ in terms of sustaining life is appreciated by even the most ignorant of patients, and many of the psychiatric symptoms that have been commonly encountered prior to or following operative procedures on the heart have been observed in nonsurgical cardiac patients and reported in the European scientific literature since the early eighteenth century. Cardiac disease, therefore, often results in a major source of fear for patients, and surgical management of cardiac disease frequently causes intensification of these fears.

A wide variety of psychiatric and psychological reactions to cardiac surgery have been reported in the literature and include depression, disorientation, confusion, hallucinations, agitation, hysteria, traumatic neurosis, psychotic reactions as well as severe catastrophic and panic reactions. The results of these studies are difficult or impossible to compare for a variety of reasons. Many studies have combined neurological, psychiatric, and cognitive dysfunction symptoms together, thereby creating syndromes, whereas others have treated specific symptoms or diagnoses as separate entities. Although many early studies concentrated on defining the incidence of either syndromes or specific symptoms in patients with the same surgical procedure (e.g., mitral commissurotomy), more recent investigators have generally included patients who have undergone a variety of different operative procedures on the heart. Methods of assessment also differ and range from prospective to retrospective and from observational to empirical. The incidence of these complications, although having experienced decreases with improved techniques and technology, gives evidence of a broad range (from 3% to 80%).

Some clinicians, including Hackett and Weisman (1960), have attempted to clarify and distinguish between the delirium and psychosis. As they explain, the signs and symptoms of delirium may include varying degrees of confusion and disorientation as well as hallucinations and rather unstructured (nonpsychotic) delusions that are frequently accompanied by hyperexcitability. In a psychotic reaction, on the other hand, disorientation is uncommon as are hallucinations, and hyperexcitability, and the major symptom is disturbance in the thought process. Patients who have experienced an early postoperative delirium may also later develop a psychotic episode, although the incidence of postoperative psychosis appears to be much lower than that of delirium.

During the early 1950s, research attention began to be devoted to the assessment of psychiatric disturbances surrounding operative procedures on patients with mitral valve disease because psychiatric symptoms were clinically observed to be quite common. Fox, Rizzo, and Gifford (1954) investigated a series of 36 patients who had cardiac surgery to correct stenosis of the mitral valve. Patients were interviewed by a psychiatrist preoperatively (generally on one or two occasions, the last of which was approximately 48 hr prior to surgery) and 1 week postoperatively. Further follow-up information was collected at 6 months postoperatively in most instances. The preoperative interview sought information concerning how patients viewed and actively coped with their progressively disabling cardiac disease and their expectations (or fantasies) concerning the illness or surgery. All interviews were tape recorded and the long-standing personality traits, usual psychological defense mechanisms, and emergency defense mechanisms of all patients were examined in association with data on the patients' medical status. The majority of patients had had their heart condition and symptoms for more than 10 years, and most of them were in the preterminal or terminal stages of their illness and were seriously ill. These patients received a "finger-fracture valvuloplasty" procedure in which the surgeon's finger was utilized to relieve the valvular stenosis with no direct visualization of the operative site. A few of the patients also had insufficiency of the mitral valve (all of whom were terminally ill), and they received a highly experimental procedure—the insertion of a plastic ball. These latter patients were, however, not directly informed of the potential risks of mortality associated with the procedure. The results of interpretation of the clinical psychiatric interview data on this series of patients indicates that although there was considerable variation in patients' reactions to becoming aware of their cardiac disease and to activity limitations resulting from symptoms, three main psychological defense mechanisms emerged as being most commonly utilized by patients to cope with the progressing disease and symptoms. These consisted of narcissism, externalization of their locus of control to a higher power (e.g., a deity), and increased activity (an attempt to deny symptoms and pursue activities). Additional defenses that were employed by patients when other coping mechanisms failed included denial, hysteric amnesia, depersonalization, and immobilization. In some patients, however, defense mechanisms proved to be totally inadequate, and these patients were observed to be in a severe state of stress and panic. Six patients in their series (19%) developed psychological disturbances after surgery, but preoperative coping behavior and psychological defense mechanisms were not consistently accurate predictors of postoperative psychological or psychiatric state. To some extent, however, the knowledge gained from the preoperative interviews was deemed useful in providing early postoperative psychiatric intervention. It was also observed that some patients who had experienced no preoperative disturbance developed unexpected psychological disturbances postoperatively when they developed serious medical complications following the operative procedure.

Following this earliest documentation of psychiatric disturbances occurring after cardiac surgery, other investigators began to report a similar incidence of postoperative psychiatric problems, including postoperative psychosis. Factors such as severity or duration of illness and perioperative complications or age or sex were not found to be related to the development of postoperative psychiatric disturbances. It was observed, however, that patients who had mitral insufficiency were more likely to experience postoperative psychiatric disturbances, and the hypothesis was advanced that the disturbance might have an organic basis that was related to the disease or surgical repair of the cardiac valve. Other researchers argued that at least some of these psychiatric disturbances were the result of the use of anesthetic agents, particularly nitrous oxide.

Early in the 1960s, Knox (1961), in Belfast, was unable to replicate the previously reported incidence of postoperative psychiatric disturbance. In a retrospective study of 50 mitral-valve-surgery patients, only 1 patient was identified as having a postoperative psychiatric disturbance. In a second series of 30 such patients examined preoperatively as well as postoperatively, 1 patient evidenced a mild confusional state of short duration; however, an unstated number of other reactions such as hysteria were also observed.

The first study in the published literature that employed the use of control groups in the investigation of psychological reactions in patients having mitral valve disease was that of Matarazzo, Bristow, and Reaume (1963). These investigators wished to explore the role of personality as well as medical factors (such as duration of chronic illness) and their potential associations with mitral valve disease patients. During the course of a 1-year period, 32 patients with a diagnosis of mitral stenosis (having a mean age of 43 years) were investigated along with a comparison group of 26 patients with coronary heart disease who had a mean age of 54 years. All patients completed the Taylor Manifest Anxiety Scale, the Saslow Psychometric Inventory, and the Cornell Medical Index. These other tests were also administered to other comparison groups: a group of 40 medical inpatients, a group of 42 medical outpatients, a group of 40 psychiatric inpatients, and a group of 40 psychiatric outpatients to examine potential differences among groups. No statistically significant differences were observed between the mitral stenosis patients and the coronary heart disease patients on any of the four tests, nor were there significant differences between either group of cardiac patients and either the inpatient or outpatient groups of medical patients. Cardiac patients scored significantly lower than the two groups of psychiatric patients on the Taylor Manifest Anxiety Scale ($p < .001$), the Saslow Psychometric Inventory ($p < .001$) and the Cornell Medical Index ($p < .001$) as well as the psychiatric subscale of the Cornell Medical Index ($p < .001$). Hospital records of the 22 mitral stenosis patients who subsequently underwent corrective cardiac surgery were then examined to search for documented postoperative behavioral disturbances. These were then compared with a control group of 32 other randomly selected surgical patients who had undergone major surgical procedures requiring a minimum postoperative hospital stay of 2 weeks. The group of mitral valve surgery patients had a much higher incidence of documented postoperative emotional disturbance than the group of patients with other types of major surgeries (68% versus 38%, $p < .05$). The most common postoperative emotional disturbances were anxiety and depression, and these two problems represented about 70% of the reactions. Severe pain accompanied by moaning and confusion, although much less frequent, accounted for the remaining documented postoperative disturbances. These disturbances occurred within the first 4 postoperative days and were of short duration, a median of 2 days. When the preoperative psychological test scores of those patients who had postoperative disturbances were compared with those who did not have evidence of documented disturbances, no differences were observed. Therefore, the investigators could not conclude that preoperative personality factors, age, sex, or length of stay, played an important role in predicting the development of subsequent postoperative emotional disturbances. These served as a quasi-measure of the severity of the trauma imposed by surgery. Because these researchers were unable to demonstrate that preoperative psychological factors were associated with the postoperative emotional disturbances, other medical factors were examined in search of an explanation for their occurrence. Severity of cardiac impairment could not be adequately examined because the majority of patients had severe preoperative cardiac impairment. Duration of cardiac illness did, however, prove to be an important medical variable in that persons who had postoperative behavioral disturbances had had their cardiac illness for a mean of 6.9 years compared with a duration of 3.6 years ($p < .001$) for the group of patients who were without psychological complications.

Abram (1965) investigated psychological responses to the threat of death experienced by a small series of 23 patients who underwent open-heart surgery, facilitated by the utilization of a pump oxygenator, for a variety of corrective cardiac surgical procedures. Psychiatric interviews of approximately 1-hr duration were conducted 1 to 2 days preoperatively to ascertain life history, attitudes toward cardiac disease, and impressions of the impending cardiac surgery. An overview of the patient's general personality structure and the defense mechanisms that were commonly utilized by the patient to cope with anxiety were also obtained. Surviving patients were interviewed by a psychiatrist postoperatively on a daily basis until patients were discharged from the hospital. The most commonly observed preoperative reactions to the impending surgery were severe anxiety that was present in 38% of the patients and denial of surgery as being a life-threatening experience in the case of 33% of the patients. One patient was so severely anxious about his impending surgery that he closed his business, had made the necessary legal preparations for his will, and he was concerned that he might be becoming insane. Of the 23 patients in this series, 8 expired during, or very shortly after, surgery (including the very severely anxious patient), and 1 patient expired after hospital discharge. The most commonly observed postoperative psychiatric reaction was the so called "catastrophic reaction" that was first described as having been observed in mitral valve surgery patients by Meyer, Blacher, and Brown (1961). Patients who developed this reaction were noted to have vacant facial expressions, remain immobilized, and they appear apathetic, fatigued, and are relatively nonverbal. These reactions have generally been reported to be of short duration, lasting only several days, and a very small percentage of patients have been observed to have also experienced a psychosis. Two of the patients in the present study had evidence of psychotic symptoms that included depersonalization and visual hallucinations; however, this state differs in one important aspect from the acute postoperative delirium described in an earlier section of this chapter in that these two patients were not disoriented. The potential etiological role of overstimulation resulting from all of the equipment, machines, procedures, and staff activity inherent in the intensive care unit environment was suggested by the author.

In a much larger series of 99 adult and 20 pediatric open-heart surgery patients (Kornfeld et al., 1965), these investigators also examined the potential contributing role of the intensive care unit in relation to the development of postoperative psychiatric complications. In their series, acute organic psychosis was determined to be present in 38% of the adult patients but in none of the pediatric patients, as determined by documentation of symptoms by physicians and nurses in the hospital charts of patients. In a subgroup of 20 patients in the series, who were interviewed postoperatively by psychiatrists, there was a 70% incidence of acute organic psychosis. In all but 2 of these patients, symptoms appeared after a lucid interval of at least 2 days, and this was defined as delirium. No statistically significant differences were observed between patients who developed psychiatric complications and those who did not in terms of age (other than the fact that none of the children developed them), sex, type of surgical procedure performed, duration of preoperative congestive heart failure, length of surgical procedure, total duration of time on cardiopulmonary bypass, or extent of hypothermia.

Patients who had operations on two separate cardiac valves did have much longer durations of surgery, total time on cardiopulmonary bypass, and a 78% incidence of delirium. The incidence of neurological complications, however, was reported to be very low both in the group of patients who encountered acute postoperative organic psychoses and the group that did not develop them. The authors attributed this finding to the use of the disc oxygenator, which should have reduced exposure to microemboli, as well as to careful monitoring and control of metabolic status of all patients. The acute psychiatric disturbances generally resolved by the sixth postoperative day, and patients were discharged from the intensive care recovery room on the average of 5.7 days postoperatively. When interviewed postoperatively and specifically queried concerning their perceptions of their experiences in the intensive care unit, the great majority of patients found the environment to be fear provoking, frightening, and not conducive to sleep. This is not surprizing, given the strange sounds produced by the monitoring devices and other equipment, the presence of other patients, and the constant presence of health care professionals.

This research contribution also very clearly illustrates some of the problems inherent in attempting to sort out and differentiate postoperative complications that are completely organic from those that are psychological or psychiatric. The 38% of patients who experienced complications in this series developed documented symptoms of illusions, hallucinations, and paranoid thoughts, but they also became disoriented. As Hackett and Weisman (1960) have suggested, the visual or auditory hallucinations that occur during delirium are much more unstructered and are generally disturbances in reality testing at the perceptual level rather than at the conceptual level that would generally be the case in psychosis. Additionally, they have observed that disorientation is uncommon in patients with psychosis. It, therefore, appears justified that these researchers have labeled the complications encountered by the patients as an "organic phenomenon." They also point out that the postoperative clinical course of the patients with these complications resembles the symptomatic course of persons who serve as subjects in studies of the effects of sleep deprivation, both in terms of symptoms and in the resolution of symptoms. Subjects in sleep deprivation studies have a similar constellation of symptoms and by the fifth day of sleep deprivation appear to have symptoms of delirium at night and symptoms of paranoid schizophrenia during the day. In both sleep deprivation studies and this study, the symptoms resolved rapidly after a period of sufficient sleep. In the cardiac surgery patients, these symptoms were observed to have resolved very shortly after patients were transferred from the intensive care unit to a general hospital floor.

Conceptually similar to the earlier work of Fox *et al.* (1954) that focused on the utilization of preoperative psychiatric adjustment as a potential predictor of postoperative psychiatric adjustment or disturbance, Kimball (1969) investigated a series of 54 adult open-heart surgery patients. All patients were interviewed 1 day prior to their cardiac surgery, utilizing a 45- to 90-min open-ended interview technique to determine the patient's previous level of psychological adjustment, the patient's general optimism, and outlook and plans for the future. Based on an evaluation of patient responses to these general areas during the course of the preoperative interviews, patients were divided into four groups (or categories of preoperative adjustment) that were then correlated with early, intermediate, and late course. During the early postoperative period, which consisted of the days when the patient was in the intensive care unit (an average of 5 to 7 days) and the intermediate postoperative period (the remainder of the postoperative stay), patients were observed for from 5 to 30 min each day, and their mental status was documented. Patients were also asked to describe how they were feeling. Medical records were examined to identify and document the observations recorded by other caretakers, and patients' relatives were, in some instances, consulted to further substantiate patients' responses and reactions. Just prior to hospital discharge, patients received a more lengthy interview to determine how they felt about the experience when they were about to leave the hospital. Long-term follow-up consisted of conducting interviews of approximately one-half hour to determine patient adjustment with regard to employment, family life, and personal satisfaction as well as any problems encountered at 1- to 3-month periods for as long as 15 months.

The four groups of patients that emerged from an evaluation of the results of the preoperative interviews were labeled the *adjusted*, the *symbiotic*, the *anxious*, and the *depressed* groups, and the characteristics of these groups of patients have been described in detail by Kimball (1969). During the early postoperative period, while in the intensive care unit, a variety of patient responses and reactions were documented by daily observations. All patients in this series experienced some degree of transient delirium persisting for as long as 36 hr, even though some had an otherwise uneventful early postoperative course. Some patients developed what Kimball and others have termed a *catastrophic reaction*, although they remained oriented. This reaction generally lasted for approximately 5 days, and then symptoms ceased, after which patients did not remember the episode. Some patients experienced a euphoric state during the early postoperative period that generally occurred within 24 hr after operation. These patients were oriented, optimistic, happy, and they tended to progress much faster, leave the intensive-care unit much sooner, and experience fewer medical complications than other patients. Although some degree of delirium could be detected in all patients in this study, 19 patients experienced more severe or prolonged altered states of consciousness. Three patients in the series developed the classic delirium observed in many other series of patients (consisting of fluctuating awareness and decreased cognitive performance) as well as hallucinations and paranoid ideation in some instances. In this series of patients, the delirium was accompanied by documented electroencephalographic evidence of slowing and reduced amplitude. Another 6 patients were either comatose or not responsive, and they had signs of focal lesions and frequently had permanent residual impairment such as hemiparesis. An additional 8 patients expired after surgery, and 2 patients expired during the first 2 postoperative days.

The early part of the intermediate postoperative period when patients were transferred from the intensive care unit to a general hospital floor normally followed a course where patients first experienced anxiety, later experienced depression, and then later spent several days sleeping, after which they began to plan to go home. At this time, some of the patients who previously had reacted with euphoria developed postoperative complications. Just prior to hospital discharge, many patients evidenced renewed anxiety and concern about elements of the recovery process and resumption of activities after hospital discharge.

In terms of long-term follow-up, patients were rated, based on their interviews, on whether their functioning was improved, the same as, or worse than their preoperative levels of functioning. Results demonstrated that the 13 patients who had been classified as "adjusted" preoperatively had a relatively uneventful early and intermediate postoperative course and generally showed an improvement in long-term functioning. However, 1 patient in this group did expire. The 15 patients who had been preoperatively classified as "symbiotic" did not fare as well postoperatively, in that they were more likely to have developed complications and required longer hospitalization, and their long-term follow-up documented that the majority of these patients had unchanged or worse levels of functioning. The 12 patients who were in the anxious group preoperatively were those who were most likely to develop catastrophic reactions during the early postoperative period. Six of the patients in this group developed these reactions, and 3 patients expired during surgery. Patients in the anxious group were also noted to be more prone to cardiac arrythmias during the intermediate postoperative period. On long-term follow-up, 3 patients demonstrated improved functioning, 3 patients remained unchanged, 2 patients had become worse, and 1 patient had expired. The 14 patients who were in the depressed group did the most poorly of all patients, and only 3 of these survived until the long-term follow-up. Of the 3 patients who did survive, only 1 had improved functioning. These findings of increased mortality in anxious patients and an even more grave prognosis in patients who are depressed preoperatively are even more noteworthy given the fact that no significant differences between the four groups could be attributed to either age differences or differences in duration of illness or severity of cardiac illness as measured by cardiologists' assessments of functional classification of cardiac disease.

As a continuation of his earlier interest in investigating patients who were undergoing cardiac operations, Kimball and several colleagues (Kimball, Quinlan, Osborne & Woodward, 1973) replicated their earlier work with a larger series of patients who were evaluated preoperatively and also received long-term follow-up interviews for a time period as long as 30 months. This research undertaking was similar in design and methodology as that previously described in this chapter with the exception that the following psychological tests were added to the preoperative assessments of the patients: the Multiple Affect Adjective Check List (for depression, anxiety, and hostility); the Cornell Medical Index; the subscales for Block Design and information from the Wechsler Adult Intelligence Scale; the Weissman-Ricks Mood Level scale; Rotter's Internal-External Locus of Control; a six-item version of the Eysenck Neuroticism Scale; as well as the Freeman-Simmons subscales for Authority/Submission and Independence/Dependence. The Multiple Affect Adjective Check List, the Mood Level Scale, and the Block Design and Information subscales were also administered a second time just prior to hospital discharge. Long-term follow-up consisted of documenting employment status at 6 months and survival at 18 months.

A total of 109 patients in this series were classified into four groups based on their preoperative interviews. Seventeen patients were classified as *adjusted*, 30 patients were classified as *symbiotic*, 26 were classified as *denying anxiety*, and 36 were classified as *depressed*. As the reader will note, the name of the third patient group has been changed from "anxious" in the earlier investigation to "denying anxiety." The authors explain that this semantic refinement is the result of the fact that patients in this group tend to actually display apparent physiological manifestations of anxiety while, at the same time, they have a tendancy to verbally deny being anxious. Sociodemographic data, medical variables, and psychological and cognitive test results were examined to determine whether differences existed between patients who had been classified in the four different groups. Statistically significant differences were found between the groups with regard to sex, in that more females were present in the group labeled symbiotic and more men were present in the denying-anxiety and depressed groups. Age was also an important variable, with the age being significantly greater for those patients who were classified as being in the symbiotic (mean age 57.8 years) and the depressed groups (mean, 51.9 years) versus the adjusted (mean, 43.5 years) or the denying-anxiety group (mean, 44.4 years). Therefore, these age and sex differences may have affected coping mechanisms. Differences among groups also existed for 4 of the 24 medical/surgical variables that were investigated, and the authors believe that these differences suggest that the patients in the adjusted group appear to have the least cardiac dysfunction followed by the denying-anxiety, symbiotic, and the depressed groups. Statistically significant differences among the four groups also occurred for five of the seven psychological tests that were administered. Patients in the adjusted group scored as having an internal locus of control on Rotter's Locus of Control Scale as opposed to the external locus of control observed in the other patient groups. Significant differences of the mean scores for the groups were also observed for the Hostility and Depression subscales of the Multiple Affect Adjective Check List; however, no significant differences were observed for the Anxiety subscale. Patients in the depressed group did demonstrate higher depression scores on the Depression subscale as well as higher Depression scores on the Wessman-Ricks Mood Level Scale. After having made the appropriate adjustments for age and intelligence on the Wechsler Adult Intelligence Scale Block Design subscale that had been administered both pre- and postoperatively, the symbiotic group was observed to demonstrate greater cognitive impairment. This was in contrast to the interviewer's assessment. Differences among the four groups were also observed with both the overall Cornell Medical Index scores and the subsection on subjective self-assessment of cardiac symptoms. The symbiotic and the depressed groups had the highest scores on these measures and appeared to be more aware of, or willing to, express their awareness of symptoms. The authors expressed disappointment with the objective psychological tests in their ability to clearly distinguish or identify the four patient groups, particularly the group classified as denying anxiety and recommend that they are clearly inadequate as a replacement for preoperative interviews conducted by psychiatrists. The results of the long-term follow-up of these four groups of patients showed that patients in the adjusted group had significantly higher rates of return to work at 6-month follow-up than the other groups. Eighteen-month survival was significantly higher in the adjusted and symbiotic groups than in the denying-anxiety or "depressed" groups. The conclusions that were drawn from this investigation concerning the prognostic value of preoperatively assigning patients to these four distinct psychological-adjustment and coping-style groups is that these preoperative group classifications are of great value for predicting long-term prognosis. Their utility in predicting short-term prognosis is very clearly diminished by the fact that other preoperative, perioperative, and early postoperative medical and surgical variables exert a statistically significant influence on the morbidity and mortality of individual patients that transcends group classifications.

Research interest and concern persisted with regard to preoperative coping behavior as a predictor of postoperative psychological status of patients who underwent open-heart surgery. A series of 72 patients who were about to undergo open-heart operations were interviewed preoperatively and were followed postoperatively in Germany (Möhlen, Davies-Osterkamp, Müller, Scheld, & Siefen, 1982). After the interviews had been completed, questionnaires were completed by the interviewer to document four general areas: overall behavior and emotional involvement while being interviewed; mechanisms utilized by the patient in coping with illness in general; mood, emotional status, and coping mechanisms with regard to the impending surgery; and any prior history of neurological or psychiatric illnesses. Patients were observed and evaluated on a daily basis while in the intensive care unit, at which time a psychopathological symptom rating scale was completed. Complications were also recorded and rated in terms of severity on a 3-point scale and total weighted sum scores were calculated. A total of 55 of the 72 patients participated in a 1-year follow-up that included a symptom inventory, a personality inventory, and questions concerning self-perception of the extent of recovery. Patients also received semistructured interviews to solicit information concerning postoperative utilization of medical care, health behavior, employment status, social participation, and family relationships. Four distinct groups of patients emerged when early postoperative psychological status was examined. A group of 17 patients had evidence of overt psychiatric symptoms; of these, 8 patients manifested anxiety and paranoid ideation, and 9 patients exhibited symptoms of delirium. Although none of the patients with anxiety and paranoid ideation had any evidence of organic brain damage, 6 of the patients who were delirious did have evidence of organic brain damage. A second group of 12 patients were classified as having a "depressive-distressed" reaction, and a third group of 12 patients were classified as having an "aggressive-hostile" reaction. The fourth group of patients were classified as having and "inconspicous" reaction. The remaining 21 patients had mixed reactions.

The investigators then sought to examine correlations between patients' preoperative coping mechanisms and the different postoperative reactions. The component of the preoperative interview that dealt with behavior and emotional involvement during the interview was subjected to factor analysis, from which three scales were derived: Emotional Withdrawal versus Openness, Depressive Inhibition versus Hypomanic Disinhibition, and Activity versus Passivity. When the results on these scales were examined for patients in the four different postoperative reaction patient groups, it was noted that the patients who experienced aggressive-hostile reactions postoperatively had demonstrated evidence of significantly greater emotional withdrawal or depressive inhibition during the preoperative interview. This group of patients also had low postoperative complication scores. No significant differences were found between the four patient groups on the Activity versus Passivity scale. Factor analysis was also performed on the component of the preoperative interview that focused on the coping mechanisms of patients. Two of the four dimensions were predictors of postoperative reactions. These were (a) viewing the cardiac surgery as a "technical event" and (b) optimistic versus pessimistic outlook for the future. Patients who postoperatively were in the group that experienced the psychiatric disturbances of anxiety and paranoid ideation were significantly more likely to view the impending surgery as a technical event and to express optimism concerning the future than were the other three groups of patients. When data from the 1-year follow-up interview were examined, it became apparent that three of the same preoperative predictors of early postoperative reactions were also correlated with long-term outcomes. These included emotional withdrawal, depressed-inhibited behavior, and a coping style that permitted the patient to view the surgery as a technical event. Patients who were emotionally withdrawn during the preoperative interview were not pleased with their recovery, and they felt that they were worse than before surgery. Those patients who preoperatively exhibited depressed-inhibited behavior were much more positive during the follow-up interview. They put little emphasis on their cardiac condition during the interview, and they reported less depression and a much more positive mental state. Those patients who preoperatively viewed their impending cardiac operations as purely technical events had poor long-term outcomes, in that they reported more depression, restlessness, and mental instability. They also perceived that they were receiving inadequate medical and psychological support from their personal physicians. The investigators concluded that preoperative behaviors and coping styles have predictive value both in terms of short-term and long-term outcomes following open-heart surgery.

In another study undertaken in Finland (Tienari *et al.*, 1982), a series of 81 open-heart surgery patients were given an extensive psychiatric, psychological, and neurological examination 3 to 4 mon preoperatively. This was repeated 3 to 6 mon postoperatively. Patients also received psychiatric interviews within 2 days prior to operation that were repeated 1 week after surgery. Additionally, postoperative psychological status was monitored and recorded on a daily basis during the first postoperative week. During the early postoperative period, 42 patients (51.9%) developed psychiatric or neuropsychiatric complications. These included psotcardiotomy delirium (22 patients), functional psychosis (7 patients), hysteric reaction (7 patients), depressive reaction (4 patients), and the remaining 2 patients had a borderline psychiatric crisis. Female patients had a much higher frequency of psychiatric complications (66.7%) than did male patients (43.1%). Age was also an important factor. The mean age of patients who experienced psychotic complications was 46.8 years, and although 31.3% of patients who were younger than 40 years of age developed a psychosis, 36.9% of patients older than 40 had a psychosis.

The preoperative psychological status of patients and the preoperative prediction of postoperative prognosis were examined in relation to postoperative status. Preoperative psychological status was rated using a scale that ranged from 1 (essentially healthy) to 6 (psychotic). Preoperative prediction of prognosis was rated on a scale that ranged from 1 (*very good*) to 5 (*very poor*). Using this latter scale, 82% of the patients who did not develop complications postoperatively were correctly predicted preoperatively to have a good prognosis. Also, patients who did develop complications had received poorer prognosis scores preoperatively than the other patients. Patients who did develop postoperative complications were divided into two groups—those who developed delirium and those who developed functional disturbances that included psychoses and neurotic reactions. No significant difference was found for preoperative psychological status between patients who developed delirium and patients who experienced no postoperative complications. There was, however, a difference between patients who developed postoperative functional disturbances and patients who did not develop postoperative complications in that the patients who experienced functional disturbances had been rated as having greater levels of psycopathology preoperatively. Psychiatrists preoperative ratings of anxiety were higher ($p < .05$) in patients who subsequently developed complications as were preoperative scores on the Hamilton Anxiety Scale ($p < .001$). Preoperative depression assessed by Beck's Depression Scale was significantly higher ($p < .01$) in patients who experienced a neurotic reaction than in those who developed delirium. Preoperative Minnesota Multiphasic Personality Inventory (MMPI) results indicated deviated profiles in patients. This was particularly evident in patients who subsequently had a postoperative functional psychosis, given the finding that five out of seven of them had preoperative t scores above 70 on three scales.

A large battery of neuropsychological tests had also been administered to patients preoperatively. These included the Wechsler Adult Intelligence Scale, the Wechsler Memory Scale, Benton's Visual Retention Test, the Bender-Gestalt Test, and Weckroth's brain damage test battery. In general, there was a trend toward poorer performance on these tests in patients who developed postoperative functional disturbances (neurotic reactions or psychosis), but the observed differences were not statistically significant with one exception (the visual pieces component of Weckroth's test battery). Upon examination of the 6-month postoperative reassessment, it was noted, in general, that patients improved their performance on the neuropsychological tests, particularly on the visual tests. Those with postoperative delirium or psychosis demonstrated less improvement. Postoperative MMPI profiles normalized both in patients without complications and in those who had only experienced neurotic reactions. Those who had postoperative delirium experienced less normalization and those patients who had had a postoperative psychosis had persistent abnormalities on three scales (Psychasthenia, Schizophrenia, and Social Introversion) as well as on the psychosis index. These patients were also much more depressed (as measured by Beck's Depression Scale) at the 6-mon reassessment.

IMPLICATIONS OF THESE FINDINGS FOR MEDICAL MANAGEMENT AND REHABILITATION

It is quite clear from a substantial number of studies that have been described in this chapter that the preoperative psychological state of the patient is extremely important because it can provide valuable clues to how the patient may react during the early postoperative course. It would appear that, at a minimum, an assessment should be made of each patient's mechanisms of coping with the impending operation as well as an assessment of the patient's expectations of the outcome of surgery. This could be performed by nursing staff who have frequent contact with patients prior to surgery. Patients who exhibit marked anxiety or depression could be identified, and interventions could be initiated prior to surgery in an attempt to reduce the severity of these symptoms and restore an improved emotional equilibrium. Most hospitals currently have patient education programs that include components specifically designed to reduce the apprehension of patients who are about to undergo major cardiac surgery. These generally include a visit to the surgical intensive care unit where the patient will be placed immediately following surgery. All of the monitoring devices and the normal routine in the unit are explained to the patient in advance. Patients are also assured that, while they are on a respirator (and will be unable to talk), they will be observed very carefully in the event that they will be trying to communicate without speaking. They are also instructed in alternative ways of communicating.

Another source of preoperative emotional support for patients that is becoming increasingly more available to patients throughout the country is the Mended Hearts Organization, a national, self-help group comprised of former cardiac surgery patients. This organization has an extensive visiting program, and in many hospitals, accredited visitors routinely make pre-operative visits to patients who will be undergoing cardiac surgery. These visits can provide a good source of reassurance not only for the patient but to any family members who happen to be present. Patients awaiting cardiac surgery should also be introduced to, and encouraged to, communicate with other hospitalized patients who are recuperating from surgery. This provides them with the opportunity of finding out directly what the experience of surgery was like, how much pain they should expect, and, in some in-stances, the preoperative patient will request to see the healing surgical incision. The patient is often relieved to see that the incision is not as large or offensive as might have been imagined.

One, not uncommon, but sometimes difficult type of patient is the pa-tient who preoperatively utilizes denial as the primary defense mechanism for coping with cardiac surgery. These patients are generally quite easily identifiable and stand out from the others by their actions and demeanor. One finds them busily engaged in activities such as talking on the telephone, reading, or entertaining visitors. They do not appear to exhibit the signs of apprehension or mild anxiety that are frequently observed to accompany impending major surgery. They can present a management problem pre-operatively, in that they can be quite disinterested in the preoperative patient teaching and preparation for the early postoperative period. These patients may be insufficiently prepared for the active participation postoper-atively in chest physical therapy and deep breathing exercises, both of which are required to prevent early postoperative medical complications. Although there is no clearly superior way of dealing with these patients, they do require perseverence and patience when one is attempting to ade-quately prepare them for surgery.

The implications for medical management during the surgery itself have already been stated throughout previous sections of this chapter. Measures to foster adequate cerebral perfusion and the prevention of emboli have been implemented. These include the provision of safe levels of hypothermia, the maintenance of adequate arterial pressures throughout the duration of surgery, and the institution of a variety of measures to prevent the formation of the different types of emboli. These safeguard measures are of even more critical importance in more elderly cardiac patients because they appear to be at greater risk for the development of cerebral damage. This may be the result of the decreased cerebral blood flow and increased cerebral vascular resistance that accompany the aging process.

During the early postoperative period, while the patient is in the surgical intensive care unit, the patient should be observed carefully for signs and symptoms that have been repeatedly reported in the literature. When patients exhibit signs or symptoms of disorientation or confusion or experience illusions or hallucinations, an attempt should be made to identify any obvious potential source of the problem and to treat accordingly whenever possible. These include fever, metabolic abnormalities, renal failure, medications, and cardiac arrythmias such as transient heart block that can result in decreased cardiac output (thereby accounting for the development of the symptoms). For those patients who experience illusions, the surrounding environment should be examined in search of a contributory source, and if found, it should be explained to the patient to alleviate apprehension. Those caring for the patient should attempt to try to verbally orient the patient. Although difficult to accomplish, given the frequency with which patients need to be monitored by the nursing staff as well as the noises associated with the equipment, every possible attempt should be made to let the patient have as many periods of uninterrupted sleep as possible. Excessively loud communication at the nurses' station and the playing of music on a radio (currently a common practice) would best be prohibited to promote patient sleep and to foster the reduction of hallucinations and confusion that have been demonstrated to be associated with sleep deprivation. Increased flexibility in the visiting schedule might also prove to be beneficial, because visitors could be requested not to awaken a sleeping patient, but they could be permitted to wait and remain past the restricted visiting period in order to see the patient after he or she awakened. Because patients are frequently in a state of semiwakefulness during much of the early postoperative period (partially as a result of pain medications), it might also prove useful to assist them in reorienting themselves to time and place each time that they awaken. Visitors might also be encouraged to orient the patient.

One controlled study examined the effectiveness of having the female spouses of male coronary artery bypass patients orient the patients and initiate verbal, visual, and tactile contact with patients three times a day, each session lasting for a period of 10 min (Chatham, 1978). Both the patients who had received this intervention and the control patients were observed and rated during each 8-hr shift of each of the first 4 postoperative days by a registered nurse who utilized a Likert-type scale to rate the 11-item behavioral checklist. The results demonstrated that patients who had received this intervention from their spouses were significantly more oriented and behaviorally appropriate, and they slept longer than did the controls. Additionally, they were observed and rated as being less confused and delusional than were patients who had not received the intervention. It would appear, therefore, that this relatively simple intervention might offer some benefit in eliminating or alleviating the early postoperative symptoms.

For those patients, however, who do develop and sustain these early transient confusional states of varying intensity, one cannot overemphasize the importance of a sympathetic and reassuring health care team. The impact of the patient's symptoms on the spouse and other close relatives can be both frightening and disturbing, and these individuals can certainly benefit from reassurance that the symptoms are not only fairly common but that they generally resolve within several days. This usually occurs within 24 hr after the patient has been transferred out of the intensive care unit and has also had a sufficient interval of uninterrupted sleep.

At the time of transfer from the intensive care unit to a general patient-care floor, some patients experience severe anxiety and fear the loss of the constant monitoring and nursing attention. The apprehensions of these patients can usually be alleviated with extra reassurance about the status of their progress combined with a little extra attention from the nursing staff during the first day after the transfer. Other patients view the transfer as evidence of their successful progress toward recovery and appear to require no additional reassurance.

After the first few days on a general hospital floor, after which considerable progress will have been made by the majority of patients, many patients will suddenly experience what appears on the surface to be a setback, in that they withdraw and sleep a lot for several days. This may be the result of prior sleep deprivation, fatigue associated with ambulation and self-care activities, a lessening of discomfort, or from a self-perception that it is finally "safe" to sleep. At this stage, the patients should be permitted to sleep as much as is possible so that they can begin to regain their stamina.

Throughout the postoperative course, prior to discharge from the hospital, a variety of psychological disturbances or reactions may be encountered. The nature and severity of these emotional responses will, in large part, depend upon the meaning of the cardiac disease to the patient and the specific coping mechanisms that are utilized by the patient to deal with the stress associated with the illness. It has been suggested that the most commonly observed meanings of illness to patients are those of challenge or threat, loss, gain or relief, and punishment (Lipowski, 1983).

Patients who perceive of their illness as a challenge will generally cope with it actively and effectively during the postoperative period. Those who perceive of the illness as a threat will tend to exhibit fear and anxiety in the postoperative period and may require psychiatric consultation or medication.

Patients who view their cardiac disease as a loss will tend to experience grief and signs and symptoms of depression. Alternatively, they may react with anger and hostility. They may require assistance with working through their grief and achieving resolution of their sense of loss. If their depression is noted to be severe, they may also require medication. It has been a personal observation that this reaction appears to be more common in younger male patients than in older patients or in female patients. The sense of loss and ensuing grief is often augmented as a result of medical recommendations for risk-factor modification. These life-style changes, including cessation of smoking, dietary restrictions, restrictions on alcohol intake, stress reduction, and changes in exercise habits may be viewed by the patient as overwhelming and as a loss of some of the pleasure in life. When multiple changes are advised, it would probably be beneficial to the patient and improve patient compliance if a plan were established to tackle and accomplish the changes one at a time.

Some patients will perceive of their illness as a source of primary or secondary gain or relief, and they will utilize it as a means of withdrawing from roles or responsibilities. Many of these individuals will have had prior previous emotional conflict over their needs for dependency. For them, the cardiac surgery provides a tangible and acceptable vehicle for resolving the conflict by giving in to their strong needs for dependency. Although these patients will often appear to be emotionally content and undisturbed, in the face of their adversity, they may present long-term management problems. They frequently fail to acknowledge their symptomatic improvement and also resist taking advantage of the benefits resulting from medical intervention.

Patients who perceive of their illness as a form of punishment may display a variety of different behaviors and emotional reactions, depending on whether or not they are experiencing guilt and believe that they deserve punishment or whether they regard the punishment as unjustified. The former will appear to accept and be resigned to the cardiac disease, whereas the latter will express extreme anger and hostility as a result of it. Under both sets of circumstances, the patients may need extra encouragement to get them to actively participate in ambulation and exercises.

The meaning of the illness to the patient and the patient coping mechanisms play a salient role in determining how the patient will react to the experience of having open-heart surgery. This should be explored preoperatively and reassessed postoperatively in the event that it should change. Specific therapeutic interventions, appropriate to the individual emotional disturbance encountered, could then be employed. When patients develop serious medical complications during the postoperiod and thus face a renewed potential threat to life, additional psychological disturbances should be anticipated and will need to be managed accordingly. Emotional support will also generally need to be provided to spouses and close family members when medical complications develop because they are frequently exhausted and depleted from the strain of the whole experience when they are faced with this renewed threat.

Prior to discharge from the hospital, patient-teaching activities will attempt to provide the patient with important information including a timetable for the resumption of exercise and employment, activities to avoid; instructions concerning any prescribed medications and their potential side effects; an explanation of necessary dietary modifications; an explanation of when sexual functioning may be resumed; a description of potential complications to observe and report; and a discussion of common emotional problems that may be encountered. Patient education has been demonstrated by many investigators to promote more rapid recovery and to contribute to a reduction in fear, anxiety, and stress during the course of recovery.

As part of our own longitudinal study of recovery and rehabilitation after open-heart surgery, we investigated patients' perceptions of the adequacy of the patient education and preparation they had received, and we examined whether a relationship existed between perceived adequacy of preparation and the extent of fears and adjustments patients encountered during the first 6 mon after cardiac surgery (Stanton, Jenkins, Savageau, Harken, & Aucoin, 1984). All patients in this study had their surgery performed at one of four large, northeastern academic medical centers. Results of this inquiry demonstrated that, in general, patients believed that they had received adequate preparation in the topical areas of resumption of exercise and work and in activities that they should avoid. However, it was clear that more attention is needed on the topics of resumption of sexual functioning, potential physical and emotional symptoms that might be encountered, and possible changes in how others may treat patients after surgery. Between one third to one half of the patients were either uncertain or critical of the adequacy of their preparation in these important areas. Fears and adjustments were very commonly experienced by patients during the first 6 months after surgery, even in patients who felt that their patient education had been adequate in most areas. There appears to be considerable room for improvement in both the scope of the content and thoroughness of coverage of patient education information and the manner in which one insures that the patient has received and understood sufficient information. Although it is a necessary and prevailing clinical practice to provide patient education prior to hospital discharge, attempts to convey important information at this time may be less than optimally fruitful, particularly for those patients who continue to have neuropsychological sequelae such as intellectual impairment, poor short-term memory, anxiety, or depression. The information that is provided should be presented slowly and repeated on several occasions to foster comprehension and retention. Written materials can be provided to supplement the instructions. Whenever possible, the spouse or other close family member should also be provided with all of the necessary information and given the opportunity to ask questions. It would probably also be useful to plan to have patients and their spouses return to the hospital 1 or 2 months after surgery to attend a group session. These could be utilized to reinforce information, answer questions, clarify misconceptions, dispel unrealistic fears, and identify patients who may need referral for additional intervention to facilitate rehabilitation.

The progress toward recovery and rehabilitation following major cardiac surgery varies considerably among patients. This is evidenced by variability in key rehabilitative outcome measures such as resumption of employment (Stanton *et al.*, 1983); functional benefits (including physical functioning, sexual functioning, recreation, and social participation) (Stanton, Jenkins, Savageau, & Thurer, 1984); and freedom from morbidity requiring rehospitalization (Stanton *et al.*, 1985). It is also evident from our own work that recovery is multidimensional rather than a unitary process. It therefore cannot be assumed that because of improvements in one area, such as reduced anginal pain, other cardiac symptoms will necessarily be accompanied by improvements in other areas, such as the patient's emotional state. Careful monitoring of the progress of recovery is necessary, and the optimal person to assume this responsibility is the patient's general internist or primary care physician. The internist will usually have known and treated the patient for some time and will be in a position to assist the patient with making any necessary life-style modifications, answer questions, and encourage the patient to resume normal activities. He or she will also usually be able to recognize subtle changes in the emotional state of the patient that may require attention.

REPRESENTATIVE CASE STUDIES

As a result of our own research efforts to document the extent of recovery and rehabilitation following cardiac surgery, we have had the opportunity to closely observe and follow over time a series of 539 patients who had elective heart surgery performed between 1979 and 1981. Patients with known psychiatric illness, substance abuse, or serious past or present severe neurological impairment were excluded from the study.

During the course of the study, we observed the wide variety of preoperative emotional reactions and coping styles that have been reported in other studies. These ranged from good adjustment accompanied by appropriate concern and adequate coping mechanisms to severe panic reaction with total failure of defense mechanisms to ameliorate the stress associated with the situation. Very early in our investigation we observed that patients who appeared to be extremely anxious preoperatively and who scored very high on Spielberger's State Anxiety Scale had a much higher risk of dying following surgery. Subsequently, patients who were identified preoperatively as being extremely anxious had their surgery postponed until such time as the anxiety was relieved. Postoperatively, we also observed a wide range of behaviors and reactions. The severe delirium reported in many of the earlier published studies was much less common in our population, whereas mild confusion or disorientation were more likely to occur. Only one patient developed a psychosis. He presented a difficult management problem, particularly for the nursing staff. He believed that the sutures in his chest and leg incisions were dirty, and he repeatedly attempted to remove them and scrub them. He also made many attempts to escape from the hospital, and he actually did so on one occasion. He was found wandering around in one of the hospital parking lots where he claimed he needed to remain to issue parking tickets.

Major neurological complications were also relatively infrequent, and this is in accord with other recently published studies. One patient developed encephalopathy, two patients developed hemiparesis, two patients experienced seizures, one patient developed a phrenic nerve palsy, and one patient had a very severe cerebral vascular accident. This latter patient never regained her functions and remains, at present, in a nursing home. One additional patient is suspected of having a fatal cerebral embolus. This particular patient had a very positive mental attitude preoperatively, and he was very optimistic about his future and the results of his surgery. His early postoperative course in the intensive care unit was uneventful with one exception. He experienced a recurring dream. In the dream, a hearse was parked in his neighbor's driveway, and it was filled with lilacs that were hanging out of all of the windows. In the dream, he went over to inspect the hearse and found that there was no body or coffin inside. It was completely filled with lilacs. He ceased having the dream just prior to leaving the intensive care unit. His remaining postoperative course, until the night prior to planned hospital discharge, was optimal. He was happy and very grateful that he had made it through the surgery. He told me of the many things that he planned to do while recuperating and waiting to go back to work. He was looking forward to updating his address book, sorting out his desk drawers, addressing his Christmas cards months ahead of time, and the like. He had made friends with many of the patients, and he helped to encourage them and uplift the spirits of several patients who were depressed. The night prior to going home, while brushing his teeth, he suddenly collapsed in his bathroom. He was successfully resuscitated twice, but within minutes suffered a third, and fatal, cardiorespiratory arrest. Permission was requested of the wife to perform an autopsy. She granted it for all of the body with the exception of the brain. Because no cause of death could be identified it was suspected that the source of the problem was the brain and that the patient probably had had a cerebral embolus. The death of this pleasant gentleman had a devastating impact on everyone who had met him, and the emotional equilibrium on the whole hospital floor was not restored for weeks.

In our study, we also commonly observed the previously reported postoperative reaction of withdrawal, fatigue, and increased daytime sleeping among the patients. This generally occurred after several days of continued progress with ambulation and resumption of self-care activities. Although this reaction was initially viewed by others as an abnormal or negative reaction, it happens so often and is frequently accompanied by a positive affective state during the times when the patient is awake that it is probably wiser to view it as a normal reaction, unless it is accompanied by depression. These patients, and others who have had other types of major surgeries, have legitimate reasons to require extra rest and sleep.

The appearance of mild depression later during the postoperative course and sometimes following hospital discharge was also fairly common in our population, whereas moderate to severe depression was very rarely encountered prior to hospital discharge. Moderate to severe depression was, however, present in some patients on long-term follow-up.

Although the great majority of studies have focused on preoperative and very early postoperative assessments of patients, the long-term physical and emotional state of the patient is also of importance. The following brief case vignettes have been included in an attempt to illustrate the fact that some of the reactions that are experienced by patients may persist over time and go unrecognized or untreated, and, therefore, interfere with optimal recovery and rehabilitation.

Case Number 1, Mr. F.

After an 18-month history of exertional chest pain, Mr. F., a 51-year-old packaging engineer, was driving home from an appointment with his physician in June of 1981. While driving, he developed a sudden onset of chest pain that was unrelieved by nitroglycerin. This was rapidly followed by an attack of syncope. Within minutes, his wife, a passenger in the car, drove him to their local hospital where cardiopulmonary resuscitation was successfully performed. After several months of persistent and severely limiting exertional angina, a triple coronary artery bypass graft procedure was performed in August.

During the course of this patient's preoperative interview, he openly expressed feelings of anxiety and depression not only concerning his recent life-threatening syncopal episode but also about the news that he had coronary artery disease. He also expressed feelings of anger and frustration with regard to the uncertainty of his future, and he stated very angrily that he had "more to do in his life." His anxiety, depression, anger, and hostility were documented empirically with his scores on these psychological scales that were part of the self-administered preoperative questionnaire. The patient did, however, have evidence of exceptionally high levels of psychosocial support. During the preoperative interview, when the patient was queried concerning major areas of overall life satisfaction, although pleased with many important areas, particularly his marriage, he was displeased with one area—his level of educational attainment. This had consisted of the completion of 2 years of college. When he was questioned directly with regard to his expectations concerning the anticipated outcome of the surgery, he was cautiously optimistic. He believed that he would feel better after the operation, but he expected that he would continue to have limitations.

While he was awaiting surgery, the hospital staff were fully aware of the patient's anxiety and depression. Attempts on the part of the nursing staff to provide additional information and reassurance, however, actually resulted in increased levels of anxiety. Prior to hospital admission, the patient had been taking valium to contain his anxiety. The drug was ordered for him while he was awaiting surgery.

The patient then shifted his attention and concern to the meals that he was being served in the hospital. He not only expressed dissatisfaction with the hospital diet and anger over the imposed restrictions, but he became totally noncompliant and took it upon himself to devise means to gain access to such restricted foods as hot dogs and bacon.

The patient's postoperative course in the hospital was basically uneventful. He experienced only very mild disorientation with regard to the correct date or day of the week, although he claimed that he was less able to remember things than prior to surgery. Repeat neuropsychological testing revealed only very minor deterioration in performance on two of the test scores. His depression had resolved, and he also appeared to be less anxious.

At the time of the 6-month follow-up interview, Mr. F. continued to have problems in spite of the fact that he reported that he had been feeling physically well and was working full time. He was able to engage in active sports and strenuous physical exertion, and he had resumed doing all of the things that he had had to give up prior to hear surgery, including horseback riding and fishing. He expressed the fact, however, that he had been experiencing frequent worries and fears. He said that he and his wife and family were worrying much more about his health than prior to surgery. This was perceived as a source of extreme stress for everyone. He said that he also frequently worried about such things as having to limit his activities, not achieving a complete recovery, and the possibility of having to have heart surgery again in the future. His problem with dietary restrictions persisted, and he claimed that he had lost his diet booklet and instructions. He also claimed that his salt- and cholesterol-restricted diet had too many restrictions and excluded his favorite foods. His most salient problem, however, centered around his fear of traveling away from home or driving on the rural road where he had had the initial syncopal episode. He had sought medical attention for a sudden attack of dizziness that he had encountered while driving on the road. He had very severe anxiety over the possibility of having another syncope attack while driving and the fear that, if he did, he may not be successfully resuscitated. In spite of all of his anxiety and fears and worries concerning the future, his depression had completely resolved, and he demonstrated dramatic improvement on a scale measuring positive well-being. The difficulty in remembering things that the patient had experienced during the early postoperative period had also resolved, and neuropsychological testing demonstrated an identical score as achieved preoperatively on the Wechsler Memory Scale. The patient actually surpassed his preoperative test scores on several other neuropsychological tests.

Both during the 1-year and 18-month follow-up interviews, it was evident that, although the patient had achieved great symptomatic relief following his cardiac surgery (having only occasional incisional discomfort), he had not achieved any emotional recovery. He continued to have persistent anxiety and concern over his physical health in spite of the fact that he was physically able to engage in any activity that he desired. The anxiety and fears progressively increased both in severity and frequency so that what he was describing appeared to resemble panic attacks. He no longer was able to walk alone. The patient had not sought any further medical attention for these problems, and he was advised to do so at the end of the interview.

During the 2-year follow-up interview, he reported that he had sought medical attention and that he was somewhat less anxious. Low-dose valium had been prescribed for him to use as necessary to alleviate his anxiety attacks. His physical condition and symptomatic status remained unchanged.

Case Number 2, Mr. G.

First having experienced angina in March of 1981, Mr. G., a 67-year-old semiretired grocer, subsequently suffered an extremely limited lifestyle. It became necessary for him to give up nearly all of his activities including his part-time job at a convenience store, where, prior to his retirement at the age of 65 years, he had worked full time as the manager for most of his life. Shortly after he retired, he became unhappy and found that his retirement was much less pleasant than he would have expected. He also encountered financial difficulties. He gradually became increasingly depressed and resentful as a result of his situation. He had taken out a large loan to assist with his living expenses, and he became both angry and remorseful over the fact that he had not made adequate financial preparation for his retirement. Also of note is the fact that at this time his wife, who suffered from severe rheumatoid arthritis, was rapidly becoming incapacitated from the progression of her disease. As a result, Mr. G. was required to perform increasing quantities of the household tasks. This he resented strongly. Eventually, he became so distraught that he sought counseling from a social worker, after which he was able to make arrangements to return to his former employer in a part-time capacity. This improved his emotional state until he developed incapacitating exertional angina that required him to stop working. After further medical evaluation, it was believed that he would benefit from cardiac surgery. A date for his hospital admission was set, and he was told to cease all smoking in preparation for his surgery in an attempt to reduce the risk of serious intraoperative complications. The patient had smoked three packs of cigarettes per day for more than 50 years. He ignored the instructions to stop smoking until the day of his hospital admission that resulted in the cancellation of his initial date for surgery. Triple coronary artery bypass graft surgery was eventually performed in June of 1981 after the patient had ceased smoking.

Preoperative psychological assessment revealed an extremely anxious, somewhat depressed individual who was appropriately concerned about how his wife was going to manage at home while he was in the hospital. He spoke at great length about his home situation and described with resentment and bitterness all of the household tasks that he had been performing. It was also obvious from some of his statements that he felt very guilty about his festering resentment. He saw his wife's illness and his financial problems as a source of extreme, chronic stress that would never end. The financial problems were viewed as a disastrous personal failure that caused a total loss of self-respect. He resented the fact that he had only stayed in school long enough to complete the sixth grade (his wife had completed high school), and he wished that he could live his life over again. He claimed that he would live very differently and make many changes. Although he did not choose to mention it during the interview, his medical record revealed that he had been an alcoholic 22 years ago. He appeared to have strong needs to be very independent and masculine, and it was clear that these needs were extremely threatened not only as the result of the financial problems and inability to work but by the performance of household tasks, especially cooking, which he viewed as "women's work." He evidenced very marginal psychosocial support mechanisms, and although he had friends in whom he could confide, he rarely chose to do so. He described his only pleasures and interests in life as those of "eating out, playing bingo, and sex." Prior to admission to the hospital, he had had to give up these activities.

His extreme self-contempt, anger, hostility, dysphoria, helplessness, and hopelessness were reflected in his scores on the psychological scales that were included in the self-administered questionnaire that was completed at the termination of the interview. On a scale measuring positive well-being, he scored a zero. Although he was extremely anxious, he elected to skip the page of the questionnaire that contained Spielbergers's State Anxiety Scale. On a scale that measured hopelessness, he endorsed the most negative items as being true (e.g., "All I can see ahead of me is unpleasantness rather than pleasantness"). Additionally, he wrote unsolicited material throughout sections of the questionnaire to further emphasize his self-hatred, repulsive obesity, lack of self-discipline, and prior irresponsible spendthrift way of living.

During the interview, when he was directly asked what his expectations were with regard to the success of the surgery, without apparent concern, he very calmly stated that he believed that he would not wake up after the operation.

Postoperatively, the patient developed multiple medical complications. Immediately after surgery, upon return to the intensive care unit, he developed multiple supraventricular cardiac arrythmias as the probable result of electrolyte disturbances. The arrythmias worsened on the day after surgery when he developed atrial flutter, atrial fibrillation, and heart block. On the third postoperative day, the patient developed intermittent confusion and disorientation. This persisted and worsened, and on the fifth postoperative day the patient had to be placed in restraints and be given Haldol as the result of severe agitation. During this time the patient was also experiencing intermittent atrial fibrillation. On the sixth postoperative day, the patient's heart returned to a normal sinus rhythm, his mental status dramatically improved, and he was transferred to a general cardiac surgery floor. When he was interviewed on the ninth postoperative day, he was no longer disoriented; however, he failed to remember anything about his 5-day stay in the intensive care unit. He claimed that he had been having dreams about having cloth on his hands (obviously, the restraints). He also stated that he was experiencing great difficulty in terms of trying to figure things out. Repeat neuropsychological testing at this time showed considerable deterioration on all test scores.

The planned 6-month follow-up interview with Mr. G. was not conducted. During the 1-year follow-up interview, the patient reported that he was feeling pretty good physically but that he was depressed. He had resumed his part-time job; however, he had been laid off 2 months prior to the interview. After being laid off, he slept late, took naps, and spent most of his time laying on his bed. He had gained 35 pounds. The weight gain was associated with considerable shortness of breath when walking, and he was uncertain of whether he could go back to work if he were requested to do so. He stated, "I seem to have no self-discipline or motivation to diet, exercise or walk. My wife is totally disabled. I do all the cooking and housework. I don't mind, but I feel I'm in a useless rut and a financial failure. I should have been mature enough to save all these years for my wife's sake. After 49 years, I have a feeling of compassion for her and her afflictions." He did however, have the discipline not to return to his former habit of heavy smoking. His only outside activity consisted of playing bingo. He continued to feel extremely stressed over finances, unpaid bills, and his future financial insecurity. In spite of this, his score on the Spielberger State Anxiety Scale was below the mean of that of the entire study population of coronary artery bypass graft patients. He did have moderately high depression, anger, and hostility scores.

At 18 month follow-up, the patient reported that he was only feeling "so-so" and that it was his own fault because he had gained another 15 pounds. He appeared quite depressed and had been unsuccessful in finding another part-time job. He was experiencing extreme financial difficulties and had further lowered his already low standard of living. He was very angry and stated, "I blame my wife's chronic illness for my weight gain; being forced to cook and housekeep is foreign to my nature." His anxiety score had increased, and his depression score had markedly increased since the previous follow-up. He was experiencing marital discord and was not very satisfied with his marriage. Since the last interview, he had found an extramarital sexual partner who afforded him increased sexual desire and satisfaction. His persistent fatigue and lack of energy continued to increase as his weight increased. He expressed a desire to attend a formal rehabilitation program, and a referral was made to a local program that included psychological counseling.

During the 2-year follow-up interview, the patient reported that he was essentially unchanged and that he was still not taking care of himself and was chronically overeating. He continued to remain a nonsmoker, and he never consumed alcoholic beverages. He failed to follow through on his plans to attend the rehabilitation program. He described feeling helpless and unable to change his situation. He remained depressed and hopeless. Although he evaluated the success of the surgery as having been good, given the fact that he had achieved complete relief of his severe chest pain, he viewed his current and future life as a hopeless pleasureless existence.

Comment, Case Number 1

This patient shows the gradual development of a simple phobic neurosis. The conscious focus is not around the major surgery nor even around his cardiac condition *per se* but concerns the dramatic episode that threatened his life and brought him to surgery. This episode occurred while *driving home from a visit to his physician*. The examination in his physician's office had included an electrocardiogram, and no signs of an impending ischemia attack were visible. Physicians know full well the unpredictability of these events and generally warn their patients in a nonalarmist manner, but patients universally want to believe in the cardiologist's omniscience and even prescience. The description of the patient's hostility to the medical directives preoperatively and his progressive phobia postoperatively suggest that he is removed from everything else but not from the psychological trauma (as opposed to the physiological one) of his ischemic attack. The framework of the study did not intend to have the researchers take part in the clinical management of patients but clearly the referral suggested at the 18-month follow-up that this would be very well advised. The use of an antianxiety medication would indeed be a judicious first step. The treatment needed to provide some relief from the anxiety symptoms before this patient would begin to hear anything that even resembled reassurance: He was anxious because his wishes to believe in the reassurance of his cardiologist had been so dramatically deceived, indeed.

Comment, Case Number 2

This patient had considerable neurotic baggage prior to his angina; the alcoholism, obesity, and three packs per day of smoking may not only be contributing factors to his coronary artery disease, but they may also reveal a lifelong pattern of poor modulation of libidinal drives. His self-accusation of having been a spendthrift may be a current depressive self-devaluating exaggeration, but to the extent that there was some truth to it, this also testifies to the same strong tendency to immediate impulsive gratification. As in Aesop's fable, having danced all summer, he had accumulated no provisions for the fall of his life. Furthermore, his wife's serious chronic illness (for which he does not blame himself) added another area of deprivation that would be major for anyone. But for this man, having to assume household chores, and especially cooking, was felt as "a woman's work." Even the casual observer will not fail to perceive the vulnerability of his masculine identification. The patient does not hide his hopelessness; he openly wishes not to wake up from the surgery, and in fact, continues to smoke to the very last moment to bring about this temporarily desired outcome.

However, thanks to the skill of the surgical and medical teams, he not only survives the surgery and the complications that follow, but he shows some definite physiological improvement. He is even capable of returning to work for several months. But psychologically, there has been no change. Although he does not return to cigarette smoking and continues his sobriety of two decades, he resumes overeating, of which he is ashamed enough to cause him to cancel the in-person follow-up interview at 6 months. He enters into an extramarital relationship which is probably meant to mitigate the anxieties mentioned earlier. Having lost his part-time employment, why does he not show indications of efforts to replace that activity with another undertaking? But there are no longer signs of preoccupation with death nor intentional conscious facilitation of it. In summary, this patient's chronic depression did not really complicate his surgery, but almost the reverse occurred. The anticipated risks of the operation provided him with an irrestible occasion to indulge in acting upon his passive death wishes. The improvement in his cardiovascular function allowed him subsequently to resume his partially adaptive and partially maladaptive lifelong patterns.

SUMMARY

The surgical treatment of acquired and congenital cardiac disease has undergone dramatic development and technological advancement during the past several decades. The increasing numbers of patients who have undergone cardiac operative procedures annually in the United States have escalated rapidly over the years. Coronary artery bypass graft operations have become second only to cholecystectomies as the most common surgical procedure performed in the United States.

In spite of the great number of changes that have occurred over time in both the nature and technique of the operation and the methods utilized to improve and insure the adequacy of cerebral protection during these surgical procedures, neuropsychological dysfunction continues to be observed in patients during the postoperative period. Psychiatric sequelae also continue to be observed in patients during the postoperative period as well, and, in some instances may persist on a long-term basis.

A large body of scientific literature attests to the fact that considerable research interest and attention has evolved and been devoted to the investigation of neurological impairment and psychological disturbances after cardiac surgery. It is evident from the literature that considerable variability exists concerning the incidence of these problems. When combined, the incidence of neurological, cognitive, behavioral, and psychiatric impairments or complications has ranged from 1.3% to 90% or greater in the published literature. This variability appears to result from differences among investigators in defining complications; differences in the focus, design, and methods of investigation; differences observed with different surgical procedures; and changes in surgical techniques with increasing advances. Scientific advances have increased the success of the surgery in terms of myocardial preservation, cerebral protection, and reduction in operative mortality and postoperative morbidity. Although difficulties are encountered when attempts are made to make comparisons among the different studies, when those that were conducted during temporal periods of similar technological refinement are compared, it becomes apparent that the incidence of these problems has declined over time. Although many fewer studies have been conducted in recent years, the incidence of all of these complications appears to be much lower than in the earlier studies.

Potential etiological factors that have been identified as contributing to neurological and neuropsychological dysfunction in numerous studies include a variety of types of emboli, hypotension, prolonged time on cardiopulmonary bypass, metabolic disturbances, cardiac arrythmias, preexisting neurological or cerebrovascular disease, and advanced age.

Potential etiological factors that have been implicated in the development of psychological disturbances or psychiatric complications include the meaning and significance of the illness and surgical procedure to the patient, inadequate defense mechanisms to cope with the threat imposed by the illness, sleep deprivation, the abnormal intensive care unit environment, and the development of medical complications in the early postoperative period.

Neuropsychological dysfunction in patients who have undergone major cardiac surgery appears to be a syndrome of multifactorial causation. Very few studies have attempted to provide anatomical verification of observed neuropsychological disturbance in nonsurvivors. Additional investigation in this area is needed. Sufficient research has also not been conducted to attempt to correlate electroencephalographic patterns with postoperative neurological and psychiatric status. In the less common studies that have employed electroencephalographic assessment of patients, results have demonstrated that focal signs were usually accompanied by electroencephalographic changes (e.g., slowing of frequencies) and the observed psychiatric abnormalities usually followed the observed neurological abnormalities and persisted longer. Additional research would appear to be warranted to define the clinical factors that determine the predictive value of the electroencephalogram in open-heart surgery patients and to further elucidate any potential relationship between the development of neuropsychological and psychiatric complications.

Because preoperative defense mechanisms, coping styles, and psychological state are not totally consistent predictors of a postoperative psychological state, and since because long-term psychological disturbances following cardiac surgery have been observed, patients should receive careful monitoring following discharge from the hospital to facilitate optimal recovery and rehabilitation.

ACKNOWLEDGMENTS

The assistance of Richard L. Goldstein in providing comments on this chapter and of Louis Vachon in providing a psychiatrist's comment on the case studies is gratefully acknowledged.

REFERENCES

Aberg, T., & Kihlgren, M. (1977). Cerebral protection during open-heart surgery. *Thorax, 32,* 525–533.

Abram, H. S. (1965). Adaptation to open heart surgery: A psychiatric study of response to the threat of death. *American Journal of Psychiatry, 122,* 659–667.

Abram, H. S. (1967). *Psychological aspects of surgery*. Boston: Little, Brown.

Allardyce, D. B., Yoshida, S. H., & Ashmore, P. G. (1966). The importance of microembolism in the pathogenesis of organ dysfunction caused by prolonged use of the pump oxygenator. *Journal of Thoracic and Cardiovascular Surgery, 52*, 706–715.

Ashmore, P. G., Svitek, V., & Ambrose, P. (1968). The incidence and effects of particulate aggregation and microembolism in pump oxygenator systems. *Journal of Thoracic and Cardiovascular Surgery, 55*, 691–697.

Blachly, P. H. (1967). Open-heart surgery: Physiological variables of mental functioning. *International Psychiatry Clinics, 4*, 133–135.

Blachly, P. H., & Starr, A. (1964). Post-cardiotomy delirium. *American Journal of Psychiatry, 121*, 371–375.

Branthwaite, M. A. (1975). Prevention of neurologic damage during open-heart surgery. *Thorax, 30*, 258–261.

Brierley, J. B. (1964). Cerebral injury following cardiac operations. *The Lancet, 1*, 175–176.

Chatham, M. A. (1978). The effect of family involvement on patients' manifestations of postcardiotomy psychosis. *Heart and Lung, 7*, 995–999.

Coons, R. E., Keats, A. S., & Cooley, D. A. (1959). Significance of electroencephalographic changes occurring during cardiopulmonary bypass. *Anesthesiology, 20*, 804–810.

Egerton, N., & Kay, J. H. (1964). Psychological disturbances with open heart surgery. *British Journal of Psychiatry, 110*, 433–439.

Egerton, N., Egerton, M. B., & Kay, J. H. (1963). Neurologic changes following profound hypothermia. *Annals of Surgery, 157*, 366–374.

Engel, G. L., & Romano, J. (1959). Delirium, a syndrome of cerebral insufficiency. *Journal of Chronic Disease, 9*, 260–277.

Fischer-Williams, M., & Cooper, R. A. (1964). Some aspects of electroencephalographic changes during open-heart surgery. *Neurology, 14*, 472–482.

Fox, H. M., Rizzo, N. D., & Gifford, S. (1954). Psychological observations of patients undergoing mitral surgery: A study of stress. *Psychosomatic Medicine, 16*, 186–208.

Frank, K. A., Heller, S. S., Kornfeld, D. S., & Malm, J. R. (1972). Long-term effects of open-heart surgery on intellectual functioning. *Journal of Thoracic and Cardiovascular Surgery, 64*, 811–815.

Freeman, A. M., Folks, D. G., Sokol, R. S., Govier, A. V., Reeves, J. G., Fleece, E. L., Hall, K. R., Zorn, G. L., & Karp, R. B. (1985). Cognitive function after coronary bypass surgery: Effect of decreased cerebral blood flow. *American Journal of Psychiatry, 142*, 110–112.

Gilberstadt, H., & Sako, Y. (1967). Intellectual and personality changes following open-heart surgery. *Archives of General Psychiatry, 16*, 210–214.

Gilman, S. (1965). Cerebral disorders after open-heart operations. *New England Journal of Medicine, 272*, 489–498.

Gonzalez-Scarano, F., & Hurtig, H. (1981). Neurologic complications of coronary artery bypass grafting: Case-control study. *Neurology, 31*, 1032–1035.

Greenspan, B., Bannett, A. D., & Pressman, M. D. (1960). Psychiatric problems in surgical practice. *Journal of The Albert Einstein Medical Center, 8*, 16–20.

Hackett, T. P., & Weisman, A. D. (1960). Psychiatric management of operative syndromes: The therapeutic consultation and the effect of noninterpretive intervention. *Psychosomatic Medicine, 22*, 267–282.

Heller, S. S., Frank, K. A., Malm, J. R., Bowman, F. O., Harris, P. D., Charlton, M. H., & Kornfeld, D. S. (1970). Psychiatric complications of open-heart surgery. A re-examination. *New England Journal of Medicine, 283*, 1015–1020.

Hill, J. D., Aguilar, M. J., Baranco, A., Lanerolle, P., & Gerbode, F. (1969). Neuropathological manifestations of cardiac surgery. *Annals of Thoracic Surgery, 7*, 409–419.

Kimball, C. P. (1969). Psychological responses to the experience of open heart surgery: I. *American Journal of Psychiatry, 126*, 96–107.

Kimball, C. P., Quinlan, D., Osborne, F., & Woodward, B. (1973). The experience of cardiac surgery. *Psychotherapy and Psychosomantics, 22*, 310–319.

Knox, S. J. (1961). Severe psychiatric disturbances in the post-operative period: A five-year survey of Belfast hospitals. *Journal of Mental Science, 107*, 1078–1096.

Knox, S. J. (1963). Psychiatric aspects of mitral valvotomy. *British Journal of Psychiatry, 109*, 656–668.

Kornfeld, D. S., Heller, S. S., Frank, K. A., Edie, R. N., & Barsa, J. (1978). Delirium after coronary artery bypass surgery. *Journal of Thoracic and Cardiovascular Surgery, 76*, 93–96.

Kornfeld, D. S., Zimberg, S., & Malm, J. R. (1965). Psychiatric complications of open-heart surgery. *New England Journal of Medicine, 273*, 287–292.

Lee, W. H., Miller, W., Rowe, J., Hairston, P., & Brody, M. P. (1969). Effects of extracorporeal circulation on personality and cerebration. *Annals of Thoracic Surgery, 7*, 562–570.

Lipowski, Z. J. (1983). Psychosocial reactions to physical illness. *Canadian Medical Association Journal, 128*, 1069–1072.

Longmore, D. (1982). The effects of prostacyclin on reducing cerebral damage following open-heart surgery. In R. Becker, J. Katz, M-J. Polonius, & H. Speidel (Eds.), *Psychopathological and neurological dysfunctions following open-heart surgery* (pp. 320–342). Berlin, Heidelberg, New York: Springer Verlag.

Matarazzo, R. G., Bristow, D., & Reaume, R. (1963). Medical factors relevant to psychological reactions in mitral valve disease. *Journal of Nervous and Mental Disease, 137*, 380–388.

Meyer, B. C., Blacher, R. S., & Brown, F. (1961). A clinical study of psychiatric and psychological aspects of mitral surgery. *Psychosomatic Medicine, 23*, 194–218.

Möhlen, K., Davies-Osterkamp, S., Müller, H., Scheld, H. H., & Siefen, G. (1982). Relationship between preoperative coping styles, immediate postoperative reactions and some aspects of the psychosocial situation of open-heart surgery patients one year after operation. In R. Becker, J. Katz, M-J. Polonius, & H. Speidel (Eds.), *Psychopathological and neurological dysfunctions following open-heart surgery* (pp. 232–237). Berlin, Heidelberg, New York: Springer Verlag.

Nussmeier, N. A., Arlund, C., & Slogoff, S. (1986). Neuropsychiatric complications after cardiopulmonary bypass: Cerebral protection by a barbiturate. *Anesthesiology, 64*, 165–170.

Priest, W. S., Zaks, M. S., Yacorzynski, G. K., & Boshes, B. (1957). The neurologic, psychiatric, and psychological aspects of cardiac surgery. *Medical Clinics of North America, 41*, 155–169.

Rabiner, C. J., & Willner, A. E. (1980). Differential psychopathological and organic mental disorder at follow-up five years after coronary bypass and cardiac valvular surgery. In H. Speidel, & G. Rodewald (Eds.), *Psychic and neurological dysfunctions after open-heart surgery* (pp. 237–249). Stuttgart: Thieme Verlag.

Raymond, M., Conklin, C., Schaeffer, J., Newstadt, G., Matloff, J. M., & Gray, R. J. (1984). Coping with transient intellectual dysfunction after coronary bypass surgery. *Heart and Lung, 13*, 531–539.

Ropper, A. H., & Martin, J. B. (1983). Coma and other disorders of consciousness. In R. Petersdorf, R. Adams, E. Braunwald, K. Isselbacher, J. Marton, & J. Wilson (Eds.), *Harrison's principles of internal medicine, Tenth Edition* (pp. 124–131). New York: McGraw-Hill.

Sachdev, N. S., Carter, C. C., Swank, R. L., & Blachly, P. H. (1967). Relationship between postcardiotomy delirium, clinical neurological changes, and EEG abnormalities. *Journal of Thoracic and Cardiovascular Surgery, 54*, 557–563.

Savageau, J. A., Stanton, B. A., Jenkins, C. D., & Frater, R. M. (1982). Neuropsychological dysfunction following elective cardiac operation. II. A six month reassessment. *Journal of Thoracic and Cardiovascular Surgery, 84*, 595–600.

Savageau, J. A., Stanton, B. A., Jenkins, C. D., & Klein, M. D. (1982). Neuropsychological dysfunction following elective cardiac operation. I. Early assessment. *Journal of Thoracic and Cardiovascular Surgery, 84*, 585–594.

Spehr, W., & Götze, P. (1982). Computerized electroencephalogram in open-heart surgery: Prediction of postoperative psychical complications. In R. Becker, J. Katz, M-J. Polonius, & H. Speidel (Eds.), *Psychopathological and neurological dysfunctions following open-heart surgery* (pp. 119–124). Berlin, Heidelberg, New York: Springer Verlag.

Stanton, B. A., Zyzanski, S. J., Jenkins, C. D., & Klein, M. D. (1982). Recovery after major heart surgery: Medical, psychological, and work outcomes. In R. Becker, J. Katz, M-J. Polonius, & H. Speidel (Eds.), *Psychopathological and neurological dysfunctions following open-heart surgery* (pp. 217–225). Berlin, Heidelberg, New York: Springer Verlag.

Stanton, B. A., Jenkins, C. D., Denlinger, P., Savageau, J. A., Weintraub, R. M., & Goldstein, R. L. (1983). Predictors of employment status after cardiac surgery. *Journal of the American Medical Association, 249,* 907–911.

Stanton, B. A., Jenkins, C. D., Savageau, J. A., Harken, D. E., & Aucoin, R. (1984). Perceived adequacy of patient education and fears and adjustments after cardiac surgery. *Heart and Lung, 13,* 525–531.

Stanton, B. A., Jenkins, C. D., Savageau, J. A., & Thurer, R. L. (1984). Functional benefits following coronary artery bypass graft surgery. *Annals of Thoracic Surgery, 37,* 286–290.

Stanton, B. A., Jenkins, C. D., Goldstein, R. L., Vander Salm, T. J., Klein, M. D., & Aucoin, R. A. (1985). Hospital readmissions among survivors six months after myocardial revascularization. *Journal of the American Medical Association, 253,* 3568–3573.

Tienari, P., Outakoski, J., Hirvenoja, R., Juolasmaa, A., Takkunen, I., & Kampman, R. (1982). Psychiatric complications following open-heart surgery: A prospective study. In R. Becker, J. Katz, M-J. Polonius, & H. Speidel (Eds.), *Psychopathological and neurological dysfunctions following open-heart surgery* (pp. 48–53). Berlin, Heidelberg, New York: Springer Verlag.

Tufo, H. M., & Ostfeld, A. M. (1968). A prospective study of open-heart surgery. *Psychosomatic Medicine, 30,* 552–553.

Tufo, H. M., Ostfeld, A. M., & Shekelle, R. (1970). Central nervous system dysfunction following open-heart surgery. *Journal of the American Medical Association, 212,* 1333–1340.

Zaks, M. S. (1959). Disturbances in psychological functions and neuropsychiatric complications in heart surgery. A four-year follow-up study. *Cardiology. An encyclopedia of the cardiovascular system.* New York: McGraw-Hill.

Zapolanski, A., Loop, F. D., Estafanous, F. G., & Sheldon, W. C. (1983). Myocardial revascularization at the Cleveland Clinic Foundation—1981. *Cleveland Clinic Quarterly, 50,* 2–5.

4

Neuropsychological Dysfunction Due to Liver Disease

RALPH E. TARTER, KATHLEEN L. EDWARDS, and
DAVID H. VAN THIEL

INTRODUCTION

Among all organs, the liver ranks first in both size and the variety of its functional accomplishments. Located between the intestine and systemic circulation, the liver is, in effect, both a filter and a metabolic factory. Through mechanisms regulated by the level of available energy substrate and the two hormones, insulin and glucagon, the liver is the organ that is responsible for determining whether ingested and absorbed nutrients in the form of chemical energy are to be either utilized immediately or to be stored for later use. The liver is also the primary site for the activation, storage, and release of several vitamins. It is additionally a major site of protein synthesis, glycogen synthesis and storage, and is the primary regulator of the plasma level of cholesterol and other fats. An additional important function performed by hepatocytes is the manufacture of bile, a unique biologic detergent containing, among many other components, bile salts and cholesterol. Thus the liver plays an integral role in maintaining the nutritional and metabolic well-being of the organism.

The liver also serves to protect the organism from disease. Kupffer cells, the phagocytic cells contained within the liver, remove, from the circulation, foreign material in the form of large cellular material (bacteria, parasites), proteins (endotoxins, bacterial cell-wall constituents) and innumerable smaller molecular species that could be harmful to the intact organism.

Portal venous obstruction present within the liver, due either to cholestatic (obstruction of bile flow) or hepatocellular disease, results in portal

RALPH E. TARTER and KATHLEEN L. EDWARDS • Department of Psychiatry, University of Pittsburgh School of Medicine, and Western Psychiatric Institute & Clinic, Pittsburgh, Pennsylvania 15213.   DAVID H. VAN THIEL • Department of Gastroenterology, University of Pittsburgh School of Medicine, Pittsburgh, Pennsylvania 15261.

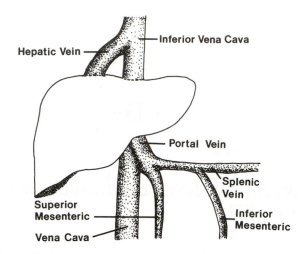

FIGURE 1. Relationship between the liver and major venous flow showing, in this case, anastomosis of the vena cava and portal vein.

hypertension and the shunting of portal venous blood around rather than
through the liver. Figure 1 illustrates the most commonly occurring portosystemic shunt, resulting in venous blood bypassing the liver. A major
consequence of this shunting of portal venous blood away from the liver is a
failure or reduced capacity of the liver to degrade a wide variety of substances present within the blood that are putative cerebrotoxins.

The liver disease has numerous potential etiological determinants, including infection, inadequate diet, alcohol abuse, and drug toxicity as well as
several inborn metabolic disorders. As a multifunctional organ, the liver
interacts with other organs and biologic systems in order to maintain the
normal physiological, biochemical, and metabolic functioning of the intact
organism. Neurological pathology occurring as either the direct result of
liver disease or occurring as an indirect result of a disruption of other organ
systems that in turn disrupt hepatic functioning comprises the basis for
interest in hepatic disease by neuropsychologists.

The ensuing discussion reviews the epidemiology of liver disease followed by an examination of the various mechanisms by which hepatic disease is known to produce neurological dysfunction and neuropsychological
sequelae. The degree to which hepatic-induced cerebral dysfunction can be
reversed is also addressed. A discussion of the effects of chronic hepatic
disease on emotional and social adjustment concludes this chapter.

EPIDEMIOLOGY OF LIVER DISEASE

The prevalence of liver disease varies widely according to the specific
type of hepatic pathology in question. Certain genetically determined meta-

bolic disorders such as alpha-1-antitrypsin deficiency and hepatolenticular degeneration (Wilson's disease) are uncommon. This latter condition, for example, has an estimated prevalence of about 5 per million. In contrast, alcoholic cirrhosis has a mortality rate (clearly less than its prevalence) of about 136 per million population (Jefferson & Marshall, 1981; Lieber & Leo, 1982). It is not uncommon, however, for individuals with chronic liver disease to be either unrecognized or misdiagnosed. Frequently the individual is asymptomatic and thus remains undiagnosed until quite late or is in the terminal stages of the disease, at which time there usually is multisystem involvement and difficulty in determining the precise etiology. In addition, no large population studies addressing liver disease have been conducted; hence, the available prevalence estimates have been based on the number of patients admitted to clinical facilities. Obviously, such data are subject to considerable referral or selection bias. The accuracy and comprehensiveness of diagnostic procedures also varies widely among physicians and institutions, and thus the validity of a given reported diagnosis cannot be accepted uncritically. For these reasons, it is very difficult to determine the exact morbidity and mortality rates for liver disease in general, let alone for any specific liver disease.

Despite the absence of precise epidemiological data concerning the prevalence and frequency of liver disease, the significant adverse consequences of liver disease for society are well recognized. For instance, cirrhosis is the fourth leading cause of death in the United States for persons between the ages of 35 to 54, ranking only behind heart disease, cancer, and accidents as a cause of death (Galambos, 1979). More importantly, cirrhosis as a nonfatal condition is associated with considerable morbidity, of which recurrent episodes of low-grade encephalopathy are common features (Conn & Lieberthal, 1979). Indeed, a significant percentage of individuals with cirrhosis are thought to be unable to competently drive an automobile (Schomerus et al., 1981). Thus, liver disease that causes premature death and is associated with major morbidity and disability is not inconsequential to society, particularly when one considers that liver diseases usually occur during the most productive period of an individual's life.

NEUROBEHAVIORAL CONSEQUENCES OF DISEASES OF THE LIVER

Wilson's Disease (Hepatolenticular Degeneration)

This inherited metabolic disease results from the liver's inability to excrete copper. The accumulation of copper occurs first in the liver and then in the brain as well as several other organs. Wilson's disease has a genetic etiology; it is transmitted as a single autosomal recessive gene. Thus if each parent is a carrier, the probablility of the offspring inheriting the disease is 25%, whereas 50% of the offspring will be carriers.

The clinical onset of this disease ranges from early childhood to young adulthood. The disease can present initially as either an acute hepatic failure or have an insidious onset that progresses into a chronic disease. With an acute onset, the disease frequently is fatal, particularly if it is not identified correctly and effectively managed. With the more usual chronic and insidious onset, the disease progresses almost imperceptively into a chronic disease; in these cases, bleeding from esophageal varices, and hypersplenism, as well as neurologic and psychiatric manifestations first characterize the disease.

The neurological functioning of patients with Wilson's disease is quite varied, but disturbances in motor functioning are most pronounced (Schienberg & Stemlieb, 1984). Intention tremor, rigidity, and bradykinesia are often found. Abnormal tendon and plantar reflexes are observed frequently. Dysarthria, gait disturbances, and impaired coordination are also frequent problems in patients with Wilson's disease. In contrast, sensory functioning is typically intact.

Neuropsychological studies measuring cognitive functioning and behavioral capacity have not been conducted on patients with Wilson's disease systematically. Because of the low prevalence of the disease in the population, the obvious limiting factor for conducting neuropsychological research has been the difficulty in accruing sufficiently large patient samples for study and analysis. In our laboratory, neuropsychological assessments are performed routinely on all patients with liver disease admitted to the gastroenterology service of a large urban university hospital. During a 3-yr period, we have been able to study 9 patients who, at the time they were studied, were asymptomatic but had been diagnosed as having Wilson's disease (Tarter, Switala, Carra, Edwards, & Van Thiel, 1987). Compared to age, education, and IQ-matched normal controls, Wilson's disease subjects performed significantly more poorly on tests of visuopractic (Trail-Making, Block Design), spatial scanning (Symbol Digit) and learning processes (Supraspan). Moreover, the subjects with Wilson's disease more frequently perform in the impaired ranges, using clinical cutoff values, than the normal subjects. These patients in our small sample were all neurologically intact in that the usual clinical signs and symptoms of neurological disturbances associated with Wilson's disease were absent. Also, they were tested at a relatively early stage of their disease and were not acutely ill at the time of the neuropsychological examination.

From these preliminary findings, it would appear that Wilson's disease, prior to the advanced stage of illness, and in the absence of clinically evident neurologic signs or symptoms, is associated with significant cognitive impairment. Whether the severity of cognitive disturbances co-varies with chronicity of the illness and whether additional areas of neuropsychological functioning become impaired remains, however, to be determined. It also remains to be determined if the manifest deficits are reversible. Tentative evidence has been presented suggesting that drug treatments such as penicillamine, lactulose, and neomycin may facilitate cognitive recovery (Rosselli, Lorenzana, & Rosselli, 1985).

Postnecrotic Cirrhosis

Postnecrotic cirrhosis is a histopathologic condition of the liver that is characterized by disruption of the normal microscopic lobular architecture as a consequence of fibrosis and hepatocellular regeneration as nodules. This advanced stage of liver disease can have a toxic (e.g., alcohol), infectious (e.g., viral hepatitis), or metabolic (e.g., glycogen storage deficiency) etiology. Apart from issues related to the etiology of the cirrhosis, the ultimate consequence of hepatic fibrosis is increased impedence of intrahepatic blood flow that results in portal hypertension and the formation of portosystemic shunts such that portal venous blood bypasses the liver rather than flowing through it prior to entering the systemic circulation. The reduced capacity of the liver to remove and detoxify a host of materials, including a wide range of putative cerebrotoxic substances present in portal venous blood, leads to the production of a neuropsychiatric condition referred to as portal-systemic encephalopathy (PSE). This encephalopathy can occur either as an acute florid neuropsychiatric disorder, as a low-grade chronic condition, or result from an acute exacerbation of a chronic disorder. Strictly speaking, the encephalopathy is not primarily caused by the diseased liver, but rather it is the presence of circulating neurotoxins that would otherwise have been removed or detoxified by the liver that are responsible for the manifest disturbances.

Differential Diagnosis and Stages of Portal-Systemic Encephalopathy (PSE)

The diagnosis of PSE can be difficult. No single clinical index or laboratory measure is by itself capable of establishing the diagnosis. Neuropsychological tests are capable of detecting the presence of cerebral dysfunction, even in the absence of overt neurological or behavioral disturbances. However, they do not identify their etiology. In the overt clinical stages, that is, in Stages 2 and 3, a specific diagnosis can usually be made based upon a constellation of findings obtained from a neuropsychiatric evaluation in conjunction with clinical and laboratory examinations for the presence of hepatic disease.

An incorrect or missed diagnosis most often occurs if the patient is either in the early stages of an acute encephalopathic episode or is suffering from an occult chronic low-grade encephalopathy. In both of these situations, patients suffering from PSE manifest features that are common to a number of "functional" psychiatric disturbances. These symptoms include euphoria, depression, mental slowing, inappropriate affect, and behavior and sleep disturbances. Not surprisingly, therefore, patients suffering from low-grade or misdiagnosed PSE are occasionally admitted inappropriately to psychiatric facilities (Havens & Child, 1955; Leevy, 1974; Summerskill, Davidson, Sherlock, & Steiner, 1956). Among the most frequent psychiatric diagnoses assigned to such patients are anxiety reaction, psychotic depression, and hysteria (Sherlock, Summerskill, White, & Pheur, 1954). Neurological misdiagnosis is also not uncommon; patients with PSE have been mistakenly diagnosed as having psychomotor epilepsy, frontal lobe tumor, narcolepsy, Parkinson's disease, multiple sclerosis, and cerebral arteriosclerosis (Sherlock *et al.*, 1954; Summerskill *et al.*, 1956).

The following characteristics are sufficient to implicate the presence of portal-systemic encephalopathy in a patient who may be otherwise thought to have a functional psychiatric illness:

1. History of hepatic disease
2. Slowing of the EEG, particularly in association with a triphasic wave pattern
3. Neuropsychological impairments on tests of cognitive and psychomotor capacity
4. Asterixis (a rapid irregular flapping of the hands when held in a dorsoflexed position)
5. Fetor hepaticus (pungent breath odor)
6. Hyperventilation
7. Elevated fasting plasma ammonia level
8. Reduced consciousness or awareness
9. Neurological signs and symptoms (see Table 1)
10. Behavioral and emotional dysregulation (see Table 1)

All of the previously listed signs and symptoms are graded phenomena that depending on the severity of the encephalopathy, are manifest to a greater or lesser degree in a given individual.

Traditionally, PSE has been graded into four broad categories based on the clinical examination (Parsons-Smith, Summerskill, Dawson, & Sherlock, 1957). If no abnormality is present, a grade of 0 is assigned; however, as will be discussed later, cerebral dysfunction is nonetheless still evidenced in such individuals when neuropsychological tests are utilized for the identification of such dysfunction. A grade of 1 is assigned if the patient exhibits a shortened attention span, is unable to perform simple mental operations efficiently, and symptoms of anxiety are present. A Grade-2 severity is given if the presentation is one of apathy, time disorientation, inappropriate behavior, and personality changes. Progression into the next stage of severity, coded as a Grade-3 encephalopathy, occurs with the emergence of features such as semistupor, somnolence, confusion, and temporal and spatial disorientation. Without medical intervention, the individual frequently lapses into Stage 4, or true coma. At this point, death may ensue if medical treatment is not initiated or if therapy is ineffective.

Neuropsychological Deficits Associated with Cirrhosis

In addition to the disturbances in affect, behavior, and neurologic functioning discussed previously, there is also considerable emerging evidence that implicates significant cognitive and psychomotor impairment in patients with cirrhosis. Impairments in neuropsychological test performance

TABLE 1. Progression of Neuropsychiatric Disturbance Associated with Acute Episode of Portal-Systemic Encephalopathy

	Severity grade of encephalopathy				
	0 (Normal)	1 (Mild)	2 (Moderate)	3 (Severe)	4 (Coma)
Consciousness	No detectable change	No clear impairment	Mild disorientation	Confusion/stupor	
Activation	Normal	Inversion of sleep pattern and/or insomnia/hypersomnia	Inversion of sleep pattern and/or insomnia/hypersomnia	Somnolence	
Behavior	Normal	Personality change; fatigue	Lethargy; disinhibition; inappropriateness	Bizarreness; depersonalization; paranoia	
Affect	Normal	Irritability; euphoria or depression	Anxiety; anger	Rage	
Cognition	Normal	Attention deficit; concentration difficulties	Impaired time sense	Amnesia	
Neurological	Normal	Tremor; incoordination	Ataxia; asterixis; slurred speech; hyperactive reflexes	Dilation of pupils; hyperactive reflexes; rigidity; nystagmus	

have been reported to occur in patients with cirrhosis who do not demonstrate an overt clinical disturbance, that is, those having a Grade 1 or 0 on ratings of the severity or stage of their portal-systemic encephalopathy.

A variety of deficits have been reported in nonalcoholic cirrhotic patients. Handwriting clarity and skill (Geffray, Segrestin, & Geffray, 1970; Reynolds, Redeker, & Davis, 1958; Simmons, Goldstein, & Boyle, 1970), figure copying and drawing accuracy (Dudrick, Mackie, & Serlin, 1968; Fung & Khoo, 1971; Geffray et al., 1970; Germain, Frezinos, Louis, & Ribet, 1973; Resnick et al., 1969; Zeegen, Drinkwater, & Dawson, 1970), and mental efficiency in performing tasks such as mental calculations (Ma, McLeod, & Blackburn, 1969; Resnick, Ishihara, Chalmers, & Schimmel, 1968; Reynolds et al., 1958; Simmons et al., 1970) have been found to be impaired in cirrhotic patients with low-grade encephalopathy when compared to normals. Employing standardized psychometric tests, deficits also have been reported in nonverbal intelligence (Dudrick et al., 1968; Gilberstadt et al., 1980), learning and memory (Atkinson & Goligher, 1960; Germain et al., 1973; Ma et al., 1969), and visuospatial capacities (Conn et al., 1977; Zeegen et al., 1970).

In addition, several investigations have been reported in which multiple measures of cognitive functioning were obtained from each patient studied. In the first of these studies, Rehnstrom, Simert, Hansson, Johnson, and Vang (1977) administered a battery of psychometric tests to alcoholic and nonalcoholic patients with established cirrhosis. The most salient results from this study were the following: (a) psychological tests of cognitive capacity were more sensitive for the detection of encephalopathy than was the clinical examination; and (b) cirrhosis, more so than the presence of alcoholism, was associated with significant cognitive impairment. Unfortunately, a group of normal subjects was not tested as part of this study, thereby making it difficult to ascertain the nature and severity of the cognitive deficits described, apart from showing that distinctions exist among the different pathologic entities comprising the various samples studied, namely nonalcoholic cirrhotics, alcoholic cirrhotics, and alcoholics without cirrhosis. The findings, however, clearly document the superior diagnostic accuracy of psychometric tests compared to the clinical examination and EEG in detecting PSE.

In a second important study, Rikkers, Jenko, Rudman, and Freides (1978) administered the Digit Symbol subtest of the WAIS, the Trail-Making Test, the Williams Visual Memory Test, and obtained several measures of reaction time performance in patients with cirrhosis. Two particularly interesting results emerged from this study. First, it was demonstrated that the EEG was a less sensitive indicator of neurological pathology than were psychometric tests of cognitive capacity. And second, not all cognitive processes were affected equally by the disease; 50% of the subjects were impaired on the Trail-Making test, whereas only 10% performed in the impaired ranges on the visual memory test. Although this study is methodologically flawed because some of the patients in this study sample had undergone surgical portacaval shunts, the findings are nonetheless important in documenting the presence of measurable cognitive deficits in individuals with advanced cirrhotic liver disease.

In yet another study, Elsass, Lund, and Ranek (1978), equating subjects for clinical severity of encephalopathy, compared eight cirrhotic patients who had undergone a portacaval shunt with eight cirrhotic patients who had not had this surgical procedure. It was found that the shunted group was more impaired than the nonshunted group on four of the seven tests of cognitive functioning utilized. The decrements were most apparent on tests of visuospatial capacity (Block Design, Hidden Patterns, Visual Gestalts) but also evident on tests of verbal memory (Story Recall). Thus, although clinical status was similar for the two groups, the surgically shunted subjects demonstrated greater cognitive impairments. However, the patients with chronic liver disease who had not been treated with surgical shunts were impaired on several measures within the battery of neuropsychological tests utilized, although not as severely or as diffusely as those treated surgically. In general, the deficits in both groups were most pronounced on measures requiring attention or concentration (Serial Subtractions, Word Fluency, and Digit Span). In contrast, memory and abstracting abilities were relatively unaffected.

In an investigation comparing alcoholics with and without biopsy-proven cirrhosis, Gilberstadt et al. (1980) obtained evidence for visuospatial deficits in the former group as evidenced by scores on the WAIS Performance subtests, Trail-Making test, a writing speed test, and a reaction time test. Significantly, none of the 36 subjects in their sample evidenced overt clinical signs of hepatic encephalopathy. Overall, 50% of the cirrhotic subjects exhibited impairment on at least one test and obtained a nonverbal IQ that was on average 10 points lower than that of the noncirrhotic subjects studied. Moreover, performance on certain of the cognitive tests correlated significantly with measures of serum liver enzyme levels and a variety of hepatic function tests utilized by these investigators. Serum Albumin correlated best with the various visuospatial tests with r values ranging from $-.47$ to $-.64$. The fasting blood ammonia level also correlated significantly with the performance on two tests, Block Design ($r = -.34$) and WAIS Performance IQ ($r = -.35$).

An association between liver functional status and cognitive capacity has been reported also by Schomerus et al. (1981) who found that the nonverbal IQ, determined using the Cattell's Culture Fair Test, correlated significantly with serum albumin level and inversely with the serum concentrations of gamma globulins. It was observed additionally that the serum bilirubin level and prothrombin time correlated with the subjects' performance on the Benton Visual Retention Test. The prothrombin time also was correlated with performance on the WAIS Block Design, Trail-Making, and motor steadiness tests. Overall, hepatic function variables were able to account for between 23% to 56% of the variance on the various cognitive tests utilized. In yet another study, Tarter, Hegedus, Van Thiel, Gavaler, and Schade (1986) observed a number of correlations between cognitive test scores and hepatic functional and injury measures in alcoholics. In a number of instances, the measured hepatic variables could explain over 50% of the variance observed in the neuropsychological test scores obtained. The best predictors of neuropsychologic test performance were albumin and fasting serum ammonia levels. In a sample of nonalcoholic cirrhotics, and employing multiple regression procedures, it was observed that a significant amount of test variance could be accounted for by albumin, prothrombin time, indocyanine green clearance at 20 min, and globulin level.

In summary, the result of several studies conducted to date indicate that nonverbal IQ and visuopractic abilities (Gilberstadt et al., 1980; Schomerus et al., 1981; Smith & Smith, 1977) are impaired in cirrhotic compared to noncirrhotic individuals. The findings are, however, not conclusive because liver pathology was studied in alcoholics; this latter condition itself is associated with marked neurologic and cognitive impairments (Tarter & Edwards, 1985). Indeed, the severity of electroencephalographic (Kardel & Stigsby, 1975) and neuroanatomic (Acker, Majumdar, Shaw, & Thomson, 1982) abnormalities that have been reported to occur in alcoholics co-vary with the severity of the hepatic pathology. The findings in this regard, however, are still not conclusive (Lee, Moller, Hardt, Haubek, & Jensen, 1979). Nonetheless, including alcoholics in any study aimed at clarifying the association between liver disease and neuropsychological test performance introduces a potentially major confounding factor because of the additional and interactive effects that chronic alcohol misuse has on neurologic functioning as well as the functioning of other organ systems, such as the liver.

More recently, controlling for the untoward effects of an alcohol abuse history, Tarter, Hegedus, Van Thiel, Schade, Gavaler, and Starzl (1984) compared a group of 30 biopsy-confirmed nonalcoholic patients with cirrhosis to a group of medically ill patients with Crohn's disease. This latter disease group was selected for study because it controls for the effects of illness chronicity as a contributing factor on cognitive functioning. Moreover, the physicians caring for such patients and the major medical therapy (glucocorticoids) utilized by individuals with Crohn's are the same as those used by cirrhotic patients. A battery of neuropsychological tests measuring intelligence as well as attention, learning and memory, and spatial, language, and perceptual-motor capacities was administered to each subject. The results revealed that the subjects with cirrhosis are deficient on tasks that measure visuospatial, praxis, and perceptual-motor capacity. Intellectual ability, assessed by the Peabody Picture Vocabulary Test and Raven's Progressive Matrices as well as language and learning and memory capacity were normal.

Similar results were obtained in a second study conducted in our laboratory in which only patients with biopsy confirmed primary biliary cirrhosis were studied (Hegedus et al., 1984). Impaired performance on spatial and psychomotor tests was noted, whereas intelligence, learning, and memory and language abilities were unaffected by their chronic liver disease. In a subsequent unpublished analysis of data by Tarter, Hays, Switala, and Van

Thiel (1987) on patients with primary biliary cirrhosis, it was found that those with an accompanying Sjogren's Syndrome were the most impaired. This finding raises the specter that the cognitive deficits found in patients with liver disease, implicating the presence of hepatic encephalopathy, may be due, in part, to the as yet unrecognized effects of the Sjogren's disease which often accompanies primary biliary cirrhosis.

Another study conducted in our laboratory compared the effects of three different types of cirrhotic disease on cognitive performance (Tarter, Hegedus, Van Thiel, Edwards & Schade, 1987). In this study, a battery of neuropsychological tests was administered to patients with either postnecrotic cirrhosis, primary biliary cirrhosis, or alcoholic (Laennec's) cirrhosis. The results indicated that both the type and severity of the identified and quantitated cognitive deficits were related to the type of liver disease. Patients with primary biliary cirrhosis were cognitively the most intact, whereas the alcoholics with cirrhosis manifested the greatest cognitive impairments. All three groups evidenced deficits on tests of attention and concentration; however, only the postnecrotic and alcoholic subjects were deficient on the tests evaluating spatial capacity. Only the alcoholics were impaired on tests of learning and memory. Thus, there are some data, with respect to the cognitive manifestations of hepatic encephalopathy, that suggest that there are both qualitative and quantitative differences in the neuropsychological disturbances that occur among patients with differing types of cirrhosis.

In conclusion, a number of studies, employing either single measures or comprehensive test batteries, have revealed the presence of cognitive impairments in individuals with cirrhosis. Significantly, deficits are manifest even in the absence of overt signs or symptoms of the neuropsychiatric syndrome of portal-systemic encephalopathy. Also noteworthy, albeit limited to date to the study of alcoholic cirrhotics, is the finding that certain liver-functional and injury-measure variables correlate with cognitive performance. These latter observations suggest that the manifest cognitive deficits are mediated, at least to some extent, by metabolic and biochemical factors relating to liver function and/or injury. For reasons that still remain to be clarified, the impairments exhibited by individuals with cirrhosis appear to be most pronounced on tests of spatial, practic, and perceptual-motor capacities. In addition, as pointed out before, there may be significant qualitative and quantitative differences among the various cirrhotic conditions, reflecting perhaps the pathophysiologic differences between the various types of advanced liver diseases.

Neuroanatomic Correlates of Cirrhosis

An examination of the gross neuroanatomic changes that occur in cirrhosis could assist in clarifying the nature of the morphologic substrate underlying the cognitive impairments identified in such populations. Patients who die as a result of fulminant hepatic coma have been found at autopsy to evidence cerebral edema (Conn & Lieberthal, 1979) as well as having pockets of necrosis or microcavitation within their cortex (Martinez, 1968). With the exception of one study recently completed in our laboratory, *in vivo* morphologic studies have not been performed in patients with portal-systemic encephalopathy. Bernthal, Hays, Tarter, Lecky, Hegedus, and Van Thiel (1987) obtained a number of quantified CT scan scores in a sample of 49 nonalcoholic cirrhotic patients. Compared to the scores obtained by controls from published reports on the same index utilized, the cirrhotic subjects exhibited evidence for both cerebral edema and cortical atrophy that was most pronounced in the anterior cerebrum. Numerous correlations between morphologic and cognitive test performance scores were obtained, indicating that the demonstrated neuropsychological test deficits are attributable, at least in part, to identifiable structural abnormalities present in the brain. It is noteworthy in this regard that the visuospatial, attentional, and psychomotor deficits found in cirrhotic individuals are consistent with the presence of anterior cerebral atrophy. Furthermore, liver-functional status in persons with nonalcoholic cirrhosis is strongly associated with gross cerebral morphological status (Tarter, Hays, Sandford, Bernthal, & Van Thiel, 1986).

Chronicity of the encephalopathy results in a number of distinctive neuropathological changes. Hypertrophy and hyperplasia of protoplasmic Alzheimer Type-II astrocytes are typically found throughout the cerebral cortex (Conn & Lieberthal, 1979). Neuronal necrosis and demyelination also occur throughout the cerebrum but with a variable degree of severity.

The previously mentioned findings suggest that in addition to biochemical factors, there are certain brain morphologic disturbances that also contribute to the manifest cognitive deficits demonstrated by individuals with liver disease and PSE. It is particularly noteworthy that patients with nonalcoholic cirrhosis exhibit deficits on neuropsychological tests and evidence cerebral morphologic disturbances that are very similar to those reported to occur in alcoholics (Tarter & Edwards, 1985). It is possible, although still not established, that the neuropsychological test performance deficits frequently reported to occur in alcoholics are mediated, at least to some degree, by a hepatic encephalopathy and do not result entirely from the direct effects of long-standing ethanol cerebrotoxicity *per se*. The extent to which alcohol induced hepatic disease underlies the neuropsychological deficits found in alcoholics is not as yet known; however, the observed correlations between hepatic and cognitive variables and the demonstration that the EEG and neuroanatomic disturbances found in such individuals covary with the severity of liver disease indicate that alcohol-induced hepatic pathology and the intrinsic neurotoxicity of ethanol probably both contribute to the cognitive deficits found in alcoholics.

Neurophysiological Correlates of Cirrhosis

The first study of the relationship between portal-systemic encephalopathy and EEG changes was reported by Adams and Foley (1953). Since then, the EEG, as a measure of brain physiologic functioning in hepatic encephalopathy, has been investigated extensively. The time course of EEG changes that occur with PSE has been well established and is known to manifest first as a slowing in the alpha frequency; however, as the patient progresses toward hepatic coma, high-amplitude delta waves become prominent as does the so-called "triphasic wave" pattern. Although not always present in patients with hepatic encephalopathy, the triphasic wave is characterized by a primary downward deflection, indicating a surface positive charge, that is preceded and followed by low-amplitude negative deflections (Bickford & Butt, 1955). The triphasic wave pattern was thought initially to be pathognomic for hepatic encepahlopathy, but subsequent research has shown clearly that it can occur in other types of metabolic encephalopathies as well (Conn & Lieberthal, 1979).

More recently, evoked response potentials (ERPs) have been recorded in patients with hepatic encephalopathy. Zeneroli, Pinelli, Gollini, Penna, Messori, Zani, and Ventura (1984) measured visual-evoked potentials in patients with hepatic encephalopathy of unstated etiology. It was found that four distinct grades of encephalopathies could be discerned by these investigators according to latency and wave morphology characteristics. It was also observed that the visual-evoked response could detect an impairment in 10 of 16 patients with subclinical encephalopathy, that is, in persons with no overt signs or symptoms of neuropsychiatric disturbances. Specifically, the latency of the N3 wave component was delayed in the subjects they studied, having evidence for hepatic encephalopathy.

Somatosensory evoked potentials also have been found to be useful for detecting subclinical or latent hepatic encephalopathy (Yang & Chu, 1985). The N3 and P3 wave latencies were longer in patients with a subclinical encephalopathy than those without encephalopathy. Moreover, it was found that the two latencies increased progressively as the severity of encephalopathy increased.

Two studies recently completed in our laboratory examined ERP latencies in patients who were not overtly encephalopathic but who had biopsy-confirmed nonalcoholic cirrhosis. Comparing the early waveform components of visual, brain stem and somatosensory ERPs revealed no striking or systematic differences between liver disease and normal controls (Sandford, Sclabassi, Tarter & Van Thiel, 1987). In our second study, it was shown, however, that liver functional status covaried with a variety of ERP measurements (Tarter, Sclabassi, Sandford, Hays, Carra & Van Thiel, 1987). Taken together, these findings suggest that the neuropsychological concomitants of liver disease are most evident in the late waveform components of the ERP, although even for the early components, hepatic functional status is correlated strongly with latency.

In summary, the EEG and more recently evoked response potentials have been recorded in patients with cirrhosis and concomitant portal-systemic encephalopathy in an effort to clarify the neurophysiological functioning in such individuals. Despite extensive research, little has been learned about the metabolic process defined as hepatic encephalopathy using the

EEG. This probably is the case because of the limitations imposed by the inherent subjective interpretation of the EEG record, the numerous clinical variations among cirrhotic individuals, and the overall lack of diagnostic specificity of this technique. Nonetheless, the severity of EEG abnormalities co-varies with the severity of neuropsychiatric disorder assessed either clinically or by the use of other techniques such as neuropsychological tests. However, for detecting the presence of encephalopathy in the latent or pre-clinical stage, the EEG does not appear to be as sensitive as are neuropsychological tests (Rehnstrom et al., 1977). Evoked response potentials appear to be a more promising research tool than the EEG based upon the two ERP investigations published to date, although the current enthusiasm for these procedures should be tempered by the lack of studies in which multiple modalities (auditory, visual, somatosensory) have been recorded simultaneously in patients with biopsy-verified nonalcoholic cirrhosis.

Psychiatric Correlates of Cirrhosis

As shown in Table 1, a variety of emotional and behavioral disturbances are manifest in patients with portal-systemic encephalopathy. Little, if any, consideration has been given to the emotional disturbances that may be present in patients with subacute or preclinical states of hepatic encephalopathy. Tarter, Hegedes, Van Thiel, Schade, Gavaler, and Starzl (1984) found that nonalcoholic cirrhotics, who do not manifest any overt signs of encephalopathy, exhibit an MMPI profile indicative of anxiety and depression. Although meaningful and potentially useful for clinical management, these findings are not particularly surprising considering the life-threatening nature of their underlying medical illness. However, it should be noted that patients with primary biliary cirrhosis, although also somewhat anxious and depressed are, in fact, less disturbed than are patients with Crohn's disease, where the disease is rarely fatal.

Psychosocial Adjustment

Quality of life is affected adversely by chronic liver disease. Employing the Sickness Impact Profile, Tarter, Hegedus, Van Thiel, Schade, Gavaler, and Starzl (1984) observed that nonalcoholic cirrhotics report impairments in the following areas of daily living: social interaction, sleep and rest, appetite, work, home management, mobility, and leisure activity. The overall dysfunction index achieved by these patients, exceeded 20%; on this scale a score at or near zero represents normal health status. Thus, nonalcoholic cirrhotics, in addition to exhibiting cognitive impairments and mild emotional disturbances, also are unable to fully meet the demands of everyday living.

Etiology of Portal-Systemic Encephalopathy

Cirrhosis is generally thought to be a necessary precondition for the development of chronic portal-systemic encephalopathy (Conn & Lieberthal,

1979). The nature of cirrhosis, involving hepatocellular dysfunction, fibrosis, nodular regeneration, cholestasis, and intra- as well as extrahepatic blood flow abnormalities, all combine to produce a variety of biochemical and physiological disturbances that culminate in the syndrome of PSE. According to Zieve (1979), the most salient metabolic aberrations include the following:

1. Brain glucose and oxygen consumption are decreased.
2. Ammonia levels are increased in the blood, brain, spinal fluid and muscles.
3. Glutamine levels are increased in brain, spinal fluid, and muscles.
4. Short chain fatty acid levels are increased in the blood and possibly the brain.
5. Normal neurotransmitter levels are decreased in the brain.
6. False neurotransmitter levels are increased in the brain, blood, urine, and muscles.
7. Mercaptan levels are increased in the brain, blood, breath, and urine.
8. Amino acid metabolism is disordered.
9. The affinity of hemoglobin for oxygen is reduced.
10. The concentration of neurotransmitter metabolites is increased both in the brain and spinal fluid.

Presumably, the resultant depressed brain energy metabolism, combined with the accumulation of a variety of cerebrotoxic substances and neurotransmitter dysregulation underlies the neuropsychiatric condition.

The point to be emphasized is that PSE is a multisystem disorder, consisting of a constellation of biochemical, physiological, and anatomical correlates. Once established, however, it may be self-perpetuating. To illustrate this point, cerebral oxygen consumption is reduced in persons suffering from PSE. Hyperventilation, is, therefore, not surprisingly, a frequent manifestation of PSE. Hyperventilation, however, results in a depression of the arterial CO_2 tension that results in a reflex reduction in cerebral blood flow that potentially could exacerbate any neuropsychiatric disturbance present due to PSE. Furthermore, the demonstration that *voluntary* hyperventilation in patients with established cirrhotic liver disease increases arterial ammonia levels (Berry, Owen, Flanagan, & Tyor, 1960), which in turn leads to further hyperventilation (James, MacDonald, & Xanalatos, 1974), demonstrates how a positive feedback loop involving the synergistic interplay of several biological systems both causes and contributes to sustaining hepatic encephalopathy once it is established.

Treatment of Portal-Systemic Encephalopathy

The medical management of PSE is a complex task, requiring attention to many aspects of the patient's overall condition. Factors that can trigger PSE and exacerbate a PSE episode include gastrointestinal bleeding, constipation, acid-base disturbances and electrolyte abnormalities such as hypokalemia, hypoxemia, azotemia, vascular volume reduction, overhydration, a diet high in protein (particulary animal protein), and malnutrition. Factors complicating the treatment can include pulmonary congestion, infection, and renal failure as well as drugs that are either metabolized by the liver or act upon the brain. Bearing these factors in mind and recognizing the need for comprehensive medical management procedures, one usually employs the following methods to treat patients with portal-systemic encephalopathy.

Antibiotics

Neomycin and other similar nonabsorbable orally administered antibiotics suppress ammonia production by reducing the bacterial flora capable of producing ammonia, which, as noted previously, is a cerebrotoxic substance implicated as a major etiological factor in the pathogenesis of PSE. Antibiotics also are used to treat infections that can have adverse effects upon renal function, blood pressure, and acid–base balance that contributes to PSE once established.

Pharmacologic Agents

Lactulose is currently the drug of choice for the medical treatment of PSE. This synthetic disaccharide both prevents and decreases the number of recurrent attacks of chronic encephalopathy. It also attenuates the severity of an acute episode of PSE. It acts both by lowering colonic pH, thereby reducing the absorption of ammonia and by increasing bacterial assimilation of ammonia into bacterial protein. Lactulose also decreases intestinal transit time and thus the availability of fecal material for the production of ammonia by bacteria and absorption of ammonia. It is particularly noteworthy that lactulose treatment has been shown to attenuate certain cognitive deficits found in cirrhotic individuals (McClain, Potter, Kromhout, & Zieve, 1984).

Neurotransmitter precursors and agonists, specifically L-dopa and bromocriptine, have also been administered in an effort to restore optimal dopaminergic neurotransmission in patients with PSE. Restoration of the optimal ratio of branched-chain amino acids (BCAA) relative to aromatic amino acids also has been attempted via intravenous infusions of BCAA in an attempt to correct or reduce the effect of false neurotransmitters upon the brain. Both of these pharmacological treatments are based on the same basic assumption—namely the excess presence of weak or false neurotransmitters in the blood and brain underlies the etiology of PSE. The efficacy of these procedures as compared to those of lactulose and neomycin is still unsettled.

Nutrition

The relationship between dietary intake of animal protein and subsequent ammonia toxicity is well documented in patients with PSE. Chronic restriction or the temporary omission of animal protein from the diet and its replacement by vegetable proteins are, therefore, prophylactic strategies occasionally used for controlling the occurrence and severity of PSE. Unfortunately, patients with PSE are not uncommonly malnourished because of disturbed storage, absorption, and utilization of essential nutrients due to their primary liver disease. Dietary restrictions tend, therefore, to enhance these disabilities even further. The provision, however, of adequate nutrients, including vitamins and minerals, is an essential and common component of the treatment regimen while maintaining protein intake at just above or at just below recommended daily intake levels.

In advanced cases, despite exhaustive medical management efforts, PSE persists. Under such circumstances, especially if the liver disease is progressive, surgical intervention may be required.

Colon Bypass and Colectomy

Total colectomy and colon bypass have both been performed on patients with PSE who are refractory to the more common medical management procedures. The purpose of these procedures is to remove the colon or the fecal stream from the colon where most of the ammonia is generated. These procedures are rarely performed any more.

Reversal of Portacaval Shunting

The surgical anastomosis of the portal vein to the vena cava is largely responsible for the PSE in patients with chronic liver disease. Thus, individuals who undergo this procedure experience an augmentation of PSE symptoms because the liver can no longer, even inefficiently, filter or remove cerebrotoxic substances from the portal venous circulation (especially ammonia and mercaptans) by virtue of the fact that the liver is bypassed. Therefore, in severe cases in which shunts have been created, eliminating or reversing the shunt has sometimes been performed. This results, however, in enhancing portal venous pressure and the risks of bleeding from varices and is a very difficult surgical procedure to accomplish, particularly in patients who are so metabolically ill. As must be obvious, therefore, this procedure is reserved only for those few patients in whom all other treatments have failed. Rather than reversing the shunt, another approach that has been tried is to arterialize the portacaval shunt, using the hepatic artery or one of its branches. Both of these procedures (shunt reversal and portal vein arterialization) are thought to enhance hepatic extraction of ammonia by increasing the effective hepatic blood flow, although their efficacy remains uncertain.

Transplantation

The most recent, innovative, and radical treatment for PSE is orthotopic liver transplantation. This procedure is reserved for individuals with advanced chronic liver disease who have not responded to any other form of medical or surgical intervention. The effects of hepatic transplantation on PSE are, as yet, undocumented. However, in one small cohort of subjects, no cognitive deficits were found in such patients when studied on an average of 1-yr postsurgery (Tarter, Van Thiel, Hegedus, Schade, Gavaler, & Starzl, 1984). Unfortunately, no pretransplant data were available in these patients; thus, the significance of this finding remains uncertain.

In summary, despite the number and variety of treatments for PSE, considerable difficulties remain in the management of this condition. Current medical and surgical techniques have been only partly effective. It should also be noted that certain of the techniques have serious drawbacks, including a high mortality rate associated with surgery in the patient population in whom it is to be applied, renal failure, nerve deafness resulting from neomycin use, malnutrition consequential to prolonged dietary restriction, and gut injury due to antibiotic exposure. Although the best available treatments may improve the patient's clinical condition, it is important to emphasize that there are no procedures that appear to be able to cure PSE; hence a chronic, low-grade encephalopathy is commonly found to persist in conjunction with chronic liver disease even when managed maximally.

Encephalopathy Associated with Fulminant Hepatic Failure

Fulminant hepatic failure, occurring as the result of hepatotoxins, drugs, or viral disease, is characterized by a rapid onset and a characteristic neuropsychiatric syndrome consisting of a sequence of aggressive or violent behavior, followed by delerium, seizures, and a progressive clouding of consciousness to coma. Within a matter of days, or even hours, the patient becomes comatose. According to Chen and Chen (1977), the mortality rate for this condition approaches 75%. Most North American hepatologists report mortality rates of 80 to 95%. Unlike chronic portal-systemic encephalopathy, the course of this illness and its concomitant neurologic deterioration is very rapid and it may not be reversible once advanced. To date, neuropsychological studies have not been conducted on patients with fulminant hepatic failure.

Acquired Chronic Hepatocerebral Degeneration

Victor, Adams, and Cole (1965) described an irreversible, although infrequent, manifestation of portal-systemic shunting, consisting of ataxia, dysarthria, dementia, grimacing behavior, intention tremor, and choreoathetosis. A permanent myelopathy, muscular rigidity, pyramidal and extrapyramidal signs, grasp reflexes, nystagmus, and paraplegia may also develop in such patients. According to Victor, Adams, and Cole (1965), this condition is irreversible, is distinct from hepatic coma, and often is present before any signs or symptoms of hepatic coma are manifest. Whether this is truly a distinct form of hepatic encephalopathy as Victor et al. (1965) claim or comprises an unusual variation of the neuropsychiatric syndrome of portal-systemic encephalopathy described previously, remains to be determined. Formal cognitive studies of patients with this latter syndrome have not been conducted.

Liver Disease in Children

Very little research has been conducted on the neuropsychological sequelae of liver disease in children, although a profound intellectual impairment has been reported to occur in children with cirrhosis (Jervis, 1979). Moreover, approximately 33% of children who survive with Reye's Syndrome (acute fatty liver) exhibit significant lifelong neurological disorders along with intellectual and cognitive deficits (Davidson, Willoughby, O'Tuama, & Swisher, 1978). There is also some indication that the earlier the age of the individual at the time of disease onset, the more severe are the persisting intellectual deficits to be expected after recovery from the illness.

It is noteworthy that the few studies of children with liver disease, unlike the findings obtained in adults, implicate the presence of a global intellectual deficit. The reason for this finding in children but not adults is unclear but suggests that the maturing brain is more vulnerable to any of a variety of potential neurologic disruptions than is the adult brain. However, comprehensive and large-scale investigations of children with hepatic disease have not been conducted; therefore, the preliminary findings reviewed in this chapter should be interpreted cautiously.

IMPLICATIONS OF LIVER DISEASE FOR COMPREHENSIVE MEDICAL MANAGEMENT

In addition to the issue of differential diagnosis, there are at least four other reasons why neuropsychologists and physicians should be familiar with the etiology and manifestations of hepatic encephalopathy. First, many individuals with cirrhosis are disabled to the point where they cannot safely drive a car (Schomerus et al., 1981) and, by analogy, use power equipment or tools that require visual spatial and psychomotor skills. Thus the potential impact of their disease on their daily living is substantial and should necessitate rehabilitation strategies that maximize autonomous living and overall functional capacity. Second, neuroleptic drugs are primarily metabolized in the liver. Safe and therapeutically effective dosages for these agents are not well established for persons with advanced liver disease; hence, usual dose levels may produce an adverse reaction due either to prolongation of drug half-life or enhanced susceptibility to drug effects. In this regard, it should be noted that individuals with cirrhosis have been reported to lapse into coma after sedative administration (Laidlow, Read, & Sherlock, 1961), become severely drowsy from chlorpromazine (Read, Laidlow, & McCarthy, 1969), and be hypersensitive to the effects of MAO inhibitors (Morgan &

Read, 1972). In view of the finding that neuropsychological tests are among the most sensitive indicators of cerebral dysfunction in hepatic disease, it is possible that cognitive tests can be used to evaluate the impact of neuroleptic drugs and to monitor their effects in situations where pharmacotherapy is required. Third, it should be pointed out that some neuroleptic drugs have been found to increase the risk for intrahepatic cholestasis (Gunderson & Amidsen, 1969). This in turn could exacerbate the encephalopathy or enhance the hepatic disease process, either of which could adversely affect the individual's quality of life. Neuropsychological tests may have the ability to distinguish the encephalopathy manifestations due to the liver disease from those due to the effects of medication. And fourth, given the high prevalence rate for liver disease in the population, especially as the result of alcohol misuse, neuropsychological tests may be useful for distinguishing the cognitive sequelae consequential to hepatic pathology from those effects that are due to the direct cerebrotoxic effects of alcohol. Because liver disease can be treated and the ensuing cognitive deficits associated with or due to the liver disease can be reversed (at least to some extent), it may be possible to cognitively rehabilitate at least some alcoholics more than is generally appreciated.

ACKNOWLEDGMENTS

The research for this chapter was partly supported by Grant RO1 32556-01 from the National Institute of Mental Health.

REFERENCES

Acker, W., Majumdar, S., Shaw, G., & Thomson, A. (1982). The relationship between brain and liver damage in chronic alcoholic patients. *Journal of Neurology, Neurosurgery and Psychiatry, 45,* 984–987.

Adams, R., & Foley, J. (1953). The neurological disorder associated with liver disease. In H. Merritt & C. Have (Eds.), *Metabolic and toxic diseases of the nervous system* (pp. 198–237). Baltimore: Williams & Wilkins.

Atkinson, M., & Goligher, J. (1960). Recurrent hepatic coma treated by colectomy and rheorectal anastomosis. *Lancet, 1,* 461–464.

Bernthal, P., Hays, A., Tarter, R., Lecky, J., Hedgedus, A., & Van Thiel, D. (1987). Cerebral CT scan abnormalities in cholestatic and hepatocellular disease and their relationship to psychometric indices of encephalopathy. *Hepatology, 7,* 107–114.

Berry, J., Owen, E., Flanagan, J., & Tyor, M. (1960). The effect of acute hyperventilation on the blood ammonia concentration of patients with liver disease. *Journal of Laboratory and Clinical Medicine, 55,* 849–854.

Bickford, R., & Butt, H. (1955). Hepatic coma: The EEG pattern. *Journal of Clinical Investigation, 34,* 790–799.

Chen, T., & Chen, P. (1977). *Essential hepatology.* Boston: Butterworth.

Conn, H., & Lieberthal, M. (1979). *The hepatic coma syndrome and lactulose.* Baltimore: Williams & Wilkins.

Conn, H., Leevy, C., Vahcevic, Z., Rodgers, J., Maddrey, W., Seeff, L., & Levy, L. (1977). Comparison of lactulose and neomycin in the treatment of chronic portal-systemic encephalopathy. A double blind controlled trial. *Gastroenterology, 72,* 573–583.

Davidson, P., Willoughby, R., O'Tuama, L., & Swisher, C. (1978). Neurological and intellectual sequelae of Reye's Syndrome. *American Journal of Mental Deficiency, 82,* 535–541.

Dudrick, S., Mackie, J., & Serlin, O. (1968). Surgical exclusion of the colon for chronic hepatic encephalopathy. *American Journal of Surgery, 115*, 57–62.

Elsass, P., Lund, Y., & Ranek, L. (1978). Encephalopathy in patients with cirrhosis of the liver. A Neuropsychological study. *Scandinavian Journal of Gastroenterology, 13*, 241–247.

Fung, W., & Khoo, O. (1971). Lactulose in the treatment of acute and chronic hepatic encephalopathy. *Singapore Medical Journal, 12*, 176–180.

Galambos, J. (1979). Cirrhosis: Epidemiology. In L. Smith (Ed.), *Major problems in internal medicine* (pp. 261–276). Philadelphia: W. B. Saunders.

Geffray, Y., Segrestin, M., & Geffray, P. (1970). Interest du lactulose dans la traitement de l'encephalopathic portocave chronique—a propos de 20 observations. *Therapeuteque, 46*, 897–901.

Germain, L., Frezinos, J., Louis, A., & Ribet, A. (1973). Effect of lactulose on post-shunt hepatic encephalopathy: A controlled trial. *Archive of Applied Digestive Diseases* (French), *62*, 293–301.

Gilberstadt, S., Gilberstadt, H., Zieve, L., Buegel, B., Collier, R., & McClain, C. (1980). Psychomotor performance deficits in cirrhotic patients without overt encephalopathy. *Archives of Internal Medicine, 140*, 519–521.

Gunderson, H., & Amidsen, A. (1969). The electrophoretic pattern of alkaline phosphatase in schizophrenic females under long-term treatment with neuroleptic drugs and in young and old healthy women. *Scandinavian Journal of Clinical and Laboratory Investigation, 24*, 173–177.

Havens, L., & Child, C. (1955). Recurrent psychosis associated with liver disease and elevated blood ammonia. *New England Journal of Medicine, 252*, 756–759.

Hegedus, A., Tarter, R., Van Thiel, D., Schade, R., Gavaler, J., & Starzl, T. (1984). Neuropsychiatric characteristics associated with primary biliary cirrhosis. *The International Journal of Psychiatry in Medicine, 14*, 303–313.

James, I., MacDonald, L., & Xanalatos, C. (1974). Effect of ammonium salts on brain metabolism. *Journal of Neurology, Neurosurgery and Psychiatry, 37*, 948–953.

Jefferson, J., & Marshall, J. (1981). *Neuropsychiatric features of medical disorders.* New York: Plenum Press.

Jervis, G. (1979). Encephalopathy in infantile hepatic cirrhosis. *Acta Neuropathologica, 48*, 273–275.

Kardel, T., & Stigsby, B. (1975). Period-amplitude analysis of the electroencephalogram correlated with liver function in patients with cirrhosis of the liver. *Electroencephalography and Clinical Neurophysiology, 38*, 605–609.

Laidlow, J., Read, A., & Sherlock, S. (1961). Morphine tolerance in hepatic cirrhosis. *Gastroenterology, 40*, 389–396.

Lee, K., Moller, L., Hardt, F., Haubek, A., & Jensen, E. (1979). Alcohol-induced brain damage and liver damage in young males. *Lancet, 2*, 759–761.

Leevy, C. (1974). Exploring the brain-liver relationship. *Modern Medicine, 42*, 17–22.

Lieber, C., & Leo, M. (1982). Alcohol and the liver. In C. Lieber (Ed.), *Medical disorders of alcoholism: Pathogenesis and treatment* (pp. 219–312). Philadelphia: W. B. Saunders.

Ma, M., McLeod, J., & Blackburn, C. (1969). Long-term treatment of portal-systemic encephalopathy with lactulose. *Australian Annals of Medicine, 18*, 117–123.

Martinez, A. (1968). Electron microscopy in human hepatic encephalopathy. *Acta Neuropathologica, 11*, 82–86.

McClain, C., Potter, T., Kromhout, J., & Zieve, L. (1984). The effect of lactulose on psychomotor performance tests in alcoholic cirrhotics without overt hepatic encephalopathy. *Journal of Clinical Gastroenterology, 6*, 325–329.

Morgan, M., & Read, A. (1972). Antidepressants and liver disease. *Gut, 13*, 697–701.

Parsons-Smith, B., Summerskill, W., Dawson, A., & Sherlock, S. (1957). The electroencephalograph in liver disease. *Lancet, 2*, 867–871.

Read, A., Laidlow, J., & McCarthy, C. (1969). Effects of chlorpromazine in patients with hepatic disease. *British Medical Journal, 3*, 497–499.

Rehnstrom, S., Simert, G., Hansson, J., Johnson, G., & Vang, J. (1977). Chronic hepatic encephalopathy. A psychometrical study. *Scandinavian Journal of Gastroenterology, 12*, 305–311.
Resnick, R., Ishihara, A., Chalmers, T., & Schimmel, E. (1968). The Boston interhospital liver
group: A controlled trial of colon bypass in chronic hepatic encephalopathy. *Gastroenterology, 54*, 1057–1069.
Reynolds, T., Redeker, A., & Davis, P. (1958). A controlled study of the effects of L-arginine on
hepatic encephalopathy. *American Journal of Medicine, 25*, 359–367.
Rikkers, L., Jenko, P., Rudman, D., & Freides, D. (1978). Subclinical hepatic encephalopathy:
Detection, prevalence and relationship to nitrogen metabolism. *Gastroenterology, 75*, 462–
469.
Rosselli, M., Lorenzana, P., & Rosselli, A. (1985). Wilson's Disease: A case of reversible demen-
tia. *Journal of Clinical and Experimental Neuropsychology, 7*, 616 (abstract).
Sandford, S., Sclabassi, R., Tarter, R., & Van Thiel, D. (1987). Sensory information processing in
nonalcoholic cirrhosis: Visual, auditory, and somatosensory event-related potentials. *Jour-
nal of the Neurological Sciences, 80*, 269–276.
Schienberg, J., & Stemlieb, J. (1984). *Wilson's disease*. Philadelphia: W. B. Saunders.
Schomerus, H., Hamster, W., Blunck, H., Reinhard, U., Mayer, K., & Dole, W. (1981). Latent
portasystemic encephalopathy. 1. Nature of cerebral functional defects and their effect on
fitness to drive. *Digestive Diseases and Sciences, 28*, 622–630.
Sherlock, S., Summerskill, W., White, L., & Pheur, E. (1954). Portal-systemic encephalopathy.
Neurological complications of liver disease. *Lancet, 2*, 453–457.
Simmons, F., Goldstein, H., & Boyle, J. (1970). A controlled clinical trial of lactulose in hepatic
encephalopathy. *Gastroenterology, 59*, 827–832.
Smith, J., & Smith, L. (1977). WAIS functioning of cirrhotic and noncirrhotic alcoholics. *Journal
of Clinical Psychology, 33*, 309–313.
Summerskill, W., Davidson, E., Sherlock, S., & Steiner, R. (1956). The neuropsychiatric syn-
drome associated with hepatic cirrhosis and an extensive portal collateral circulation.
Quarterly Journal of Medicine, 25, 245–266.
Tarter, R., & Edwards, K. (1985). Neuropsychology of alcoholism: In R. Tarter & D. Van Thiel
(Eds.), *Alcohol and the brain: Chronic effects* (pp. 217–242). New York: Plenum Press.
Tarter, R., Hegedus, A., Van Thiel, D., Schade, R., Gavaler, J., & Starzl, T. (1984). Nonalcoholic
cirrhosis associated with neuropsychological dysfunction in the absence of overt evidence
of hepatic encephalopathy. *Gastroenterology, 86*, 1421–1427.
Tarter, R., Van Thiel, D., Hegedus, A., Schade, R., Gavaler, J., & Starzl, T. (1984). Liver transplantation: Long-term neuropsychiatric status. *The Journal of Laboratory and Clinical Medicine, 103*, 776–782.
Tarter, R., Hegedus, A., Van Thiel, D., Gavaler, J., & Schade, R. (1986). Hepatic dysfunction and
neuropsychological test performance in alcoholics with cirrhosis. *Journal of Studies on
Alcohol, 47*, 74–77.
Tarter, R., Hays, A., Sandford, S., Bernthal, P., & Van Thiel, D. (1986). Cerebral morphologic
status is predicted by liver injury severity in patients with nonalcoholic cirrhosis. *Lancet, 2*,
893–895.
Tarter, R., Hegedus, A., Van Thiel, D., Edwards, N., & Schade, R. (1987). Neurobehavioral
correlates of cholestatic and hepatocellular disease: Differentiation according to disease
specific characteristics and severity of the identified cerebral dysfunction. *International
Journal of Neuroscience, 32*, 901–910.
Tarter, R., Sclabassi, R., Sandford, S., Hays, A., Carra, J., & Van Thiel, D. (1987). Relationship
between hepatic injury status and event related potentials. *Clinical Electroencephalography, 18*, 15–19.
Tarter, R., Switala, J., Carra, J., Edwards, N., & Van Thiel, D. (1987). Neuropsychologic impairment in patients with Wilson's Disease who do not exhibit overt encephalopathy. *International Journal of Neuroscience*.
Tarter, R., Hays, A., Switala, J., & Van Thiel, D. (1987). The influence of Sjogren's Syndrome on
the manifest neuropsychiatric disturbances concomitant to primary biliary cirrhosis. Unpublished manuscript.

Victor, M., Adams, R., & Cole, M. (1965). The acquired non-Wilsonian type of chronic hepatocerebral degeneration. *Medicine, 44*, 345–396.

Yang, S., & Chu, Y. (1985). Somatosensory evoked potentials in hepatic encephalopathy. *Gastroenterology, 89*, 625–630.

Zeegen, R., Drinkwater, J., & Dawson, A. (1970). Method for measuring cerebral dysfunction in patients with liver disease. *British Medical Journal, 2*, 633–636.

Zeneroli, M., Pinelli, G., Gollini, G., Penna, A., Messori, E., Zani, G., & Ventura, E. (1984). Visual evoked potentials: A diagnostic tool for the assessment of hepatic encephalopathy. *Gut, 25*, 291–299.

Zieve, L. (1979). Hepatic encephalopathy: Summary of present knowledge with an elaboration on recent developments. In H. Popper & F. Schaffner (Eds.), *Progress in liver diseases* (pp. 88–104). New York: Grune & Stratton.

5

Renal System

ROBERT P. HART and JEFFREY S. KREUTZER

INTRODUCTION

The incidence of renal disorders requiring end-stage care (e.g., dialysis or transplantation) is approximately 59 per million person yr (Sugimoto & Rosansky, 1984). The present chapter considers the neuropsychological impairments associated with renal failure and chronic hemodialysis. Research findings on renal transplantation, though limited, are also included. The chapter is organized into three major sections. First, discussion focuses on clinical syndromes associated with renal failure and hemodialysis treatment and the behavioral changes that occur between individual dialysis sessions. Next, research findings pertaining to neuropsychological impairments in chronic renal failure and chronic hemodialysis are summarized. Within this section, studies are organized in terms of (a) general intelligence, (b) memory, and (c) attentional processes. The final sections discuss rehabilitation, summarize methodological issues, and propose directions for future research. Behavioral research on renal disorders has been beset by methodological problems related to the complex interactions between chronic medical conditions and central nervous system dysfunction. Additional methodological issues are of particular relevance in the renal population, for example, short-term changes in toxic uremic status in assessing the effect of dialysis treatment on neuropsychological function.

Tables 1 and 2 are provided to facilitate comparison of studies and to provide an overview of methodological adequacy as specified by Parsons and Prigatano (1978). Table 1 denotes educational levels, age, sex, duration of disease and dialysis treatments, frequency of dialysis sessions, and whether control subjects were used. Research reports should also include the following information to allow accurate data interpretation and com-

ROBERT P. HART • Departments of Psychiatry and Neurology, and Division of Neurological Surgery, Medical College of Virginia, Virginia Commonwealth University, Richmond, Virginia 23298.   JEFFREY S. KREUTZER • Departments of Rehabilitation Medicine and Psychiatry, Medical College of Virginia, Virginia Commonwealth University, Richmond, Virginia 23298.

TABLE 1. Sample Characteristics

Authors	Education (years)	Age (years)	N	Sex	Duration disease (months)	Duration dialysis (months)	Frequency of dialysis	Controls
Alexander, Hightower, Anderson, & Snow, 1980	–	18–69	56	–	–	–	–	+
Blatt & Tsushima, 1966	8–17	x̄ = 43	17	M = 17	–	N.A.	N.A.	–
Comty, Leonard & Shapiro, 1974	–	x̄ = 41	49	M = 29 F = 20	–	x̄ = 19	–	–
English, Savage, Britton, Ward, & Kerr, 1978	–	x̄ = 40	29	M = 15 F = 14	–	x̄ = 36	–	–
Fishman & Schneider, 1972	8–18	x̄ = 47	12	M = 6 F = 6	–	–	–	–
Freeman, Sherrard, Calsyn, & Paige, 1980	–	–	137	M = 134 F = 3	–	–	–	+
Gentry & Davis, 1972	–	x̄ = 44	18	M = 17 F = 1	x̄ = 96	x̄ = 8	–	–
Gilli & DeBastiani, 1983	x̄ = 6	x̄ = 51	54	M = 17 F = 37	–	x̄ = 30	–	–
Ginn et al., 1975	–	–	7	–	x̄ = 6	–	–	–
Hagberg, 1974	–	13–60	23	M = 9 F = 14	–	6–12	–	–
Hart, Pederson, Czerwinski, & Adams, 1983	x̄ = 12	x̄ = 40	20	M = 16 F = 4	x̄ = 60	x̄ = 30	–	+
Kaplan, De-Nour, Shanan, & Garty, 1977	6–12	20–51	47	M = 31 F = 16	–	–	–	–
Malmquist et al., 1972	10–19	24–42	13	M = 12 F = 1	–	N.A.	N.A.	–

Study								
McKee, Burnett, Raft, Batten, & Bain, 1982	$\bar{x} = 10$	$\bar{x} = 46$	34	M = 18 / F = 16	—	6–51	3/wk	—
Rabinowitz & van der Spuy, 1978	$\bar{x} = 8.4$	—	28	—	—	—	—	—
Ryan, Souheaver, & DeWolfe, 1980	$\bar{x} = 9$	$\bar{x} = 52$	72	M = 72	—	N.A.	N.A.	+
Ryan, Souheaver, & DeWolfe, 1981	$\bar{x} = 10$	$\bar{x} = 47$	48	M = 48	—	—	2–3/wk	+
Ryan, Souheaver, & DeWolfe, 1981	—	18–45	48	M = 48	—	35	2–3/wk	+
Schupak, Sullivan, & Lee, 1967	—	13–57	25	—	—	5–21	2–3/wk	—
Souheaver, Ryan, & DeWolfe, 1982	$\bar{x} = 9$	$\bar{x} = 11$	12	F = 12	—	N.A.	N.A.	—
Spehr et al., 1977	—	$\bar{x} = 41$	20	F = 11 / M = 9	—	—	2/wk	—
Teschan et al., 1974	—	—	—	—	—	—	—	—
Teschan et al., 1975	—	—	4	F = 4	—	—	—	—
Teschan et al., 1976	—	—	47	—	—	—	—	—
Teschan et al., 1977	—	—	—	—	—	—	—	—
Teschan et al., 1979	3–20	17–70	132	—	—	—	—	—
Trieschmann & Sand, 1971	$\bar{x} = 12$	$\bar{x} = 37$	83	M = 52 / F = 31	—	N.A.	N.A.	—
Winokur, Czaczkes, & Kaplan De-Nour, 1973	—	—	38	—	—	1.1.5	—	—
Ziesat, Logue, & McCarty, 1980	$\bar{x} = 10$	$\bar{x} = 48$	28	M = 21 / F = 7	—	12	2.5/wk	—

TABLE 2. Methodological Variables

Authors	Race	Diagnoses	Other systemic medical illness	Drug/ alcohol Hx.	Psychiatric Hx.	Medication	Emotional status	Multivariate stats	Age/education partialed in r	Testers experience
Alexander, Hightower, Anderson, & Snow, 1980	−	−	−	−	−	−	−	−	N.A.	−
Blatt & Tsushima, 1966	−	−	+	−	−	−	−	N.A.	−	−
Comty, Leonard, & Shapiro, 1974	−	−	−	−	−	−	+	−	−	+
English, Savage, Bretton, Ward, & Kerr, 1978	−	−	−	−	−	−	−	N.A.	−	−
Fishman & Schneider, 1972	−	−	−	−	−	−	−	−	−	−
Freeman, Sherrard, Calsyn, & Paige, 1980	−	−	+	−	−	−	N.A.	+	N.A.	−
Gentry & Davis, 1972	−	−	−	−	−	−	−	−	−	−
Gilli & DeBastiani, 1983	+	+	+	−	−	−	−	N.A.	+	+
Ginn et al., 1975	−	−	−	−	−	−	−	N.A.	N.A.	−
Hagberg, 1974	−	−	−	−	−	−	−	N.A.	N.A.	−
Hart, Pederson, Czerwinski, & Adams, 1983	+	+	+	+	+	+	+	+	+	−
Kaplan, De-Nour, Shanan, & Garty, 1978	−	+	−	−	−	−	−	−	−	−
Malmquist et al., 1972	+	−	−	−	−	−	−	N.A.	N.A.	−

Study										
McKee, Burnett, Raft, Batten, & Bain, 1982	−	−	−	+	+	−	+	−	N.A.	+
Rabinowitz & van der Spuy, 1978	+	+	−	−	−	−	−	−	−	−
Ryan, Souheaver, & DeWolfe, 1980	−	+	+	−	+	−	+	−	N.A.	+
Ryan, Souheaver, & DeWolfe, 1981	−	+	+	−	+	−	+	−	−	+
Ryan, Souheaver, & DeWolfe, 1981	−	+	−	−	−	−	+	−	N.A.	+
Sand, Livingston, & Wright, 1966	−	−	−	−	−	−	−	N.A.	N.A.	−
Schupak, Sullivan, & Lee, 1967	+	+	−	−	−	−	−	N.A.	N.A.	−
Souheaver, Ryan, & DeWolfe, 1982	−	+	−	−	−	−	+	−	N.A.	−
Spehr et al., 1977	−	+	−	−	−	−	−	−	−	−
Teschan et al., 1974	−	+	−	−	−	−	−	−	−	−
Teschan et al., 1975	−	+	−	−	−	−	−	−	−	−
Teschan et al., 1976	−	+	−	−	−	−	−	−	−	−
Teschan et al., 1977	−	−	−	−	−	−	−	−	−	−
Teschan et al., 1979	−	−	−	−	−	−	−	−	−	−
Trieschmand & Sand, 1971	−	−	+	−	+	−	−	−	−	+
Winokur, Czaczkes, & Kaplan De-Nour, 1973	−	−	−	−	−	−	−	N.A.	N.A.	−
Ziesat, Logue, & McCarthy, 1980	−	−	−	−	−	−	−	N.A.	−	−

parisons between findings utilizing different samples: subject race, medical diagnosis, the presence or absence of other significant illnesses, history of psychiatric treatment, alcohol/drug abuse, experience levels of those who administer neuropsychological tests, and the emotional status of the patient during evaluation. From a statistical point of view, variance attributable to age and education should be partialed out in relevant analyses, and multivariate statistics should be used in cases of multiple comparisons. Table 2 denotes whether studies meet these methodological criteria.

CLINICAL SYNDROMES

Uremia

The neurobehavioral symptoms of uremia are generally similar, regardless of the underlying renal disease. Manifestations of acute renal failure tend to be more severe and progress more rapidly than those associated with chronic renal failure. Symptoms also vary with degree of renal failure. Reduced mental alertness, fatigability, intellectual impairment, decreased concentration, memory deficits, and diminished perceptual-motor coordination are characteristic clinical features (Ginn, 1975; Marshall, 1979). Vegetative, mood, and personality changes are also likely to be present. Untreated renal failure may result in delirium, focal neurological signs, coma, and death. Dialysis treatment often permits at least temporary reversal of the neurobehavioral symptoms of uremia, but mental status does not necessarily improve with normalization of blood chemistries in acute renal failure (Arieff, 1981).

There are a number of factors that contribute to uremic encephalopathy, although the significance of each is largely speculative. Biochemical changes associated with acute renal failure include alteration of brain electrolyte concentrations (Ca^{++}, Na^{+}, Al^{+++}), changes in brain permeability, alterations in cerebral metabolism, decreased cerebral oxygen consumption, disruption of transport mechanisms, and an increase in brain urea concentration (Arieff, 1981). Plasma parathyroid hormone (PTH) elevations have been related to EEG and mental status changes. Given the multitude of factors, it is not surprising that there may be a poor correlation between neurobehavioral changes and commonly measured indexes of renal failure such as BUN, serum creatinine, bicarbonate, and pH (Arieff, 1981). Because factors other than renal failure affect BUN and serum creatinine levels (e.g., protein intake, catabolic metabolism, liver function, muscle mass), these measures may be inconsistent co-variates of a "uremic toxin."

Pathologic cerebral changes associated with chronic renal failure are nonspecific. Biochemical brain changes tend to be less severe and extensive than those associated with acute renal failure. Part of the CNS dysfunction found in chronic renal failure may be due to PTH-mediated increases in brain Ca^{++} or the effect of PTH itself (Arieff, 1981). There are also effects of associated physical illnesses such as diabetes, hypertension and ischemic events, and effects of antihypertensive medications (Solomon et al., 1983).

Dialysis Disequilibrium

Mental status changes of acute onset may occur during or within several hours after hemodialysis (Burnett, McKee, Raft, Lipton, & Blythe, 1980; Marshall, 1979). Symptoms include restlessness, headache, nausea, weakness, fatigue, and muscle cramps. There may be vomiting, hypertension, blurred vision, muscular twitching, tremors, disorientation, and seizures. Changes are usually limited and of short duration. If delirium is present, symptoms may persist for days. The syndrome generally occurs in patients with acute renal failure but has also been reported in patients with chronic renal failure treated by maintenance hemodialysis. Elevated CSF pressure, acid-base abnormalities, and a rise of brain intracellular osmolarity leading to tissue swelling can follow rapid hemodialysis and may underlie the pathophysiology of the syndrome (Arieff, 1981). The syndrome can be largely prevented by attention to techniques of dialysis, that is, low blood flow rates and short duration of hemodialysis at frequent intervals.

Neuropsychological Function between Dialysis Treatment Sessions

Fluctuations in electrophysiological and neuropsychological measures between dialysis sessions reflect short-term changes in toxic uremic status. Evoked potentials of shorter latency 24 hr following dialysis compared to 1, 42, and 66 hr after dialysis (Lewis, O'Neill, Dustman, & Beck, 1980) and EEG changes from 14 hr after to 14 hr before dialysis (Spehr et al., 1977) indicate increased neural efficiency or arousal. Reaction time and psychomotor speed improve significantly within 24 hr of dialysis (Lewis, et al., 1980). Memory and sensory-perceptual functions may also improve (Lewis et al., 1980; Teschan et al., 1974; Spehr et al., 1977), but these findings should be considered tentative because of the small number of subjects and lack of detail in research reports. Overall, both electrophysiological and behavioral data indicate changes in mental alertness and efficiency occur between individual dialysis sessions.

Progressive Dialysis Encephalopathy or Dialysis Dementia

Dialysis dementia or encephalopathy is a progressive and generally fatal neurological syndrome with characteristic EEG disturbance and neurobehavioral signs. Alfrey et al. (1972) first described five chronically dialyzed patients who developed an encephalopathy with a rapidly progressive course. Soon, additional cases of dialysis dementia were reported by investigators (Barratt & Lawrence, 1975; Burks, Alfrey, Huddlestone, Noremberg, &

Lewin, 1976; Chokroverty, Bruetman, Berger, & Reyes, 1976; Mahurkar *et al.*, 1973; Scheiber & Ziesat, 1976; Silke, Fitzgerald, Hanson, Carmody, & O'Dwyer, 1978; Weddington, 1978). The initial symptom is often stuttering speech that may progress to dysarthria or dyspraxia. Speech impairment is followed by myoclonus, apraxia, and seizure activity. Impaired memory, poor concentration, personality changes, and psychotic symptoms may all be observed in the course of progressive mental deterioration. Symptom onset generally occurs after at least 2 yr of treatment, and the illness usually progresses to coma and death within 12 mon. There is also an epidemic variety of dialysis dementia involving the majority of patients at a dialysis center in which symptom onset can occur after a short period of treatment. Early clinical features of dialysis dementia include changes in personality and cognitive functioning (Madison, Baehr, Bazell, Hartman, Mahurkar, & Dunea, 1977; Mahurkar, Meyers, Cohen, Kamath, & Dunea, 1978; Schriber & Ziesat, 1976). Agitation, hostility, paranoia, depression or flat affect, and diminished interest and spontaneity are often reported. Disorientation, impaired judgment, confusion, memory problems, and decreased attention have also been noted. These findings are generally based on clinical impressions rather than quantitative neuropsychological assessment. Madison *et al.* (1977) documented language and perceptual-motor deficits and deterioration of memory and intellectual functions in two patients. Schreiber and Ziesat (1976) also reported impaired perceptual-motor functions on the Bender-Gestalt in a patient with dialysis dementia.

Pathological studies of brain tissue have not revealed any consistent abnormalities that could account for the mental deterioration in dialysis dementia (Alfrey *et al.*, 1972; Alfrey, Hegg, & Craswell, 1980; Barratt & Lawrence, 1975; Burks *et al.*, 1976). The most extensively studied proposed etiological factor is the accumulation of trace metals, particularly aluminum (Alfrey *et al.*, 1972, 1980; Alfrey, LeGendre, & Kaehny, 1976; Bloomfield, 1973; Lyle, 1973; McDermott, Smith, & Ward, 1978). Major sources of aluminum include dialysate water, diet, and aluminum-containing antacids. Tissue aluminum concentration is higher in dialyzed than nondialyzed uremic patients. Alfrey *et al.* (1980) found a correlation between brain aluminum concentration and duration of dialysis in patients who died of causes other than dialysis dementia. Brain aluminum was highest in dialyzed patients with dementia, but there was no significant relationship between aluminum level and duration of dialysis. Patients with dialysis dementia tended to have higher brain aluminum levels at any interval of dialysis than patients dying of other causes. The evidence for a role of aluminum in the pathogenesis of dialysis dementia is stronger for the epidemic form than for the sporadic form of the disorder. In either case, the actual contribution of brain aluminum to the encephalopathy remains unclear. Elevated brain aluminum may be a nonspecific finding associated with dementia and blood–brain barrier abnormalities (Arieff, 1981). Other proposed causes of dialysis dementia include slow central nervous system virus, normal pressure hydrocephalus, dopamine deficiency, phosphate depletion, and the accumulation of drugs (Arieff, 1981; Tacob & Needle, 1970).

NEUROPSYCHOLOGICAL FUNCTION AND RENAL FAILURE

General Intelligence

In a series of well-controlled studies Ryan and co-workers (Ryan, Souheaver, & De Wolfe, 1980; Ryan, Souheaver, & De Wolfe, 1981; Souheaver, Ryan, & De Wolfe, 1982) assessed renal patients using Wechsler intelligence scales and the extended Halstead-Reitan battery. Other investigators have reported Weschler IQ scores, subtest patterns, or results from other tests of intelligence such as Raven's Progressive Matrices, but methodological shortcomings make these findings difficult to interpret.

Ryan and co-workers (1980, 1981; Souheaver et al., 1982) demonstrated global intellectual-cognitive impairment in renal failure patients prior to dialysis onset. Renal patients had lower Full Scale and Performance IQs and lower scores on 9 of 12 measures from the extended Halstead-Reitan battery than patients with medical and/or psychiatric illnesses. Average impairment ratings (AIR) (Russell, Neuringer, & Goldstein, 1970) fell in the moderately impaired range. The degree of impairment in renal patients was similar to that for patients having chronic neurological disorders (Ryan et al., 1980; Souheaver et al., 1982). Although there were no significant differences in IQ scores or in AIR, renal patients demonstrated relatively more impairment than neurological patients on constructional tasks such as Block Design and Object Assembly and relatively less impairment on tests of perceptual and motor function. These patterns may reflect differences in the nature (progressive versus static) of brain dysfunction (Ryan et al., 1980). The use of a medical-psychiatric comparison group and matching on MMPI Depression scores (Ryan et al., 1981; Souheaver et al., 1982) help to control for nonspecific effects of chronic medical illness such as reactive depression. Nevertheless, the general medical status of renal patients and associated deficits in mental alertness and stamina may contribute to lowered performance on a lengthy neuropsychological test battery.

Uncontrolled studies demonstrating intrasubject patterns of lower Performance than Verbal IQ or selective impairments on Block Design, Digit Symbol and Object Assembly subtests (Blatt & Tsushima, 1966; Hagberg, 1974; Trieschmann & Sand, 1971) also suggest that intellectual impairments accompany renal failure. Degree of renal failure as assessed by blood urea nitrogen (BUN) and serum creatinine did not correlate with IQ or individual subtest scores, although Trieschmann and Sand (1971) showed a relationship between overall sickness level (defined in part by serum creatinine) and WAIS performance.

Numerous studies report Wechsler IQ scores or results of related intelligence tests in renal failure patients prior to the onset of dialysis treatment (Comty, Leonard, & Shapiro, 1974; Fishman & Schneider, 1972; Greenberg, Davis, & Massey, 1973; Kaplan De-Nour, Shanan, & Garty, 1977; Malmquist *et al.*, 1972; Rabinowitz & van der Spuy, 1978; Sand, Livingston, & Wright, 1966). Unfortunately, some studies are confounded by the inclusion of subjects who were tested after initiation of dialysis treatment (e.g., Sand *et al.*, 1966; Malmquist *et al.*, 1972). Several articles were descriptive, and many of the studies were primarily designed to answer other research questions (e.g., identify variables useful for prediction of adjustment to dialysis). Mean IQ scores varied from 115 to 82.8 with lower scores for some poor adjustment subgroups. Due to unspecified subject selection variables, incomplete demographic data, and incomplete information pertaining to duration and severity of renal failure, medical status, and emotional status, these scores are difficult to interpret meaningfully. The study by Rabinowitz and van der Spuy (1978) demonstrates the dangers of selection bias. Patients accepted into renal programs had higher Verbal IQs, socioeconomic status, and educational achievement than patients who were not accepted despite having met medical criteria.

Memory

There has been wide variation in the type of tests and experimental designs employed to assess memory functions in renal failure patients. Test procedures have included standardized clinical measures of verbal recall, (e.g., logical memory, paired-associated learning), reproduction of designs (visual reproduction, Benton Visual Retention Test), and incidental recall of stimuli presented tactually (Tactile Performance Test). Comparison groups have also varied, and examination of the literature revealed no study assessing renal patients longitudinally that employed a control group.

Despite methodological variations, memory deficits have been demonstrated in numerous studies. Hart, Pederson, Czerwinski, and Adams (1983) found deficits on three of five memory tests, including logical memory and visual reproduction from the Wechsler Memory Scale and a test of facial recognition. Patients performed less well than matched controls with chronic physical disabilities on all three tests and less well than dialysis patients on one test. Measures of incidental memory from the Halstead-Reitan Battery were equally impaired in patients with renal and chronic brain dysfunction (Souheaver *et al.*, 1982), but these same tests did not differentiate renal patients from dialysis and medical-psychiatric patients in another study (Ryan *et al.*, 1981). Renal patients with serum creatinine values above 10 mg/dl performed less well than normal controls on a continuous memory test, but they did not differ from dialysis or transplant patients (Teschan *et al.*, 1979). For nondialyzed patients, memory performance correlated with serum creatinine levels. Unfortunately, it is unclear whether groups in the Teschan *et al.* (1979) study were matched on demographic variables, renal illness variables (e.g., diagnosis and duration of renal failure), and general medical or emotional status.

Uncontrolled studies also suggest memory deficits in renal failure, although methodological problems make the findings difficult to interpret. In particular, longitudinal studies have not assessed practice effects and the potential role of changes in emotional status. Hagberg (1974) studied renal patients judged to be impaired on tests of verbal and visual memory based on normative data. The patients approached expected performance levels after 6 mon of dialysis treatment, improving significantly on a paired-associate learning test. There was no evidence of impairment 12 mon after dialysis treatment because Benton Visual Retention Test scores improved over both retest intervals. McKee, Burnett, Raft, Batten, and Bain, (1982) studied five renal patients longitudinally. Although statistical comparisons were not made given the small number of subjects, initial scores of renal patients were lower than those of dialysis patients. Delayed recall for stories improved significantly over a period of 22 mon with the onset of dialysis. The change in performance over time in this study was not attributable to changes in emotional status as assessed by the Hopkins Symptom Checklist. Nevertheless, this finding is at best suggestive, given the subjects-to-variables ratio and absence of improvement on three other memory measures as well as the lack of control for practice effect. Four renal patients studied by Teschan et al. (1979) improved their performance on the continuous memory test following dialysis onset, although similar methodological problems existed.

It is difficult to generalize from studies that compare renal patients to dialysis patients or which study renal patients longitudinally because of variance regarding time of assessment relative to individual dialysis treatment sessions. For example, several studies evaluated dialysis patients 1 day postdialysis (Hart et al., 1983; Ryan et al., 1981); some examined patients prior to a dialysis run (McKee et al., 1982; Teschan et al., 1979); and others did not specify when patients were tested (Hagberg, 1974).

Mental Efficiency, Psychomotor Speed, and Attention

In a series of studies, Teschan, Ginn, and co-workers (Ginn, 1975; Ginn et al., 1975; Teschan et al., 1974; Teschan, Ginn, Bourne, & Ward, 1976; Teschan et al., 1979) and Murawski (1975) examined renal patients on tests measuring psychomotor speed, sustained attention, speed of arithmetic calculation and decision-making, choice reaction time, and speed of access to memory storage. These tests were intended to assess mental alertness. Other investigators have assessed attention, psychomotor speed and reaction time, but there has been minimal overlap in the tests employed (Trail-Making and Digit Symbol). Simple reaction time, Digit Vigilance from the Rennick Repeatable Battery, and measures of sustained attention from the Halstead-Reitan Battery (Speech Sound Perception and Seashore Rhythm) have also been used by different groups of investigators. Most of these studies are complicated by serious methodological problems.

Among renal patients not undergoing dialysis, scores on all five measures employed by Teschan and co-workers were related to the degree of renal failure as measured by serum creatinine (Ginn et al., 1975; Teschan et al., 1979). Hart et al. (1983) also found significant correlations between BUN and serum creatinine levels and performance on tests requiring sustained attention and psychomotor speed in renal patients. In the studies by Teschan, Ginn, and co-workers and the study by Murawski (1975), renal patients performed less well than normal controls, and, in some instances, the tests differentiated renal patients with low versus high serum creatinine levels. Dialysis patients generally performed better than renal patients with high serum creatinine levels. Larger group differences may have been demonstrated if Teschan and co-workers had evaluated patients 1-day postdialysis rather than prior to treatment sessions. Renal transplant patients performed at levels comparable to normals and in some instances did significantly better than dialysis or renal patients. Unfortunately, some studies (e.g., Murawski, 1975; Teschan et al., 1974) did not provide raw data or statistical results. In other studies, statistical adjustments were apparently not made for increased Type I error arising from multiple comparisons. It is also unclear from studies by Teschan and co-workers whether groups were closely matched on demographic and illness variables (see Tables 1 and 2). The use of a normal comparison group, furthermore, did not control for nonspecific effects of chronic medical illness.

Teschan and co-workers studied small numbers of renal patients longitudinally, using measures of mental alertness. Findings were generally consistent with those discussed earlier, that is, improvements following the onset of dialysis and occasional further improvements after renal transplantation. Unfortunately, neither raw data nor statistics were presented in several reports. Furthermore, control data were not available, making it difficult to assess the contributions of practice effect and changes in emotional status.

The work of other investigators has also demonstrated deficits in attention, psychomotor speed, and reaction time, although some negative findings have been reported in uncontrolled studies employing single measures or small samples (Hagberg, 1974; McKee et al., (1982). Relative to their own mean performance level, renal patients performed less well on the Trail-Making Test than a matched group of medical-psychiatric patients (Souheaver et al., 1982). Relative to medical-psychiatric controls, renal failure patients demonstrated impairments on Halstead-Reitan Battery measures of sustained attention and perceptual-motor speed (Ryan et al., 1981). Differences between renal and dialysis patients did not reach statistical significance, although there was a tendency for renal patients to perform less well. Hart et al. (1983) found consistent differences between renal patients and dialysis patients and/or controls on measures of sustained attention and psychomotor speed that included Trail Making, Digit Symbol, and Digit Vigilance.

Summary and Conclusions

Although complicated by serious methodological shortcomings, research findings indicate that deficits in general intelligence, memory, and mental alertness often accompany renal failure. Deficits in sustained attention and psychomotor speed appear to be related to degree of renal failure. The onset of dialysis treatments and renal transplantation have beneficial effects on attention and psychomotor speed. Other cognitive abilities such as memory tend to improve with dialysis and transplantation, although research findings are less consistent.

NEUROPSYCHOLOGICAL FUNCTIONING AND CHRONIC HEMODIALYSIS

General Intelligence

No two studies of dialysis patients employ both the same measures of intellectual-cognitive functioning and similar experimental designs. It is therefore not surprising that findings are inconsistent across studies. Some investigators report Wechsler IQ scores or subtest patterns, but, as in the case of renal patients, methodological problems make these findings difficult to interpret.

Ryan et al. (1981) compared patients tested 20 to 24 hr postdialysis to a matched sample of medical-psychiatric patients on the Halstead-Reitan Battery. Dialysis patients performed less well than controls on 6 of 12 measures, including tests of attention, nonverbal abstract reasoning, language, and sensory perceptual functions. However, they performed better than renal patients on 3 other measures. It is unclear whether individuals with complicating medical illness excluding hypertensive or diabetic nephropathy or with a history of drug or alcohol abuse were excluded from the patient sample. Although the overall performance trend was clear, statistical adjustments were apparently not made for multiple follow-up comparisons, contributing to an uncertain reliability of findings. In contrast to these data, Freeman, Sherrard, Calsyn, and Paige (1980) did not find differences on WAIS subtests between groups of 107 dialysis patients and 33 orthopedic patients, although many variables were unspecified.

Results from uncontrolled longitudinal studies have also been equivocal. Gilli and DeBastiani (1983) reported that 21 dialysis patients tested at intervals of at least 1-yr duration showed a deterioration in Verbal but not Performance and Full Scale IQ. The magnitude of change in Verbal IQ was only 2 points and thus was not clinically meaningful. Hagberg (1974) reported improved Block Design scores to expected levels in renal patients following 6 months of dialysis treatment and higher scores on verbal measures of intelligence over 12 mon of treatment. The absence of controls to assess practice effect, lack of alternate forms for Block Design, and absence of measures of emotionality make these findings difficult to interpret.

A number of investigators report Wechsler IQ or subtest scores for di-
alysis patients (e.g., English, Savage, Britton, Ward, & Kerr, 1978; Gilli &
DeBastiani, 1983; Schupak, Sullivan, & Lee, 1967; Winokur, Czaczkes, &
Kaplan De-Nour, 1973), but, in some instances, findings were confounded by
inclusion of patients tested prior to dialysis onset (Gilli & DeBastiani, 1983).
Mean Full Scale IQs ranged from 86.6 to 99.9 in these studies. Although
some investigators reported comparable Verbal and Performance IQ scores
(Gilli & DeBastiani, 1983), others found subtest patterns associated with
mild diffuse brain damage (English et al., 1978). Findings were difficult to
interpret for a number of reasons. There was great variability among studies
as regards the duration of dialysis treatment at the time of testing, ranging
from an average of several weeks to 3 yr. Frequency of dialysis treatment was
either unspecified or variable within a study. Time of examination relative
to a dialysis treatment session was often unspecified or reported as a range
(e.g., 12 to 36 hr). The latter point is particularly important because dialysis
patients appear to perform least well on a WAIS subtest (Digit Symbol)
shown to be sensitive to the time since the last dialysis treatment (Lewis et
al., 1980). Further complications in data interpretation are related to unspecified subject selection variables, incomplete demographic data, and incomplete information pertaining to duration and severity of renal failure,
general medical status, and emotional status.

There is no clear evidence of a relationship between Wechsler IQs and
duration of dialysis treatment (Gilli & DeBastiani 1983; English et al., 1978).
Gentry and Davis (1972) reported no correlation between Quick Test IQ
score and length of dialysis treatment or number of dialysis treatments.
Negative findings in the latter study are complicated by the fact that patients
had generally been on dialysis for short periods of time and were examined
during a dialysis run. Additionally, the Quick Test provides no specific
information about patients' cognitive functioning.

Memory

A variety of tests have been employed to assess memory function in
patients undergoing chronic hemodialysis. Methodological variations as
well as lack of comparison groups or appropriate norms precludes meaningful data interpretation in many studies.

Studies by Hart et al. (1983), Ryan et al. (1981), and Teschan et al. (1979)
comparing the performance of dialysis patients to that of nondialyzed renal
patients were described earlier. There was a trend for dialysis patients to
perform better on memory tests than renal patients, although few differences
reached statistical significance. Evaluation of dialysis patients prior to a
treatment session may have minimized differences in some studies (Teschan
et al., 1979). Renal transplant patients tend to perform intermediate to normals and to both dialysis and renal patients, although transplantation did
not improve memory performance of eight dialysis patients in a study by

Teschan *et al.* (1979). Ryan *et al.* (1981) found no evidence of memory impairment relative to medical controls, and Hart *et al.* (1983) found significant impairment on only one of five tests with a tendency for impairment on second. Although Teschan *et al.* (1979) reported deficits based on a continuous memory test relative to normal controls, they examined patients immediately prior to a dialysis run when uremia is most severe. Use of a normal comparison group did not control for nonspecific effects of chronic medical illness.

Uncontrolled studies relying on normative data have yielded equivocal findings. English *et al.* (1978) found that performance of patients 12 to 48 hr postdialysis was within the normal range on both verbal and visuospatial learning tasks. Gilli and DeBastiani (1983) reported Wechsler Memory Quotients that tended to be higher than Wechsler IQ scores. Ziesat, Logue, and McCarty (1980) reported mild memory impairments for both prose material and geometric figures, but there are several problems interpretating these data. First, the mean age of dialysis patients was 12 yr older than that of the normative group (Russell, 1975), and the patients averaged 2 yr less formal education. Second, the percentage of material retained over a 30-min delay period was within the normal range. Third, the authors did not report when testing was conducted relative to a dialysis treatment session.

Ziesat *et al.* (1980) reported a negative correlation between nonverbal memory performance and duration of dialysis treatment. Age and education were not partialed out in these correlations, but there was no statistically significant relationship between age and the number of dialysis sessions. There is no clear evidence from other studies of deterioration in memory functions as time on dialysis increases. Hart *et al.* (1983) found no correlation between memory performance and duration of dialysis treatment. English *et al.* (1978) reported that Block Design learning was negatively related to duration of dialysis treatment, although the strength of the association was not reported and effects of age and education were not partialed out. It is also difficult to interpret such a correlation when the mean scores of dialysis patients fell within the normal range. Gilli and DeBastiani (1983) found a negative correlation between Memory Quotient and duration of dialysis treatment, but this may have been a spurious finding because only 3 of 24 correlations were significant. As in the English *et al.* study, it is difficult to interpret the correlation when memory performance for the group was within the expected range (Memory Quotients were greater than or equal to IQ scores).

Longitudinal studies do not indicate cognitive deterioration in dialysis patients, although methodological problems including lack of comparison groups make these findings difficult to interpret. Gilli and DeBastiani (1983) reported a decline in Memory Quotient over periods of at least 1 year, but McKee *et al.* (1982) and Hagberg (1974) found no evidence of deterioration in memory over periods of 22 mon and 6 mon, respectively. Patients on dialysis for 6 mon versus 4.3 yr performed similarly, although the latter group did tend to score lower on a test of prose recall (McKee *et al.*, 1982).

Mental Efficiency, Psychomotor Speed, and Attention

These functions were studied in dialysis patients as well as renal patients by Teschan, Ginn, and co-workers and by other investigators. The tests and experimental designs employed are generally the same as those previously described for renal patients. As discussed in an earlier section, dialysis patients tend to perform better than nondialyzed renal patients on tests sensitive to mental alertness. Renal transplant patients tend to perform at levels comparable to those of normal controls, and, in some instances, transplant patients have performed better than dialysis and renal patients. Dialysis patients performed less well than normal controls on several of the tests from the battery employed by Teschan and co-workers (1979). In addition to the methodological issues raised earlier, it should again be emphasized that these differences may be attributable to short-term changes in uremic status because patients were tested prior to a treatment session. Alexander, Hightower, Anderson, and Snow (1980) evaluated patients prior to a dialysis session and found impaired reaction time on a vigilance test. There is inconsistent evidence of deficits in attention and psychomotor speed when patients are examined 1 day postdialysis (Hart *et al.*, 1983; Ryan *et al.*, 1981).

There is no evidence to suggest an inverse relationship between mental efficiency and duration of dialysis treatment. Hart *et al.* (1981) found no significant correlation between scores on Trail-Making, Digit Symbol, Digit Vigilance, and the duration of dialysis treatment. Hagberg (1974) found no change in simple reaction time over 12 mon of dialysis treatment. McKee *et al.* (1982) reported improvements on Trail-Making and Digit Symbol over 22 mon, although this may have been attributable to improved emotional status or possibly to practice effect. The same authors found no significant differences on similar measures between patients who had been on dialysis for 6 mon versus 4 yr.

Summary and Conclusions

No clear, consistent evidence exists demonstrating global cognitive deficits in dialysis patients independent of the effects of short-term fluctuations in uremic status. Inconsistencies across studies are not surprising, given the numerous methodological problems. Dialysis patients generally perform better than nondialyzed renal patients on tests of intelligence, memory, psychomotor speed, and attention. There is relatively little evidence of cognitive impairment in dialysis patients relative to medical or normal controls, although significant group differences and tendencies are all in the direction of poorer performance for dialysis patients. The data generally do not support a relationship between cognitive performance and duration of dialysis treatment, suggesting that progressive dementia is not a necessary consequence of dialysis treatment.

REHABILITATION

The potential disabilities associated with chronic renal disease include cognitive dysfunction, depression, blindness, and muscular atrophy (Osberg, Meares, McKee, & Burnett, 1980). Considering the long-term nature of these effects, renal disease patients would appear to make excellent candidates for rehabilitation programs. Unfortunately, research investigating potential benefits of both physical and vocational rehabilitations is limited. The few studies available suffer from serious methodological flaws (Osberg et al., 1980). Kaplan De-Nour et al. (1977) and other investigators (see Osberg et al., 1982, for review) have suggested that IQ scores and memory are related to outcome in rehabilitation and to level of psychosocial adjustment. Patients with greater mental capacity are more likely to integrate and learn from rehabilitation therapies. Osberg et al. (1980) have also commented on the gross categorization schemes employed in rehabilitation outcome studies. Typically, patients are assigned an outcome level on a 1 to 4 scale. This single number conveys little information because it reflects performance in a wide variety of areas. Future research should focus on providing more specific information by incorporating a diversity of outcome variables related to quality of life, including measures of neuropsychological functioning, emotional status, medical status, work and leisure activities, and ability to carry out daily living skills independently.

Chronic renal patients would appear to be excellent candidates for rehabilitation therapies directed toward improving quality of life and daily living skills. Interdisciplinary inpatient rehabilitation programs would permit patients to participate in psychological, physical, occupational, and leisure skills therapies in a single setting. Unfortunately, the numerous physical limitations imposed by chronic disease as well as the requirement of 2 to 3 times/weekly dialysis ensures minimal participation in therapies. Fluctuations in mental status as well as physical exhaustion associated with time-consuming dialysis procedures also contribute to limited participation. Consequently, brief inpatient rehabilitation or therapy on an outpatient basis is a more feasible alternative. A second issue that has likely limited rehabilitation for chronic renal patients has also plagued cancer victims. Considering the limited rehabilitation resources available in most communities, physicians are less likely to admit patients with either a poor prognosis or a multiplicity of medical problems. Very likely, lobbying efforts will be required to ensure the availability of rehabilitation programs for patients with chronic renal disease.

FUTURE RESEARCH

Future research in this area should more carefully specify or control relevant subject variables (i.e., demographics, medical status, emotional status, psychiatric history), illness variables (diagnosis, duration and severity of renal failure, duration of treatment), and the time of measurement relative to individual treatment sessions. A number of factors likely to influence performance on neuropsychological measures are unrelated to the disease process (Parsons & Prigitano, 1978). Examination of Tables 1 and 2 indicates that a large proportion of studies reviewed have failed either to eliminate patients with confounding problems or have failed to provide important descriptive information. Consequently, data in many of the studies do not allow for reliable interpretation, nor are direct comparisons between studies possible. The importance of specifying descriptive information and eliminating patients with certain coexisting illnesses or histories is clear. Heterogeneity in any of these areas will diminish discriminability of treatment or illness effects. Examination of the tables also reveals a large degree of variability in the methods utilized to assess neuropsychological functioning. Ideally, each researcher would use some of the same methods to assess attention, memory, intelligence, and other important cognitive functions. The reliance on WAIS-R Full Scale IQ scores in many of the studies provides limited information and ignores patterns of deficit.

The effect of dialysis treatment and uremia on neuropsychological function is confounded by the effects of nonspecific factors associated with chronic physical illness. A particularly important factor is depression, a common characteristic of chronic hemodialysis patients (Gentry & Davis, 1972; Glassman & Siegel, 1970; Maher et al., 1983; Short & Wilson, 1969; Wright, Sand, & Livingston, 1966). Depression may impact neuropsychological functions in several ways. First, depression may decrease compliance with the medical regimens, impairing the general medical status of the patient. The suicide rate among dialysis patients may be more than 100 times that of the normal population and much higher when deaths from overt noncompliance are included (Abram, Moore, & Westervelt, 1971). Second, depression affects performance on memory and learning tasks and may decrease intellectual efficiency (Miller, 1975; Sternberg & Jarvik, 1976). Deficits are particularly noticeable for cognitive processes requiring sustained effort (Cohen, Weingartner, Smallberg, Pickar, & Murphy, 1982). Therefore, it is important in future research that patients with other chronic medical illnesses are routinely included for comparison and that emotional status is evaluated quantitatively. The relationship between cognitive and emotional variables should be explored statistically.

The relationship between cognitive, emotional, and physiological measures of functioning needs to be carefully examined. The "uremic toxin" remains unidentified, and various physiological measures are not highly sensitive indicators of degree of renal failure. Nevertheless, correlations between physiological variables and neuropsychological data can generate meaningful hypotheses.

Examination of the literature reveals the virtual absence of well-controlled longitudinal studies of patients with chronic renal failure. More research is also needed in those patients undergoing renal transplantation or chronic ambulatory peritoneal dialysis (CAPD). Studies of CAPD and transplant patients should pay particular attention to specifying selection criteria and descriptive subject information. Both known and unknown biases influence selection of patients for CAPD programs and transplantation. Comparisons between CAPD and hemodialysis patients or between samples of hemodialysis patients prior to, versus after, the initiation of CAPD programs can be misleading. Studies of transplant patients also need to take into account the effect of steroids on neuropsychological performance.

We recognize that strict compliance with a scientifically rigorous research design is difficult or impractical in studying patients with a chronic medical illness such as renal failure. Specification of variables such as those listed in Tables 1 and 2 would increase the reliability of conclusions about the neuropsychological status of chronic renal failure and dialysis patients.

ACKNOWLEDGMENTS

We would like to thank James Levenson, Gregory O'Shanick, and Susan Glocheski for their helpful comments during the preparation of the manuscript.

REFERENCES

Abram, H. S., Moore, G. L., & Westervelt, F. B. (1971). Suicidal behavior in chronic dialysis patients. *American Journal of Psychiatry, 127,* 1199–1204.

Alexander, L., Hightower, M. G., Anderson, R. P., & Snow, N. E. (1980). Suitability of vigilance test data as a neurobehavioral measure of uremic status. *Perceptual Motor Skills, 50,* 131–135.

Alfrey, A. C., Mishell, J. M., Burks, J., Contiguglia, S. R., Rudolph, H., Lewin, E., & Holmes, J. H. (1972). Syndrome of dyspraxia and multifocal seizures associated with chronic hemodialysis. *Transactions, American Society for Artificial Internal Organs, 18,* 257–261.

Alfrey, A. C., LeGendre, G. R., & Kaehny, W. C. (1976). The dialysis encephalopathy syndrome: Possible aluminum intoxification. *New England Journal of Medicine, 294,* 184–188.

Alfrey, A. C., Hegg, A., & Craswell, P. (1980). Metabolism and toxicity of aluminum in renal failure. *The American Journal of Clinical Nutrition, 33,* 1509–1516.

Arieff, A. I. (1981). Neurological complications of uremia. In B. Brennan & F. Rector (Eds.), *The kidney* (pp. 2307–2343). Philadelphia: W. B. Saunders.

Barratt, L. J., & Lawrence, J. R. (1975). *Australian and New Zealand Journal of Medicine, 5,* 62.

Blatt, B., & Tsushima, W. T. (1966). A psychological survey of uremic patients being considered for the chronic hemodialysis program: Intellectual and emotional patterns in uremic patients. *Nephron, 3,* 206–208.

Bloomfield, J. (1973). Dialysis and lead absorption. *Lancet, 2,* 666.

Burks, J. S., Alfrey, A. C., Huddlestone, J., Noremberg, M. D., & Lewin, E. (1976). A fatal encephalopathy in chronic hemodialysis patients. *Lancet, 1,* 764–768.

Burnett, G. B., McKee, D. C., Raft, D., Lipton, M. A., & Blythe, W. B. (1980). Neuropsychiatric syndromes in hemodialysis: A review. *Dialysis and Transplantation, 9:10,* 925–926.

Chokroverty, S., Bruetman, M. E., Berger, V., & Reyes. M. G. (1976). Progressive dialytic encephalopathy. *Journal of Neurology, Neurosurgery and Psychiatry, 39,* 411–419.

Cohen, R. M., Weingartner, H., Smallberg, S. A., Pickar, D., & Murphy, D. L. (1982). Effort and cognition in depression. *Archives of General Psychiatry, 39,* 593–597.

Comty, C. M., Leonard, A., & Shapiro, F. C. (1974). Psychosocial problems in dialyzed diabetic patients. *Kidney International, 1,* 144–151.

English, A., Savage, R. D., Britton, P. G., Ward, M. K., & Kerr, D. N. S. (1978). Intellectual impairment in chronic renal failure. *British Medical Journal, 1,* 888–890.

Fishman, D. B., & Schneider, C. J. (1972). Predicting emotional adjustment in home dialysis patients and their relatives. *Journal of Chronic Disease, 25,* 99–109.

Freeman, C. W., Sherrard, D. J., Calsyn, D. A., & Paige, A. B. (1980). Psychological assessment of renal dialysis patients using standard psychometric techniques. *Journal of Consulting and Clinical Psychology, 48:4,* 537–539.

Gentry, W. D., & Davis, G. C. (1972). Cross-sectional analysis of psychological adaptation to chronic hemodialysis. *Journal of Chronic Disease, 25,* 545–550.

Gilli, P., & DeBastiani, P. (1983). Cognitive function and regular dialysis treatment. *Clinical Nephrology, 19,* 188–192.

Ginn, H. E. (1975). Neurobehavioral dysfunction in uremia. [Paper presented at Conference on Adequacy of Dialysis, March, 1974.] *International Society of Nephrology,* 217–221.

Ginn, H. E., Teschan, P. E., Walker, P. J., Bourne, J. R., Fristoe, M., Ward, J. W., McLain, L. W., Johnston, H. B., Jr., & Hamel, B. (1975). Neurotoxicity in uremia. *Kidney International, 7,* 357–360.

Glassman, B., & Siegel, A. (1970). Personality correlates of survival in a long-term hemodialysis program. *Archives of General Psychiatry, 22,* 566–574.

Greenberg, R. P., Davis, G., & Massey, R. (1973). The psychological evaluation of patients for kidney transplant and hemodialysis program. *American Journal of Psychiatry, 130,* 274–277.

Hagberg, B. (1974). A prospective study of patients in chronic hemodialysis—III. Predictive value of intelligence, cognitive deficit and ego defense structures in rehabilitation. *Journal of Psychosomatic Research, 18,* 151–160.

Hart, R. P., Pederson, J. A., Czerwinski, A. W., & Adams, R. L. (1983). Chronic Renal Failure, Dialysis, and Neuropsychological Function. *Journal of Neuropsychology, 4,* 301–312.

Kaplan De-Nour, A., Shanan, J., & Garty, I. (1977). Coping behavior and intelligence in the prediction of vocational rehabilitation of dialysis patients. *International Journal of Psychiatry in Medicine, 8,* 145–158.

Lewis, E. G., O'Neill, W. M., Dustman, R. E., & Beck, E. C. (1980). Temporal effects of hemodialysis on measures of neurol efficiency. *Kidney International, 17,* 357–363.

Lyle, W. H. (1973). Dialysis dementia. *Lancet, 2,* 271.

Madison, D. P., Baehr, E. T., Bazell, M., Hartman, R. W., Mahurkar, S. D., & Dunea, G. (1977). Communicative and cognitive deterioration in dialysis dementia: Two case studies. *Journal of Speech and Hearing Disorders, 42,* 238–246.

Maher, B. A., Lamping, D. L., Dickinson, C. A., Murawski, B. J., Olivier, D. C., & Santiago, G. C. (1983). Psychosocial aspects of chronic hemodialysis: The National Cooperative Study. *Kidney International, 23* (Suppl. 13), S50–S57.

Mahurkar, S. D., Dhar, S. K., Salta, R., Meyers, L., Jr., Smith, E. C., & Dunea, G. (1973). Dialysis dementia. *Lancet, 1,* 1412–1415.

Mahurkar, S. D., Meyers, L., Jr., Cohen, J., Kamath, R. V., & Dunea, G. (1978). Electroencephalographic and radionuclide studies in dialysis dementia. *Kidney International, 13,* 306–315.

Malmquist, A., Kopfstein, J., Frank, E. T., Picklesimer, D., Clements, G., Ginn, E., & Cromwell, R. L. (1972). Factors in psychiatric prediction of patients beginning hemodialysis. *Journal of Psychosomatics Research, 16,* 19–23.

Marshall, J. R. (1979). Neuropsychiatric aspects of renal failure. *Journal of Clinical Psychiatry, 40,* 81–85.

McDermott, J. R., Smith, A. I., & Ward, M. K. (1978). Brain aluminum concentration in dialysis encephalopathy. *Lancet, 1,* 901–904.

McKee, D. C., Burnett, G. B., Raft, D. D., Batten, P. G., & Bain, K. P. (1982). Longitudinal study of neuropsychological functioning in patients on chronic hemodialysis: A preliminary report. *Journal of Psychosomatics Research, 26*, 511–518.

Miller, W. R. (1975). Psychological deficit in depression. *Psychological Bulletin, 82*, 238–260.

Murawski, B. J. (1975). Psychological approaches to study the uremic state. [Presented at Conference on Adequacy of Dialysis, March, 1974.] *International Society of Nephrology*, 206–209.

Osberg, J. W., Meares, G. J., McKee, D. C., & Burnett, G. B. (1980). Research issues in psychological studies of chronic dialysis. *Psychiatry Research, 3*, 307–314.

Osberg, J. W., Meares, G. J., McKee, D. C., & Burnett, G. B. (1982). Intellectual functioning in renal failure and chronic dialysis. *Journal of Chronic Disease, 35*, 445–457.

Parsons, O. A., & Prigatano, G. P. (1978). Methodological considerations in clinical neuropsychological research. *Journal of Consulting and Clinical Psychology, 46*, 608–619.

Rabinowitz S., & van der Spuy, H. (1978). Selection criteria for dialysis and renal transplant. *American Journal of Psychiatry, 135*, 861–863.

Russell, E. W. (1975). A multiple scoring method for the assessment of complex memory function. *Journal of Consulting and Clinical Psychology, 43*, 800–809.

Russell, E. W., Neuringer, C., & Goldstein, G. (1970). *Assessment of brain damage: A neuropsychological approach.* New York: Wiley-Interscience.

Ryan, J. J., Souheaver, G. T., & DeWolfe, A. S. (1980). Intellectual deficit in chronic renal failure. A comparison with neurological and medical psychiatric patients. *The Journal of Nervous and Mental Disease, 168:12*, 763–767.

Ryan, J. J., Souheaver, G. T., & DeWolfe, A. S. (1981). Halstead-Reitan test results in chronic hemodialysis, *The Journal of Nervous and Mental Disease, 16*, 311–314.

Sand, P., Livingston, G., & Wright, R. G. (1966). Psychological Assessment of candidates for a hemodialysis program. *Annals of Internal Medicine, 64*, 602–610.

Scheiber, S. C., & Ziesat, H. (1976). Brief Communication: Clinical and psychological test findings in cerebral dyspraxia associated with hemodialysis. *The Journal of Nervous and Mental Disease, 162*, 212–214.

Schupak, E., Sullivan, J. F., & Lee, D. Y. (1967). Chronic hemodialysis in 'unselected patients.' *Annals of Internal Medicine, 67*, 708–717.

Short, M. J., & Wilson, W. P. (1969). Roles of denial in chronic hemodialysis. *Archives of General Psychiatry, 20*, 433–437.

Silke, B., Fitzgerald, G. R., Hanson, S., Carmody, M., & O'Dwyer, W. F. (1978). Clinical aspects of dialysis dementia. *Journal of the Irish Medical Association, 71*, 10–12.

Solomon, S., Hotchkiss, E., Saravay, S. M., Bayer, C., Ramsey, P., & Blum, R. S. (1983). Impairment of memory function by antihypertensive medication. *Archives of General Psychiatry, 40*, 1109–1112.

Souheaver, G. T., Ryan, J. J., & DeWolfe, A. S. (1982). Neuropsychological pattern in uremia. *Journal of Clinical Psychology, 38:3*, 490–496.

Spehr, W., Sartorius, H., Berglund, K., Hjorth, B., Kablitz, C., Plog, U., Widenman, P. H., & Zapf, K. (1977). EEG and hemodialysis. A structural survey of EEG spectral analysis, Hjorth's EEG descriptors blood variables, and psychological data. *Electroencephalography Clinical Neurophysiology, 43*, 787–797.

Sternberg, D. E., & Jarvik, M. E. (1976). Memory functions in depression. *Archives of General Psychiatry, 33*, 219–224.

Sugimoto, T., & Rosansky, S. J. (1984). The incidence of treated end stage renal disease in the Eastern United States: 1973–1979. *American Journal of Public Health, 74*, 14–17.

Tacob, L., & Needle, M. (1970). Drug-induced encephalopathy in patients on maintenance hemodialysis. *Lancet, 2*, 704–706.

Teschan, P. E., Ginn, H. E., Walker, P. J., Bourne, J. R., Fristoe, M., & Ward, J. W. (1974). Quantified functions of the nervous system in uremic patients on maintenance dialysis. *Transactions, American Society for International Organs, 20*, 388–389.

Teschan, P. E., Ginn, H. E., Bourne, J. R., & Ward, J. W. (1976). Neurobehavioral responses to "middle molecule" dialysis and transplantation. *Transactions, American Society for Artificial International Organs, 22*, 190–194.

Teschan, P. E., Ginn, H. E., Bourne, J. R., Ward, J. W., Baruch, H., Nunnally, J. C., Musso, M., & Vaughn, V. K. (1979). Quantitative indices of clinical uremia. *Kidney International, 15,* 676–697.

Trieschmann, R. B., & Sand, P. L. (1971). WAIS and MMPI correlates of increasing renal failure in adult medical patients. *Psychological Reports, 29,* 1251–1262.

Weddington, W. W. (1978). Dementia dialytica. *Psychosomatics, 19,* 267–370.

Winokur, M. Z., Czaczkes, J. W., & Kaplan De-Nour, A. (1973). Intelligence and adjustment to chronic hemodialysis. *Journal of Psychosomatic Research, 17,* 29–34.

Wright, R. G., Sand, P., & Livingston, G. (1966). Psychological stress during hemodialysis for chronic renal failure. Annuals of Internal Medicine, 64, 611–621.

Ziesat, H. A., Logue, P. E., & McCarty, S. M. (1980). Psychological measurement of memory deficits in dialysis patients. *Perceptual and Motor Skills, 50,* 311–318.

6

Neurobehavioral Disturbances Associated with Disorders of the Pancreas

CHRISTOPHER M. RYAN

INTRODUCTION

Concerned primarily with the digestion of food and the metabolism of carbohydrates, the pancreas appears at first glance to be a most unlikely source of neuropsychiatric disturbances. Yet an extensive clinical literature has reported significant mental-status changes in individuals with several different pancreatic disorders. Severe depression and anxiety are often seen in patients with cancer of the pancreas long before any other somatic symptoms of their carcinoma are evident. Profound impairments affecting both emotional and intellectual domains have been reported in patients with pancreatitis, and severe inflammation of the pancreas is said to produce a "pancreatic encephalopathy." Impairments on various cognitive measures are also seen in children and adults with diabetes mellitus, though these intellectual changes tend to be far less severe than those associated with pancreatitis, and they appear to be restricted to a relatively small subset of diabetic patients. In addition, mental confusion, slurred speech, motor incoordination, and a number of other symptoms of central nervous system (CNS) dysfunction are typically found in patients with hyperinsulinism secondary to islet cell tumors (insulinomas).

It is likely that diverse biochemical and physiological mechanisms are responsible for the development and expression of the neurobehavioral disturbances observed to occur in patients with different types of pancreatic disorders. In this chapter, I review the four pancreatic diseases that are most often associated with neuropsychiatric dysfunction: pancreatic carcinoma,

CHRISTOPHER M. RYAN • Department of Psychiatry, University of Pittsburgh School of Medicine, and Western Psychiatric Institute & Clinic, Pittsburgh, Pennsylvania 15213.

pancreatitis, diabetes mellitus, and insulinoma. Although several recent electrophysiological studies of children with cystic fibrosis have suggested that there is an increased incidence of EEG abnormalities in patients with this genetically determined pancreatic disorder (see Benos, 1976, for review), I will not discuss this disease because the neurobehavioral status of such individuals has not been examined in any systematic manner.

My goal is to provide answers to three basic questions. First, is it possible to describe a constellation of behavioral deficits, or a "neuropsychiatric syndrome," that is characteristic of, or unique to, each of these four diseases? Second, to what extent are these behavioral changes a consequence of central nervous system dysfunction, and to what extent are they an emotional reaction to stressors associated with having a painful and/or chronic disease? Third, when CNS damage *is* detected, what is the means by which certain disease-related variables (e.g., release of pancreatic enzymes into bloodstream; development of pulmonary fat embolism; serious episodes of hypoglycemia) either produce or facilitate this outcome?

THE PANCREAS: ANATOMICAL AND PHYSIOLOGICAL CONSIDERATIONS

Varying in length from 10 to 15 cm and weighing from 90 to 120 g in the adult human, the pancreas rests in the retroperitoneal region of the upper abdomen and is covered anteriorly by portions of the stomach, liver, transverse colon, and small intestine (Volk & Allen, 1985). This lobulated organ is generally subdivided into a large head, an elongated body, and a narrower tail (see Figure 1) and extends from the duodendum, at the right of midline, to the spleen. Pancreatic secretions are carried primarily by the main pancreatic duct, or the duct of Wirsung, which traverses the length of the pancreas until it empties into the duodenum. The pancreas is innervated by fibers from the vagus and splanchnic nerves. It receives a rich arterial blood

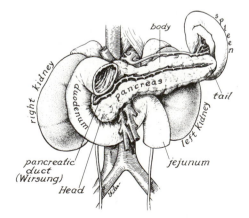

FIGURE 1. The pancreas.

supply from the anterior and posterior pancreaticoduodenal arcades, and from several branches of the splenic artery.

The pancreas has both exocrine and endocrine functions. As an exocrine organ, it facilitates digestion of foodstuffs by secreting various amylolytic, lipolytic, and proteolytic enzymes into the gastrointestinal tract by way of the main pancreatic duct. These enzymes hydrolyze complex food molecules into smaller molecules that are then either digested further or are absorbed by the small intestine. The exocrine pancreas also secretes sufficient biocarbonate to neutralize gastric acid and to produce the alkaline environment needed for the optimal activity of the pancreatic enzymes that have been released into the duodenum. Production of these so-called pancreatic juices occurs mainly in the acinar cells and is under both hormonal and neural control.

As an endocrine organ, the pancreas secretes a number of hormones that are necessary for efficiently regulating the metabolism of glucose. This function occurs in the islets of Langerhans, which occupy only 2% of the total volume of the pancreas. At least four types of islet cells have been identified. The majority of islet cells are B cells (or as they are more traditionally known, beta cells), which secrete insulin. Approximately 18 to 25% of the islet cells are A, or alpha, cells, which release glucagon. Located in close proximity to the alpha cells are a smaller number (approximately 3 to 8%) of D cells, which secrete somatostatin. In addition, there are a small number of pancreatic polypeptide (PP) cells, whose biological function remains poorly understood.

Each of these islet cell hormones has a number of very different actions. Perhaps the most important function of insulin is to facilitate the uptake of glucose into cells (and thus reduce blood glucose levels). On the other hand, glucagon increases blood glucose levels both by initiating the process of glycogenolysis and by augmenting the formation of glucose from fatty acids in the liver (Cahill & Arky, 1983). Because somatostatin is released by a large number of extrapancreatic cells, including neurons, it affects a wide variety of functions, including growth processes, gastrointestinal functions, and CNS activity. Within the pancreas, however, it plays a major role in a negative feedback loop and appears to inhibit the secretion of glucagon, and to a lesser extent, insulin (Reichlin, 1983). More detailed, very readable descriptions of the anatomy and physiology of the pancreas can be found in recent publications by Volk and Allen (1985), Greenberger, Toskes, and Isselbacher (1983), Keynes and Keith (1981), and Fitzgerald (1980).

CARCINOMA OF THE PANCREAS

Epidemiology and Etiology

Cancer of the pancreas is a devastating disorder that is difficult to diagnose and nearly impossible to treat successfully. It has been estimated that 25,500 new cases will be diagnosed and 24,000 deaths will result from it in

1986. In the United States, it is the fourth most frequent cause of death from a malignant neoplasm, after cancer of the lung, the colorectal region, and the breast, respectively (Cancer Statistics, 1986). The incidence of this disorder is highest for both men and women between the ages of 55 and 74. The average age at diagnosis is 60 yr. This disease is somewhat more common in males than in females and occurs significantly more often in black and native Hawaiian males than in white males.

Studies of the yearly incidence of pancreatic carcinoma demonstrate that it has increased 300% since 1930. These figures have been interpreted as evidence that a number of environmental agents may play an important role in the etiology of this disease. A recent case-control study encompassing more than 115 hospitals has demonstrated that for males, occupational exposure to gasoline and degreasing agents or employment in the dry cleaning industry significantly increases the risk of pancreatic cancer. This was most apparent when the exposure exceeded 10 yr. Other significant risk factors include the consumption of caffeine-free coffee (in which trichlorethylene is used to remove caffeine), habitual drinking of wine (> 2 glasses/day) and in women, a prior history of oophorectomy or uterine myomata, or heavy cigarette smoking (> 10/day) (Lin & Kessler, 1981). Although the relative risk for any single factor is quite small, the risk of pancreatic cancer increases dramatically when several factors are combined—sixfold in men and 34-fold in women.

Pathology and Clinical Presentation

Most pancreatic tumors are adenocarcinomas that arise from ductal epithelial cells. The head of the pancreas is the most common initial site of carcinoma, though the body or tail is affected initially in approximately 25% of the cases. As the tumor grows, it tends to be associated with a large zone of fibrosis and produces a pattern of inflammation that may be identical to that seen in patients with chronic pancreatitis. There is a marked tendency for carcinoma of the body or tail to metastasize to distant sites, with regional lymph nodes, lungs, liver, and bones being the sites most often affected; extensive metastasis prior to diagnosis is less likely to occur with carcinoma of the head of the pancreas.

The classic symptoms of pancreatic cancer include weight loss (20 to 30 lb is not unusual), a dull abdominal pain that is poorly localized or radiates to the back, anorexia, weakness, and fatigue. Jaundice may also be a prominent symptom—particularly as tumors in the pancreatic head frequently produce an obstruction of the common bile duct. Because these changes usually develop insidiously, patients may wait several months before consulting a physician. Indeed, it has been estimated that only 15% of patients seek medical advice within the first month of symptom appearance, and nearly half wait 6 mon before obtaining a medical evaluation (Gray, 1983). The nature of pancreatic carcinoma is such that laboratory tests (e.g., serum amylase and lipase values) and diagnostic procedures (e.g., CT scan, sonograms) are relatively unreliable at the earliest stages of the disease. This is especially true in cases involving the body and tail of the pancreas. By the time a correct diagnosis is made, the carcinoma has usually progressed to such an extent that surgical resection is not possible. No effective non-surgical therapy currently exists for pancreatic carcinoma. In one study of patients with histological evidence of incurability (Moertel, 1969), median survival was only 3.5 months; at 1 year, only 8% of the sample were alive.

Neuropsychiatric Disturbances

The first clinical evidence that pancreatic carcinoma may be associated with a distinctive neuropsychiatric syndrome was provided by Yaskin in 1931. He described detailed case histories from four patients, 50 to 59 years of age, who had no history of previous nervous disease yet began to experience general weakness, fatigability, insomnia, anxiety, and depression. Often the patients had inexplicable crying spells, and they frequently reported feeling that something terrible was about to befall them. Because no medical disease was found on initial examination, these patients were diagnosed as having a psychiatric disorder. Over time, however, their abdominal symptoms gradually worsened and when they were reexamined, several months later, pancreatic carcinoma was diagnosed.

Yaskin's (1931) description of EC provides an excellent illustration of this syndrome.

> *History:* EC, a woman, aged 59, . . . without any history of deviation in personality or psychotic episodes. In April, 1928, she began to lose appetite, could not sleep, and became restless, nervous, and anxious. There were vague lower abdominal pains, and the constipation that had existed for 10 years became more pronounced. In July, she was admitted to a teaching hospital, where exhaustive investigations, including complete gastrointestinal studies, failed to disclose any organic disease, and she was discharged early in September with a diagnosis of neurasthenia and anxiety neurosis.
>
> *Examination:* Examination about the middle of September revealed the following: The patient complained of insomnia, general weakness, nervousness, a feeling of some imminent danger to her life, depression with crying spells, lack of appetite, and vague abdominal pain not related to the intake of food. There was no disturbance of perception or of memory. She looked somewhat reduced in weight and had actually lost 10 lbs. . . .
>
> *Course:* By the early part of November the pain became pronounced; she lost considerable weight, and a hard mass, which moved with respiration, could be felt in the left hypochondrium. Curiously, at this time she became less anxious and depressed and was rather apathetic and listless. . . . Laparotomy was performed, December 11. . . . A carcinoma of the pancreas with a minimum of involvement of the head was found. The patient received radium treatment, made a satisfactory surgical recovery, and was discharged from the hospital, February 5, 1929. The mental attitude continued to be one of apathy. She died at home within a few weeks. (p. 1664)

Since Yaskin's initial presentation of these four cases, a number of published reports have described the occurrence of an affective disorder that precedes, or is contemporaneous with, the obvious physical signs and symptoms associated with pancreatic carcinoma (Arbitman, 1972; Dumphy, 1940; Kant, 1946, Latter & Wilbur, 1937; Pelner, 1947; Perlas & Faillace, 1964; Pomara & Gershon, 1984; Rickles, 1948; Savage & Noble, 1952; Ulett & Parsons, 1948). As Salmon (1967) has pointed out in his meta-analysis of many of these cases, the most commonly occurring psychiatric symptoms include depression, anxiety, insomnia, nervousness, and restlessness or agitation. Pain—often poorly localized—usually accompanies these mental symptoms, as does a variety of nonspecific physical symptoms such as weakness, diarrhea, and weight loss. In contrast, patients typically do not manifest clinically obvious disturbances in reasoning, memory, or concentration. However, no investigator has ever used a formal battery of neuropsychological tests to systematically assess the cognitive status of such patients.

Although most patients undergo an extensive series of physical and laboratory investigations, results are usually within normal limits and, as a consequence, a diagnosis of gastrointestinal disease is generally *not* made initially. Rather, physicians tend to focus on the so-called "functional" symptoms and make psychiatric diagnoses that range from "nervous breakdown" and neurasthenia to involutional melancholia and agitated depression. To a certain extent, this failure to diagnose pancreatic cancer at an early stage reflects the relatively low incidence of clinically significant jaundice in these cases and the absence of any compelling evidence of pancreatic dysfunction. The problem of detecting pancreatic dysfunction is compounded by the fact that the pancreas is anatomically buried in the abdomen and therefore difficult to examine and study. It is interesting to note, however, that the mental status of a number of cases, including Yaskin's (1931) EC, *changed significantly* from depression and anxiety to apathy after the definitive diagnosis of pancreatic carcinoma was made—that is, at that point when the cancer had spread sufficiently to produce a major disruption of gastrointestinal functions.

In an effort to estimate the incidence of psychiatric symptoms associated with pancreatic carcinoma, Jacobsson and Ottosson (1971) conducted a retrospective study of all patients diagnosed with pancreatic carcinoma between 1959 and 1968 at Umea University Hospital. They located a close family member of each patient and interviewed them about the patient's mental and somatic symptoms. These results were compared with those from a group of patients having carcinoma of the stomach. In contrast to the impression provided by case studies, Jacobsson and Ottosson (1971) found a relatively low incidence of mental symptoms associated with pancreatic cancer. Only 16% of their 50 pancreatic cancer patients were thought to have evidence of irritability, weakness, and mild depression in the absence of somatic symptoms. Although only 4% of patients with stomach cancer were thought to have similar mental symptoms, this apparent between-group difference failed to reach statistical significance, probably as a consequence of the rather small sample size.

Unfortunately, this study is seriously flawed because of its reliance on a retrospective methodology. In certain cases, as many as 10 yr had elapsed between the time the patient died and the time at which a close relative was actually interviewed about the patient's mental and physical complaints *prior* to the diagnosis of carcinoma. Given the various problems associated with retrospective studies, including the obvious unreliability of the average person's memory of a deceased relative's mental symptoms, it is unlikely that the incidence of psychiatric symptoms reported by Jacobsson and Ottosson (1971) was very accurate.

The most compelling information to date on psychiatric symptoms associated with pancreatic carcinoma comes from a prospective study conducted by Fras and his associates (Fras, Litin, & Pearson, 1967; Fras, Litin, & Bartholomew, 1968). They interviewed three groups of subjects: 46 consecutive patients with histologically verified evidence of carcinoma of the pancreas, 64 patients with carcinoma of the colon, and 15 patients with other diagnoses ("mixed" group). Using a semistructured interview technique, they obtained a detailed psychiatric and medical history from each patient. In addition, they specifically asked each patient, "What was the very first thing you noticed wrong with your health?" and followed this up by having the patient free-associate about various aspects of his or her illness. Severity of depression was estimated with the Depression Rating Scale, and all subjects were asked to complete the Minnesota Multiphasic Personality Inventory (MMPI).

Nearly 50% of the patients with carcinoma of the pancreas reported that mental symptoms were the *first* signs of illness and that these preceded the physical symptoms by 1 to 43 mon (median = 6 mon). Symptoms of depression—particularly loss of ambition or loss of initiative—were reported most frequently. Although these patients did not report feelings of guilt or worthlessness, they were likely to describe themselves as feeling sad or "down in the dumps." In contrast, symptoms of depression were reported in only 13% of the patients with carcinoma of the colon and in only 7% of patients in the mixed control group. According to their analyses, the onset of depression almost always preceded, and never followed, the onset of pain, whereas the onset of anxiety occurred with, or after, pain onset. There was no relationship between the duration of illness or knowledge of diagnosis and the manifestation of various psychiatric symptoms.

Both the Depression Rating Scale and the MMPI profiles corroborated the results from the clinical interview. On the Depression Rating Scale, patients with pancreatic carcinoma had a significantly higher score (mean = 63.4; SD = 12.8) than either the group of patients with carcinoma of the colon (mean = 46.7) or the mixed group (mean = 51.0). On the MMPI, the Depression (2) scale was the most elevated clinical scale, and was significantly higher for the pancreatic group (mean *t* score = 65.8) than for either the colon carcinoma (mean = 58.1) or the mixed (mean = 55.2) groups. Not surprisingly, the Hypochondriasis scale was elevated in all three groups.

Differential Diagnosis

Results from this study and from the extensive series of case histories suggest that there may be a distinctive psychiatric syndrome associated with pancreatic carcinoma and that this syndrome can be distinguished from a number of other psychiatric or medical disorders. It is particularly critical to differentiate this from what has been termed *involutional depression* because both disorders first appear late in life. Fras and his associates have made such a comparison and have delineated a number of important differences that are based primarily on the severity of the symptoms. As indicated in Table 1, there is a delusional quality to the late life depression that is absent from, or at least considerably less evident in, the depressive disorder associated with cancer of the pancreas. There are also signs of serious concentration and mnestic disturbances in patients with involutional depression that are absent (or minimal) in patients with pancreatic cancer.

Very important differences in responsiveness to antidepressant medications may also distinguish patients with involutional depression from those

TABLE 1. Differential Diagnosis between the Depression Associated with Cancer of the Pancreas and Late Life Depression[a]

Cancer of the pancreas	Late life depression
Depression is usually mild or moderate.	Depression is severe.
Feelings of worthlessness are absent or mild.	Feelings of worthlessness predominate.
Guilt feelings are absent or mild.	Guilt feelings and self-accusatory ideas are common.
Delusions are absent.	Delusions are often present.
Although the future may appear bleak, hopelessness is never complete, and help is realistically sought.	Complete all-encompassing hopelessness is present that is unresponsive to external circumstances.
Paranoid trends or mechanisms are absent.	Paranoid trends or mechanisms are often found.
Restlessness or agitation is rare.	Restlessness or agitation is frequently seen.
Suicidal ideation is infrequent.	Suicidal ideation is not unusual.
Insomnia is related to pain and characteristically responds only to aspirin.	Early morning awakening is common and responds to adequate sleeping medications.
Impairment of concentration or memory is rare and mild.	Concentration and memory are often impaired.
Somatic complaints are localized.	Somatic complaints may be bizarre, variable, or appear in different places.

[a]Adapted from "Comparison of Psychiatric Symptoms in Carcinoma of the Pancreas with those of some other Intraabdominal Neoplasms" by I. Fras, E. M. Litin, & J. S. Pearson, 1967, *American Journal of Psychiatry*, *123*, 1553–1562.

whose depression is secondary to pancreatic carcinoma. For example, Pomara and Gershon (1984) found that their patient with a 9-year history of moderately severe depression showed no therapeutic responsiveness to trials with zimelidine or imipramine. He was subsequently diagnosed as having carcinoma of the head of the pancreas, and the size and location of the tumor was such (38 g) as to suggest that it had been growing slowly for approximately 9 years. Remarkably, following surgical resection of the patient's adenocarcinoma, they observed a significant therapeutic response to antidepressants and an obvious improvement in his affective state. Others (Fras, Litin, & Bartholomew, 1968) have commented that neither medications nor electroconvulsive therapy ameliorates the depression associated with pancreatic cancer.

Subjective descriptions of pain can also be used to differentiate the psychiatric complaints voiced by patients with pancreatic carcinoma from those with other medical disorders, or from patients who have what would now be termed a *conversion disorder* or a *psychogenic pain disorder*. Patients with pancreatic carcinoma describe the pain as being located deep in the abdomen or back. They rarely describe pain moving from one region to another, nor do they typically report pain in the extremities, face, or head, as is commonly observed in patients with a primarily psychogenic disorder. Moreover, patients with pancreatic cancer may, like patients with pancreatitis, obtain relief by sitting and leaning forward. This is rarely, if ever, reported in patients with a psychogenic pain disorder.

The temporal relationship between the first evidence of depressive symptomatology and pain may also provide important diagnostic information. Unlike patients with other forms of cancer, patients with pancreatic carcinoma usually describe feelings of depression and impending doom *long before* their diagnosis and often at a point when their pain is only slight or intermittent. Although it is widely assumed that virtually any type of carcinoma will trigger serious psychiatric disturbances, this belief is not supported by data obtained from several recent studies. For example, although Levine and his associates reported that 25% of cancer patients referred for psychiatric consultation met diagnostic criteria for a depressive syndrome, only 1.9% of patients hospitalized with cancer were *ever referred* for psychiatric consultations. Presumably, the other 98.1% of the cancer patients in their hospital did not show sufficiently severe neuropsychiatric disturbances to warrant a psychiatric consultation.

In another study, Plumb and Holland (1977) compared Beck Depression Inventory responses from cancer patients, relatives of the patients, and a group of psychiatric patients hospitalized because of a recent suicide attempt. Although the cancer patients were seriously ill with advanced stage solid tumors, their Beck scores were no different from those of their relatives. Not surprisingly, both groups were significantly less depressed than the psychiatric patients. It is becoming increasingly clear that the incidence of depression in cases of pancreatic carcinoma is significantly higher than expected, despite the obvious methodological problems associated with the ascertainment of psychiatric distress in medically ill patients (Lipowski, 1975).

Possible Underlying Mechanisms

Several hypotheses have been advanced to explain the development of psychiatric disturbances in patients with pancreatic carcinoma, but none are very compelling. Fras and associates have speculated that patients with pancreatic carcinoma who develop depression may have a distinctive personality style and/or have a particular psychiatric history that increases the likelihood that they may react to the effects of a neoplastic disorder in a particular manner. For example, they found that 63% of the patients in their pancreatic cancer group, but only 30 to 40% of patients in their other two groups, could be characterized as having an "anger-in" personality, that is, these patients were more likely to handle angry feelings by depression. Moreover, a higher proportion of the pancreatic cancer patients had experienced a significant "object loss" in the preceding 4 years. Exactly how these psychological factors would produce the depressive disorder was not, unfortunately, specified by these authors. Although an extensive literature suggests that preexisting personality organization may influence the development of certain neoplastic diseases, particularly breast cancer (LeShan, 1959), there has been little support for this view from studies of patients with pancreatic carcinoma.

We believe that some type of biochemical process is responsible for the psychiatric disturbances seen in these patients. One can imagine that the neoplastic process—or the mild pancreatitis associated with the carcinoma— triggers a variety of local hormonal and biochemical changes that ultimately are capable of disrupting certain CNS functions. For example, Jacobsson and Ottosson (1971) have argued that pancreatic carcinoma may somehow interfere with the metabolism of 5-Hydroxy-tryptomine (5-HT) or its precursors and in that way produce an affective disorder. Fras and associates, on the other hand, suggest that the tumor may interfere with the normal activity of the autonomic nervous system and in that way initiate symptoms of depression. These possibilities are, however, purely speculative because there have been no biochemical studies that have systematically examined the relationship between the affective state and the metabolic state of such patients. We must admit that currently we have no idea why depression and anxiety are found so frequently in the early stages of pancreatic carcinoma, nor do we know why it is that some patients are more likely than others to develop a psychiatric syndrome.

PANCREATITIS

Epidemiology and Etiology

Pancreatitis is an inflammation of exocrine pancreatic tissue that may be acute, relapsing, or chronic. Although the number of patients with relapsing or chronic pancreatitis is not well established, approximately 5,000 new cases of acute pancreatitis are diagnosed in the United States each year (Greenberger & Toskes, 1983). The most common causes of pancreatitis in this country are alcohol abuse and biliary tract disease (gallstones), though the disease can also be triggered by hypercalcemia, hyperlipoproteinemia, blunt abdominal trauma (e.g., steering wheel injury), certain viral infections (e.g., mumps; viral hepatitis), a variety of drugs (e.g., sulfonamides, estrogens, tetracycline), or a penetrating peptic ulcer. Gray (1983) reports that 10 to 20% of alcoholics show evidence of chronic pancreatitis at autopsy. It now appears that alcoholic pancreatitis is more likely to be seen in individuals who started drinking excessively at a relatively young age (before the age of 25), have been drinking heavily for approximately 10 years, and consume large amounts of fat and protein. Alcoholic males are 5 to 10 times more likely to be affected than females.

Pathology and Clinical Presentation

By definition, acute pancreatitis refers to an isolated episode of inflammation that appears to produce no permanent structural damage to that gland. In contrast, relapsing and chronic pancreatitis are characterized by permanent necrotic changes occurring primarily in the acinar tissue; it is unusual for the islets of Langerhans to be affected histopathologically. The precise pathophysiological mechanisms that underlie the development of pancreatitis remain poorly understood, though it is widely believed that the acute inflammatory disorder occurs when the normally inactive proteolytic enzymes are somehow activated *within* the pancreas (rather than within the intestine) and begin to digest pancreatic tissue. In this situation, some of the activated pancreatic enzymes are absorbed and enter the bloodstream, where they are subsequently distributed more widely. Because of the proteolytic action of certain pancreatic enzymes—particularly trypsin, chymotrypsin, elastase, and lipase—the resulting enzymatic toxemia produces damage in a number of structures distant from the pancreas, including the lungs and the brain (Sharf & Levy, 1976). On the other hand, the structural changes associated with chronic pancreatitis—particularly those found in alcoholics—appear to be due to the precipitation of protein within the ducts and ultimately leads to acinar cell atrophy, fibrosis, and tissue calcification (Greenberger, et al., 1983).

The most common presenting symptoms of acute or chronic pancreatitis is abdominal pain, often accompanied by low grade fever, abdominal tenderness, and tachycardia. The onset of pain is usually sudden and frequently occurs several hours after a large meal or a prolonged period of heavy drinking. Although this pain appears most commonly in the epigastric region, it may also radiate to the back. It tends to be constant, rather than intermittant, and although some patients have only a mild, rather tolerable pain, the majority experience pain that is considered to be among the most severe and pernicious encountered in medical practice (Brooks, 1979). In chronic pancreatitis, the patient may also manifest weight loss and, in the later stages of the disease, may show evidence of glucose intolerance.

Neuropsychiatric Disturbances

The first detailed description of a profound neuropsychiatric disorder associated with pancreatitis was published by Rothermich and von Haam (1941). They described eight cases of patients with acute pancreatitis who manifested a syndrome characterized by clouding of consciousness, anxiety, psychomotor agitation, language disturbances, and muscle spasticity or rigidity. Since that time, the publication of a number of other case histories has confirmed the existence of a "pancreatic encephalopathy." It now appears that this disorder, which is characterized by clinically obvious emotional, intellectual, and neurological changes, may have somewhat different presentations, depending on whether patients are experiencing their first *acute* episode of pancreatitis or whether they are having a recurring attack of *chronic* pancreatitis.

According to Benos (1973, 1974, 1976), the neuropsychiatric changes found in patients with acute pancreatitis typically occur 48 to 74 hr after the initiation of the pain and abdominal tenderness that signals an attack. Patients manifest the classic signs of a delirium: They are disoriented in time and place, show extreme psychomotor restlessness, and often experience visual and, to a lesser extent, auditory hallucinations. Neurological disturbances, including ocular and vestibular abnormalities and cerebellar signs, are common, as are affective changes—particularly the occurrence of anxiety or depression. The electroencephalogram usually shows generalized abnormalities. Although this syndrome may progress to coma and death in a small number of very severe cases, the vast majority begin to show recovery within 3 to 5 days. Indeed, Benos (1973) maintains that there is *complete recovery* of neuropsychiatric status following normalization of pancreatic functions. Unfortunately, the possibility of subtle residual neurobehavioral disturbances cannot be completely ruled out because none of the patients studied to date have ever been evaluated formally with a comprehensive battery of sensitive neuropsychological tests.

Because so many patients with pancreatitis have a history of excessive alcohol abuse, it is tempting to consider alcoholism as a risk factor for the development of encephalopathy. There is, however, no evidence to support such a belief. For example, in a prospective study of 17 *nonalcoholic* cases of acute pancreatitis, one group of investigators (Estrada, *et al.*, 1979) found that 6 (35%) showed a classic, deliriumlike reversible encephalopathy similar to delirium tremens. Thus, the behavioral similarities between this syndrome and that associated with an alcohol-withdrawal delirium, or delirium tremens, may be expected to cause much diagnostic confusion. Benos (1973) suggests that in questionable cases, the presence of overt tremors can substantially aid in the differential diagnosis: Such tremors are rarely if ever seen in patients with "pure" pancreatic encephalopathy.

A somewhat different constellation of symptoms may be found in patients who have a history of chronic relapsing pancreatitis (Benos, 1974). Although these patients can present with a dramatic clouding of consciousness that is characteristic of a delirious state, the most common manifestation is depression or anxiety, usually accompanied by agitation. Unlike patients with a pancreatic carcinoma, the individual whose neuropsychiatric disorder is secondary to chronic pancreatitis also shows evidence of language or memory disturbances as well as a variety of neurological abnormalities, including seizures, hemiparesis, and abnormal reflexes. The electroencephalogram is inevitably abnormal. In a number of cases, the patient's level of consciousness cycles between periods of profound impairment and relative lucidity (Sharf & Levy, 1976).

An illustration of the neuropsychiatric changes associated with what appears to be a chronic case of pancreatitis is provided by Rothermich and von Haam (1941), in their report of Case 5:

> *History.* KS, a white female, was first admitted to the Columbus State Hospital in July 1932, at the age of 59. She voluntarily applied for commitment and was diagnosed psychoneurosis, neurasthenic type. The patient stated that 7 years ago she developed a persistent pain of varying intensity in the right upper quadrant for which she consulted a dozen or more physicians. At the time of this admission, she had innumerable complaints. . . . Mentally, she was well oriented in all spheres; the memory was impaired; the general information and knowledge good, the judgment fair, her insight questionable. She was quite irritable, complaining and critical. She was discharged in October 1932. . . . [She was periodically admitted and discharged over the ensuing 5 years.] In November 1939 she began showing some ataxia and a diminution of mental clarity. Her speech became incoherent and she obstinately refused to take nourishment of any kind. Her temperature elevated to 105 °F, and she died shortly after.
> *Autopsy Results.* The pancreas was small, weighing only 40 gm. The glandular substance was markedly decreased and replaced in good part by fat tissue. The organ showed numerous adhesions and considerable gross scarring. Numerous small whitish and yellow pinhead-sized spots were scattered throughout the organ. The brain weighed 1,100 gm. The precentral area on the left side was shrunken, and the sulci appeared widened. The ventricles were not dilated. (p. 871)

Although this particular patient expired, those patients who survive and show improved pancreatic functioning often manifest a parallel improvement in mental status (Savage, Butcher, & Noble, 1952), though some residual symptoms may persist over time (Benos, 1973).

The true incidence of pancreatic encephalopathy remains controversial. Sharf and Levy (1976) state that they have been able to identify only 26 cases of pancreatic encephalopathy reported in the literature and conclude that this is an exceedingly rare complication of pancreatitis. In the most extensive literature review to date, Benos (1973; 1974) has identified "at least" 168 cases of pancreatic encephalopathy, though he also concludes that the actual incidence of this disorder is relatively rare. It should be obvious that the number of cases observed depends not only on whether one is actually looking for evidence of neuropsychiatric disturbance but on the diagnostic criteria used to identify "encephalopathy" (Estrada et al., 1979; Lipowski, 1975). As a consequence, the estimates of incidence for this condition have ranged from a high of 53% (Schuster & Iber, 1965) to a low of 1.3% (Trapnell, 1972). Most estimates cluster at the lower end of this range. For example, in a discussion of data from two of the largest studies conducted thus far, Benos (1974) notes that Lastchevker (1965) found that 4.18% of 287 cases of pancreatitis met criteria for an encephalopathy, whereas Sharafeev (1961) found evidence for significant neuropsychiatric impairment in 14.9% of 283 cases.

Possible Underlying Mechanisms

At least one study has indicated that psychodynamic factors may be related to the development of neuropsychiatric symptomatology (Lawton & Phillips, 1955), though most discussions of the pathogenesis of pancreatic encephalopathy have attributed the structural and biochemical damage occurring within the central nervous system to the action of some proteolytic substance released by the damaged pancreas.

An early study by Vogel (1951a) suggested that certain pancreatic enzymes may cause the encephalomalacia and extensive demyelinization that are typically found at autopsy in the brains of individuals dying of pancreatitis. Lipase has been implicated as the principal toxin not only because very high levels of lipase and other pancreatic enzymes are usually found in the bloodstream and cerebrospinal fluid (CSF) of patients with acute pancreatitis but because a similar pattern of demyelinization can be induced experimentally by injecting lipase directly into the brain of rabbits (Vogel, 1951b). Additional support for such a hypothesis is provided by a report by Estrada and associates (1979) that delineates a clear relationship between measured CSF–lipase levels and neuropsychiatric dysfunction. Eleven of their 17 cases showed no evidence of neuropsychiatric symptoms and had CSF–lipase levels that were within normal limits. The remaining 6 cases showed clinical evidence of encephalopathy (e.g., visual and auditory hallucinations; disorientation in time and place), nonspecific EEG abnormalities, and CSF–lipase levels that were elevated more than 2 standard deviations beyond the mean. Of special note is their observation that as CSF–lipase levels normalized over time; there was a parallel normalization of both neuropsychiatric and electroencephalographic parameters. Whether lipase is the sole toxic agent or whether other enzymes such as trypsin and chymotrypsin also play a role in the pathogenesis of pancreatic encephalopathy remains to be determined. Neuropsychiatric status may also be influenced by serum electrolyte disturbances or by the nutritional abnormalities that are associated with pancreatic disease. Indeed, Rothermich and von Haam (1941) have speculated that the primary agent may be a nicotinic acid deficiency. There are certainly similarities between the neurological (e.g., ophthalmoplegia) and behavioral disturbances (e.g., delirium) associated with pancreatic encephalopathy and those associated with the so-called Wernicke's encephalopathy seen in patients with a vitamin B deficiency (Victor, Adams, & Collins, 1971).

A very different pathogenic mechanism has been proposed by Johnson and Tong (1977). They report that extensive fat embolism occurs in the lungs and kidneys as a complication of acute pancreatitis and postulate that the structural brain damage often seen in patients with pancreatitis may be a direct or indirect consequence of fat embolization. Two somewhat different scenarios have been elaborated by them. On the one hand, pulmonary fat embolism may produce hypoxemia that, in turn, produces a distinctive neuropathologic change. As they point out, the pattern of spotty demyelinization found in patients with a pancreatic encephalopathy is identical to that seen in patients who have experienced extensive hypoxia. Moreover, it is now well known that a large proportion of patients with acute pancreatitis show arterial hypoxia within the first 48 hs of their illness (Ranson, Roses, & Fink, 1973). On the other hand, it is possible that brain damage may be a *direct consequence* of fat embolization occurring within the cerebral circulation. The resulting widespread cerebral infarctions could explain some of the focal neurologic deficits (e.g., visual field deficits, language disturbances) that are sometimes associated with the pancreatic disease. Although Johnson and Tong (1977) have described autopsy results from one case that is consonant with this possibility, most other neuropathological studies have not found a significant degree of cerebral fat embolization (Rothermich & von Haam, 1941; Vogel, 1951a).

DIABETES MELLITUS

Epidemiology and Etiology

The term *diabetes mellitus* has been applied to several different disorders that produce chronically high blood glucose levels (hyperglycemia). The most carefully studied of these is characterized by a complete inability to secrete insulin and is commonly known as "juvenile-onset," or "insulin-dependent," or "Type I" diabetes. Without insulin, individuals are unable to metabolize carbohydrates efficiently and, as a consequence, will experience dangerously high blood glucose levels several hours after a meal unless that hormone is supplied exogenously. The etiology of Type I diabetes is not completely understood, though some interplay between genetic and environmental factors most certainly appears to have occurred (Craighead, 1978). Recent studies have demonstrated that this form of diabetes is associated with specific histocompatibility markers (i.e., Human Lymphocyte Antigen—HLA) that reside on Chromosome 6. Most investigators now believe that certain, yet unidentified, viral agent(s) may trigger, in genetically susceptible individuals, an autoimmune process that destroys the beta cells within the pancreas (Cahill & McDevitt, 1981).

It has been estimated that there are 435,000 people in the United States with Type I diabetes. After asthma, this disorder is the most prevalent chronic disease of childhood, and at least one study has suggested that its prevalence has been doubling every decade since 1946 (Stewart-Brown, Haslum, & Butler, 1983). Each year approximately 19,000 new cases are diagnosed in this country; virtually all of those individuals are under the age of 30 (Carter Center, 1985). In fact, the incidence is highest in children who are between 10 and 14 years of age (LaPorte, *et al.*, 1981).

In contrast, "maturity-onset," or "non-insulin-dependent," or "Type II" diabetes is found most commonly in individuals who are over the age of 40 and whose body weight is higher than normal. Approximately 93% of the more than 5.5 million Americans who have been diagnosed as having diabetes are afflicted with this form of the disease, and 586,000 new cases are diagnosed each year. The incidence and prevalence of this disorder are 1.8 and 1.4 times greater in women than in men (Carter Center, 1985).

It is now believed that this disorder occurs when chronic overeating stimulates excessive production of insulin by the pancreas. This, in turn, causes a loss of sensitivity to insulin at peripheral cell receptor sites and may ultimately lead to damage of the insulin-secreting beta cells themselves such that they release less than normal amounts of insulin. Both of these changes decrease the effective bioavailability of insulin and, as a result, the efficient metabolism of carboyhdrates is reduced, and blood glucose levels rise. Because the beta cells continue to release a *moderate* (albeit inadequate) amount of insulin, most patients with this form of diabetes can function without daily insulin injections. Again, genetic factors play an important role in pathogenesis. Although the locus of the genes mediating a vulnerability to Type II diabetes has not been identified, family studies indicate that this form of the disease is more strongly inherited than is Type I diabetes (Barnett, Eff, Leslie, & Pyke, 1981).

Pathology and Clinical Presentation

Type I Diabetes

The onset of this form of diabetes is an acute medical crisis that is marked by excessive urination, excessive water and food intake, and by rapid weight loss. If this illness is not treated immediately, patients may experience severe dehydration and ketoacidosis that may, in turn, eventuate in diabetic coma and death (Drash & Becker, 1978). Because of a complete lack of endogenous insulin, the patient with Type I diabetes must obtain exogenous insulin and regulate his or her diet and exercise patterns in such a manner as to "normalize" carbohydrate metabolism. Excessive amounts of insulin or a failure to balance one's self-administered insulin with both food intake and amount of exercise can lead to extremely low blood glucose levels. The resulting hypoglycemia, or so-called "insulin reaction," produces a generalized sense of discomfort that is characterized by sweating, weakness, irritability, anxiety, fine motor tremor. mental confusion, and motor incoordination. If left untreated, loss of consciousness ("insulin coma") may occur, or a hypoglycemic seizure may be initiated.

In contrast, inadequate amounts of insulin or excessive carbohydrate consumption will cause blood glucose levels to become extremely high. There are two reasons for diabetic patients to avoid excessive hyperglycemia. An acute episode may lead to life-threatening ketoacidosis. Chronic hyperglycemia, on the other hand, appears to damage small and large blood vessels and thereby increases the likelihood of developing a variety of serious medical complications. Diabetic patients have a greatly increased risk of heart attacks, stroke, and gangrene of the feet because of their predisposition to develop atherosclerosis in the large arteries of the heart, brain, and legs. Microvascular damage occurring within the retina increases the risk of impaired vision or blindness, whereas the microangiopathy that frequently occurs within the glomerular loops of the kidneys increases the likelihood of developing end-stage renal disease. In addition, these patients may lose fine motor control or experience painful and/or reduced sensation in the extremities because of peripheral neuropathy or develop impotence, cardiac arrhythmias, or loss of urinary bladder sensation as a consequence of autonomic neuropathy. More detailed discussions of these problems can be found in past reviews by Cahill and Arky (1983), Pohl, Gonder-Frederick, and Cox (1984), and Santiago (1984).

In Type I diabetes, the primary therapeutic goal is to maintain good "metabolic control" by avoiding excessively high or low blood glucose levels. It is now possible to estimate the patient's degree of metabolic control over the previous several months by measuring the glycosylated fraction of hemoglobin—also known as the hemoglobin A_{1C} (Daneman, Wolfson, Becker, & Drash, 1981). The greater the degree and duration of chronic hyperglycemia, the higher this value and the more "out of control" the patient is. To avoid the vascular complications of this disease, most diabetologists now counsel their patients to maintain "tight" control and keep blood glucose levels as close to the normal range as possible by frequently monitoring blood glucose levels and adjusting their insulin dosage accordingly.

Type II Diabetes

The onset of this form of diabetes is rarely signaled by a clinically obvious medical crisis. Rather, it may "sneak up" on the individual over a number of years and be noted only after certain medical complications appear. Like patients with Type I diabetes, these individuals have a greatly increased risk of stroke, heart attacks, kidney disease, blindness, and neuropathy. On the other hand, they rarely experience ketoacidosis following an episode of extreme hyperglycemia. Their treatment is directed at maintaining blood glucose levels close to normal, but, because the pancreas continues to secrete insulin, it is unusual for insulin injections to be prescribed for any prolonged time period. The most common treatments are dietary (reduce body weight and decrease carbohydrate intake) control alone or in combination with oral hypoglycemic drugs that promote insulin production and secretion by the pancreas.

Psychiatric Symptomatology

Clinicians have repeatedly commented that children and adolescents with Type I diabetes seem to be more difficult to manage and appear to have more psychosocial problems than do youngsters with other chronic medical disorders. Given the nature of diabetes, however, an unusually high incidence of emotional disturbances would not be at all surprising. Young diabetic patients must take responsibility for daily, self-administered injections of insulin, maintain careful attention to their diet, and periodically test their urine and blood for its glucose content. These tasks not only differentiate them from their healthy peers but also provide them with a constant reminder that they have a chronic, incurable disease (Maddison & Raphael, 1971). Moreover, they are faced with the distinct possibility that no matter how meticulously they monitor these biological variables, their life span may be shortened, and the quality of their life may be compromised by the advent of diabetes-related degenerative complications (Pirart, 1978; Santiago, 1984).

The possibility that diabetic youngsters and their families have an increased incidence of emotional and behavioral disturbances has been discussed by a number of reviewers (Greydanus & Hofmann, 1979; Hauser & Pollets, 1979; Johnson, 1980; Kimball, 1971; Tattersall, 1981). Although all agree that there is no empirical evidence for a unique "diabetic personality" that would predispose an individual to diabetes (Dunn & Turtle, 1981), there is less unanimity about the nature and extent of psychosocial problems *following* diagnosis. Some investigators have observed increased hostility and social maladjustment (Delbridge, 1975; Fällström, 1974; Tavormina, Kastner, Slater, & Watt, 1976), lower levels of ego development (Hauser, Jacobson, Noam, & Powers, 1983), poor self-esteem (Grey, Genel, & Tamborlane, 1980) and heightened anxiety in diabetic youngsters (Fällström, 1974; Swift, Seidman, & Stein, 1967), though others have not (Kubany, Danowski, & Moses, 1956; McCraw & Tuma, 1977; Simonds, 1977; Steinhauser, Borner, & Koepp, 1977; Sterky, 1963; Sullivan, 1978; Zeltzer, Kellerman, Ellenberg, Dash, & Rigler, 1980). Similarly, despite the clinical impression that depression is more prevalent in diabetic youngsters, results from several studies have not borne out such a conclusion. For example, Kovacs and her associates (Kovacs, et al., 1985) have used a series of semi-structured psychiatric interview schedules with both newly diagnosed diabetic children and their parents to determine the incidence of major psychiatric disorders associated with the development of diabetes. Although this longitudinal study is still in progress, preliminary data analyses suggest that the rate of psychiatric illness—particularly major depression—is low in this group and is comparable to that reported to occur in the general population.

It is likely that this lack of consensus reflects differences in types of measures used (e.g., projective tests, self-report inventories), the composition of control groups (e.g., healthy subjects, normative data from standardization samples), variability among diabetic subjects in their degree of metabolic control, or other methodological problems (for critical review, see Johnson, 1980). There is no doubt that *some* diabetic youngsters, like *some* nondiabetic youngsters, show serious depression, anxiety, hostility, or various behavioral problems and that many of these problems have a common etiology (e.g., inadequate or disturbed parenting, family life events, etc.). At the present time, however, results from the most methodologically sound studies (e.g., Kovacs *et al.*, 1985) provide little empirical support for the clinical belief that diabetes *per se* significantly increases the risk of manifesting emotional problems. Whether diabetic individuals go on to develop serious psychiatric disturbances later in life is a somewhat different issue that has not yet been addressed. We have been unable to find any studies that report the incidence of psychiatric symptomatology in *adults* with either Type I or Type II diabetes.

Neuropsychological Disorders in Childhood and Adolescence

Studies of Intelligence

Unlike pancreatic carcinoma and pancreatitis, diabetes mellitus is a disorder that has been studied extensively by neuropsychologically oriented investigators. To a certain extent, this may have been motivated initially by clinical observations and results from single case studies (Dashiell, 1930) that indicated that the typical diabetic experiences rather dramatic fluctuations in mental efficiency over the course of the day. One might expect this to have a significant impact on learning, memory, and problem-solving abilities and ultimately affect the measured intelligence of these individuals over time. As a consequence, beginning in the 1930s, and continuing until about 1965, a large number of studies were conducted in which the IQ scores of small groups of diabetic children were compared with either the published norms or with some sort of control group. Results from these early studies were not very edifying. Depending primarily on their sampling strategies, different investigators were able to demonstrate either that diabetic children were somewhat brighter than the general population (Grishaw, West, & Smith, 1939; Joslin, Root, White, & Marble, 1940) or were somewhat less intelligent (Shirley & Greer, 1940; Teagarden, 1939) or were no different (Brown, 1938; Hiltmann & Lüking, 1966; Kubany, *et al.*, 1956; McGavin, Schultz, Peden, & Bowen, 1940).

Effects of Age at Onset on Performance

One early study is noteworthy, however, because it explicitly examined the relationship between IQ scores and three specific diabetes-related variables: the age at onset of the disease, the duration of the disease, and the number of acute metabolic crises (i.e., hypoglycemic seizures and episodes of ketoacidosis). In their study, Ack, Miller, and Weil (1961) administered the Stanford-Binet Intelligence Test to both diabetic children and their siblings and calculated the mean difference in IQ scores between each of the 38 pairs of sibs. Although scores were not apparently affected by the duration of the disease, there was a strong relationship between intelligence and age at diagnosis. Those children who developed diabetes *before* the age of 5 earned IQ scores that were significantly lower than their nondiabetic sibs—10 points lower, on the average. In contrast, those who were diagnosed *after* the age of 5 were intellectually comparable to their siblings because the mean difference was less than 1 IQ point. Neither hypoglycemic seizures nor episodes of ketoacidosis were apparently related to the IQ scores of the diabetic group as a whole. In the early onset subgroup, however, there was a nonsignificant trend for IQ scores to be negatively correlated with number of metabolic crises.

These early studies offered few insights into the neuropsychological status of diabetic youngsters, perhaps because they were so limited. Rather than using a comprehensive series of neuropsychological measures, investigators tended to rely instead on only a single, global measure of cognitive competence—the IQ score. For whatever reason, this research had remarkably little scientific impact either on diabetologists or on psychologists working with chronically ill children, and essentially no neuropsychological investigations were conducted in this field between 1961 and 1980. It was in this context, in 1980, that a series of neurobehavioral studies was begun by our group at Children's Hospital of Pittsburgh. Drawing on the earlier (and unreplicated) findings of Ack *et al.* (1961), we attempted to delineate the nature and extent of neuropsychological disturbances manifested by diabetic adolescents and test the hypothesis that these deficits were related to the child's age at diagnosis (Ryan, Vega, & Drash, 1985).

To that end, we administered a comprehensive battery of neuropsychological tests to 125 randomly selected diabetic outpatients and to 83 demographically similar nondiabetic control subjects. All subjects were white, were between the ages of 10 and 19 (mean = 14.8 years), and tended to come from relatively well-educated, middle-class families. No subject in any group had a history of any neurologic or psychiatric disorder. Those 46 diabetic subjects who were diagnosed before the age of 5 years were assigned to an "early onset" subgroup; the remaining 79 subjects who were diagnosed at or after the age of 5 were assigned to a "later onset" subgroup. The test battery included subtests from the Wechsler Intelligence Scales, the Wechsler Memory Scale, and the Wide Range Achievement Test as well as a number of more specialized neuropsychological tests. A factor analysis of the entire data set demonstrated that the battery tapped five cognitive domains: General Intelligence, Visuospatial Processes, Learning and Memory, Attention and School Achievement, and Mental and Motor Speed.

Multivariate data analyses revealed that the early onset group was significantly impaired, relative to the other two groups, on each of the five clusters of tests. That is, adolescents who became diabetic before the age of 5 learned new information less efficiently than either later onset diabetics or nondiabetic control subjects and remembered less of that information over a 30-min retention interval. They also made more errors on a number of visuo-spatial tests, were slower on tasks that required dexterity and eye–hand coordination, and earned lower scores on those tasks used to estimate general intelligence. When clinical ratings of impairment were carried out, it was found that a significantly larger proportion of the early onset subjects (24%) met criteria for clinically evident impairment, compared to either the later onset diabetic subjects (6%) or the nondiabetic controls (6%). Because children who developed diabetes earlier in life have typically had the disease longer than those who were diagnosed at a later age, it is tempting to attribute these changes not to age at onset but duration of diabetes. However, results from a series of regression analyses that attempted to statistically disentangle those two correlated variables have indicated that duration predicts performance on only a small subset of tests—those measuring school achievement and verbal intelligence. In contrast, many more test scores—particularly those measuring "fluid intelligence"—were affected more by age at diagnosis.

A recent study by Rovet, Ehrlich, and Hoppe (1987) has essentially replicated many of our findings and demonstrated that neurobehavioral deficits are not restricted to adolescents but may also be found in younger diabetic children. Rovet et al. administered an extensive series of neuro-psychological tests to 27 diabetic children who were diagnosed before the age of 4 years ("early onset"), 24 children who developed the disease after age 4 ("later onset"), and 30 sibling control subjects. All subjects were between the ages of 6 and 16 years (mean = 10 years) at the time of assessment, and there were nearly equal numbers of girls and boys in each subgroup. Their test battery was composed of subtests from the WISC-R, the Verbal Meaning and Spatial Reasoning subtests from the SRA Primary Mental Abilities Test, the Beery-Buktenica Test of Visual Motor Integration, and the Wide Range Achievement Test.

Although the three groups of subjects did not differ on measures of verbal intelligence or school achievement, a significant age-at-onset effect was found on spatial tasks, but only for girls. That is, early-onset girls earned significantly lower scores than did either later-onset or nondiabetic girls; in contrast, no between-group differences were found for boys. A statistically reliable negative correlation was also found between age at onset and performance IQ—but again, only in the female subgroups. Like us, Rovet and her colleagues (1987) found that neither duration of disease nor degree of recent metabolic control (as determined by glycosylated hemoglobin values) was a potent predictor of performance. The authors have speculated that the tendency for young diabetic girls to show more pronounced neuropsychological deficits than boys may merely reflect the increased sensitivity of females to cerebral disease (Taylor & Ounstead, 1972). Spatial skills may be particularly vulnerable because those cognitive abilities may be less well represented within the female brain (McGlone, 1980).

Possible Underlying Mechanisms

These data, as well as our own, demonstrate that the age at onset of diabetes significantly increases the risk of developing clinically apparent neuropsychological deficits in children and adolescents. We suspect that a similar age-at-onset effect would be found in diabetic adults, although no one has yet tested that hypothesis. It is likely that the relationship between neuropsychological dysfunction and the occurrence of diabetes early in life is the product of two very different processes. First, the young diabetic child is more likely to experience hypoglycemic seizures because of a heightened responsiveness to insulin. Ternand, Go, Gerich, & Haymond (1982) found that diabetic children who were diagnosed before the age of 3 years experienced a greater frequency of hypoglycemic seizures or coma than did those diagnosed after the age of 5 years. These data are consonant with our findings (Ryan et al., 1985) and with those of Rovet and associates (1987). For example, when we compared the number of serious hypoglycemic episodes in both early- and later-onset diabetic subjects, we found that a significantly higher proportion of the early-onset subjects had experienced one or more such episodes. Similarly, Rovet and her colleagues also found that the incidence of hypoglycemic seizures was higher among the early-onset subjects, and though it just failed to reach statistical significance, there was a marked tendency for girls to have more seizures than boys.

A second phenomenon that contributes to the increased likelihood of cognitive impairments in early-onset diabetic children is the fact that the brain of the very young child is unusually sensitive to the deleterious effects of any type of metabolic or physiologic insult. As a consequence, hypoglycemic seizures may be more likely to have a marked effect on neuropsychological processes when they occur early in life. For example, nondiabetic children who experience multiple hypoglycemic seizures have an increased risk of significant brain dysfunction (Hirabayashi, Kitahara, & Hishida, 1980; Ingram, Stark, & Blackburn, 1967). Moreover, the severity of impairment is negatively correlated with the age when the child first had a seizure or otherwise sustained brain damage (Ernhart, Graham, Eichman, Marshall, & Thurston, 1963; Teuber & Rudel, 1962). Results from several studies of epileptic children suggest that the first 5 years of life may be a particularly sensitive "critical period" for the development of serious neurologic dysfunction because the most severe cognitive disturbances invariably were found in those children whose seizures began before the age of 5 years (Dikman, Matthews, & Harley, 1975; O'Leary et al., 1983).

If the neuropsychological disturbances found in diabetic children reflect some type of central nervous system dysfunction, one ought to find parallel evidence of structural or functional changes within the brain. Neither we, nor Rovet and associates, have evaluated our patients with either electrophysiologic or neuroradiologic techniques. On the other hand, three European research groups have recorded electroencephalograms (EEGs) from diabetic children and adolescents and have found a significantly higher incidence of abnormality than that characteristically seen in the general population. For example, Gilhaus, Daweke, Lülsdorf, Sachsse, and Sachsse (1973) recorded EEGs from more than 300 diabetic youngsters and found that 23.3% of their sample showed nonspecific abnormalities, an additional 14% had "questionable" EEGs, and 3.7% showed clear evidence of focal or generalized seizure activity. When they evaluated the relationship between hypoglycemia and incidence of EEG anomalies, they found that those children who had experienced an episode of severe hypoglycemia were nearly twice as likely to show EEG pathology as compared to youngsters who had never had such an episode (30.8% versus 16.5%). In contrast, the number of previous hyperglycemic (ketotic) comas did not predict presence or absence of EEG abnormality. Of particular note is the finding that children who were diagnosed with diabetes between the ages of 2 and 5 years were far more likely to show anomalies than those who were diagnosed at a somewhat later age.

Very similar findings have been reported by Eeg-Olofsson and Petersen (1966) and by Haumont, Dorchy, and Pelc (1979). All three of these studies demonstrated that diabetic youngsters are more likely to manifest mild, diffuse brain dysfunction than are their nondiabetic peers. Although duration of diabetes does not appear to be a critical variable, the data overwhelmingly indicate that multiple episodes of severe hypoglycemia are at least partially responsible for the development of a "diabetic encephalopathy" (Eeg-Olofssen, 1977). Evidence that this intellectual dysfunction may also be accompanied by structural damage within the brain has been provided by Reske-Nielsen, Lundbaek, and Rafaelsen (1965). Results from an autopsy study of brain tissue obtained from 16 diabetic young adults led them to conclude that poorly controlled diabetes may somehow affect CNS metabolism and produce a unique pattern of diffusely distributed neuronal damage.

Neuropsychological Disorders in Adulthood

Type I Diabetes

Although the relationship between age at diagnosis and cognitive functioning has not been formally evaluated in adults with Type I diabetes, several other disease-related variables have been examined in this patient population. One variable that has received much scrutiny is the degree of metabolic control. Many investigators have argued that a long history of poor metabolic control (i.e., a tendency toward excessive hyperglycemia) greatly increases the risk of micro- and macrovascular diabetic complications, including retinopathy, nephropathy, and neuropathy (Jackson, Ide, Guthrie, & James, 1982; Raskin, Pietri, Unger, & Shannon; 1983; Young, Ewing, & Clarke, 1983). Given the well-known relationship between cerebrovascular disturbances and cognitive dysfunction (Lishman, 1978), one might expect to see an analogous deterioration in the neuropsychological functioning of older diabetic adults, particularly those with clinical evidence of small and large vessel pathology.

One of the earliest studies to demonstrate such an association was reported by Rennick, Wilder, Sargent, and Ashley (1968). They evaluated a group of 30 diabetic adults (mean age = 40 years) with a number of tests from the Halstead-Reitan Neuropsychological Battery and the Wechsler Adult Intelligence Scale. Those 15 patients who had no evidence of microvascular complications performed within normal limits on *all* tests. On the other hand, the 15 demographically similar patients who had mild to moderate retinopathy performed normally on vocabulary and general information tests and on basic sensory and motor function tests but showed evidence of mild impairment on tests requiring complex problem-solving and abstract reasoning skills. Interestingly, their level of performance was *not* related to their past history of hypoglycemic seizures.

Using the same test battery, Skenazy and Bigler (1984) have reported that neuropsychological test scores are related to the severity of the disease. They found that non-visually-impaired diabetic subjects (mean age 32) performed more poorly than an age-matched group of nondiabetic medical patients on measures of mental flexibility (Trail-Making, Part B), problem-solving ability (Category Test) and nonverbal intelligence (WAIS Performance IQ). When diabetic patients were assigned to "less severe" and "more severe" subgroups based on incidence of various medical complications and disease-related problems, those patients with a more severe medical course (presumably as a result of being in poorer metabolic control) manifested a greater number of neuropsychological deficits. Although problem-solving ability was not affected, there was a marked decline in performance on measures of grip strength, motor speed, and mental flexibility. Unlike Rennick and associates, however, Skenazy and Bigler also found association between the number of severe hypoglycemic reactions and performance on a variety of tests.

Evidence of impairment on measures of memory, abstract reasoning, and visuoconstructional ability has been reported by Franceschi et al. (1984). They administered an extensive battery of tests to a group of 37 diabetic patients 18 to 35 years of age (mean = 26) and to 26 demographically similar normoglycemic control subjects, and found pronounced between-group differences on the WAIS Block Design and Similarities subtests and on the Wechsler Memory Scale (WMS). No correlation was found between performance and either duration or severity of disease, though it must be kept in mind that all of these patients were in relatively poor control when they were studied. The investigators make the very important point that though they observed statistically significant effects, the "abnormalities" they detected seemed to have little clinical significance and did not appear to have any obvious impact on the patients' daily functioning.

A somewhat different approach has been taken in a very recent study by Holmes (1986). Rather than estimating metabolic control from the incidence of vascular complications, she used glycosylated hemoglobin levels to assign 27 young (mean age = 22) diabetic males to a "good control" or "poor control" subgroup. Despite the fact that the two groups were comparable in age and educational background, the men in the poor control subgroup earned significantly lower scores on WAIS Information and Vocabulary subtests and performed more slowly on simple reaction time tests. Although it is known that excessively high, or excessively low, blood glucose levels at the time of testing can interfere with attentional processes (Holmes, Hayford, Gonzalez, & Weydert, 1983), the simple reaction times recorded from these patients were unrelated to their ambient blood glucose levels.

A similar reduction in mental efficiency has been noted by Lichty and Klachko (1985) who administered tasks that required either "effortful" (e.g., paired-associate learning) or "automatic" (e.g., word frequency judgment) processing to 32 diabetic college students and an equal number of nondiabetic subjects. Although both groups performed equally well when asked to estimate word frequency, the diabetic group learned the list of word pairs somewhat more slowly than did the nondiabetic group. When diabetic subjects were subsequently assigned to "good control" or "poor control" subgroups on the basis of past medical history, a reanalysis of the data demonstrated that only those with a history of poor control were impaired: Those in good control learned as efficiently as the nondiabetic subjects. Both Holmes and Lichty interpret their findings as evidence that a recent history of excessive hyperglycemia may be associated with a decrement in general information-processing ability.

Other investigators, using very different tasks, have often but not always found relatively subtle cognitive deficits in diabetic adults. For example, Bale (1973) administered the Walton-Black Modified New Word Learning Test to 100 diabetic adults (mean age = 47 years) and to age- and sex-matched control subjects and found that 17% of the diabetic patients, but none of the controls, scored in the brain-damaged range. Although there was no relationship between brain damage and the patient's age or the duration of the disease, there was a significant correlation between low test scores and severity of past hypoglycemic episodes. Meuter, Thomas, Gruneklee, Gries, & Lohmann (1980) compared the neuropsychological performance of a group of 112 Type I diabetic patients (mean age = 38) with age- and education-matched nondiabetic control subjects and found the diabetic patients to be somewhat less efficient on measures of memory, and significantly slower on reaction time tasks. Unfortunately, insufficient information is provided by the authors to determine which specific diabetes-related variables (e.g., metabolic control) may have been affecting test performance.

In contrast, Lawson and co-workers (1984) concluded that diabetic adults (mean age = 38) performed as well as nondiabetic control subjects on a variety of standard neuropsychological tests, including the WAIS, the WMS, and the Repeated Figures and Repeated Words tests. Further, they observed no relationship between test scores and age at onset, duration, or severity of disease (indexed by degree of peripheral and autonomic neuropathies). Although they reported that diabetic patients earned WMS Memory Quotients that were significantly lower than controls, they attributed this isolated finding to chance, unaware that Franceschi and associates (1984) had made a similar observation. Perhaps the greatest problems with Lawson's study are its inclusion of an extremely wide age range (16 to 60 years) of subjects and its failure to differentiate patients with Type I diabetes from those with the Type II form of the disease. A somewhat different pattern of results might have been obtained had more homogeneous subsamples been analyzed.

Type II Diabetes

To date, only two studies have explicitly examined the neuropsychological status of adults with Type II diabetes. In an extensive assessment of diabetic patients, Meuter and his associates (1980) compared a group of 35 adults with Type II diabetes to a group of age-matched controls and to a group of adults with Type I diabetes. They found that patients with maturity-onset diabetes showed a dramatic decline in response time as well as serious impairments on a number of learning and memory tests.

Significantly disrupted mnestic functions have also been observed by Perlmuter et al. (1984). In their detailed study of elderly patients with Type II diabetes, they evaluated 140 diabetic patients, 55 to 74 years of age, and compared them to 38 age-matched nondiabetic controls. Each subject was tested by an examiner who was unaware of the subject's medical condition. Tests included a serial learning test, a digit span test, a reaction time test, and the WAIS Vocabulary Test. In addition, mood was assessed with the Zung Depression Survey; peripheral neuropathy was determined by measuring vibratory threshold; and degree of recent metabolic control was estimated from glycosylated hemoglobin levels. Although the serial learning scores of the diabetic patients were found to improve over successive trials, they learned significantly fewer concrete and abstract words than the nondiabetic subjects and recalled a smaller proportion of words. Moreover, fewer of the diabetic patients mastered the list (42%) than controls (71%), and those diabetic patients who reached criterion required significantly more study trials. This pattern of results cannot be attributed to between-group differences in mood, educational level, verbal knowledge, or reaction times because the diabetics were comparable to controls on those measures. Similarly, the immediate memory span (forward digit span) of the diabetic subjects did not differ from that of controls, though their backward span was significantly smaller. Two disease-related variables were negatively correlated with learning scores: degree of peripheral neuropathy and degree of metabolic control. On the other hand, neither duration of disease nor blood glucose level at the time of test was related to performance. This overall pattern of results is quite similar to that reported by Lichty and Klachko (1985).

Possible Underlying Mechanisms

Although a past history of serious hypoglycemic episodes has sometimes been associated with the development of cognitive disturbances, it appears that poor metabolic control (hyperglycemia) may have a potent effect on cognitive functioning in diabetic adults. This appears to be true in the case of both Type I and Type II diabetes. Patients with clinically significant diabetes-related medical complications (especially retinopathy and neuropathy) have a much higher risk of cognitive impairments—as measured by standard neuropsychological tests—than those without such problems. Moreover, those who have a history of poor control (estimated by glycohemoglobin values) manifest a variety of subtle information-processing deficits.

Exactly *how* poor control would produce neuropsychological dysfunction remains poorly understood. Perlmuter *et al.* (1984) have suggested that some, yet unknown, cerebral metabolic derangement may play a role or, alternately, microvascular disease may be somehow responsible. At least one study of cerebral blood flow has demonstrated that the reactivity of cerebral blood vessels is altered in diabetic patients (Dandona, James, Newbury, Woollard, & Beckett, 1978). Specifically, when diabetic and non-diabetic control subjects were challenged with a 5% CO_2 inhalation, 86% of the control subjects showed increased cerebral blood flow, but only 39% of the diabetic subjects showed a similar increase. That is, when the metabolic requirements of the brain are increased, the diabetic patients are less able to respond effectively. Dandona and associates attribute these changes to some type of neurohumoral dysregulation and suggest that they are unique to diabetic patients. It is unfortunate that these investigators did not evaluate the neuropsychological status of their subjects and correlate decrements in performance with changes in cerebrovascular reactivity.

INSULINOMA

Epidemiology and Etiology

An insulinoma, or nesidioblastoma, is a small insulin-secreting tumor of the beta (islet) cells of the pancreas. Although there is no accurate estimate of its incidence or prevalence, insulinoma is generally considered to be a rare endocrine disorder. For example, during a 30-year period, only 39 cases of insulinoma were found in the records of 16 Seattle hospitals (Glickman, Hart, & White, 1980). It is most frequently diagnosed in individuals who are 40 to 60 years old, though it may occur at any age. Men and women are affected equally. To date, few risk factors have been identified. Approximately 25% to 30% of patients with this disorder have a family history of diabetes. Individuals with a preexisting endocrinopathy (e.g., tumors in the pituitary, parathyroid, or adrenal gland) are also more likely to have an insulinoma (Freinkel, 1979).

Pathology and Clinical Presentation

Functioning beta cell tumors are usually encapsulated adenomas that range in size from 0.14 to 15 cm in diameter, though most are 0.5 to 3 cm. Less than 10% are metastatic; the vast majority are firm, highly vascularized, solitary tumors that are not limited to a single region of the pancreas but are as likely to be found in the head or body as in the tail (Fajans & Thorn, 1970). The treatment of choice is surgical enucleation of the tumor or partial pancreatectomy; 90% of the patients so treated are reported to be cured (Shatney & Grage, 1974).

By definition, the insulinoma autonomously secretes an excessive amount of insulin that will lead to a hypoglycemic state during fasting or exercise. In most cases, the blood sugar level drops slowly over several hours. As a consequence, the signs of hypoglycemia are most likely to be seen only in the morning before breakfast or late in the afternoon or evening when a meal has been delayed, or following vigorous physical exercise. The resulting symptoms are most likely to appear when blood glucose levels fall below 40 mg/dl. During an "episode," patients find themselves becoming increasingly fatigued, report headaches, and may experience blurred or double vision. If glucose is not made available, more serious neuropsychiatric disturbances will appear, including slurred speech, paresthesias, mental confusion, hallucinations, and strange or psychotic behavior. Ultimately, coma may result. The traits known as "Whipple's triad" continue to be the best criteria for making an accurate clinical diagnosis: (a) the appearance of symptoms of hypoglycemia after an overnight or prolonged fast; (b) neurobehavioral symptoms that are associated with a blood glucose value of 40 mg/dl or lower; and (c) the immediate relief of symptoms following oral or intravenous glucose administration.

Neuropsychiatric Disturbances

Perhaps the most intriguing aspect of insulinoma is that patients with this disorder most often present with a series of neuropsychiatric symptoms in the absence of other signs of physical disease (e.g., gastric pain). As a consequence, they are frequently misdiagnosed as having a neurological disorder like epilepsy or a purely "functional" psychiatric disorder (Breidahl, Priestly, & Rynearson, 1955). For example, of the 13 cases of beta cell tumors diagnosed at Vanderbilt-affiliated hospitals over a 20-year period, one young patient had been incarcerated, and an additional 6 (46%) had sought psychiatric consultation or treatment for a variety of "nervous conditions" that were, in retrospect, secondary to their insulinoma (Clarke, Crofford, Graves, & Scott, 1972).

Although the specific constellation of symptoms seems to be relatively constant within a patient from one attack to another, there is much variability between patients. The appearance of various symptoms is affected by a number of factors and is known to depend more on the *rate* of blood glucose decline, rather than on the *absolute value*. Symptomatology is also related to age. Infants are most likely to show convulsive seizures, whereas adolescents with an insulinoma are more likely to have school behavior problems. The most common manifestation in adults is some type of neuropsychiatric problem—most often mental confusion or psychotic behavior, whereas elderly patients frequently show focal neurologic signs that are similar to those seen after a stroke (Steinke, 1971). Occasionally, adults will show a predominantly or entirely motor peripheral neuropathy that affects the upper limbs (Jaspan, Wollman, Bernstein, & Rubenstein, 1982).

Retrospective studies of the natural history of insulinoma suggest that in the early stages of the disease, hypoglycemic attacks occur only rarely. Over time, however, as the tumor grows, these attacks become more frequent and patients often learn to avert such episodes by eating every 3 to 4 hrs. Not only may this behavior result in a weight gain of 50 to 100 lb, it may also delay diagnosis for several years because patients may interpret this as being a trivial problem that they can control or a normal part of growing older. Crain and Thorn (1949) have reported that 25% of the patients they reviewed had had symptoms of hypoglycemia for more than 5 years prior to surgery.

A large number of excellent case reports have been published (Best, Chisholm, & Alford, 1978; Clarke *et al.*, 1972; Illangasekera, 1981; Sparagana & Rubnitz, 1972). The following case, described by Camperlengo (1961) illustrates the classic pattern of neuropsychiatric symptoms and the typical course of an insulinoma.

> *Examination.* On December 6, 1959, a 47-year-old female was brought to the emergency room for "nervous spells." After an examination by a busy house officer, the impression obtained was "schizophrenia, catatonic type," and the psychiatry resident was summoned. . . . The patient had a motor-type aphasia but showed comprehension of spoken commands. . . . Nystagmus was present in all directions. There was a bilateral facial paresis, flaccid quadraparesis, bilateral extensor plantar reflexes, and generalized hyperreflexia as well as sustained clonus in both lower extremities.
>
> *Past History.*She had complained of intermittent episodes of diplopia for 2 years prior to admission. However, it was not until 6 months prior to admission that the following signs and symptoms were noted: a personality change marked by irritability, "moodiness," and sometimes inappropriate behavior. In the mornings especially, the patient was noted to stagger "like a drunk." On one occasion, she began barking at the family cat, pursued it outdoors in a doglike fashion, and chased it up a tree. When confronted with the unseemliness of her behavior, the patient would often smile incongruously and repeat, "There is nothing wrong with me." Her first major "attack" came on 5 months prior to admission. Several hours after an early start and no breakfast, the patient began to roll and writhe from side to side. Mental clouding was noted, and motor

activity decreased progressively to the point where the patient was in a rigid posture. These symptoms were entirely dissipated in 20 min to a half hour after a voraciously eaten meal, during which it was noted that the patient could not manipulate her fork because her hands were "rigid and clasped." (pp. 3327–3328)

In an analysis of their own cases as well as the literature, Daggett and Nabarro (1984) found the most frequently observed symptoms were confusion (69% of cases), coma (37% of cases), and convulsions (26% of cases). In contrast, paralyses, dizziness, and dysarthria tended to be rather uncommon, as were other speech disorders.

To my knowledge, there have been no studies in which patients with insulinoma have been evaluated with formal neuropsychological tests. We might, however, expect these patients to show information-processing deficits on various attentional, sensorimotor, and verbal fluency tests because those processes are most often disrupted in the hypoglycemic state. In a series of elegant studies, Holmes and her collaborators artificially maintained the blood glucose levels of diabetic patients at a hypoglycemic (55–60 mg/dl), a euglycemic (110 mg/dl), or a hyperglycemic level (300 mg/dl) and found a significant decrement in performance associated with hypoglycemia. This appeared when subjects were required to perform simple mental arithmetic (Holmes et al., 1983), generate words beginning with particular letters of the alphabet (Holmes, Koepke, Thompson, Gyves, & Weydert, 1984), or rapidly respond in a go–no-go or a choice reaction time paradigm (Holmes, Mann Koepke, & Thompson, 1986). Using a very different experimental procedure, Russell and Rix-Trott (1975) found a similar reduction in motor coordination, immediate memory, and mental problem-solving speed. On the basis of results from studies of diabetic patients who have had multiple episodes of serious hypoglycemia, we might also predict that insulinoma patients would have difficulty on memory tests (Bale, 1973) and on a wide range of complex cognitive tasks (Ryan et al., 1985). Until the neuropsychological status of insulinoma patients is assessed in a systematic manner, however, these predictions must be considered to be purely speculative.

It is generally assumed that, once the insulinoma is removed, the patient's hypoglycemic disorder is cured and mental status returns to normal. Unfortunately, this belief is not entirely supported by results from several surgical follow-up studies. In what may be the largest study to date, Galbut and Markowitz (1980) found that 28% of the patients who were followed up for more than 6 months postsurgery showed evidence of significant neuropsychiatric disorders. The most common disturbances included "emotional problems" requiring long-term psychotherapy, "erratic behavior, manic-depression, and paranoid psychosis." Although Galbut and Markowitz wish to attribute these disturbances to the patients' long history of serious hypoglycemia, other interpretations are possible. An extensive literature has indicated that surgical patients—particularly middle aged or elderly patients— have an increased risk of manifesting neuropsychiatric problems and that this risk appears to be secondary to certain intra- and postsurgical variables, rather than to the disease process that has motivated the surgery (Kupfer, Detre, Swigart, & Southwick, 1971; Titchener *et al.*, 1956).

NEUROPSYCHOLOGICAL DISTURBANCES AND PANCREATIC DISEASE: SOME FINAL THOUGHTS

We began this review with three questions. Do different pancreatic diseases produce characteristic neurobehavioral disturbances? Are these disturbances secondary to CNS dysfunction, or are they primarily psychogenic? What disease-related variables underlie the development of these disturbances? It should be clear from our survey of the literature that we do not yet have completely satisfactory answers to any of these questions. To a very large extent, this situation reflects the absence of large-scale studies having a major neuropsychological component. Of the four pancreatic disorders we have discussed, only diabetes mellitus has been investigated systematically by neuropsychologists, and virtually all of that research has been carried out since 1980. Our knowledge of the neurobehavioral aspects of pancreatic carcinoma, pancreatitis, and insulinoma has come almost exclusively from clinical observations that focused on only the most obvious neurobehavioral changes. Subtle information-processing deficits would have been missed in most of the studies.

Nevertheless, there are a number of tentative generalizations that emerge from the available literature.

First, each pancreatic disorder has associated with it a somewhat different constellation of neurobehavioral or neuropsychiatric signs and symptoms. Carcinoma is associated with an affective disorder that closely resembles an involutional depression. Pancreatitis is associated with an acute confusional state that is accompanied by ocular, vestibular, and cerebellar signs. Diabetes is associated with several different patterns of neurobehavioral disturbances, the exact picture being determined by certain disease-related variables (e.g., past history of hypoglycemia, recent history of metabolic control). Insulinoma is associated with mental confusion and erratic behavior as well as by neurological disturbances like diplopia or paresthesias.

Second, though patients with pancreatic disorders often manifest emotional disorders that may be secondary to pain or to the realization that they have a terminal or serious chronic disease, it is not possible to attribute their neurobehavioral disturbances simply to their emotional distress. Neurologic, neuroradiologic, and electrophysiologic studies have provided evidence of CNS dysfunction in cases of pancreatitis, insulinoma, and diabetes. There is no doubt that the depressive disorder found in patients with pancreatic carcinoma is also a consequence of some type of CNS disturbance, though sophisticated neurohumoral studies may be needed to delineate the connection between depression and brain dysfunction in those patients.

Third, the actual biochemical link between pancreatic disease and CNS

dysfunction remains incompletely understood. It is likely that fat embolization or various pancreatic enzymes have triggered the CNS disturbances seen
in patients with acute pancreatitis. Similarly, hypoglycemia-induced hypoxic processes are probably responsible for the neuropsychiatric changes
found in the patient with insulinoma. The cognitive disturbances seen in
children or adolescents who became diabetic at a very young age are also
most likely a consequence of the effects of serious hypoglycemia. On the
other hand, how *hyper*glycemia in adults might produce subtle information-
processing deficits is unknown. Also unknown is the mechanism by which
pancreatic carcinoma initiates the affective changes that are characteristic of
that disease.

Fourth, having said all of these things, it is also very apparent that the
incidence of serious neuropsychological disturbance is quite low for *any* type
of pancreatic disorder except insulinoma. Relatively few diabetic children or
adults show clinically significant impairments, and most clinicians would
agree that both the depressive disorder associated with pancreatic carcinoma
and the encephalopathy associated with pancreatitis are rarely seen.

Why is it that only certain individuals with pancreatitis (or diabetes, or
carcinoma) develop neurobehavioral problems? Are there specific medical
treatment strategies that can prevent the occurrence of these neuropsychiatric disturbances? Does the neuropsychological status of patients successfully treated for pancreatitis or insulinoma revert to normal following treatment, or do subtle neurobehavioral sequalae persist for years after? Efforts to
answer these and similar questions should guide future research on the
relationship between pancreatic disorders and neuropsychological dysfunction.

ACKNOWLEDGMENTS

The preparation of this manuscript was supported in part by Grant AM
26069 from the National Institute of Arthritis, Diabetes, and Digestive and
Kidney Disease.

REFERENCES

Ack, M., Miller, I., & Weil, W. B. (1961). Intelligence of children with diabetes mellitus. *Pedi-
atrics, 28,* 764–770.
Arbitman, R. (1972). Psychiatric manifestations of carcinoma of the pancreas. *Psychosomatics,
13,* 269–271.
Bale, R. N. (1973). Brain damage in diabetes mellitus. *British Journal of Psychiatry, 122,* 22–39.
Barnett, A. H., Eff, C., Leslie, R. D. G., & Pyke, D. A. (1981). Diabetes in identical twins: A study
of 200 pairs. *Diabetologia, 20,* 87–93.
Benos, J. (1973). Encephalopathia pancreatica: Zwei weitere Fälle korperlich begründbarer
Psychosen bei akuter und chronish rezidivierender Pankreatitis. *Münchener medizinische
Wochenschrift, 115,* 1842–1844.
Benos, J. (1974). Funktionspsychosen und neurologische Ausfälle bei Pankreatitis. *Medizinishe
Klinik, 69,* 1185–1192.

Benos, J. (1976). Neuropsychiatrische Storüngen bei Erkrankungen des exokrinen Pankreas. *Fortschritte der Neurologie Psychiatie, 44*, 683–701.

Best, J. D., Chisholm, D. J., & Alford, F. P. (1978). Insulinoma: Poor recognition of clinical features is the major problem in diagnosis. *Medical Journal of Australia, 2*, 1–5.

Breidahl, H. D., Priestley, J. T., & Rynearson, E. H. (1955). Hyperinsulinism: Surgical aspects and results. *Annals of Surgery, 142*, 698–708.

Brooks, F. P. (1979). Diseases of the pancreas. In P. B. Beeson, W. McDermott, & J. B. Wyngaarden (Eds.), *Cecil textbook of medicine: Vol. 2* (15th ed., pp. 1550–1560). Philadelphia: W. B. Saunders.

Brown, G. W. (1938). The development of diabetic children, with special reference to mental and personality comparisons. *Child Development, 9*, 175–183.

Cahill, G. F., & Arky, R. A. (1983). Diabetes mellitus. In E. Rubenstein & D. D. Federman (Eds.), *Medicine* (pp. 1–21). New York: Scientific American.

Cahill, G. F., & McDevitt, H. O. (1981). Insulin-dependent diabetes mellitus: The initial lesion. *New England Journal of Medicine, 304*, 1454–1465.

Camperlengo, H. A. (1961). Pancreatic islet cell adenoma presenting as neuropsychiatric problems. *New York Journal of Medicine, 61*, 3327–3331.

Cancer Statistics. (1986). *CA: A Cancer Journal for Clinicians, 36*, 9–25.

Carter Center. (1985). Closing the gap: The problem of diabetes mellitus in the United States. *Diabetes Care, 8*, 391–406.

Clarke, M., Crofford, O. B., Graves, H. A., & Scott, H. W. (1972). Functioning beta cell tumors (insulinomas) of the pancreas. *Annals of Surgery, 175*, 956–974.

Craighead, J. E. (1978). Current views on the etiology of insulin-dependent diabetes mellitus. *New England Journal of Medicine, 299*, 1439–1445.

Crain, E. L., & Thorn, G. W. (1949). Functioning pancreatic islet cell adenomas: A review of the literature and presentation of two new differential tests. *Medicine, 28*, 427–446.

Daggett, P., & Nabarro, J. (1984). Neurological aspects of insulinomas. *Postgraduate Medical Journal, 60*, 577–581.

Dandona, P., James, I. M., Newbury, P. A., Woollard, M. L., & Beckett, A. G. (1978). Cerebral blood flow in diabetes mellitus: Evidence of abnormal cerebrovascular reactivity. *British Medical Journal, 2*, 325–326.

Daneman, D., Wolfson, D. H., Becker, D. J., & Drash, A. (1981). Factors affecting glycosylated hemoglobin values in children with insulin-dependent diabetes. *Journal of Pediatrics, 99*, 847–853.

Dashiell, J. F. (1930). Variations in psycho-motor efficiency in a diabetic with changes in blood-sugar level. *Journal of Comparative Psychology, 10*, 189–197.

Delbridge, L. (1975). Educational and psychological factors in the management of diabetes in childhood. *Medical Journal of Australia, 2*, 737–739.

Dikmen, S., Matthews, C. G., & Harley, J. P. (1975). The effect of early versus late onset of major motor epilepsy upon cognitive-intellectual performance. *Epilepsia, 16*, 73–81.

Drash, A. L., & Becker, D. (1978). Diabetes mellitus in the child: Course, special problems, and related disorders. In H. M. Katzen & R. J. Mahler (Eds.), *Diabetes, obesity, and vascular disease: Metabolic and molecular interrelationships* (pp. 615–643). New York: Wiley.

Dunn, S. M., & Turtle, J. R. (1981). The myth of the diabetic personality. *Diabetes Care, 4*, 640–646.

Dumphy, J. E. (1940). Early diagnosis of cancer of the pancreas. *American Journal of Digestive Diseases, 7*, 69–70.

Eeg-Olofsson, O. (1977). Hypoglycemia and neurological disturbances in children with diabetes mellitus. *Acta Paediatrica Scandinavica* (Suppl. 270), 91–95.

Eeg-Olofsson, O., & Petersen, I. (1966). Childhood diabetic neuropathy: A clinical and neurophysiological study. *Acta Paediatrica Scandinavica, 55*, 163–176.

Ernhart, C. B., Graham, F. K., Eichman, P. L., Marshall, J. M., & Thurston, D. (1963). Brain injury in the preschool child: Some developmental considerations: II. Comparisons of brain injured and normal children. *Psychological Monographs: General and Applied, 77*, 17–33.

Estrada, R. V., Moreno, J., Martinez, E., Hernandez, M. C. Gilsanz, G., & Gilsanz, V. (1979). Pancreatic encephalopathy. *Acta Neurologica Scandinavica, 59*, 135–139.

Fajans, S. S., & Thorn, G. W. (1970). Hyperinsulinism, hypoglycemia, and glucagon secretion. In M. M. Wintrobe, G. W. Thorn, R. D. Adams, I. L. Bennett, E. Braunwald, K. J. Isselbacher, & R. G. Petersdorf (Eds.), *Harrison's principles of internal medicine* (6th ed., pp. 542–549). New York: McGraw-Hill.

Fällström, K. (1974). On the personality structure of diabetic children aged 7–15 years. *Acta Paediatrica Scandinavica* (Suppl. 251), 1–70.

Fitzgerald, P. J. (1980). Medical anecdotes concerning some diseases of the pancreas. In P. J. Fitzgerald & A. B. Morrison (Eds.), *The Pancreas* (pp. 1–29). Baltimore: Williams & Wilkins.

Franceschi, M., Cecchetto, R., Minicucci, F., Smizne, S., Baio, G., & Canal, N. (1984). Cognitive processes in insulin-dependent diabetes. *Diabetes Care, 7*, 228–231.

Fras, I., Litin, E. M., & Pearson, J. S. (1967). Comparison of psychiatric symptoms in carcinoma of the pancreas with those in some other intra-abdominal neoplasms. *American Journal of Psychiatry, 123*, 1553–1562.

Fras, I., Litin, E. M., & Bartholomew, L. G. (1968). Mental symptoms as an aid in the early diagnosis of carcinoma of the pancreas. *Gastroenterology, 55*, 191–198.

Freinkel, N. (1979). Hypoglycemic disorders. In P. B. Beeson, W. McDermott, & J. B. Wyngaarden (Eds.), *Cecil textbook of medicine: Vol. 2* (15th ed., pp. 1989–1995). Philadelphia: W. B. Saunders.

Galbut, D. L., & Markowitz, A. M. (1980). Insulinoma: Diagnosis, surgical management, and long-term follow-up. *American Journal of Surgery, 139*, 682–690.

Gilhaus, K. H., Daweke, H., Lülsdorf, H. G., Sachsse, R., & Sachsse, B. (1973). EEG-Veränderungen bei diabetischen Kindern. *Deutsche Medizinische Wochenschrift, 98*, 1449–1454.

Glickman, M. H., Hart, M. J., & White, T. T. (1980). Insulinoma in Seattle: 39 cases in 30 years. *American Journal of Surgery, 140*, 119–123.

Gray, G. M. (1983). Diseases of the pancreas. In E. Rubenstein & D. D. Federman (Eds.), *Medicine* (pp. 1–10). New York: Scientific American.

Greenberger, N. J., & Toskes, P. P. (1983). Approach to the patient with pancreatic disease. In R. G. Petersdorf, R. D. Adams, E. Braunwald, D. J. Isselebacher, J. B. Martin, & J. D. Wilson (Eds.), *Harrison's principles of internal medicine* (10th ed., pp. 1832–1836). New York: McGraw-Hill.

Greenberger, N. J., Toskes, P. P., & Isselbacher, K. J. (1983). Diseases of the pancreas. In R. G. Petersdorf, R. D. Adams, E. Braunwald, D. J. Isselebacher, J. B. Martin, & J. D. Wilson (Eds.), *Harrison's principles of internal medicine* (10th ed., pp. 1836–1848). New York, McGraw-Hill.

Grey, M. J., Genel, M., & Tamborlane, W. V. (1980). Psychosocial adjustment of latency-aged diabetics: determinants and relationship to control. *Pediatrics, 65*, 69–73.

Greydanus, D. E., & Hofmann, A. D. (1979). Psychological factors in diabetes mellitus: A review of the literature with emphasis on adolescence. *American Journal of Disease in Childhood, 133*, 1061–1066.

Grishaw, W. H., West, H. F., & Smith, B. (1939). Juvenile diabetes mellitus. *Archives of Internal Medicine, 64*, 787–799.

Haumont, D., Dorchy, H., & Pelc, S. (1979). EEG abnormalities in diabetic children: Influence of hypoglycemia and vascular complications. *Clinical Pediatrics, 18*, 750–753.

Hauser, S. T., & Pollets, D. (1979). Psychological aspects of diabetes mellitus: A critical review. *Diabetes Care, 2*, 227–232.

Hauser, S. T., Jacobson, A. M., Noam, G., & Powers, S. (1983). Ego development and self-image complexity in early adolescence: Longitudinal studies of psychiatric and diabetic patients. *Archives of General Psychiatry, 40*, 325–332.

Hiltmann, H., & Lüking, J. (1966). Die Intelligenz bei diabetischen Kindern im Schulalter. *Acta Paedopsychiatrica, 33*, 11–24.

Hirabayashi, S., Kitahara, T., & Hishida, T. (1980). Computed tomography in perinatal hypoxic and hypoglycemic encephalopathy with emphasis on follow-up studies. *Journal of Computer Assisted Tomography, 4*, 451–456.

Holmes, C. S. (1986). Neuropsychological profiles in men with insulin-dependent diabetes. *Journal of Consulting and Clinical Psychology, 54,* 386–389.

Holmes, C. S., Hayford, J. T., Gonzalez, J. L., & Weydert, J. A. (1983). A survey of cognitive functioning at different glucose levels in diabetic persons. *Diabetes Care, 6,* 180–185.

Holmes, C. S., Koepke, K. M., Thompson, R. G., Gyves, P. W., & Weydert, J. A. (1984). Verbal fluency and naming performance in Type I diabetes at different blood glucose concentrations. *Diabetes Care, 7,* 454–459.

Holmes, C. S., Mann Koepke, K., & Thompson, R. G. (1986). Simple versus complex performance impairments at three blood glucose levels. *Psychoneuroendocrinolgy, 11,* 353–357.

Illangasekera, V. L. U. (1981). Insulinoma masquerading as carotid transient ischemic attacks. *Postgraduate Medical Journal, 57,* 232–234.

Ingram, T. T. S., Stark, G. D., & Blackburn, I. (1967). Ataxia and other neurological disorders as sequels of severe hypoglycemia in childhood. *Brain, 90,* 851–862.

Jackson, R. L., Ide, C. H., Guthrie, R. A., & James, R. D. (1982). Retinopathy in adolescents and young adults with onset of insulin-dependent diabetes in childhood. *Ophthalmology, 89,* 7–13.

Jacobsson, L., & Ottosson, J-O. (1971). Initial mental disorders in carcinoma of pancreas and stomach. *Acta Psychiatrica Scandinavica* (Suppl. 221), 120–127.

Jaspan, J. B., Wollman, R. L., Bernstein, L., & Rubenstein, A. H. (1982). Hypoglycemic peripheral neuropathy in association with insulinoma: Implication of glucopenia rather than hyperinsulinism. *Medicine, 61,* 33–44.

Johnson, D. A., & Tong, N. T. (1977). Pancreatic encephalopathy. *Southern Medical Journal, 70,* 165–167.

Johnson, S. B. (1980). Psychosocial factors in juvenile diabetes: A review. *Journal of Behavioral Medicine, 3,* 95–116.

Joslin, E. P., Root, H. F., White, P., & Marble, A. (1940). *Treatment of Diabetes Mellitus* (7th ed.). Philadelphia: Lea & Febiger.

Kant, O. (1946). A deceptive psychoneurosis. *Psychiatric Quarterly 20,* 129–134.

Keynes, W. M., & Keith, R. G. (1981) *The Pancreas.* London: William Heinemann.

Kimball, C. H. (1971). Emotional and psychosocial aspects of diabetes mellitus. *Medical Clinics of North America, 55,* 1007–1018.

Kovacs, M., Fineberg, T. L., Paulauskas, S., Finkelstein, R., Pollock, M., & Crouse-Novak, M. (1985). Initial coping responses and psychosocial characteristics of children with insulin-dependent diabetes mellitus. *Journal of Pediatrics, 106,* 827–834.

Kubany, A. J., Danowski, T. S., & Moses, C. (1956). The personality and intelligence of diabetics. *Diabetes, 5,* 462–467.

Kupfer, D. J., Detre, T. P., Swigar, M. E., & Southwick, W. O. (1971). Adjustment of patients after hip surgery. *Journal of the American Geriatrics Society, 19,* 709–720.

LaPorte, R. E., Fishbein, H. A., Drash, A. L., Kuller, L. H., Schneider, B. B., Orchard, T. J., & Wagener, D. K. (1981). The Pittsburgh insulin-dependent diabetes mellitus registry: The incidence of insulin-dependent diabetes mellitus in Allegheny county, Pennsylvania (1965–1976). *Diabetes, 30,* 279–284.

Lastchevker, V. (1965). Les troubles mentaux au cours de la pancreatite aigue. *Z. Nevropat. Psickiat. Korsakow, 65,* 434 [Russian with French summary].

Latter, K. A., & Wilbur, D. L. (1937). Psychic and neurologic manifestations of carcinoma of the pancreas. *Proceedings of the Mayo Clinic, 12,* 457–463.

Lawson, J. S., Williams Erdahl, D. L., Monga, T. N., Bird, C. E., Donald, M. W., Surridge, D. H. C., & Letemendia, F. J. J. (1984). Neuropsychological function in diabetic patients with neuropathy. *British Journal of Psychiatry, 145,* 263–268.

Lawton, M. P., & Phillips, R. W. (1955). Psychopathological accompaniments of chronic relapsing pancreatitis. *Journal of Nervous and Mental Disease, 122,* 248–253.

LeShan, L. (1959). Psychological states as factors in the development of malignant disease: A critical review. *Journal of the National Cancer Institute, 22,* 1–18.

Levine, P. M., Silberfarb, P. M., & Lipowski, Z. J. (1978). Mental disorders in cancer patients: A study of 100 psychiatric referals. *Cancer 42,* 1385–1391.

Lichty, W. & Klachko, D. (1985). Memory in Type 1 diabetics [abstract]. *Diabetes, 34* (Suppl. 1). 19.

Lin, R. S., & Kessler, I. I. (1981). A multifactorial model for pancreatic cancer in man. *Journal of the American Medical Association, 245,* 147–152.

Lipowski, Z. J. (1975). Psychiatry of somatic diseases: Epidemiology, pathogenesis, classification. *Comprehensive Psychiatry, 16,* 105–124.

Lishman, W. A. (1978). *Organic psychiatry.* Oxford: Blackwell Scientific Publications.

MacMahon, B., Yen, S., Trichopoulos, D., Warren, K., & Nardi, G. (1981). Coffee and cancer of the pancreas. *New England Journal of Medicine, 304,* 630–633.

Maddison, D., & Raphael, B. (1971). Social and psychological consequences of chronic disease in childhood. *Medical Journal of Australia, 2,* 1265–1270.

McCraw, R. K., & Tuma, J. M. (1977). Rorschach content categories in juvenile diabetics. *Psychological Reports, 40,* 818.

McGavin, A. P., Schultz, E., Peden, G. W., & Bowen, B. D. (1940). The physical growth, the degree of intelligence, and the personality adjustment of a group of diabetic children. *New England Journal of Medicine, 223,* 119–127.

McGlone, J. (1980). Sex differences in human brain asymmetry: A critical survey. *Behavioral and Brain Sciences, 3,* 215–227.

Meuter, F., Thomas, W., Gruneklee, D., Gries, F. A., & Lohmann, R. (1980). Psychometric evaluation of performance in diabetes mellitus. *Hormone and Metabolic Research* (Suppl. 9), 9–17.

Moertel, C. S. (1969). Natural history of gastrointestinal cancer. In C. G. Moertel & R. J. Reitemeier (Eds.), *Advanced gastrointestinal cancer: Clinical management and chemotherapy* (pp. 1–14). New York: Harper & Row.

O'Leary, D. S., Lovell, M. R., Sackellares, J. C., Berent, S., Giordani, B., Seidenberg, M., & Boll, T. J. (1983). Effects of age of onset of partial and generalized seizures on neuropsychological performance in children. *Journal of Nervous and Mental Disease, 171,* 624–629.

Pelner, L. (1947). Carcinoma of the pancreas—A disease that may closely mimic a psychosomatic illness. *Gastroenterology, 8,* 92–94.

Perlas, A. P., & Faillace, L. A. (1964). Psychiatric manifestations of carcinoma of the pancreas. *American Journal of Psychiatry, 121,* 182.

Perlmuter, L. C., Hakami, M. K., Hodgson-Harrington, C., Ginsberg, J., Katz, J., Singer, D. E., & Nathan, D. M. (1984). Decreased cognitive function in aging non-insulin-dependent diabetic patients. *American Journal of Medicine, 77,* 1043–1048.

Pirart, J. (1978). Diabetes mellitus and its degenerative complications: A prospective study of 4,400 patients observed between 1947 and 1973. *Diabetes Care, 1,* 252–263.

Plumb, M. M., & Holland, J. (1977). Comparative studies of psychological function in patients with advanced cancer: I. Self-reported depressive symptoms. *Psychosomatic Medicine, 39,* 264–276.

Pohl, S. L., Gonder-Frederick, L., & Cox, D. J. (1984). Area review: Diabetes mellitus. *Behavioral Medicine Update, 6,* 3–7.

Pomara, N., & Gershon, S. (1984). Treatment-resistant depression in an elderly patient with pancreatic carcinoma: Case report. *Journal of Clinical Psychiatry, 45,* 439–440.

Ranson, J. H. C., Roses, D. G., & Fink, S. D. (1973). Early respiratory insufficiency in acute pancreatitis. *Annals of Surgery, 178,* 75–79.

Raskin, P., Pietri, A. O., Unger, R., & Shannon, W. A. (1983). The effect of diabetic control on the width of skeletal-muscle capillary basement membrane in patients with Type I diabetes mellitus. *New England Journal of Medicine, 309,* 1546–1550.

Reichlin, S. (1983). Somatostatin. *New England Journal of Medicine, 309,* 1495–1501, 1556–1563.

Rennick, P. M., Wilder, R. M., Sargent, J., & Ashley, B. J. (1968). Retinopathy as an indicator of cognitive-perceptual-motor impairment in diabetic adults [Summary]. *Proceedings of the 76th Annual Convention of the American Psychological Association, 3,* 473–474.

Reske-Nielsen, E., Lundbaek, K., & Rafaelsen, O. J. (1965). Pathological changes in the central and peripheral nervous system of young long-term diabetics. *Diabetologia, 1,* 232–241.

Rickles, N. K. (1948). Functional symptoms as first evidence of pancreatic disease. *Journal of Nervous and Mental Disease, 101,* 566–571.

Rothermich, N. O., & von Haam, E. (1941). Pancreatic encephalopathy. *Journal of Clinical Endocrinology, 1,* 872–881.

Rovet, J. F., Ehrlich, R. M., & Hoppe, M. G. (1987). Specific intellectual deficits associated with the early onset of insulin-dependent diabetes mellitus in children. *Diabetes Care, 10,* 510–515.

Russell, P. N., & Rix-Trott, H. M. (1975). An exploratory study of some behavioural consequences of insulin-induced hypoglycaemia. *New Zealand Medical Journal, 81,* 337–340.

Ryan, C., Vega, A., & Drash, A. (1985). Cognitive deficits in adolescents who developed diabetes early in life. *Pediatrics, 75,* 921–927.

Salmon, P. A. (1967). The significance of psychic symptoms in the early diagnosis of carcinoma of the pancreas. *Canadian Medical Association Journal, 97,* 767–772.

Santiago, J. V. (1984). Effect of treatment on the long term complications of IDDM. *Behavioral Medicine Update, 6,* 26–31.

Savage, C., Butcher, W., & Noble, D. (1952). Psychiatric manifestations in pancreatic disease. *Journal of Clinical and Experimental Psychopathology, 13,* 9–16.

Savage, C., Noble, D. (1954). Cancer of the pancreas: Two cases simulating psychogenic illness. *Journal of Nervous and Mental Disease, 120,* 62–65.

Schuster, M. M., & Iber, F. L. (1965). Psychosis with pancreatitis: A frequent occurrence infrequently recognized. *Archives of Internal Medicine, 116,* 228–233.

Sharafeev, A. G. (1961). General cerebral disorders in acute pancreatitis. *Klin. Med.* (Moscow), *39,* 86 [Russian with English summary].

Sharf, B., & Levy, L. (1976). Pancreatic encephalopathy. In P. J. Vinken & G. W. Bruyn (Eds.), *Handbook of clinical neurology: Metabolic and deficiency diseases of the central nervous system,* (Vol. 27, Pt. I, pp. 449–458). Amsterdam: North-Holland.

Shatney, C. H., & Grage, T. B. (1974). Diagnostic and surgical aspects of insulinoma: A review of twenty-seven cases. *American Journal of Surgery, 127,* 174–184.

Simonds, J. F. (1977). Psychiatric status of diabetic youth matched with a control group. *Diabetes, 26,* 921–925.

Shirley, H. F., & Greer, I. M. (1940). Environmental and personality problems in the treatment of diabetic children. *Journal of Pediatrics, 16,* 775–781.

Skenazy, J. A., & Bigler, E. D. (1984). Neuropsychological findings in diabetes mellitus. *Journal of Clinical Psychology, 40,* 246–258.

Sparagana, M., & Rubnitz, M. E. (1972). Hypoglycemia presenting with neuropsychiatric symptoms. *Postgraduate Medicine, XX,* 192–196.

Steinhauser, H., Borner, S., & Koepp, P. (1977). The personality of juvenile diabetics. In Z. Laron, (Ed.), *Pediatric and adolescent endocrinology,* (Vol. 3, pp. 1–7).

Steinke, J. (1971). Hypoglycemia. In A. Marble (Ed.), *Joslin's diabetes mellitus* (11th ed., (pp. 797–817). Philadelphia: Lea & Febiger.

Sterky, G. (1963). Family background and state of mental health in a group of diabetic schoolchildren. *Acta Paediatrica, 52,* 377–390.

Stewart-Brown, S., Haslum, M., & Butler, N. (1983). Evidence for increasing prevalence of diabetes mellitus in childhood. *British Medical Journal, 286,* 1855–1857.

Sullivan, B. J. (1978). Self-esteem and depression in adolescent diabetic girls. *Diabetes Care, 1,* 18–22.

Swift, C. R., Seidman, F., & Stein, H. (1967). Adjustment problems in juvenile diabetes. *Psychosomatic Medicine, 29,* 555–571.

Tattersall, R. B. (1981). Psychiatric aspects of diabetes: A physician's view. *British Journal of Psychiatry, 139,* 485–493.

Tavormina, J. B., Kastner, L. S., Slater, P. M., & Watt, S. L. (1976). Chronically ill children: A psychologically and emotionally deviant population. *Journal of Abnormal Child Psychology, 4,* 99–110.

Taylor, D. C., & Ounstead, C. (1972). The nature of gender differences explored through ontogenetic analysis of sex ratios in disease. In C. Ounstead & D. C. Taylor (Eds.), *Gender*

Differences: Their ontogeny and significance (pp. 215–240). Edinburgh: Churchill Livingstone.

Teagarden, F. M. (1939). The intelligence of diabetic children with some case reports. *Journal of Applied Psychology, 23,* 337–346.

Ternand, C., Go, V. L. W., Gerich, J. E., & Haymond, M. W. (1982). Endocrine pancreatic response of children with onset of insulin-requiring diabetes before age 3 and after age 5. *Journal of Pediatrics, 101,* 36–39.

Teuber, H-L., & Rudel, R. G. (1962). Behavior after cerebral lesions in children and adults. *Developmental Medicine and Child Neurology, 4,* 3–20.

Titchener, J. L., Zwerling, I., Gottschalk, L., Levine, M., Culbertson, W., Cohen, S., & Silver, H. (1956). Psychosis in surgical patients. *Surgery, Gynecology, & Obstetrics, 102,* 59–65.

Trapnell, J. (1972). The natural history and management of acute pancreatitis. *Clinical Gastroenterology, 1,* 147–166.

Ulett, G., & Parsons, E. H. (1948). Psychiatric aspects of carcinoma of the pancreas. *Journal of the Missouri Medical Association, 45,* 490–493.

Victor, M., Adams, R. D., & Collins, G. H. (1971). *The Wernicke-Korsakoff syndrome.* Philadelphia: F. A. Davis.

Vogel, F. S. (1951a). Cerebral demyelination and focal visceral lesions in a case of acute hemorrhagic pancreatitis. *Archives of Pathology, 53,* 355–362.

Vogel, F. S. (1951b). Demyelinization induced in living rabbits by means of a lipolytic enzyme preparation. *Journal of Experimental Medicine, 93,* 297–304.

Volk, B. W., & Allen, R. A. (1985). Embryology, anatomy, histology, and anomalies of the pancreas. In J. E. Berk (Ed.), *Gastroenterology* (4th ed., pp. 3834–3843). Philadelphia: W. B. Saunders.

Yaskin, J. C. (1931). Nervous symptoms as earliest manifestations of carcinoma of the pancreas. *Journal of the American Medical Association, 96,* 1664–1668.

Young, R. J., Ewing, D. J., & Clarke, B. F. (1983). Nerve function and metabolic control in teenage diabetics. *Diabetes, 32,* 142–147.

Zeltzer, L., Kellerman, J., Ellenberg, L., Dash, J., & Rigler, D. (1980). Psychological effects of illness in adolescence. II. Impact of illness in adolescents—crucial issues and coping styles. *Journal of Pediatrics, 97,* 132–138.

7

The Pituitary Axis
Behavioral Correlates

HAROLD W. GORDON, PETER A. LEE, and LISA K. TAMRES

INTRODUCTION

Pituitary disease manifests itself with a variety of different signs and symptoms, any of which can be the impetus for the patient to seek help. Disease may come to attention because of growth retardation in youth, amenorrhea, visual disturbances, headache, other evidence of hormone deficiencies, or even emotional symptoms. Pituitary disease may be related to tumors of various types or to defects of hypothalamic stimulation. Because the pituitary is made up of different cell types, many of which are associated with the secretion of specific hormones, the types of diseases and related symptoms are dependent on how hypothalamic function is disrupted. In the case of a tumor, symptoms depend on the nature, location, and treatment of the mass.

In contrast to the more striking physical manifestations, the psychological and neuropsychological deficits associated with pituitary disease have been studied relatively little. It has yet to be determined how closely the behavioral effects are associated with the specific hormones secreted by the pituitary, with resulting derangements of other hormones, or with neurotransmitters associated with the hypothalamic-pituitary end organ function. A variety of factors, including the incompletely understood feedback mechanisms of pituitary hormones, unknown properties of hypothalamic and central nervous system hormones and peptides, and the relatively unknown neurochemical bases of cognitive behavior prevent satisfactory conclusions of brain–behavior relationships on the basis of hormone levels. Nevertheless, the observations that follow are an attempt to relate pituitary phys-

HAROLD W. GORDON • Department of Psychiatry, University of Pittsburgh School of Medicine, and Western Psychiatric Institute & Clinic, Pittsburgh, Pennsylvania 15213. PETER A. LEE • Department of Pediatrics, University of Pittsburgh School of Medicine, and Children's Hospital of Pittsburgh, Pittsburgh, Pennsylvania 15213.   LISA K. TAMRES • Department of Psychiatry, University of Pittsburgh School of Medicine, and Western Psychiatric Institute & Clinic, Pittsburgh, Pennsylvania 15213.

iology and pathophysiology to the study of the neurochemical bases of higher cortical functions.

ANATOMY OF THE PITUITARY

The pituitary or hypophysis consists of an anterior lobe and a posterior lobe. The anterior lobe (adenohypophysis) includes (see Figure 1) the pars tuberalis, pars intermedia, and pars distalis. The bulk of the hormone-secreting cells lie within the pars distalis. The three main sections of the posterior lobe (neurohypophysis) are the infundibulum, the infundibular stem, and the median eminence of the tuber cinerium. The anterior and posterior lobes have separate embryonic origins. There are direct neural tracts that connect in the posterior lobe via the infundibular stem to the hypothalamus. In contrast, the anterior lobe has no direct neural connection but is stimulated by hormones secreted by the hypothalamus into the blood stream that pass through an anastomasing vascular plexus. These hypothalamic hormones stimulate or suppress the synthesis and secretion of the anterior pituitary hormones.

Secretion of the hypothalamic hormones are, in turn, regulated by brain neurotransmitters such as dopamine, norepinephrine, serotonin, histamine, and melatonin. Hormones synthesized and secreted by the anterior pituitary

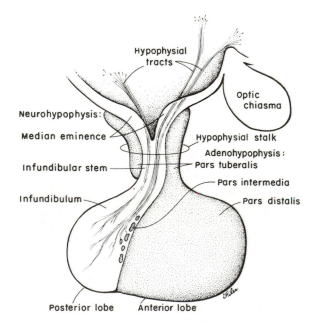

FIGURE 1. The pituitary: Sketch of the main anatomy.

are polypeptides: growth hormone (GH), thyrotropin, or thyroid-stimulating hormone (TSH), adrenocorticotrophic hormone (ACTH), prolactin and the gonadotropins, follicle-stimulating hormone (FSH), and luteinizing hormone (LH). These hormones act on target cells by stimulating adenylate cyclase activity.

Cells are currently classified according to the hormones that are within them as demonstrated by specific immunofluorescent techniques rather than by the former histochemical categorization. Each cell type tends to be clustered or localized within the same general region of the anterior pituitary.

Growth Hormone

Growth hormone (somatotropin) is a polypeptide hormone necessary for normal growth. It stimulates protein synthesis, causes breakdown of body fats (lipolysis), and is a counterregulatory hormone to insulin in carbohydrate metabolism. It causes the body to accumulate nitrogen and minerals and increases the uptake of amino acids into cells. Growth hormone synthesis and release is regulated by at least two hypothalamic hormones: growth hormone (or somatotropin) releasing factor (SRF) and somatotropin release-inhibiting factor (SRIF), or somatostatin. Growth hormone is released in a pulsatile fashion stimulated by exercise, eating, and sleep. Generally, growth hormone release occurs shortly after the onset of sleep and is greatest during the slow wave stage. Sex steroids stimulate greater growth hormone secretion. The action of growth hormone is largely via somatomedin, a hormone synthesized under growth hormone stimulation, primarily in the liver. Both growth hormone and somatomedin have a negative feedback effect upon growth hormone secretion.

Adrenocorticotropin (ACTH)

ACTH stimulates secretion of the adrenal cortical steroids. The major hormone secreted is cortisol. The ACTH molecule is derived from a much larger molecule that is also the precurser of several other peptide hormones, including melanocyte-stimulating hormone (MSH) that stimulates skin pigmentation. ACTH is secreted under the stimulation of the hypothalamic hormone, corticotropin-releasing hormone (CRH), in a diurnal or circadian pattern. The greatest amount is released at the end of the sleep cycle, usually morning, and the least amount is released at the end of the waking phase, usually late evening. Superimposed upon this pattern is ACTH released in association with physical or emotional stress.

ACTH binds to receptors of cells of the adrenal cortex, and the metabolic stimulation results in increased adrenal steroid production, especially cortisol. High levels of cortisol suppress CRH and ACTH release; lower levels of cortisol have the reverse effect.

Prolactin

Prolactin release is also pulsatile, greater with sleep and regulated by at least two hypothalamic hormones, prolactin-inhibiting factor (PIF) and prolactin-releasing factor (PRF). Prolactin is released by exogenous administration of thyrotropin-releasing hormone (TRH). The PIF has a dramatic influence on prolactin secretion; hyperprolactinemia is a common indicator of hypothalamic dysfunction. One of the functions of prolactin is to maintain lactation.

Glycopeptides: LH, FSH, and TSH

The other three hormones synthesized and secreted by the anterior pituitary are glycopeptides consisting of two polypeptide chains, one chain being identical in all three. These hormones are luteinizing hormone (LH), follicle-stimulating hormone (FSH), and thyroid-stimulating hormone (TSH).

Secretion of the gonadotropins, LH and FSH, is a result of stimulation of the hypothalamic hormone, gonadotropin-releasing hormone (GnRH or LHRH). Both LH and FSH are secreted in a episodic fashion; the episodic rise of the gonadotropin is a reflection of the release of LHRH from the hypothalamus. There is greater release of gonadotropins during sleep. At the onset of puberty, a dramatic rise of sleep-related episodic release occurs as well as a significant elevation in total secretion.

LH stimulates the gonad to produce sex steroids that in turn stimulate the physical growth and the developmental changes of puberty and subsequently maintain sexual and reproductive function in adults. In males, LH stimulates the Leydig cells to secrete testosterone. In females, theca cells or luteal cells are stimulated to secrete female sex steroids. FSH, by stimulating the Sertoli cells, causes spermatogenesis in the male. In females, granulosa cell stimulation by FSH contributes to the maturation of the ovarian follicle. Gonadotropin production is controlled by a negative feedback effect so that the greater gonadal activity the more suppression of gonadotropin release and vice versa. There is also a positive feedback mechanism that results in an acute release of gonadotropins when the gonadotropin and ovarian sex steroid levels are just right.

The release of TSH from the pituitary occurs after stimulation by thyrotropin-releasing hormone (TRH) from the hypothalamus. TSH, in turn, binds to receptors in thyroid gland cells causing increased synthesis of thyroid hormones. The thyroid hormone negative feedback is at both the pituitary and hypothalamic levels. Thyroid hormone limits the TSH release after TRH stimulation so TSH secretion is controlled by TRH secretion and circulating levels of thyroid hormone. With lower thyroid hormone levels, there is a greater TSH response to TRH. There is also a nocturnal rise of TSH secretion with the onset of sleep.

DISEASES RELATED TO THE PITUITARY

Neuropsychological manifestations of pituitary disease can range from psychiatric disorders to changes in intellectual ability. Emotional problems commonly include depression, lability, or apathy, but can also extend over the whole spectrum of mood and behavioral states. Changes in basic behaviors such as libido, sleep, and eating habits are often reported.

Intellectual capacity is the most commonly studied cognitive function, although changes in more specific functions such as memory, verbal, or visuospatial abilities also occur. It is notable that diseases associated with changes in the hormone levels of the pituitary may produce enhancement as well as decrement of specific cognitive performance. Furthermore, both long-term and short-term effects on cognitive function may be found.

The neuropsychological changes of pituitary disease may be due to hormonal abnormalities. If a tumor is involved, there may be other effects such as tunnel vision due to pressure on the optic chiasm. The patient is often aware of such changes, thereby producing secondary reactions. Emotional problems are inevitable when the consequences of pituitary disease impede day-to-day functioning, cause abnormalities in physique, and change lifestyle. Therefore, emotional sequelae from hormonal dysfunction are often difficult to differentiate from secondary psychological reactions. For example, depression in Cushing's disease is likely to be related to hormonal levels, whereas depression in short stature is probably more related to situational problems.

In order to emphasize the hormonal abnormalities, the following descriptions of the pituitary disorders have been divided into *hyper*pituitary syndromes and *hypo*pituitary syndromes. Hyperpituitary states include excessive secretion of GH resulting in acromegaly and gigantism, excessive prolactin secretion that may be present with galactorrhea and amenorrhea, ACTH hypersecretion, or Cushing's disease, and rarely superphysiologic secretion of TRH and TSH causing so-called pituitary hyperthyroidism. Pituitary hypersecretion is much less common in childhood than in adults. Hypopituitary diseases include LH and FSH deficiency (hypogonadotropic hypogonadism), growth hormone deficiency, lack of adequate secretion of ACTH (secondary hypoadrenalism), and TSH (secondary hypothyroidism). In spite of the specificity of the hormone defect in relation to the physical evidence of the disease, there is commonly multiple hormone involvement due to the feedback mechanisms and other interrelated hormonal stimuli. For example, excess secretion of growth hormone may potentiate the effect of thyroid hormone, or decreased secretion of thyroid hormone and growth hormone may mask the effects of inadequate secretion of ACTH. The hyperpituitary and hypopituitary categories described next refer to the *primary* endocrine disturbance with the understanding that observed behavioral and physical symptoms may be related to the secondary effects as well.

HYPERPITUITARY SYNDROMES

Acromegaly/Gigantism

Excessive secretion of growth hormone is usually associated with tumors of the anterior pituitary made up of cells that secrete growth hormone. If the growth-hormone excess occurs before skeletal growth is complete, excessive linear growth results. This state is called *gigantism*. After growth is complete, the condition is referred to as *acromegaly*. Growth-hormone excess occurs among adults with about equal frequency between men and women but occurs among children predominantly in males.

The growth-hormone excess results in overgrowth of virtually all organs. In adults, because linear growth of long bones is no longer possible, bone overgrowth is manifested as increased thickness. Children with gigantism may have excessive linear growth with heights in excess of 7 ft (210 cm). In addition to excess growth, symptoms include headache, easy fatigue, joint and muscle pains, profuse sweating, and oily skin. There may be a loss of libido and impotence in men and amenorrhea in women. Early symptoms are usually present long before recognition of the disease. Patients often seek help after a dramatic change such as a sudden increase in hat, shoe, and ring size. As the disease progresses, the overgrowth results in a coursening of physical features. Notably, the supraorbital ridges and lower jaw become more prominent, and the nose, hands, and feet enlarge. In the later stages, hypertension and diabetes mellitus may further complicate the disorder.

As with most pituitary diseases, the reason for the changes seen in acromegaly vary. Excessive growth of soft tissues and bone, increased sweating, weight gain, and occasional voice deepening are due to excess secretion of growth hormone. Local effects of the tumor mass itself may cause headaches, visual defects, cranial nerve palsies, and even temporal lobe epilepsy. Secondary imbalances of ACTH, FSH, LH, prolactin, and TSH may have their own associated symptomologies. Examples of these include galactorrhea, amenorrhea, infertility, and loss of libido.

Psychological symptoms in acromegaly include irritability, depression, and other emotional symptoms. Cognitive effects, in particular problems with memory, are occasionally reported (Lishman, 1978). It is unclear whether the changes are due to hormonal imbalance *per se* or to a psychological reaction to the disfigurement and pain that accompanies the condition, or both. However, a hormonal etiology is suggested because apathy has often been retrospectively reported to have occurred prior to any observed physical manifestations. Sleep apnea is a common disturbance in acromegaly that may also have hormonal association because its occurrence cannot be fully explained by other common causes (Perks *et al.*, 1980). However, frequent wakenings result in sleep loss that may produce secondary effects of emotional distress, changes in life-style, and problems with memory, spatial and visual perception, and concentration (Kales et al., 1985).

Hyperprolactinemia

This entity is rare in childhood and adolescents. In adult females, it commonly presents with amenorrhea, with or without galactorrhea. Women with both symptoms have a high incidence of pituitary tumors. There is no relationship of prolactinomas to oral contraceptive use. Hyperprolactinemia may be secondary to interference with the action of the hypothalamic prolactin inhibitory hormone, related to excessive TSH secretion in primary hypothyroidism, or be a side effect of dopamine receptor-blocking drugs.

The symptoms of hyperprolactinemia can be subtle and may often go unreported. Women with this problem most frequently complain of amenorrhea. In fact, hyperprolactinemia is a not infrequent cause of infertility in women. In men, the signs and symptoms are less noticeable and include obesity, often with a feminized distribution of body fat, decreased facial and body hair, small, soft testes, loss of libido, and sometimes galactorrhea (Franks, Jacobs, Martin, & Nabarro, 1978). The frequency among men has generally been considered to be less than women, although evidence suggests that this may not be true. Evidence of the disease is often subtle enough in men so as not to be recognized (Burrow, Wortzman, Rewcastle, Holgate, & Kovacs, 1981). In both men and women, the nonendocrine symptoms of a large tumor include headache, visual field loss, or palsies, as well as emotional lability.

There is frequently apathy and loss of libido associated with hyperprolactinemia. Ninety percent of the men show some degree of sexual dysfunction (Schwartz, Bauman, & Masters, 1982). However, it may be the apathy that explains why males often fail to seek medical attention (Cohen, Greenberg, & Murray, 1984).

Women with hyperprolactinemia tend to experience more difficulty with emotional symptoms. In a study comparing women with amenorrhea secondary to hyperprolactinemia and women with primary amenorrhea, the hyperprolactinemic women reported greater levels of depression, anxiety, and hostility. (Fava, Fava, Kellner, Serafini, & Mastrogiacomo, 1981; Fava, Fava, Kellner, Serafini, & Mastrogiacomo, 1982). Hyperprolactinemic men did not report any greater levels of general depression or hostility, and only slightly higher levels of anxiety, when they were compared with a control group of male inpatients with nonendocrinological problems (Fava et al., 1982).

It has been hypothesized that the prolactin interacts with ovarian hormones to produce the different emotional effects. One suggestion has been that high prolactin levels in conjunction with low progesterone levels in women produce symptoms of anxiety and hostility (Fava et al., 1982). Also, it has been shown that high prolactin and low estrogen produce depressive symptoms. (Carroll & Steiner, 1978). Because estrogen levels are often so low in these patients that osteoporosis occurs in some cases, the levels may be sufficiently deficient to have an emotional effect as well (Von Werder, 1985).

Although these hormone relationships have not been shown conclusively to cause the emotional disturbances, they do provide a model with which to understand the discrepancy between the male and female symptoms.

Bromocryptine is a dopamine (DA) agonist that acts on regulatory mechanisms to inhibit prolactin and is used in the treatment of hyperprolactinemia. The side effects from this class of drug includes dyskinesia, erythromelalgia, and psychiatric disorders, as seen in patients with Parkinson's disease, but these were thought to be rare in hyperprolactinemic patients (Thorner, Flückiger, & Caine, 1980; Von Werder, 1985). However, in a past study, 8 patients out of 600 (1.3%) developed serious drug-related psychosis without having any previous disposition toward psychiatric problems (Turner, et al., 1984). This occurred even with low doses of DA agonists, as is typically used for pituitary tumors. Not only are much larger doses generally used in patients with Parkinson's disease, but the population is typically older and are frequently taking other drugs. Therefore, although psychotic reactions in Parkinsonism, similar to those seen in the hyperprolactinemic patients, do occur more frequently, it cannot be inferred that hyperprolactinemic patients have a lesser potential for side effects from the DA agonists. Accordingly, these patients should be monitored for psychiatric symptoms.

Cushing's Syndrome and Disease

Cushing's disease refers specifically to the condition resulting from the hypothalamic-pituitary defects resulting in increased pituitary ACTH secretion that causes bilateral adrenal hyperplasia and excessive cortisol secretion. Pituitary adenomas are the most common cause of Cushing's disease. This disease is rare in childhood, more common in females, and occurs most frequently in middle-aged women. Cushing's syndrome refers to the manifestations of excessive cortisol, whether the primary deficit is hypothalamic, pituitary or adrenal, or secondary to exogenous drug administration. The administration of exogenous cortisol is the most common cause of this syndrome because it is a frequent treatment of a variety of diseases.

The most visible evidence of glucocorticoid excess includes truncal obesity with a round face. There may also be a loss of height due to dorsal kyphosis in adults. Growth failure is a characteristic early finding among children. In adults, not children, protein (muscle) wasting resulting in thin extremeties and purple striae in the skin frequently occurs. Children may develop sexual hair and adults hirsutism. Amenorrhea or oligomenorrhea, hypertension, and hyperglycemia may also occur in Cushing's syndrome. Glycosuria, muscular weakness, and osteoporosis can further complicate the disease.

Psychiatric problems are common in Cushing's disease, occurring in some degree in as many as two-thirds of patients (Whelan, Schteingart, Starkman, & Smith, 1980). They may manifest as affective disorders such as depressed mood, easy irritability, and crying episodes. Cognitive functions such as concentration, comprehension, memory, and orientation may also be disturbed. Insomnia, decreased libido, and changes in appetite often occur (Starkman & Schteingart, 1981).

Although the depression seen frequently in Cushing's disease may be in reaction to the patient's physical changes, a primary endocrine cause is also suspected. For example, irritability and decreased libido are seen often before the patient has experienced enough symptoms to recognize illness. Furthermore, mood disorders are described as being similar to those of a primary depressive disorder. However, crying episodes and depressed mood are without depressing thought content (Starkman, Schteingart, & Schork, 1981). Additionally, severe psychiatric symptoms are seen three to four times more frequently in Cushing's disease than in the iatrogenic syndrome in which the same physical conditions are caused by cortisol drug therapy (Lishman, 1978). The psychiatric disturbances remit as the endocrine disturbances are treated, suggesting a primary hormone effect. The patient can be expected to return to predisease stability following successful treatment (Lishman, 1978).

Further indications of a primary hormonal neuropsychiatric impairment are found in a study correlating severity of psychiatric impairment with plasma concentrations of ACTH and cortisol (Starkmann et al., 1981). Impairment covered a range of deficits including affective, cognitive, and vegetative functions. In a series of 35 Cushing's patients, 34% had a mild deficit, 26% moderate, 29% severe, and 11% a very severe deficit. In contrast to relationships to hormone levels alone, ratios among different hormones are correlated with psychiatric symptoms. For example, a high cortisol level with a lower ACTH level was related to the milder depressive symptoms. The reverse—low cortisol to high ACTH—reflected a higher degree of depression (Starkman et al., 1981). A higher cortisol to ACTH ratio tended to reflect more cognitive than emotional difficulties, especially in the degree of problems with concentration. Finally, the high levels of both ACTH and cortisol were associated with the patients experiencing the most severe depression, including paranoid or confusional states (Starkman et al., 1981).

It appears reasonable that the higher frequency of psychiatric deficits associated with the pituitary–ACTH-related Cushing's syndrome (Cushing's disease), as compared with the adrenal Cushing's syndrome, is related to the characteristic difference in cortisol/ACTH ratios, although altered CNS levels of other hormones or neurotransmitters in this CNS disease may be involved. Adrenal adenomas, which tend to produce high cortisol/ACTH ratios compared with the lower ratios of pituitary hyperfunction, generally result in milder psychopathology. However, there were some subjects with high ACTH without elevation of cortisol levels (low cortisol/ACTH ratios), who do not show the same frequency of psychiatric deficit. Thus, it has been suggested that a low cortisol/ACTH ratio may act to allow deficit, but it is not sufficient to cause deficit (Starkman et al., 1981).

Precocious Puberty

The onset of pubertal development at or before the age of 8 years in females and 9.5 years in males is defined as precocious puberty. True precocious puberty is characterized by premature activation of the hypothalamic-pituitary function with an increased secretion of gonadotropins stimulating sex steroid secretion by the gonads. Most instances of true precocious puberty are idiopathic, although frequently cases are related to hypothalamic or other CNS tumors.

Regardless of the cause, precocious puberty produces secondary sex characteristics such as pubic and axillary hair, breast enlargement in girls, and genital growth in boys. Children are tall for chronological age with advanced skeletal maturity, although adult height may be below average due to early completion of bone growth. Isolated characteristics of puberty such as early breast development (premature thelarche) or pubic hair growth (premature adrenarche) may occur without other growth disturbance. This is in contrast to full precocious puberty in which all the physical growth and development characteristics of normal puberty occur. Precocious puberty typically follows the usual course of pubertal development except for the earlier age of onset that may be as young as the first year of life.

Although somatic pubertal development is advanced, psychological and social development follow chronological age rather than physical age. Although it is generally agreed that precocious puberty does not cause any severe primary emotional or cognitive disturbances, secondary social difficulties can arise from enhanced expectations of maturity more befitting the child's physical than chronological age. The greater social pressure often leads to disappointment and a feeling of failure on the part of the child. On the other hand, children with precocious puberty are found to adjust better than children with partial maturational precocity such as premature adrenarche or thelarche. (Solyom, Austad, Sherick, & Bacon, 1980).

Pituitary Hyperthyroidism

Hyperthyroidism, only in rare instances, is caused by extreme secretion of TSH from a pituitary tumor (Tolis, Bird, Bertrand, McKenzie, & Ezrin, 1978). The feedback mechanism is overridden by an autonomous secretion of TSH, resulting in elevated thyroid hormone levels. The hyperthyroid symptoms are often mild. Patients may present with symptoms more directly related to pituitary tumor than to hyperthyroidism.

HYPOPITUITARY SYNDROMES

The signs and symptoms associated with hypopituitary disorders vary, depending upon which hormones are deficient. Possible causes for decreased hormonal secretion include disturbed hypothalamic regulation involving stimulatory and inhibitory hormones. Hypopituitarism can refer to the deficiency of a single hormone or several. In childhood, hypopituitarism is most commonly idiopathic or congenital, whereas among adults the most common cause is a tumor of the pituitary or hypothalamus. In childhood, growth-hormone deficiency is the most common single defect. Generally, the next most common defect is TSH secretion. Congenital hypopituitarism, manifest during infancy, commonly involves all anterior pituitary hormones. Gonadotropin deficiency is not apparent until puberty unless recognized in infancy. A particular entity known as septo-optic-dysplasia involves hypopituitarism. Such patients have optic nerve hypoplasia. There is also an association with midline facial (cleft palate) and CNS malformations, particularly the absence of the septum pellucidum. An interesting variation is the hypopituitary child who has only a single central maxillary incisor.

Among adults, in whom multiple endocrine failure is usually due to tumor, deficiencies usually occur in a particular sequence. First LH will be deficient, then GH, followed by FSH. ACTH and TSH are the most resistant to change. Thus symptoms of hypogonadism are usually an early presentation of hypopituitarism (Belchetz, 1984). If the tumor causing the pituitary dysfunction may be expanding, hypopituitarism dysfunction may be readily treatable with chemotherapy directed at the appropriate hormone deficits rather than surgical intervention. Enlarged tumors that cause visual deficit or other local difficulties would require surgery.

In infancy, hypopituitarism may present with small genitalia (evidence of gonadotropin deficienty) and hypoglycemia (evidence of ACTH and GH deficiency). In childhood, hypopituitarism presents with short stature. The characteristic appearance is a combination of normal body proportions, for size not age, and short stature. The child looks young for chronological age, has soft skin, and mild truncal obesity. Skeletal maturation is usually retarded (Smith, 1984).

Signs and symptoms among adults are related to the consequent hormonal deficits of thyroid, cortisol, and sex steroids. They experience weakness, tire easily, develop an increased sensitivity to cold, loss of pubic hair, and eventually develop pale, finely wrinkled skin. Women may experience amenorrhea and men a loss of libido and impotence. Growth hormone deficiency seems to add little to the overall symptomatology. Replacement therapy with growth hormone is the standard treatment for children; there is no clear indication for replacement therapy for adults after completion of growth.

There seems to be a broad range from mild to extreme in the degree of psychiatric impairment involved with hypopituitarism. Symptoms are more obvious with a more abrupt onset and can be very subtle otherwise (Smith, Barish, Correa, & Williams, 1972). Included most commonly is the symptomatology of depressive symptoms, such as apathy, confusion, drowsiness, and poor concentration. Although less common, symptoms such as irritability, unreasonable fears, and paranoid ideas are also found. More severe hypopituitarism, involving marked deficiencies in both ACTH and TSH, seems to be characterized by a more extreme apathy and lack of initiative (Belchetz, 1984).

Short Stature

Although much literature has been devoted to understanding the neuropsychological manifestations of short stature in various populations, little is clear. There are many contradicting studies that center around problems with either personality development, emotional disorders and depression, intelligence, and specific cognitive deficits.

Personality development presents the most coherent picture within the literature. Mild deficits have been seen in relation to maturation and coping behaviors. Typically, cases have a lack of aggression and withdrawallike behaviors. There is rarely a tendency toward severe thought disorders. These general adjustment problems are largely related to the degree of social support within the patient's environment rather than to any endocrine imbalance (Abbott, Rotnem, Genel, & Cohen, 1982; Drotar, Owens, & Gotthold, 1980; Money & Pollitt, 1966; Rotnem, Genel, Hintz, & Cohen, 1977; Steinhausen & Stahnke, 1976, 1977). In particular the degrees to which families were able to maintain a normal attitude toward the dwarfed child appropriate to chronological age predicted the ease with which the child developed (Abbott *et al.*, 1982; Money & Pollitt, 1966).

Problems in other areas include reports of children with short stature having difficulty with school achievement and having to repeat grades (Abbott, *et al.*, 1982; Money & Pollitt, 1966). However, there have been occasional reasons for average or better achievement (Rosenbloom, Smith, & Loeb, 1966). The achievement levels correlate more with intellectual ability, social and economic backgrounds, and, in particular, the educational network rather than the condition of short stature itself (Abbott *et al.*, 1982). Similarly, studies have shown either low IQs (Frankel & Laron, 1968; Shurka & Laron, 1975) or average to above average IQ performance (Brust, Ford, & Rimoin, 1976; Drash, Greenburg, & Money, 1968; Meyer-Bahlburg, Feinman, MacGillivray, & Aceto, 1978; Steinhausen & Stahnke, 1976) that correlates more with background and socioeconomic status than with short stature or associated hormonal influences.

Another series of studies demonstrated a specific cognitive deficit in visual-motor ability for patients with short stature (Abbott *et al.*, 1982; Frankel & Laron, 1968; Steinhausen & Stahnke, 1976). Lower scores than would have been predicted by IQ were found in such visuospatial tests as Spatial Relations, Speed of Closure, and Bender-Gestalt tests. In general, a developmental lag is suggested. However, the patients never catch up. The older the subject, the larger the discrepancy between chronological and developmental age.

Psychosocial Dwarfism

Short stature patients who do not respond to GH may be exhibiting an "emotional deprivation syndrome," or "psychosocial dwarfism." The symptoms mimic idiopathic hypopituitarism (Powell, Brasel, Raiti, & Blizzard,

1967). Not only does retardation occur as in pituitary dwarfs, but there are other unique symptoms including polydypsia, polyphagia, and poor speech and behavior development (Hung, August, & Glasgow, 1978). The most characteristic feature of psychosocial dwarfs is a history of emotional problems. For example, there are unusual eating and drinking behaviors such as food stealing, hoarding, eating garbage, drinking from stagnant or dirty water, and gorging and vomiting. There is usually social withdrawal, apathy, and poor interpersonal interaction. Insomnia is present, and sometimes patients cause self-injury. Home life is almost always unstable, often with an abusive or emotionally disturbed parent (Green, Campbell, & David, 1984; Powell, Brasel, & Blizzard, 1967; Powell, Brasel, Raiti, & Blizzard, 1967).

Although IQs generally fall in the low to borderline retarded range, these values probably do not represent actual intellectual capacity. Complicating factors in assessing intelligence are delays in speech and psychomotor development (Powell, Brasel, & Blizzard, 1967).

There is evidence of deficient GH and ACTH secretion in most psychosocial dwarfs. However, almost immediately upon removal from the pathologic environment, GH and ACTH return to normal levels and catch-up growth begins (Green et al., 1984). Patients will continue to flourish in a stable alternative home situation, but, upon return to the original home environment, growth failure recurs.

COGNITIVE FUNCTION AND PITUITARY HORMONES

Clinical descriptions of patients with pituitary diseases have provided only a glimpse of accompanying behavioral deficits that may be related to hormone imbalances of the pituitary axes. However, only for a limited number of these patient groups have specific cognitive functions been studied. Other groups, including patients with psychopathology in which the pituitary axis is implicated and normal subjects in whom there are hormone–behavior variations, will provide an additional framework in which to study hormonal correlates of cognitive behavior. Hormones are more readily available for measurement than are neurotransmitters. There is growing evidence that the two are related, directly or indirectly. Evaluation of patients offer an opportunity to form hypotheses regarding hormone deficiency and cognitive dysfunction. Unfortunately, patient studies are limited because their diverse etiologies and complicating secondary symptoms can obscure the relationships under study. Yet, once patient groups provide the direction, more controlled studies in normals can be initiated.

There are two broad areas in which human cognitive behavior has been associated with hormones of the pituitary axis. One is in psychopathology in which various hormone abnormalities have been reported for patients with affective or schizophrenic behavior. This area has a large literature; only some of the early and current issues will be sketched. The second area is the variation in performance on specialized cognitive tasks in patients whose hormone differences are measured both across and within subjects. Specialized cognitive tasks include tests of spatial relations, form perception, mental rotation, verbal fluency, and sequencing. Unfortunately, most studies do not delve into these individual cognitive factors too deeply; most of the data are comprised of subtests of intelligence tests. These are only partial measures of specialized cognitive skills. Nevertheless, analysis of these subtests can give insight to the more specific factors. Also, there are scattered studies that directly address the issue of cognitive performance in relation to hormonal variation. The task for the remainder of the chapter will be to outline these studies for the purpose of providing the groundwork for future research in this area.

PSYCHOPATHOLOGY
TRH/TSH

A major emphasis in the recent literature regarding psychopathology and hormone dysfunction is to understand the defective neurotransmitter mechanisms underlying the behavioral disturbances. As an index of neurotransmitter function, studies in both affective and schizophrenic patients concentrate not only on abnormal baseline measures of hormones and abnormal pituitary responses to drug or hormone stimulation but also on long-term changes in these factors following a drug treatment program. An early attempt to remediate psychiatric disorders was to influence the hormonal axis directly. Because it was observed that thyroid-stimulating hormone (TSH) was involved in depression because of the blunted TSH response from the anterior pituitary to the thyroid-releasing hormone (TRH), it was thought there would be a therapeutic effect from administering TRH, thereby increasing TSH levels. The results were mixed. A number of investigators reported no effect (Hollister *et al.*, 1974; Schmidt, 1977; Vogel, Benkert, Illig, Müller-Oerlinghausen, & Poppenberg, 1977), whereas others reported a reduction in depressed symptomatology in some patients, suggesting that a subgroup may benefit from TRH therapy (Furlong, Brown, & Beeching, 1976; Karlberg, Kjellman, & Kågedal, 1978; Pecknold, Ban, & Lehmann, 1976). A cause and effect relationship was not established, and the treatment has not been adopted.

Inconsistency for the blunted thyrotropin (thyroid-stimulating hormone, TSH) response seemed to be the rule in endogenous depression. Apparently, patients presenting with the same behavioral symptomatology, according to standard diagnostic criteria, did not have equivalent pituitary responses. There is an inconsistancy of response to other chemical challenge procedures such as in the dexamethazone suppression test (DST), which had been designed to aid in differential diagnosis of endogenous depression. In one study on 54 depressed patients, only one-third exhibited a blunting of TSH; no blunting was observed in nondepressed controls (Targum, Sullivan, & Byrnes, 1982). Nearly half of the depressed patients responded abnormally on the DST, but only 11% of these overlapped with the blunted TSH. It was concluded that both the hypothalamic-pituitary-thyroid and hypothalamic-pituitary-adrenal axes were disregulated but that the mechanisms were independent even though both are associated with depressive symptomatology.

Confirmation of the independence of these mechanisms was provided in a study of 24-hr serum levels of TSH. These levels were reduced and less variable in patients with depression than in controls (Kjellman, Beck-Friis, Ljunggren, & Wetterberg, 1984), but the levels were not correlated with either symptomatology or severity, nor were they related to results on the DST. The findings on this and other TSH studies are not conclusive in relating the disordered mechanism in depressives to the pituitary axis. However, the differential effect on TSH in these patients, relative to controls, suggests an involvement of the regulatory mechanism for at least some subjects.

Prolactin

Prolactin is another anterior pituitary hormone that has reportedly blunted secretory patterns in depression. As had been the case for TSH, the reports are variable. Findings include features such as blunted response to methadone (Judd, Risch, Parker, Janowsky, Segal, & Huey, 1982), increase in baseline levels after recovery (Asnis, Nathan, Halbreich, Halpern, & Sachar, 1980), and abnormal rhythm including an *increase* in prolactin levels in the evening relative to controls (Halbreich, Grunhaus, & Ben-David, 1979). These studies suggest there is yet an undefined abnormality of the anterior pituitary regulatory system associated with depressive disorders.

Prolactin levels are also affected in chronic schizophrenics. After administration of TRH, increases in prolactin suggest a relationship with the catecholaminergic system in the hypothalamus (Brambilla et al., 1976). Other reports of excess prolactin in schizophrenia, especially at the time of admission, have been related to the "nonspecific" effects of stress rather than a direct psychopathological connection (Gruen et al., 1978; Meltzer, Sachar, & Frantz, 1974). As with TRH, the interest in prolactin levels in psychopathological patients is to have an index for the neurochemical mechanisms underlying the psychopathology. Unfortunately, the relationships are complicated; evidence for cause and effect is not yet available.

Growth Hormone

Growth hormone is regulated by a number of neurosystems and accordingly is also affected in psychopathological illness. Because the dopaminergic neurotransmitter system has an influence on growth hormone regulation, common abnormalities of growth hormone levels are seen in schizophrenia, in which dopamine plays a major pathological role. For example, elevated basal levels of growth hormone are seen in some schizophrenic patients after neuroleptic withdrawal; however, inadequate responses were also seen after administration of a dopamine agonist (Ettigi, Nair, Lal, Cervantes, & Guyda, 1976). In a study of acutely schizophrenic adolescents, LRH and TRH induced increases in growth hormone in most schizophrenic subjects before initial neuroleptic treatment (Gil-Ad *et al.*, 1981); GH was not elevated in control subjects. After antipsychotic treatment, however, LRH did not cause a rise in GH, whereas TRH did. Prolactin and gonadotropin responses were normal.

These studies demonstrate that hormonal levels (in this last case, growth hormone) are regulated in part by neurotransmitter systems that are also related to neurosystems involved in psychopathology. It is of interest that the same abnormal increase in growth hormone, following acute administration of TRH, has been observed in other patients, including those with acromegaly (Irie & Tsushima, 1972). Acromegalic patients are not known to be psychotic, but the question arises as to whether the common denominator between the pituitary disorder and psychopathology would lead to an understanding of both diseases.

Multiple Hormone Involvement

One study, responding to the confusion and the mixed results found previously, followed the course of several pituitary hormones (Winokur *et al.*, 1983). Responses of FSH, LH, TSH, and prolactin to TRH were measured in 45 depressed patients and 32 controls. The dominant finding was that the *variance* of the responses from the patients was greater than for the controls, especially for TSH, prolactin, and FSH. Second, the abnormalities were not consistent. In contrast to controls who had little or no response to the TRH challenge, the patients usually had abnormal responses by one, two, and as many as three different hormones. Although the possibility could not be ruled out that each response type represented a different subtype of endogenous depression, the alternative viewpoint favored was that the anterior pituitary was affected in a nonspecific way.

Conclusion

The picture sketched by this outline of studies in which hormones of the pituitary axes are related to etiologies of psychopathologic illness is incomplete. On the one hand, there is the unquestionable connection whereby pituitary hormones are unregulated in psychopathological cases, as is evidenced by excess baseline levels, and blunted or increased responses to challenges by releasing hormones. The difficulties in understanding the systems arise from inconsistencies of response across subjects within diagnostic groups. Either the neurotransmitter–pituitary connection is relatively nonspecific, or the relationship between the underlying disorders in psychopathology and the hormonal mechanisms are too far removed. A closer look at the cognitive function in specific patient groups who have hormonal abnormalities of the pituitary axis is the next step for investigating a relationship between hormones and behavior.

COGNITIVE DYSFUNCTION IN PATIENTS
WITH GENETIC ABNORMALITIES

Gonadal Dysgenesis

Gonadal dysgenesis (Turner's syndrome) is characterized by a completely or partially deleted sex chromosome (45,X) and is associated with a number of physical features. These include a webbed neck, short stature, shieldlike chest, and sometimes more complicating symptoms such as heart deformities. The gonads are rudimentary, and consequently there are very low peripheral levels of estrogen and progesterone but markedly elevated levels of luteinizing hormone (LH) and follicle-stimulating hormone (FSH). This condition indicates an imbalance of the entire pituitary-gonadal-hypothalamic feedback loop.

These patients present the most striking example of hormonal (and genetic) abnormalities associated with a deficit in a specific cognitive function. There have been numerous reports of spatial difficulties in these patients because the disorder was first reported as a deficit in Performance IQ (Shaffer, 1962) that was confirmed by subsequent studies (Buckley, 1971; Money, 1964). The Performance IQ includes tests of form perception and manipulation, concept formation, and attention. In an extensive study in both children and adults (Garron, 1977), gonadal dysgenesis patients were grouped according to whether they had the "pure" 45,X karotype or a mosaic (e.g., 45,X/XX). Each patient was matched with a control according to age, sex, race, and social class and given the appropriate (child or adult) Wechsler IQ test. Most of the verbal tests were performed at the level of controls, except Arithmetic and Digit Span, whereas all the subtests of the Performance IQ, especially Block Design and Object Assembly, were performed significantly lower. The same pattern was observed regardless of karotype and regardless of age.

Continued investigation into the specific deficits associated with gonadal dysgenesis demonstrated deficits in direction sense, as measured by a test of map reading (Alexander, Walker, & Money, 1964) and drawing (Alexander, Ehrhardt, & Money, 1966). These tests narrowed the deficit to be one of space–form perception and not poor memory nor a distorted self-image. This is important because it meant that the disorder was not psychiatric but one of either a perceptual or perceptuomotor nature. Past neuropsychological studies redefined the defect to be one of mental rotation (Netley & Rovet, 1982), generating hypotheses that the pattern of difficulties in gonadal dysgenesis was related to dysfunction of the right cerebral hemisphere (Kolb & Heaton, 1975; Silbert, Wolff, & Lilienthal, 1977). This notion was supported, in part, by a study in which no specific deficits were found in sequential tasks that are skills that are associated with the left hemisphere (Gordon & Galatzer, 1980). Although it has not been settled whether the hormone deficiencies or the genetic abnormalities are the cause of the spatial deficit, it is apparent that the defect is related to functions associated with the right hemisphere.

One additional neuropsychological difference between gonadal dysgenesis patients and controls should be mentioned. In tests of both cerebral laterality ("sidedness" or location of cerebral function) and laterality of manual performance, patients with gonadal dysgenesis tended to be less lateralized (Gordon & Galatzer, 1980; Netley & Rovet, 1982). This means that functions such as speech comprehension normally dominant in the left hemisphere may be more shared by both hemispheres. Similarly, tests of manual dexterity that usually favor the preferred hand were performed equally well by both hands. However, the cerebral mechanisms that may be responsible for differential brain organization in these patients have not been described.

Trisomy X and Klinefelter's Syndrome

It is important to contrast the relatively normal verbal skills and deficient spatial ability in gonadal dysgenesis patients (genotype 45,X) with the reverse cognitive profile demonstrated in patients of both sexes with extra X chromosomes: 47,XXX and 47,XXY (Klinefelter's syndrome). Hormonal abnormalities are minor in patients with Klinefelter's syndrome prior to puberty. After puberty, testosterone is reduced, whereas follicle-stimulating hormone tends to be elevated. How the pituitary may be involved is not clear, but the effect is certainly in the gonadal-hypothalamic-pituitary axis.

In a study using the Verbal and Performance subtests of the Wechsler Intelligence Scale for Children (WISC), Verbal IQs (VIQ) were lower than Performance IQs (PIQ) in five of six prepubertal XXY patients (Wesner, Spangler, Petrides, Baker, & Telfer, 1973). Consistent with verbal dysfunction, reports of these cases often mention the presence of learning disabilities. In a larger, sibling-controlled study of supernumerary X-chromosome children, both males 47,XXY and females 47,XXX performed worse on verbal tests but not on performance tests of the Wechsler IQ scale (Netley & Rovet, 1983). The discrepancy between patients and controls was about the same for both 47,XXY and 47,XXX, although the 47,XXX had slightly reduced performance scores as well. The VIQ–PIQ difference for the patients was on the order of one standard deviation.

The lowered verbal score for 47,XXY (Klinefelter's) patients continues into adulthood. In early reports on these patients (Pasqualini, Vidal, & Bur, 1957), the Verbal IQ was usually lower than the PIQ. Subsequent studies have tended to confirm these findings although the data are not as strong as those reported for the children (Burnard, Hunter, & Hoggart, 1967; Wakeling, 1972). One problem in early studies such as these is that patient selection is from pools of low-IQ groups that may represent a multiply deficited sample.

Relatively few studies extend the findings for the behavioral deficits in these patients beyond the IQ measures. Instead, learning disabilities are often just reported; personality disorders are a main focus. However, there is one study, in which verbosequential skills (including word fluency and sound or number sequencing) were contrasted with visuospatial tests of form perception and mental rotation. The typical profile of verbal inferiority found in the previous IQ studies was replicated: The verbosequential tests were performed less well than the visuospatial tests (Galatzer & Gordon, 1982). A relationship between hemisphere laterality and hormone levels failed to be established when the hemispheric function was assessed with dichotic listening, tachistoscopic viewing, and dichaptic manipulation (Netley & Rovet, 1986). Although the expected hemispheric asymmetries of left dysfunction and right superiority was supported from the laterality data, only the group defined by high right hemisphere performance for nonverbal tests had low Verbal IQs. There was no relationship to hormone levels.

Androgen Insensitivity Syndrome (Testicular Feminization)

Patients with normal ability to synthesize hormones but with defects in androgen receptor structure or function are an interesting group whose test performance suggests a hormonal influence on cognitive function. These genetic male, phenotypic females perform IQ tests with a pattern resembling that of normal women. Namely, they perform better on verbal skills than they do on spatial skills (Masica, Money, Ehrhardt, & Lewis, 1969). The discrepancy is especially apparent in comparing the Verbal Comprehension and Similarities subtests of the Wechsler IQ test with Block Design and Object Assembly. Although there is debate as to which verbal skills normal females excel in and which spatial skills males excel in, the sex differences are consistently reported (Harshman, Hampson, & Berenbaum, 1983). The same findings of a cognitive asymmetry were reported for another group of phenotypic females whose genotype was a gonadal dysgensis/male mosaic: 45,X/46,XY (Rovet & Netley, 1979). By contrast, phenotypic males whose genotype was 46,XX (apparently containing at one time a now-deleted Y chromosome) performed better on the Performance IQ. In other words, the pattern of cognitive performance was concordant with that typical for the phenotype, not the genotype. Unfortunately, hormone abnormalities on these patients were not reported.

HORMONAL ABNORMALITIES RELATED
TO COGNITIVE FUNCTION

If hormonal considerations are more salient than chromosome aberrations for individual differences in cognitive function, then cognitive performance should be altered in patients with hormonal but not chromosomal abnormalities. Unfortunately, not many studies exist on such patients, but there are some indications that hormonal levels do reflect performance on specialized cognitive tasks.

Hypogonadotropic Hypogonadism

Patients with hypogonadotropic hypogonadism have a deficiency of pituitary gonadotropin levels related to the pituitary axis. Frequently these patients also have hyposmia or anosmia. Six males and 3 females of such patients were tested with several perceptual tests, including response time, field independence (Rod and Frame; Hidden Figures), size perception, and Category Estimation (e.g., What's the length of the longest whale if the average is 65 ft?) (Buchsbaum & Henkin, 1980). The patients had low urinary FSH levels and had been off replacement therapy for 2 months prior to study. Also tested were 12 phenotypic females with gonadal dysgenesis (hypergonadotropic hypogonadism), 8 of whom had elevated urinary FSH levels. There were 20 male and 11 female normal controls matched for parents' socioeconomic and educational levels.

Although the main findings focused on confirming perceptual deficits for gonadal dysgenesis patients, the hypogonadotropic patients also tended to have the same low performance on spatial perception. However, none of the differences between the hypogonadotropic males and the normals was significant except for the Rod and Frame test and the Category Estimation test. The Rod and Frame test is considered a measure of field independence and has been shown to be related to visuospatial function (Kanter & Schreiner, 1986); it is unclear what is measured by Category Estimation other than a type of reasoning. It appears from these data that there may be a specific deficit in spatial skills for the hypogonadotropic patients. However, simple response time was also slower for both patient groups, although the gonadal dysgenesis were significantly slower than the hypogonadotropic patients. This makes interpretation somewhat difficult because response time is usually an indication of general functioning level. Had the results been covaried for this measure, it is not clear whether the hypogonadotropic subjects would have differed from controls. Also, no tests of verbal, sequential, or perceptuomotor tests were given to determine if the deficits were specific to spatial skills. These missing data make it difficult to hypothesize what, if any, are the effects of the abnormal hormone levels. Both groups had abnormally lower circulating sex steroids (normally produced by the gonads); the hypogonadotropic patients also had low circulating LH and FSH.

Both verbal and spatial cognitive tests were given in a study on 19 men with idiopathic hypogonadotropic hypogonadism who had been under androgen replacement therapy for presumably 10 years (Hier & Crowley, 1982), although treatment had been suspended 3 months prior to testing. Spatial abilities were performed less well than verbal abilities by about one standard deviation. This pattern of performance differed from both normal controls and 5 patients with hypogonadotropic hypogonadism that was *acquired* due to hypothalamic destruction by some disease process. The interpretation is that androgenization of the brain during fetal or childhood development is required for normal acquisition of spatial function. Without it, brain development for spatial skills suffers. This viewpoint is often cited as a reason why males in general are superior in performance on tasks of spatial ability.

This is consistant with superior verbal abilities, in relation to spatial function, reported for patients with androgen insensitivity in whom androgens are unrecognized by receptors.

In contrast to the apparently lowered spatial skills in idiopathic hypogonadotropic hypogonadism patients who had undergone replacement therapy, relatively better spatial ability was seen in 22 adolescent patients with either hypogonadotropic hypogonadism or isolated gonadotropin deficiency who had not undergone treatment (Galatzer & Gordon, 1982). In these patients, along with contrast groups described in later sections, a battery of tests chosen to assess visuospatial and verbosequential functions attributed to specialized functions of the right and left cerebral hemispheres (Gordon & Harness, 1977) was given. The test battery had been normed on a relatively unbiased selection of children and adults so that the tests could be conveniently cross-compared.

Contrary to the results for the adult posttreatment patients, these hypogonadotropic patients performed slightly below average overall but were worse on the verbosequential tests than on the visuospatial tests (see Table 1).

TABLE 1. Performance on Cognitive Tests by Patients with Hormonal Abnormalities

	N	Average verbosequential Z-score	Average visuospatial Z-score	Cognitive profile	Average overall performance
Constitutional delay of puberty: Reduced (for age) gonadotropins and sex steroids[a]					
Male	11	−0.58	0.12	0.44	−0.20
Female	7	−0.82	−0.06	0.99	−1.11
Total	18	0.67	0.05	0.66	−0.56
Hypogonadotropic hypogonadism: Reduced (for age) gonadotropins and sex steroids[a]					
Male	12	−0.73	0.10	0.90	−0.65
Females	6	−1.22	−0.34	0.93	−1.55
Total	18	−0.89	−0.05	0.91	−0.95
Isolated gonadotropin deficiency: Reduced (for age) gonadotropins[a]					
Male	4	−0.24	−0.57	−0.33	−1.10
Precocious puberty: Increased (for age) gonadotropins and sex steroids[a]					
Female	7	−0.24	−0.57	−0.33	−1.10
Gonadal dysgenesis: Genotype 45,XO or mosaic; no sex steroids; normal or increased gonadotropins[a]					
Female	8	−0.22	−0.71	−0.49	−0.92
Klinefelter's syndrome: Genotype 47,XXY[a]					
Male	7	−0.94	−0.26	0.67	−1.05
Delayed puberty[b]					
Male	5	0.44	1.07	0.63	1.51
Female	1	−0.33	−0.11	0.22	−0.44
Precocious puberty[b]					
Female	1	−0.08	−0.97	−0.89	−1.05

[a]Adapted from Galatzer & Gordon, 1982.
[b]Adapted from Gordon & Gutai, unpublished data.

The same asymmetry was seen in 18 patients of the same series with constitutional delay of puberty; both sexes performed verbosequential skills worse than visuospatial skills. The results were replicated in a small-scale, pilot study in another population (Gordon & Gutai, unpublished data) on 6 untreated patients with delayed puberty (see Table 1). It is possible that the low endogenous hormone levels for patients of this age were related to the observed performance. It remains to be determined whether subsequent androgen therapy would have altered the direction of the cognitive asymmetry.

Precocious Puberty

Patients with precocious puberty are characterized by early pubertal development usually due to early maturation of the hypothalamus and pituitary. Excess secretion of gonadotropin for age caused increased sex steroid secretion by the gonads resulting in premature pubertal development. There is no reason to believe abnormal levels of hormones are present during prenatal development. Therefore, any influence on cognitive function would have occurred at the time of pubertal development during childhood.

Performance by patients with precocious puberty tends to be enhanced, especially in the verbal and academic areas. Data on advanced school achievement were collected on an entire clinic population who could be contacted for follow-up (Money & Neill, 1967). Twenty subjects constituting more than half of the sample had been advanced or recommended for advancement to a higher grade because of their high potential for achievement. Although this fact alone does not prove enhanced verbal skills, such abilities are usually most strongly related to achievement (Gordon, 1983). The IQ data were based on a study of 27 girls and 8 boys with sexual precocity in the same clinic population who had been given the Wechsler or Stanford-Binet IQ test (Money & Meredith, 1967). On the average, performance tests were performed normally, whereas verbal tests were performed at least one standard deviation above normal. In an unusual twist, the male patients outperformed the female patients overall and on the Verbal IQ. The opposite pattern of results was reported in 8 girls with idiopathic precocious puberty who were tested by a German translation of the Wechsler IQ test (Schambach, Schneemann, & Müller, 1979). In 7 out of 8 of the patients, the "action" part of the test was performed better than the verbal part. No subtest scores were reported, nor was there a control or contrast group in order to evaluate selection bias. However, in confirmation of the general observation, the Full Scale IQ was elevated in virtually all of the cases.

In a more recent study, the originally reported finding of the high verbal, normal visuospatial profile was replicated (Galatzer, Beth-Halachmi, Kauli, & Laron, 1984). Care was taken in this study to control for selection bias. Patients were selected in the course of normal follow-up in a large neuroendocrine unit. In all, 52 girls with precocious puberty were invited to participate in psychological testing; none refused. Controls were matched for age, socioeconomic status of the family, father's occupation, and ethnic origin. In addition, 8 subjects with "fast maturity" were tested. Fast maturity patients are ones who achieve first indications of secondary sexual characteristics at the proper time (i.e., after age 8) but who progress quickly through normal pubertal development. Verbal IQs were consistently higher for the precocious puberty patients relative to controls, especially for the Vocabulary, Information, and Similarities subtests of the Wechsler IQ (Hebrew translation and norms). No differences were seen for the distribution and level of performance in the Performance IQ subtests. The fast maturers performed like the controls, suggesting that it may be the time of the maturity rather than the rate of maturation that is crucial. It is of interest that the verbal superiority disappeared when the scaled IQ scores were recalculated on the basis of bone age rather than chronological age.

Additional support for the verbal-performance dichotomy in precocious puberty was found in a study where the patients were administered the same battery of verbosequential and visuospatial tests that had been administered to patients with delayed puberty (Galatzer & Gordon, 1982) (see Table 1). The asymmetry favored the verbosequential skills.

The role of excess hormones for cognitive behavior in early maturing patients is not clear. Because the precocious subjects probably did not have prenatal exposure to excess hormones, the increased hormonal activity prior to normal development presumably exerted specific effects on brain mechanisms subserving verbal function while leaving unaffected mechanisms subserving visuospatial function. It is important to add that patients with congenital adrenal hyperplasia who had prenatal exposure to excess androgens have not demonstrated cognitive abnormalities when compared to their siblings as controls (Baker & Ehrhardt, 1974).

Tall Stature

More support for the mutual influence of hormone action and puberty on increased verbal ability is demonstrated in a retrospective study on patients with tall stature (Galatzer, Beth-Halachmi, & Topper, 1979). This was defined as individuals whose height is greater than four standard deviations above the mean for age. Growth hormone is not elevated in these patients; no hormonal etiology of tall growth is known; and their height may be due to genetic predisposition or biologic variation. Cognitive performance on verbal skills was enhanced in postpubertal but not prepubertal patients of tall stature. The Verbal IQ (VIQ) scores for postpubertal patients was significantly greater than Performance IQ (PIQ); there was no difference, as is usually expected, between these IQ scores for the prepubertal patients. Eight out of 10 postpubertal patients showed a VIQ–PIQ discrepancy ranging from one to three standard deviations; 2 had the reverse profile. Eight out of 11 prepubertal patients also had greater verbal than performance scores but the difference in the two scores was only a few scaled points (see Figure 2). So far, there has been no cross-validation report, and these data have not been explained. It is left for future research to determine whether the similarity of

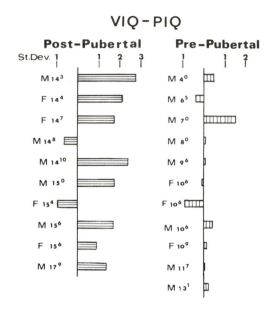

FIGURE 2. VIQ-PIQ in patients with tall stature.

increased verbal performance in both the tall stature patients and those with precocious puberty is meaningful.

NORMAL HORMONAL VARIATION AND COGNITIVE FUNCTION

Rate of Maturation at Normal Puberty

There is one often-referenced study on early and later maturing children in the normal age range of puberty whose results parallel those for the more extreme idiopathic hypogonadotropic hypogonadism at the one extreme and precocious puberty at the other (Waber, 1976). The subjects were male and female children at two pubertal ages (11 and 13 for females; 13 and 15 for males), half of whom had matured early at the time of testing and half of whom had not yet progressed in their pubertal development to the level of Tanner Stage 2. Tests of verbal and spatial ability were given to all subjects along with a test of dichotic listening that measures cerebral dominance of verbal perception.

The groups did not differ among themselves on verbal skills, but visuo-spatial ability was performed significantly better by all the groups delayed in their maturation, regardless of age or sex. Because the test scores could be converted to standard scores according to group performance, the results may also be interpreted as a relatively better performance on verbal skills than spatial skills for the early maturers and a better spatial than verbal performance for the late maturers. In a broad sense, therefore, the results resemble the better verbal skills of the precocious puberty patients and the better visuospatial skills in the untreated patients with delayed puberty (Galatzer & Gordon, 1982; Gordon, 1980). In addition, the dichotic listening test revealed a greater lateral dominance toward the left hemisphere that was seen in the older late maturers rather than in the older early maturers. The superiority for spatial ability in late maturers was replicated in another study on eighty-five 11-year-old girls (Newcombe & Bandura, 1983). In this study, the relationship was demonstrated by correlating the scores on the spatial test with a continuous measure of maturation (defined as the ratio between total body water and body weight). However, the relationship was weak, explaining only 5% of the variance. Verbal tests were not given that would have aided in the interpretation.

The results in both studies were interpreted to be the result of maturation rate. However, the rate explanation is not concordant with the normal cognitive performance reported for fast maturers (Galatzer et al., 1984). Another related hypothesis that has not been ruled out is that the time of maturation is the important variable. If either time of puberty or rate of maturation determines cognitive profile, the profile should be unchanged after pubertal development is complete. That is, subjects tested several years after pubertal development should have the same cognitive preference as they had at the time of pubertal development. Such was not found to be the case in a study on normal women tested at college age (Strauss & Kinsbourne, 1981). In this study, there was no correlation between age at onset of menarche and performance on a spatial task or verbal fluency task.

More significantly, the pattern of improved cognitive performance failed to replicate for precocious maturers tested postpubertally on a battery of verbal and spatial tasks. Precocious patients performed worse on most tasks relative to controls, especially Vocabulary and Similarities subtests of the Wechsler IQ (Rovet, 1983). Males did worse on a mental rotation task than controls, whereas females did better. Results were also contrary to expectation for patients with delayed development as judged by bone age. No satisfactory explanation could be offered for these findings other than to suggest sampling biases, test conditions, or age differences. Once again the possibility of a moderating influence by endogenous hormone levels must be considered.

Endogenous Hormones and Cognitive Ability

The importance of endogenous hormones in relation to performance of specialized cognitive skills was demonstrated in a study on 32 normal males and 28 females (Gordon & Lee, 1986). The subjects were tested on a battery of visuospatial and verbosequential tests (Gordon, 1986) at which time small blood samples were drawn as each test was performed. For the males, FSH, LH, and testosterone were assayed; for the females, FSH, LH, estradiol, and progesterone were assayed. The results for the males demonstrated a high negative correlation between FSH and the visuospatial tests with rs $\cong$ −.5.

The visuospatial tests measured a variety of abilities including point localization, mental rotation, and form closure, all of which were negatively related. LH tended to have a modest positive correlation not only with the visuospatial tests but also with the verbosequential tests as well. Testosterone did not have any consistent relationship to any test. A multiple regression of the three hormones and the sum of the tests of visuospatial function had a value of $r = .67$, explaining nearly 40% of the variance for the 32 subjects. The results were replicated a week later when the subjects returned for a second session.

The results for females in this study were considerably weaker. A negative correlation was again found between FSH and the one mental rotation test but only when the levels of estradiol and progesterone were statistically held constant. A multiple regression was not significant. The time of testing was counterbalanced to coincide with the menstrual, follicular, or luteal phases of the cycle. It is possible that the weak result was due to the higher mean gonadotropin levels in women, the variance of which was not related to cognitive function.

If the results of this study are accurate, they not only explain the results for the early and late pubertal children but also explain the failure to find the effect in postpubertal subjects as well. FSH was certainly higher in early maturers at the time of testing than in late maturers. This is consistent with the poorer visuospatial skills found in the early maturers. Neither time nor rate of pubertal maturation would be able to predict FSH levels in postpubertal years, thus explaining why cognitive function was not related to onset of puberty in the postpubertal subjects.

In spite of the fact that the relationships described for FSH were consistent with most observations, the results were serendipitous. The expectation for most studies in this area is that sex steroids would play the major role in specialized cognitive behavior, especially spatial skills (Geschwind & Behan, 1982). One study focused on just this relationship in normal subjects. Testosterone was measured from blood samples and correlated to spatial behavior in both male and female college students (Shute, Pellegrino, Hubert, & Reynolds, 1983). Three spatial factors—closure, mental rotation, and visualization—were tested in 91 subjects about equally split between the sexes. Males outperformed females on each of the tests, but the relationship between testosterone levels and spatial performance was found only for males and only when fitted to a third-order polynomial. These results were partially supported in a follow-up study for one of the spatial tests in which a sex-by-testosterone interaction was found for the test scores.

Physical Androgyny

As a substitute for measuring circulating hormones, especially in earlier studies where assays were less accurate and more expensive, physical characteristics have been related to cognitive function. In the most well-known study (Petersen, 1976), both male and female adolescents at three different ages were assessed for muscle/fat distribution, overall body shape, genital or breast size, and amount of pubic hair. These variables were compared to performance on two tests of spatial ability and two tests of fluency. It was found that the more physically masculine males were better on the tests of fluent production than on spatial ability; the less physically masculine males showed the reverse trend. By contrast, the more masculine females (in the older age group only) were the more capable on spatial ability; fluency was not related to physical parameters. These findings support an earlier study on males only, in which these same general relationships were reported for a different set of verbal and spatial tests (Klaiber, Broverman, & Kobayashi, 1967). Namely, the relationship between physical measures of androgens and cognitive behavior was positive for verbal ability and negative for spatial skills. In addition to physical characteristics, levels of urinary 17-ketosteroids were measured. These were supposed to confirm the relationships found with the physical characteristics. As expected, the relationships held, strengthening the androgen-behavior connection. It is disappointing, however, that replication of the result has not been widely reported. Therefore caution should be exercised before coming to conclusions regarding the relationship between physical characteristics of the body and the behavioral variables.

VARIATION IN HORMONE LEVELS AND COGNITIVE FUNCTION

If there is cognitive behavior that can be related to endogenous hormone levels, then it should be possible to observe changes in performance of neuropsychological tasks following natural or induced changes in hormone levels. To some extent this was attempted in patients with psychopathology as described previously. There have also been a number of studies in which ACTH or vasopressin has been administered to enhance memory and cognitive performance. Finally, and in keeping with the studies involving the pituitary-gonadal axis, a few findings relating cognitive changes to natural variation of the menstrual and other cycles or to exogenous administration of gonadal hormones will be reported.

ACTH

Adrenocorticotropic hormone has been well-studied in the rat where increased levels are believed to improve performance for learning and memory. Consistent with that view, intellectual deficits in patients with ACTH deficiency have been reported (Laron, Karp, Pertzelan, & Frankel, 1970). However, compounds that are believed to be the active fragments of ACTH, ACTH 4-10, have met with equivocal success in trying to improve performance in humans.

Two studies on the elderly demonstrated a significant improvement in one particular memory test but failed to produce improvements in others.

Subjects improved in remembering a first name of a person when cued with a surname (Ferris, Sathananthan, Gershon, Clark, & Moshinsky, 1976). However, there was no improvement in a similar paired-associate test with noun words or other memory and performance tests including recognition of faces, paragraph recall, digit span, and recall of simple line drawings. Another study demonstrated significant improvement of memory of geometric figures but not for memory of names and faces, nor was there improvement in a common scale of memory testing (Miller, Groves, Bopp, & Kastin, 1980). These studies are not exhaustive but are typical of the problems in relating ACTH to intellectual or memory factors in human performance. At best, the results suggest that effects are subtle and require a specific type of memory test to demonstrate the effect. A more skeptical conclusion would be that findings are plagued with Type I error where the majority of studies produce no effect but go unreported in the literature.

Vasopressin

Vasopressin is another hormone released from the pituitary that has demonstrated improvement in learning and memory in rats. Like ACTH, it was hoped the apparent improvements in memory tasks in animals might also be found in humans. Some success has been reported for serial learning of word lists, prompted free recall, and recall of semantically related words (Weingartner *et al.*, 1981). These studies were carried out on unimpaired subjects in which treatment by vasopressin was compared to a placebo condition. Similar positive findings were reported for depressed patients in whom improvement in memory and learning was independent of changes in mood. Improvement in performance has also been seen in a qualitatively different task of concept learning (Beckwith *et al.*, 1982). The concept task was of the usual type in which the subject is asked to sort forms of different shapes and colors according to an undisclosed category (i.e., shape, color) using feedback from the examiner. The dependent variable is the number of trials needed to "catch on" to the correct concept. The concept is then changed without warning, and the subject has to switch strategies. Treatment by an analog of 8-arginine vasopressin (desmopressin acetate) prior to learning enhanced performance relative to placebo. In a task of pattern memory with the same subjects, there was no improvement, suggesting the drug action to be somewhat specific.

These small successes encouraged an attempt to use vasopressin to improve memory in elderly normal subjects and in young, healthy controls. In a double blind crossover study, vasopressin facilitated subjects' responses to search in memory for a correct answer (Nebes, Reynolds, & Horn, 1983). However, improvement was not any greater for the elderly subjects than for the controls, suggesting the effect is not one of compensation for lost function but an enhancement of baseline performance. In a group of subjects ranging in age from 50 to 65, increased attention in task performance and enhanced recall was observed following intramodal administration of vasopressin (Legros & Gilot, 1979). There was no improvement on a visual memory test and no changes in mood. The results were interpreted to reflect a CNS action of vasopressin that affects the consolidation memory in which engrams are permanently encoded in cortical substrate. In another study, it was reported that vasopressin acted to focus attention on a specific task at the expense of attention to the periphery (Jennings, Nebes, & Reynolds, 1986).

These studies suggest that vasopressin may produce some improvement in cognitive processing, but the results are modest. The nature of behavioral change appears to be for memory processes rather than for specialized skills of a verbal, spatial, or sequential nature. Also contrary to most other pituitary hormone effects thus far studied, vasopressin or ACTH is related to neurosystems farther removed from the hypothalamic-pituitary-gonadal (or adrenal) axis. It is in these reports where most of the concern is with effects on specialized cognitive function.

Menstrual Cycle

The most dramatic natural fluctuation of hormones other than during puberty is the female menstrual cycle. There are large variations in the gonadotropins and multifold changes in estrogen and progesterone throughout the 28-day period. The highest levels for most of the hormones occur at the follicular phase; the lowest levels are during menstruation.

One of the clearest examples of shifts in verbal function and spatial performance was demonstrated in 14 normally cycling women (Komnenich, Lane, Dickey, & Stone, 1978). In this study, the two verbal tests—color naming and color reading—tended to be performed best during the preovulatory phase when hormones were elevated relative to the other phases. These tests were also performed better during this period by the experimental women than at any time by two control groups: men and women on birth control pills in whom hormones have low fluctuations. By contrast, a spatial test (Embedded Figures) and a test of Serial 7's and Serial 3's (counting backward) were performed significantly worse during the preovulatory phase, suggesting a negative correlation. As is usual for spatial tasks, the Embedded Figures test was performed best by the male controls at each of four testings. Women on birth control pills performed consistently at the median level throughout. The nonpill (experimental) women performed worse on this test at every cycle phase except during menstruation when hormones were the lowest.

Another example of fluctuation of cognitive performance during the menstrual cycle was in 12 normally cycling women given a test of dot detection and one of dot-pattern discrimination (Ward, Stone, & Sandman, 1978). Opposite effects were seen for the two tasks. The best performance of dot detection occurred during menstruation when hormones were low. Perception of dot patterns was best performed during the premenstrual period when estrogen and progesterone were higher, but LH and FSH were the lowest. If the Dot Pattern test can be favorably compared to the Embedded Figures test of the previous experiment, then these results are consistent with those in which FSH is negatively correlated with spatial ability. It is also consistent with the data that these hormones or the steroids are positively correlated with the verbal skills. A third study (Wuttke *et al.*, 1975) demonstrated faster simple response times, and faster, more accurate arithmetic calculations during the premenstrual period. However, performance was considerably lower during the preovulatory period when all the related hormones but progesterone are reasonably higher. In another study with fewer subjects, performance on verbosequential and visuospatial tests varied considerably in the different menstrual phases, although not in any consistent way (Gordon, Corbin, & Lee, 1986).

Diurnal and Other Cycles

Mean levels of testosterone in males decrease about 20% from morning to afternoon. If performance on cognitive tests is related to testosterone levels, then consistent diurnal shifts are expected. In support of this hypothesis, names of colors were read quicker in the morning than in the afternoon (Klaiber, Broverman, Vogel, & Mackenberg, 1974). In this study, however, these shifts were significant only for adolescent age groups and only for subjects whose basal testosterone levels were generally low to begin with. A follow-up study demonstrated that speed of naming did not increase when testosterone was injected during the morning session. Presumably, the induced increase in testosterone by afternoon counteracted the normal diurnal decrease, thereby producing no change in speed-naming performance.

Unfortunately, an attempt at replicating these findings has not been successful. There were no changes in either verbal fluency, sequencing, or visuospatial cognitive performance after administration of either testosterone or placebo (Gordon *et al.*, 1986). It is possible the cognitive tests used to assess performance levels may have been less sensitive than speed of naming. Also, the subjects of the latter study were college-age students who had not demonstrated the morning–afternoon shift in performance as had the subjects in the previous study for color naming. If the age-related effects of testosterone are replicated in future studies, one conclusion would be that this or related hormones have a greater effect on cognitive performance for the maturing brain than the matured brain.

Other studies have shown that shifts in cognitive function are related to ultradian variation in which periods of fluctuation are less than 24 hr. Performance on a verbal test and spatial test rose and fell in 90-min cycles in a study that tested subjects three times an hour throughout an 8-hr day (Klein & Armitage, 1979). In addition, the performances were 180° out of phase, such that good performance on the spatial test corresponded to low performance on the verbal, and vice versa. In another series of studies, essentially the same results were seen to follow the 90-min REM/NREM sleep cycle (Gordon, Frooman, & Lavie, 1981; Lavie, Metanya, & Yehuda, 1984). Visuospatial tasks were performed better after awakening from REM sleep, and verbosequential tasks were performed better after awakening from NREM sleep. Neither the daytime nor the REM/NREM cycle has been related to hormone changes as yet, but the acute shifts in functional performance support the hypothesis that specialized cognitive function is related to neurochemical systems because only these could change so rapidly as to reflect the rapid shifts in cognitive performance. The fact that there may be hormonal correlates to cognitive function also reflects the presence of these neurosystems, but caution dictates that the issue of causation is far from settled.

Conclusion

These studies in patients with genetic and hormonal abnormalities and in normal males and females imply that hormones related to the pituitary axes are involved in cognitive behavior and performance on tests of specialized cognitive function. For many researchers, testosterone, androgen, or androgenization is the important hormone class. These are somehow negatively related in men to spatial ability, visualization, spatial orientation, and other similar tasks all of which are usually associated with male superiority. For females, androgenization predicts the opposite, positive correlation, at least for spatial ability. On the other hand, in females, high levels of both estrogen and gonadotopins have been related to good performance on verbal-type skills.

It is not always easy to distinguish between the importance of sex steroids and gonadotropins in relation to cognitive function. There are high levels (for age) of gonadotropins in precocious and early maturers and in normal women during the follicular phase of the menstrual cycle at which time these subjects perform well on verbal tests and poorly on spatial tests. There are low levels of these hormones in males and females with delayed puberty and in normals with late development who perform well on spatial abilities relative to verbal functions.

The current level of research is only at the stage of establishing relationships among hormones and behavior. Cause and effect, not to mention neural mechanisms, have not yet been established. For one thing, and as might be expected from behavioral studies, the pattern of relationships is not consistently clear. There are patients whose hormone levels and cognitive function contradict findings supporting the general picture. Examples are Klinefelter patients who, with lowered testosterone and elevated gonadotropins, perform better on spatial skills than verbal skills. There are also patients such as those with congenital adrenal hyperplasia in whom major developmental and endogenous hormonal alterations do not seem to play a specific role in cognitive performance at all. And finally, there are nonconfirming or contradictory reports on the same subjects. An example is the change or lack of change in cognitive performance that has been reported to coincide with the menstrual cycle.

Cognitive behavior is difficult to measure with the same strict criteria as, for example, hormone assays. The variables are less well-defined, and the test instruments are less pure. The purpose of this survey is to focus on the range of research bearing on the topic in order to stimulate the experimentalist to form hypotheses in search of hormonal correlates of cognitive behavior.

EPILOGUE: IMPLICATIONS AND SPECULATIONS

Clinical Implications

For cases that reach the endocrine clinic, the usual reason for a person to seek help is physical. Patients present with growth or maturational abnormalities, sexual dysfunction, or other physical changes. Behavioral difficulties or cognitive changes are much less noticeable and are usually considered secondary. They are rarely assessed in the clinic. However, difficulties in school, the workplace, or home, reflecting learning disability, depression, or apathy, are not unusual. The implication from a number of studies in this survey is that regular assessment of these behavioral issues in clinic patients is desirable.

Research findings are sufficiently consistent to warrant a closer look at behavioral and cognitive changes that may accompany endocrine disease. On the one hand, any cognitive changes may aid in differential diagnosis of the type of illness as well as serve as an index of severity. Second, full documentation of cognitive ability will enhance research efforts in establishing hormonal correlates of cognitive behavior.

Research Speculations

The last issue that emerges from the experimental studies is to offer an hypothesis for the cerebral basis of cognitive performance with the idea that hormonal correlates of behavior are related either directly or indirectly to neuronal mechanisms. The working hypothesis is that there are several neurosystems, each one underlying a specific class of cognitive function such as verbal fluency, sequencing, three-dimensional visualization, or form perception. Based on the fact that these functions are differentially related by hormone levels or other rapidly changing factors, it is presumed that each neurosystem is qualitatively different from other neurosystems in the nature of its neurochemical mechanisms. These differences could be the neurotransmitters themselves, their receptors, or metabolites. The theory does not exclude neuroanatomical differences such as structure, interconnections of neurons, or location of nuclei, nor the possibility that developmental influences have altered brain structure. But the reason the focus is on neurochemical rather than on the neuroanatomical bases of cognitive function is the persistent evidence of hormone–behavior relationships that are reported for various subject groups. Even stronger support is derived from the behavioral changes that seem to be related to hormonal fluctuations within subjects. Also, the rapid behavioral fluctuations described for various diurnal and ultradian cycles reflect a chemical basis rather than an anatomical basis although the connection to hormones, *per se*, is less clear.

It is too early to go beyond the working hypothesis to suggest a mechanism. It is not known, for example, whether the cognitive fluctuations reported for awakenings from REM and NREM sleep are related to the same mechanisms as the cognitive fluctuations related to the menstrual cycle. Do hormones play a direct role or are they only indirectly influenced by, and related to, the critical neurosystems?

It should also be pointed out that many of the specialized cognitive functions that are related to hormone concentrations and hormone changes are the same functions associated with specialized processing by either the left or right cerebral hemisphere. Language skills, verbal fluency, and sequencing are associated with processing by the left hemisphere; visuospatial skills are associated with processing in the right. The differential relationship between hormones and verbosequential or visuospatial behavior and the connections to the separate cerebral hemispheres may not be accidental. Asymmetrical concentration and action of neurotransmitters or their metabolites is well documented in both animals and humans. Several studies have demonstrated that gonadal hormones differentially and asymmetrically are recognized by receptors in the cerebral cortex. Consistent with these data, it is proposed that neurochemical systems are the basis of right–left hemispheric differences in cognitive functioning. It is attractive to focus on the neurochemical basis of specialized cognitive functions with the caution that the nature of the neurotransmitter systems and the role of hormones have not yet been proposed. This chapter is intended to be a stimulant to this end.

ACKNOWLEDGMENTS

We wish to thank E. Avery and A. Schwartz for research help and Sandra Ballantyne for technical assistance in preparation of this chapter. The authors are supported in part by Grant HD 16264 from the National Institutes of Health.

REFERENCES

Abbott, D., Rotnem, D., Genel, M., & Cohen, D. J. (1982). Cognitive and emotional functioning in hypopituitary short-statured children. *Schizophrenia Bulletin, 8* 310–319.

Alexander, D., Ehrhardt, A., & Money, J. (1966). Defective figure drawing, geometric and human, in Turner's syndrome. *The Journal of Nervous and Mental Disease, 142,* 161–167.

Alexander, D., Walker, H. T., & Money, J. (1964). Studies in direction sense. *Archives of General Psychiatry, 10,* 337–339.

Asnis, G. M., Nathan, R. S., Halbreich, U., Halpern, F. S., & Sachar, E. J. (1980). Prolactin changes in major depressive disorders. *American Journal of Psychiatry, 137,* 1117–1118.

Baker, S. W. & Ehrhardt, A. A. (1974). Prenatal androgen, intelligence, and cognitive sex differences. In R. C. Friedman, R. M. Richart, & R. L. Vande Wiele (Eds.), *Sex differences in behavior* (pp. 153–176). New York: Wiley.

Beckwith, B. E., Petros, T., Kanaan-Beckwith, S., Couk, D. I., Haug, R. J., & Ryan, C. (1982). Concept learning in human males. *Peptides, 3*, 627–630.

Belchetz, P. E. (1984). Hypopituitarism. In P. E. Belchetz (Ed.), *Management of pituitary disease* (pp. 103–158). New York: Wiley.

Brambilla, F., Guastalla, A., Guerrini, A., Rovere, C., Legnani, G., Sarno, M., & Riggi, F. (1976). Prolactin secretion in chronic schizophrenia. *Acta Psychiatry Scandinavica, 54*, 275–286.

Brust, J. S., Ford, C. V., & Rimoin, D. L. (1976). Psychiatric aspects of dwarfism. *American Journal of Psychiatry, 133*, 160–164.

Buchsbaum, M. S., & Henkin, R. I. (1980). Perceptual abnormalities in patients with chromatin negative gonadel dysgenesis and hypogonadotropic hypogonadism. *International Journal of Neuroscience, 11*, 201–209.

Buckley, F. (1971). Preliminary report on intelligence quotient scores of patients with Turner's syndrome: A replication study. *British Journal of Psychiatry, 119*, 513–514.

Burnard, G., Hunter, H., & Hoggart, K. (1967). Some psychological test characteristics of Klinefelter's syndrome. *British Journal of Psychiatry, 113*, 1091–1096.

Burrow, G. N., Wortzman, G., Rewcastle, N. B., Holgate, R. C., & Kovacs, K. (1981). Microadenomas of the pituitary and abnormal sellar tomograms in an unselected autopsy series. *The New England Journal of Medicine, 304*, 156–158.

Carroll, B. J. & Steiner, M. (1978). The psychobiology of premenstrual dysphoria: The role of prolactin. *Psychoneuroendocrinology, 3*, 171–180.

Cohen, L. M., Greenberg, D. B., & Murray, G. B. (1984). Neuropsychiatric presentation of men with pituitary tumors (the four a's). *Psychosomatics, 25*, 925–928.

Drash, P. W., Greenberg, N. E., & Money, J. (1968). Intelligence and personality in four syndromes of dwarfism. In D. B. Cheek (Ed.), *Human growth: Body composition, cell growth, energy, and intelligence* (pp. 568–581). Philadelphia: Lea & Febiger.

Drotar, D., Owens, R., & Gotthold, J. (1980). Personality adjustment of children and adolescents with hypopituitarism. *Child Psychiatry and Human Development, 11*, 59–66.

Ettigi, P., Nair, N. P. V., Lal, S., Cervantes, P., & Guyda, H. (1976). Effect of apomorphine on growth hormone and prolactin secretion in schizophrenic patients, with or without oral dyskinesia, withdrawn from chronic neuroleptic therapy. *Journal of Neurology, Neurosurgery, and Psychiatry, 39*, 870–876.

Fava, G. A., Fava, M., Kellner, R., Serafini, E., & Mastrogiacomo, I. (1981). Depression, hostility and anxiety in hyperprolactinemic anenorrhea. *Psychotherapy and Psychosomatics, 36*, 122–128.

Fava, M., Fava, G. A., Kellner, R., Serafini, E., & Mastrogiacomo, I. (1982). Depression and hostility in hyperprolactinemia. *Neuropsychopharmacol and Biological Psychiatry, 6*, 479–482.

Ferris, S. H., Sathananthan, G., Gershon, S., Clark, C., & Moshinsky, J. (1976). Cognitive effects on ACTH 4-10 in the elderly. *The Neuropeptides: Pharmacology, Biochemistry, and Behavior, 5*, 73–78.

Frankel, J. J., & Laron, Z. (1968). Psychological aspects of pituitary insufficiency in children and adolescents with special reference to growth hormone. *Israel Journal of Medical Science, 4*, 953–961.

Franks, S., Jacobs, H. S., Martin, N., & Nabarro, J. D. N. (1978). Hyperprolactinaemia and impotence. *Clinical Endocrinology, 8*, 277–287.

Furlong, F. W., Brown, G. M., & Beeching, M. F. (1976). Thyrotropin-releasing hormone: Differential antidepressant and endocrinological effects. *American Journal of Psychiatry, 133*, 1187–1190.

Galatzer, A., & Gordon, H. W. (1982). *Cognitive asymmetries in patients with hormones and genetic abnormalities.* Paper presented at the 5th European Meeting of the International Neuropsychological Society, Deauville, France.

Galatzer, A., Beth-Halachmi, N., & Topper, E. (1979). *Intellectual functions in patients with tall stature.* Paper presented at the 2nd European Meeting of the International Neuropsychological Society, Noordwijderhout, The Netherlands.

Galatzer, A., Beth-Halachmi, N., Kauli, R., & Laron, Z. (1984). Intellectual function of girls with precocious puberty. *Pediatrics, 74,* 246–249.

Garron, D. C. (1977). Intelligence among persons with Turner's syndrome. *Behavior Genetics, 7,* 105–127.

Geschwind, N., & Behan, P. (1982). Left-handedness: Association with immune disease, migraine, and developmental learning disorder. *Proceedings of the National Academy of Science USA, 79,* 5097–5100.

Gil-Ad, I., Dickerman, Z., Weizman, R., Weizman, A., Tyano, S., & Laron, A. (1981). Abnormal growth hormone response to LRH and TRH in adolescent schizophrenic boys. *American Journal of Psychiatry, 138,* 357–360.

Gordon, H. W. (1980). Genetic and hormonal aspects of hemispheric asymmetries. *Neuroscience Letters Supplement, 5(S8).*

Gordon, H. W. (1983). The learning disabled are cognitively right. *Topics in Learning and Learning Disabilities, 3,* 29–39.

Gordon, H. W. (1986). The Cognitive Laterality Battery: Tests of specialized cognitive function. *International Journal of Neuroscience, 29,* 223–244.

Gordon, H. W., & Galatzer, A. (1980). Cerebral organization in patients with gonadal dysgenesis. *Psychoneuroendocrinology, 5,* 235–244.

Gordon, H. W., & Harness, B. Z. (1977). A test battery for diagnosis and treatment of developmental dyslexia. *DASH, Speech and Hearing Disabilities, 8,* 1–5.

Gordon, H. W. & Lee, P. (1986). A relationship between gonadotropins and visuospatial function. *Neuropsychologia, 24,* 563–576.

Gordon, H. W., Frooman, B., & Lavie, P. (1981). Shift in cognitive asymmetries between waking from REM and NREM sleep. *Neuropsychologia, 29,* 99–103.

Gordon, H. W., Corbin, E. D., & Lee, P. A. (1986). Changes in specialized cognitive function following changes in hormone levels. *Cortex, 22,* 319–422.

Green, W. H., Campbell, M., & David, R. (1984). Psychosocial dwarfism: A critical review of the evidence.*Journal of the American Academy of Child Psychiatry, 23,* 39–48.

Gruen, P. H., Sachar, E. J., Altman, N., Langer, G., Tabrizi, M., & Halpern, F. S. (1978). Relation of plasma prolactin to clinical response in schizophrenia patients. *Archives of General Psychiatry, 35,* 1222–1227.

Halbreich, U., Grunhaus, L., & Ben-David, M. (1979). Twenty-four-hour rhythm of prolactin in depressive patients. *Archives of General Psychiatry, 36,* 1183–1186.

Harshman, R. A., Hampson, E., & Berenbaum, S. A. (1983). Individual differences in cognitive abilities and brain organization, Part I: Sex and handedness differences in ability. *Canadian Journal of Psychology, 37,* 144–192.

Hier, D. B., & Crowley, W. F. (1982). Spatial ability in androgen-deficient men. *The New England Journal of Medicine, 306,* 1202–1205.

Hollister, L. E., Berger, P., Ogle, F. L., Arnold, R. C., & Johnson, A. (1974). Protirelin (TRH) in depression. *Archives of General Psychiatry, 31,* 468–470.

Hung, W., August, G. P., & Glasgow, A. M. (1978). The hypothalamus and anterior pituitary gland. In W. Hung, G. P. August, & A. M. Glasgow (Eds.), *Pediatric endocrinology* (pp. 38–102). New York: Medical Examination Publishing.

Irie, M., & Tsushima, T. J. (1972). Increase in serum GH concentration following TRH injection in patients with acromegaly or gigantism. *Clinical Endocrinology Metabolism, 35,* 97–100.

Jennings, J. R., Nebes, R. D., & Reynolds, C. F. (1986). Vasopressin peptide (DDAVP) may narrow the focus of attention in normal elderly. *Psychiatry Research, 17,* 31–39.

Judd, L. L., Risch, S. C., Parker, D. C., Janowsky, D. S., Segal, D. S., & Huey, L. Y. (1982). Blunted prolactin response. *Archives of General Psychiatry, 39,* 1413–1416.

Kales, A., Caldwell, A. B., Cadieux, R. J., Vela-Bueno, A., Ruch, L. G., & Mayes, S. D. (1985). Severe obstruction sleep apnea—II: Associated psychopathology and psychosocial consequences. *Journal of Chronic Disease, 38,* 427–434.

Kanter, M. F., & Schreiner, L. A. (1986). *Comparison of cognitive laterality with field independence and the implications for display design.* Paper presented at the IEEE 1986 National Aerospace and Electronics Conference (NAECON, 1986).

Karlberg, B. E., Kjellman, B. F., & Kägedal, B. (1978). Treatment of endogenous depression with oral thyrotropin-releasing hormone and amitriptyline. *Acta Psychiatry Scandanavica, 58,* 389–400.

Kjellman, B. F., Beck-Friis, J., Ljunggren, J. S., & Wetterberg, L. (1984). Twenty-four-hour serum levels of TSH in affective disorders. *Acta Psychiatry Scandanavica, 69,* 491–502.

Klaiber, E. L., Broverman, D. M., & Kobayashi, Y. (1967). The automatization cognitive style, androgens, and monoamine oxidase. *Psychopharmacologia, 11,* 320–336.

Klaiber, E. L., Broverman, D. M., Vogel, W., & Mackenberg, E. J. (1974). Rhythms in cognitive functioning and EEG indices in males. In M. Ferin, F. Halberg, R. M. Richart, & R. L. Vande Wiele (Eds.), *Biorhythms and human reproduction* (pp. 481–493). New York: Wiley.

Klein, R., & Armitage, R. (1979). Rhythms in human performance: 1 1/2 hour oscillations in cognitive style. *Science, 204,* 1326–1328.

Kolb, J. E., & Heaton, R. K. (1975). Lateralized neurologic deficits and psychopathology in a Turner syndrome patient. *Archives of General Psychiatry, 32,* 1198–1200.

Komnenich, P., Lane, D. M., Dickey, R. P., & Stone, S. C. (1978). Gonadal hormones and cognitive performance. *Physiological Psychology, 6,* 115–120.

Laron, Z., Karp, M., Pertzelan, A., & Frankel, J. (1970). ACTH deficiency in children and adolescents (clinical and psychological aspects). In D. De Wied & J. A. W. M. Weignen (Eds.), *Progress in brain research* (Vol. 32, pp. 305–315). New York: Elsevier.

Lavie, P., Metanya, Y., & Yehuda, S. (1984). Cognitige asymmetries after wakings from REM and NREM sleep in right-handed females. *International Journal of Neuroscience, 23,* 111–116.

Legros, J., & Gilot, P. (1979). Vasopressin and memory in the human. In D. T. Krieger, M. J. Brownstein, & J. B. Martin (Eds.), *Brain peptides* (pp. 347–364). New York: Wiley.

Lishman, W. A. (1978). Endocrine diseases and metabolic disorders. In W. A. Lishman (Ed.), *Organic psychiatry* (pp. 595–672). Oxford: Blackwell Scientific Publications.

Masica, D. N., Money, J., Ehrhardt, A. A., & Lewis, V. G. (1969). IQ, fetal, sex hormones and cognitive patterns: Studies in the testicular feminizing syndrome of androgen insensitivity. *Johns Hopkins Medical Journal, 124,* 34–43.

Meltzer, H. Y., Sachar, E. J., & Frantz, A. G. (1974). Serum prolactin levels in unmedicated schizophrenic patients. *Archives of General Psychiatry, 31,* 564–569.

Meyer-Bahlburg, H. F. L., Feinman, J. A., MacGillivray, M. H., & Aceto, T. (1978). Growth hormone deficiency, brain development, and intelligence. *American Journal of Disabled Children, 132,* 565–572.

Miller, L. H., Groves, G. A., Bopp, M. J., & Kastin, A. J. (1980). A neuroheptapeptide influence on cognitive functioning in the elderly. *Peptides, 1,* 55–57.

Money, J. (1964). Two cytogenetic syndromes: Psychologic comparisons I. Intelligence and specific factor quotients. *Journal of Psychiatric Research, 2,* 223.

Money, J., & Meredith, T. (1967). Elevated verbal IQ and idiopathic precocious sexual maturation. *Pediatric Research, 1,* 59–65.

Money, J., & Neill, J. (1967). Precocious puberty, IQ and school acceleration. *Clinical Pediatrics, 6,* 277–280.

Money, J., & Pollitt, E. (1966). Personality maturation and response to growth hormone treatment in hypopituitary dwarfs. *The Journal of Pediatrics, 68,* 381–390.

Nebes, R. D., Reynolds, C. F., & Horn, L. C. (1983). The effect of vasopressin on memory in the healthy elderly. *Psychiatry Research, 11,* 49–59.

Netley, C., & Rovet, J. (1982). Verbal deficits in children with 47,XXY and 47,XXX karyotypes: A descriptive and experimental study. *Brain & Language, 17,* 58–72.

Netley, C., & Rovet, J. (1983). Relationships among brain organization, maturation rate, and the development of verbal and nonverbal ability. In S. Segalowitz (Ed.), *Language functions and brain organization* (pp. 245–266). New York: Academic Press.

Netley, C. & Rovet, J. (1987). Relations between a dermatoglyphic measure, hemispheric specialization and intellectual abilities in 47,XXY males. *Brain & Cognition, 6,* 153–160.

Newcombe, N., & Bandura, M. M. (1983). Effect of age at puberty on spatial ability in girls: A question of a mechanism. *Developmental Psychology, 19*, 215–224.

Pasqualini, R. Q., Vidal, G., & Bur, G. E. (1957). Psychopathology of Klinefelter's syndrome. *The Lancet, II*, 164–167.

Pecknold, J. C., Ban, T. A., & Lehmann, H. E. (1976). Thyrotropin releasing hormone in depression: Clinical and endocrinological findings. *Psychopharmacology Bulletin, 12*, 44–48.

Perks, W. H., Horrocks, P. M., Cooper, R. A., Bradbury, S., Allen, A., Baldock, N., Prowse, K., & Van't Hoff, W. (1980). Sleep apnea in acromegaly. *British Medical Journal, 1*, 894–897.

Petersen, A. C. (1976). Physical androgyny and cognitive functioning in adolescence. *Developmental Psychology, 12*, 524–533.

Powell, G. F., Brasel, J. A., & Blizzard, R. M. (1967). Emotional deprivation and growth retardation simulating idiopathic hypopituitarism I. Clinical evaluation of the syndrome. *The New England Journal of Medicine, 276*, 1271–1278.

Powell, G. F., Brasel, J. A., Raiti, J. A., & Blizzard, R. M. (1967). Emotional deprivation and growth retardation simulating idiopathic hypopituitarism II. Endocrinologic evaluation of the syndrome. *The New England Journal of Medicine, 276*, 1279–1283.

Rosenbloom, A. L., Smith, D. W., & Loeb, D. G. (1966). Scholastic performance of short statured children with hypopituitarism. *Journal of Pediatrics, 69*, 1131–1133.

Rotnem, D., Genel, M., Hintz, R., & Cohen, D. J. (1977). Personality development in children with growth hormone deficiency. *Journal of American Academy of Child Psychiatry, 16*, 412–426.

Rovet, J. (1983). Cognitive and neuropsychological test performance of persons with abnormalities of adolescent development: A test of Waber's hypothesis. *Child Development, 54*, 941–950.

Rovet, J., & Netley, C. (1979). Phenotype vs. genotypic sex and cognitive abilities. *Behavior Genetics, 9*, 317–322.

Schmidt, J. (1977). Treatment of endogenous depressions with Thyrotropin-Releasing Hormone (TRH) under oral administration. *Acta Psychiatry Scandinavica, 55*, 142–146.

Schwartz, M. F., Bauman, J. E., & Masters, W. H. (1982). Hyperprolactinemia and sexual disorders in men. *Biological Psychiatry, 17*, 861–876.

Schambach, H., Schneemann, K., & Müller, E. (1979). Psychic and intellectual development in girls with precocious puberty. *Endokrinologie, 74*, 47–51.

Shaffer, J. W. (1962). A specific cognitive deficit observed in gonadal aplasia (Turner's syndrome). *Journal of Clinical Psychology, 8*, 403–406.

Shurka, E., & Laron, Z. (1975). Adjustment and rehabilitation problems of children and adolescents with growth retardation. I. Familial dwarfism with high plasma immunoreactive human growth hormone. *Israel Journal of Medical Science, 11*, 352–357.

Shute, V. J., Pellegrino, J. W., Hubert, L., & Reynolds, R. W. (1983). The relationship between androgen levels and human spatial abilities. *Bulletin of the Psychonomic Society, 21*, 465–468.

Silbert, A., Wolff, P. H., & Lilienthal, J. (1977). Spatial and temporal processing in patients with Turner's syndrome. *Behavioral Genetics, 7*, 11–21.

Smith, C. K., Barish, J., Correa, J., & Williams, R. H. (1972). Psychiatric disturbance in endocrinologic disease. *Psychosomatic Medicine, 34*, 69–86.

Smith, C. S. (1984). Clinical features and growth hormone deficiency. In P. E. Belchetz (Ed.), *Management of pituitary disease* (pp. 461–486). New York: Wiley.

Solyom, A. E., Austad, C. C., Sherick, I., & Bacon, G. E. (1980). Precocious sexual development in girls: The emotional impact and the child and her parents. *Journal of Pediatric Psychology, 5*, 385–392.

Starkman, M. N., & Schteingart, D. E. (1981). Neuropsychiatric manifestations of patients with Cushing's syndrome. *Archives of Internal Medicine, 141*, 215–219.

Starkman, M. N., Schteingart, D. E., & Schork, M. A. (1981). Depressed mood and other psychiatric manifestations of Cushing's syndrome: Relationship to hormone levels. *Psychosomatic Medicine, 43*, 3–18.

Steinhausen, H. C., & Stahnke, N. (1976). Psychoendocrinological studies in dwarfed children and adolescents. *Archives of Disease in Childhood, 51,* 778–783.

Steinhausen, H. C. & Stahnke, N. (1977). Negative impact of growth hormone deficiency on psychological functioning in dwarfed children and adolescents. *European Journal of Pediatrics, 126,* 263–270.

Strauss, E., & Kinsbourne, M. (1981). Does age of menarche affect the ultimate level of verbal and spatial skills? *Cortex, 17,* 323–325.

Targum, S. D., Sullivan, A. C., & Byrnes, S. M. (1982). Neuroendocrine interrelationships in major depressive disorder. *American Journal of Psychiatry, 139,* 282–286.

Thorner, M. O., Flückiger, E., & Calne, D. B. (1980). Adverse reactions to bromocriptine. In M. O. Thorner, E. Flückiger, & D. B. Calne (Eds.), *Bromocriptine: A clinical and pharmacological review* (pp. 143–153). New York: Raven.

Tolis, G., Bird, C., Bertrand, G., McKenzie, J. M., & Ezrin, C. (1978). Pituitary hyperthyroidism: Case report and review of the literature. *The American Journal of Medicine, 64,* 177–181.

Turner, T. H., Cookson, J. C., Wass, J. A. H., Drury, P. L., Price, P. A., & Besser, G. M. (1984). Psychotic reactions during treatment of pituitary tumours with dopamine agonists. *British Medical Journal, 289,* 1101–1103.

Vogel, H. P., Benkert, O., Illig, R., Müller-Oerlinghausen, B., & Poppenberg, A. (1977). Psychoendocrinological and therapeutic effects of TRH in depression. *Acta Psychiatry Scandanavica, 56,* 223–232.

Von Werder, K. (1985). Recent advances in the diagnosis and treatment of hyperprolactinemia. In H. Imura (Ed.), *The pituitary gland* (pp. 405–439). New York: Raven.

Waber, D. P. (1976). Sex differences in cognition: A function of maturation rate? *Science, 192,* 572–574.

Wakeling, A. (1972). Comparative study of psychiatric patients with Klinefelter's syndrome and hypogonadism. *Psychological Medicine, 2,* 139–154.

Ward, M. M., Stone, S. C., & Sandman, C. A. (1978). Visual perception in women during the menstrual cycle. *Psychology & Behavior, 20,* 239–243.

Weingartner, H. W., Gold, P., Ballenger, J. C., Smallberg, S. A., Summers, R., Rubinow, D. R., Post, R. M., & Goodwin, F. K. (1981). Effects of vasopressin on human memory functions. *Science, 211,* 601–603.

Wesner, C. E., Spangler, P., Petrides, A., Baker, D., & Telfer, M. A. (1973). Prepubertal Klinefelter syndrome: A report of six cases. *Journal of Mental Deficiency Research, 17,* 237–246.

Whelan, T. B., Schteingart, D. E., Starkman, M. N., & Smith, A. (1980). Neuropsychological deficits in Cushing's syndrome. *The Journal of Nervous and Mental Disease, 168,* 753–757.

Winokur, A., Amsterdam, J. D., Obler, J., Mendels, J., Synder, P. J., Caroff, S. N., & Brunswick, D. J. (1983). Multiple hormonal responses to protirelin (TRH) in depressed patients. *Archives of General Psychiatry, 40,* 525–531.

Wuttke, W., Arnold, P., Becker, D., Creutzfeldt, O., Langenstein, S., & Tirsch, W. (1975). Circulating hormones, EEG, and performance in psychological tests of women with and without oral contraceptives. *Psychoneuroendocrinology, 1,* 141–151.

8

Thyroid Disorders

BILL E. BECKWITH and DON M. TUCKER

INTRODUCTION

Caleb Parry was the first to describe hyperfunction of the thyroid gland in 1825 when he attributed the disorder to traumatic fear (Whybrow & Ferrell, 1974). Graves, 10 years later, again suggested psychogenic origins of hyperthyroidism in his description of the illness in 1835. Finally, in 1886, Mobius clearly differentiated a hyperthyroid syndrome of endocrine origin from the neuroses. Gull characterized a syndrome of hypothyroidism in 1873, but it remained for a report by the Committee of the Clinical Society of London in 1888 to identify symptoms of mental disturbance. Most of the myxedematous patients described in this report had symptoms "ranging from irritability to agoraphobia to dementia and melancholia" (Whybrow & Ferrell, 1974, p. 6).

Several other events during the early part of the twentieth century contributed to growing clinical interest in diseases of the thyroid (Whybrow & Ferrell, 1974). Cannon was conducting experiments to explore the relationship between environmental stimulation and the thyroid gland. Goetsch observed the sensitivity of hyperthyroid patients to epinephrine. More precise and reliable techniques for measurement of hormones and related compounds were being developed. Cannon set the stage for Selye's popularization of the dynamic link between hormones and emotion. Finally, psychodynamic thought sought to explain the differential susceptibility of individuals to stress. All of these trends led to the classical formulation by Ham, Alexander, and Carmichael (1951), proposing that thyrotoxicosis became manifest following the breakdown of adaptive psychological mechanisms. Although this theory has since been proven incorrect (Hermann & Quarton, 1965; MacCrimmon, Wallace, Goldberg, & Streiner, 1979; Wallace,

BILL E. BECKWITH • Department of Psychology, University of North Dakota, Grand Forks, North Dakota 58202. DON M. TUCKER • Department of Psychology, University of Oregon, Eugene, Oregon 97403.

MacCrimmon, & Goldberg, 1980), these events allowed for the study of thyroid dysfunction by psychologically as well as medically trained researchers and clinicians.

DISORDERS OF THE THYROID GLAND

For recent reviews of the major disorders of the anatomy and physiology of the thyroid gland, see Greenspan and Rapoport (1983), Ingbar and Woeber (1981), and DeGroot, Larsen, Refetoff, and Stanbury (1984). Hyperthyroidism, also known as Graves' disease and thyrotoxicosis, is the result of heightened concentrations of thyroid hormones. Although the cause is uncertain, it is believed that autoimmunity is important as well as heredity. The incidence is reported to be about 0.3 cases per 1,000 in the United States, and the prevalence is estimated to be about 0.4% of the population in the United States. Although hyperthyroidism may occur at any time during the life span, it appears to peak during the third and fourth decades. Seven to 10 times as many women as men develop hyperthyroidism; the reason for this sex difference is unknown. Classical features of hyperthyroidism are weight loss, weakness, dyspnea, palpitations, increased thirst or appetite, irritability, profuse sweating, sensitivity to heat or intolerance of cold, and tremor. Occasionally, symptoms may include prominence of the eyes or diplopia, and goiter may precede for some time the development of all other symptoms.

Adult hypothyroidism, also known as Gull's disease and myxedema, results from a depletion in the concentration of thyroid hormones. Although full-blown myxedema is uncommon, hypothyroidism occurs at a rate of about one eighth that of hyperthyroidism. As was the case for hyperthyroidism, this illness is also more common in women: Four to seven times more women than men develop hypothyroidism. Hypothyroidism often occurs as a product of treatment for Graves' disease or as a result of Hashimoto's thyroiditis. Prominent clinical signs of hypothyroidism are puffy face, marked cold intolerance, and coarse, dry skin and hair. The diagnosis of myxedema is often missed, often for periods of several years, because the onset of symptoms is so gradual.

The final major subtype of thyroid disorder is known as Hashimoto's thyroiditis. This disorder is manifested as an often painless, diffuse enlargement of the thyroid gland. It occurs most often in women who are often euthyroid. Occasionally, patients (about 20% of these patients when first seen) present with mild thyrotoxicosis but eventually the thyroid atrophies, hypothyroidism develops, and myxedema may appear. The incidence of Hashimoto's thyroiditis is believed to be equal to that of Graves' disease or about 0.3 to 1.5 cases per 1,000. Women are 15 to 20 times more likely to develop Hashimoto's thyroiditis than men. Although this disorder may appear at any age, it is most likely to occur in individuals 30 to 50 years of age.

ANATOMY AND PHYSIOLOGY OF THE THYROID GLAND

The thyroid gland is one of the largest endocrine glands, weighing about 20 g in an adult human. It consists of two lobes that are roughly 2 to 2.5 cm in both width and thickness and about 4 cm in length. The two lobes are connected by means of an isthmus, and the right lobe is generally larger and more vascularized than the left lobe. Arterial blood is supplied by the superior thyroid arteries, arising from the external carotoids, and by the inferior thyroid arteries, arising from the subclavan arteries. Autonomic innervation is provided by both adrenergic (sympathetic) and cholinergic (parasympathetic) neurons. Microscopic analysis of the gland indicates that it is composed of closely packed follicles served by an elaborate capillary network. These follicles contain large stores of thyroglobin that provides the major constituent of total thyroid mass and that stores about 100 days of the average output of thyroid hormones.

Synthesis and Metabolism of Thyroid Hormones

Synthesis of thyroid hormones is dependent upon the availability of adequate quantities of exogenous iodine. The iodine used in the formation of thyroid hormones is provided by inorganic iodide from the diet, iodide leak (passive loss of iodide from the thyroid into the blood), and peripheral deiodination of thyroid hormones. Iodide is concentrated in extracellular fluid, from which it is drawn during the synthesis of thyroid hormones, at 1 to 1.5 micrograms per 100 ml of serum with a total pool of about 250 micrograms. Iodide is stored in red blood cells and intraluminal fluids such as saliva and gastric juice and is cleared predominately through the thyroid and kidney. However, the kidney reabsorbs iodide passively; so it is not considered as sharing in thyroidal homeostasis. About 500 micrograms of iodine, which is slightly less than the average daily intake in the United States, is lost through the urine daily. The major channel for removal of iodide from the extracellular fluid is the thyroid gland that contains about 8,000 micrograms of iodine that turns over at a rate of about 1% per day. The thyroid gland is unique among endocrine glands in this respect, in that it has a large store of hormone and a slow rate of turnover. This large reservoir provides extended protection against depletion of circulating thyroid hormone in the event of termination of synthesis of thyroid hormones.

The basic process by which thyroid hormones are synthesized begins with the active transport, which is increased in the presence of thyroid-stimulating hormone (TSH), of iodine into the thyroglobulin within the follicles of the thyroid gland. Next, iodide is oxidized, and oxidized tyrosyl residues are iodinated to yield the iodotyrosines monoiodotyrosine (MIT) and diiodotyrosine (DIT). MIT and DIT are then coupled to form hormonally active the iodothyronines 3,5,3′,5′-tetraiodothyronine (L-thyroxine) (T4) and 3,5,3′-triiodothyronine (T3). T3 and T4 are held within the thyroglobulin, which serves as a prohormone for T4, by peptide bonds until their release. Release of thyroid hormones involves hydrolysis of thyroglobulin by thyroid protease and peptidases that liberate free iodinated amino acids and passes the iodothyronines into the general circulation.

Once in the plasma, T4 is found in the highest concentration of any thyroid hormone or metabolite. It is the only iodotyronine or derivative that arises solely from the thyroid gland. Some T3 comes directly from the thyroid gland, but most is believed to originate in peripheral tissue where it is formed by removal of a single iodine atom from T4. T3 is several times more potent in all classical thyromimetic actions than T4. With about one-third of all T4 converted into T3 during its metabolism, the question arises as to whether all metabolic activity of T4 can be attributed to T3. In other words, is T4 a prohormone for T3 as thyroglobulin is a prohormone for T4? This issue remains unresolved. Most of the T4 released by the thyroid is bound to inter-alpha-globulin (TBG) and T4-binding prealbumin (TBPA) and to a lesser extent albumin in the plasma, whereas most T3 is bound to TBG and to a lesser extent albumin. The free T4 is 0.03% of the total in normal plasma and is concentrated at about 2 nanograms per 100 ml. Most believe that it is the free hormone that is available to tissue and, therefore, may induce metabolic changes and undergo metabolic degradation. This concept is called the "free thyroid hypothesis" and implies the existence within the cell or on its surface of receptors that engage the hormone in a reversible interaction. Indeed, receptors that bind T3 and T4 have been discovered in the cytosol of many tissues. These receptors have been found in cell nuclei, mitochondria, and plasma membranes of many organs.

About 80% of the metabolism of T4 and its derivatives takes place by enzymatic monodeiodination, that is, removal of one iodine at a time. T4 is metabolized either by 5'-monodeiodinase that removes an iodine atom from the outer ring of the parent molecule to form T3 or by 5-monodeiodinase that removes an iodine molecule from the inner ring of the parent molecule to form reverse T3 (rT3), which is believed to be metabolically inert. T3 and rT3, in turn, are acted on by 5'- and 5-monodeiodinases to yield the three diiodo-L-thyronines (T2) that are monodeiodinated to yield the two possible monoiodo-L-thryronines (T1). Deaminated and decarboxylated derivatives of T3 and T4, tetrac and triac, are also formed in the plasma and metabolized by deiodination and conjugation before being excreted in bile.

The level of activity of thyroid hormones is complex and multiply determined. First, activity is a function of the rate of secretion of T3 and T4 from the thyroid gland, the rate that target tissue receives T3 generated by other organs, and the rate at which the target tissue can convert T4 into T3. Second, according to the free thyroid hypothesis, alterations in interaction of thyroid hormones with their binding proteins (especially TBG that is the main binding protein for thyroid hormones) should also determine activity. This appears to be the case as several conditions have been found to increase the concentration of TBG (e.g., pregnancy, estrogens, oral contraceptives, neonatal state, treatment with perphenazine) and decrease it (e.g., androgens, glucocorticoids, major systemic illness). Interestingly, although these changes force a shift in hormone from the free to the bound state or vice versa, alter the metabolic clearance rate, and alter the quantity of hormone removed from the plasma, the concentration of free hormone is soon returned to normal by altering the release of hormone from the thyroid gland. Thus these changes alter the total hormone concentration and the kinetics of hormone metabolism, but they do not, in the long run, alter absolute quantity of the hormone that enters the cell, acts, and is metabolized.

However, the consequence of an alteration in the rate of supply of thyroid hormone is entirely different. For example, in hyperthyroid states, the total concentration of thyroid hormone is increased that leads to a decrease in unoccupied TBG-binding sites and an increase in the concentration of both free and bound hormone. Because there is a fixed quantity of TBG, the concentration of free thyroid hormone would increase beyond normal values. The converse happens during hypothyroidism, leading to a decrease in the concentration of free thyroid hormone. Thus pathology appears to be a consequence of alteration of the rate of production rather than an alteration in the binding of thyroid hormone.

Regulation of Thyroid Function

Regulation of thyroid function is accomplished by means of both classical negative feedback control by the pituitary and the hypothalamus and autoregulatory mechanisms not found in other endocrine glands. The hypothalamic-pituitary-thyroid complex is governed by concentration changes in hormones of thyroid, pituitary, and hypothalamic origins. The activity of the thyroid gland is predominately regulated by thyroid-stimulating hormone (TSH). TSH is a glycoprotein hormone that has a molecular weight of about 28,000 daltons. It consists of two subunits, an alpha and a beta chain. The alpha chain is identical to the alpha chain in follicle-stimulating hormone, luteinizing hormone, and human chronic gonadotropin; whereas the beta chain is unique to TSH and, therefore, mediates its specific actions. TSH is synthesized and released by basophilic cells, thyrotrops, of the anterior pituitary. From there it enters the general circulation to stimulate the synthesis and release of thyroid hormones from the thyroid gland. TSH is transported in an unbound state and has a plasma half-life of about 60 min. Concentration of TSH, in turn, is regulated by the concentration of thyroid hormone and thyrotropin-releasing hormone (TRH) and possibly somatostatin.

TRH is a tripeptide that is synthesized in the hypothalamus (possibly in the dorsomedial, suprachiasmatic, ventromedial and/or paraventricular nuclei and/or the preoptic and/or periventricular regions of the hypothalamus). TRH enters the adenohypophysis via the median eminence and hypophysial portal system. Once in the adenohypophysis, it stimulates the synthesis and release of TSH in the thyrotrops. TRH is, in turn, regulated by multiple controls including serotonin, histamine, dopamine, norepinephrine, cold, and stress. Dopamine may also directly stimulate the release of TSH from the adenohypophysis. Somatostatin, on the other hand, is a tetradecapeptide that is synthesized in the hypothalamus (probably mainly in the periventricular and the preoptic areas) and also enters the adenohypophysis via the median eminence and hypophysial portal system. Once in the adenohypophysis, it inhibits the release of TSH.

All known properties of TSH regulation are well explained by the actions of TRH and thyroid hormone interaction with the pituitary alone. Thyroid hormones mediate the negative feedback regulation of the secretion of TSH, whereas TRH, and possibly somatostatin, determine the set point for release of TSH. It is still not entirely clear whether T4, T3, or some combination of each, acts to regulate TSH. It is clear that the pituitary does actively convert T4 into T3, but it is not clear whether both hormones regulate the output of TSH or whether this is a property of T3 alone.

The thyroid gland is also capable of autoregulation, that is, by intrathyroidal mechanisms that are independent of TSH. For example, when increasing amounts of iodide are given, there appears some critical value after which the thyroid blocks further incorporation of iodide and further synthesis of thyroid hormones independent of concentration of TSH. The converse appears to occur during iodide insufficiency. Furthermore, the thyroid gland appears to be able to monitor its own iodide concentration and alter its own sensitivity to TSH. During iodide insufficiency, the thyroid gland can increase the ratio of T3 to T4 secreted and, thereby, enhance its efficiency (remember that T3 is more potent than T4). Other examples of autoregulation are described in Ingbar and Woeber (1981) and Degroot et al. (1984).

Actions of Thyroid Hormones

> The thyroid hormones play upon a great multiplicity of metabolic processes, influencing the concentration and activity of numerous enzymes; the metabolism of substrates, vitamins and minerals; the secretion and degradation rates of virtually all other hormones; and the response of their target tissues to them. As a consequence, it can truly be said that no tissue or organ system escapes the adverse effects of thyroid hormone excess or insufficiency. (Ingbar & Woeber, 1981, p. 171)

The classical action of thyroid hormones is the stimulation of calorigenesis and is measured as increased oxygen consumption. This action has an onset latency of hours to days after alteration of concentration of thyroid hormones and occurs in most tissues with the exception of the spleen, testis, and brain. Although the specific mechanism mediating this action is uncertain, it is believed to result from effects of these hormones either on mitochondrial metabolism or on transport of sodium and potassium across cellular membranes.

Thyroid hormones also stimulate protein, carbohydrate, lipid, and vitamin metabolism. The most notable sequelae of thyroid hormone modulation of protein synthesis occur in the athyreotic infant and child who suffers profound and enduring retardation in growth and intellectual development. Modulation of protein synthesis by thyroid hormones may also underlie many of the metabolic actions of thyroid hormones. Thyroid hormones also appear to regulate all aspects of carbohydrate metabolism. Of interest here is the ability of thyroid hormones to regulate the magnitude of glycogenolytic and hyperglycemic effects of epinephrine. This may account for the thyroid hormone potentiation of insulin's effect on the synthesis of glycogen and the utilization of glucose. Additionally, thyroid hormones stimulate all aspects of lipid metabolism, with the greatest effect on degradation. Thus there is a net decrease in the stores and plasma concentration of lipids in hyperthyroid states. Finally, the thyroid-induced stimulation of metabolic processes increases the demand for co-enzymes and the vitamins from which they are derived. This produces an increased requirement for both water and fat-soluble vitamins in hyperthyroidism.

The similarities between the manifestations of thyrotoxicosis and activation of the sympathetic nervous system have been noted for some time. This action is not a result of increased activity of the sympathetic nervous system as evidenced by the failure to find alterations in catecholamines or their metabolites in either plasma or urine. It may be that thyroid hormones produce effects that are similar to and/or additive to those of catecholamines, which would account for only partial alleviation of sympathomimetic manifestations of thyrotoxicosis by anticholinergic drugs.

An important hypothesis for the action of thyroid hormones on brain function has been proposed by Whybrow and Prange (1981). They suggest that thyroid hormones may increase the sensitivity of beta-adrenergic receptors to norepinephrine. The catecholamine neurotransmitters and the thyroid hormones are derivatives of the biochemical precursor tyrosine. Whybrow and Prange suggest that these substances have been used in vertebrate evolution as synergists in regulating beta-adrenergic neurotransmission. They have parallel effects on several physiologic functions, including oxygen consumption and energy metabolism. Both the thyroid and beta-adrenergic systems respond to mediate nonshivering thermogenesis in response to cold.

Whybrow and Prange emphasize the importance of thyroid action for neural function by pointing out that an increase in thyroid output occurs not only in response to a physiologic stressor, such as cold, but also in response to perception of an adaptive challenge. They suggest that the thyroid-induced increase in the sensitivity of beta-adrenergic receptors may occur in the brain as well as the periphery and may represent an adaptive self-regulatory mechanism for augmenting neural function.

Probably the most important clinical evidence for this hypothesis is the finding that for some depressed patients, administration of thyroid hormone improves the efficacy of treatment with tricyclic antidepressant drugs

(Loosen & Prange, 1984). Recently, observations have been reported in the popular press linking a decrease in thyroid activity prior to menstruation to the psychological dysfunctions of premenstrual syndrome. High levels of thyroid function have been found to produce anxiety or a "tense dysphoria" (Whybrow & Prange, 1981). In some patients, administration of thyroid hormone may precipitate an attack of mania (Josephson & MacKenzie, 1979). Given the general view that dysfunction of the CNS beta-adrenergic pathways is involved in the affective disorders, the Whybrow and Prange (1981) hypothesis has clear relevance for the role of thyroid function in the regulation of affect. Given the importance of catecholamine neurotransmitter systems in recent models of memory (McGaugh, 1983) and attention (Tucker & Williamson, 1984), the Whybrow and Prange hypothesis may also suggest mechanisms for participation of thyroid hormones in altered cognitive function.

Many of the changes in affect and behavior that are routinely seen in hyper- and hypothyroidic patients are generally attributed to hormone-mediated events, such as those outlined before, that originate outside of the central nervous system (Sourkes, 1976). Recent studies have again raised the possibility that T4, either itself or after being converted to T3, may directly influence function of the mature brain. For example, Leonard, Kaplan, Visser, Silva, and Larsen (1981) demonstrated that thyroidectomy induced a marked increase in iodothyronine 5'-deiodinase activity in the rat cerebral cortex within 24 hr, which could be normalized within 4 hr in animals receiving thyroxine replacement. These results indicate that the central nervous system is capable of very rapid response to concentration of thyroid hormone. Dratman et al. (1982) demonstrated that iodine-125-labeled triiodothyronine is selectively concentrated in nerve cells and neuropil in the hippocampus, cortical gray matter, and the choroid plexis of the mature brain of the rat. Evidence such as this suggests that thyroid hormones must be added to the growing list of substances currently known as neuromodulators that act to regulate brain function and behavior (Barchas, Akil, Elliot, Holman, & Watson 1978).

Finally, mention should be made of the mechanism by which thyroid hormones act on cell metabolism. In contrast to the steroid hormones that bind to a cytosolic receptor with subsequent translocation of the hormone receptor complex to the cellular nucleus, thyroid hormones appear to bind directly to receptors on the nucleus of the cell. This action induces cellular effects through both transcriptional and posttranscriptional events. Also, thyroid hormones are known to act on the mitochondria to influence the respiratory chain at the cellular level. Finally, thyroid hormone receptors have been found on cellular membranes, which suggests a primary action at the level of the cellular membrane as has been demonstrated for peptide hormones (e.g., TSH). In short, it may be that thyroid hormones exert their action at multiple sites within the cell by a complex regulated series of cellular events.

Congenital Hypothyroidism

The effects discussed so far relate to the actions of thyroid hormone in a mature brain. These actions of hormones have been referred to as activational (Levine & Mullins, 1966) or baseline hormonal states (Leshner, 1978). In addition, many hormones, including thyroid hormones, have unique actions on the developing organism; these are referred to as organizational (Levine & Mullins, 1966) or early hormonal state (Leshner, 1978). Activational effects are seen as behavioral manifestations of altered metabolic processes, altered sensitivity of peripheral sensory receptors, or alteration of CNS functions. On the other hand, organizational effects occur as a result of permanent alteration of the endocrine and/or nervous system. According to the model presented by Leshner (1978), the concentrations of hormones during critical periods that occur early in life, especially during fetal or neonatal surges, alter sensory receptors, general metabolic state, endocrine systems, and/or brain circuits to determine the pattern of responses available to the adult. Once these neuroendocrine systems are established, they shape the responses of the organism to future situations. It is widely known that hypothyroidism has profound and permanent effects on developing neural and skeletal systems.

The organizational effects of hypothyroidism appear to be localized during the final stages of gestation through infancy (Underwood & van Wyk, 1981). Childhood and adolescent hypothyroidism are comparable to adult hypothyroidism, if detected and treated relatively early. Hypothyroidism in infancy may lead to either "sporadic cretinism" or "endemic cretinism" (DeGroot et al., 1984). In the latter, hypothyroidism is a result of living in a part of the world where nutritional deficiency of iodine is common. The former is a result of thyroid dysgenesis in 80% to 90% of the cases seen (DeGroot et al., 1984). It may also be caused by thyroid dyshormonogenesis (e.g., resistance to TSH), hypothalamic or pituitary hypothyroidism, maternal antithyroid drug ingestion, maternal autoimmunity, immaturity, or iodide exposure. The prevalence of sporadic congenital hypothyroidism has been estimated to be about 1 in 4,000. The term cretin is applied in the case where hypothyroidism in infancy is quite complete and prolonged. Cretinism is usually accompanied by the classical symptoms of mental retardation, short stature, puffy appearance of the face and hands, deaf mutism, and pyramidal tract signs.

Impairment of intelligence is the most obvious sign of congenital hypothyroidism on the CNS (DeGroot et al., 1984). This effect occurs as a result of hypothyroidism during the first 6 months of life and perhaps up to the first 30 months of life. Once incurred, this deficit is permanent. Although the number of autopsies studied is small due to the nonlethal nature of this disorder, in cases where the brain has been studied in humans, it has been shown to be small with retarded development of the cerebral cortex, the cerebellar cortex, the basal ganglia, and the thalamus. EEG studies have shown a slowing of the alpha rhythm and signs of diffuse cerebral dysfunction. In a past study, Hrbek, Fallstrom, Karlberg, and Olsson (1982) reported that the visual evoked response of congentital hypothyroidal patients (aged 1 week to 17 months) was immature and had long latencies compared to the pattern of evoked visual response seen in normally developing children.

The greater the delay in treatment to replace thyroid hormones is begun, the worse the eventual impairment (DeGroot et al., 1984). It appears that signs of intelligence, as measured by standard IQ tests, return to normal in most cases where treatment is begun before 1 month of age but, although gross tests of motor impairment appear to be normal, there seems to be a disturbance of fine motor and cerebellar function (Birrell, Frost, & Parkin, 1983). Based upon evidence from long-term effects of neonatal hypothyroidism on animal learning (Schalock, Brown, & Smith, 1979), more detailed investigation of specific neuropsychological and cognitive functions may indicate deficits not detectable by means of gross IQ assessment. It should also be noted in passing that neonatal hyperthyroidism, though neglected in the clinical literature, has been found also to produce learning deficits in rats (Davenport, Hagquist & Hennies, 1975) and is in need of study in appropriate clinical populations.

If gross hypothyroidism produces gross neurodevelopmental deficits, it is difficult not to think that more subtle hypothyroid conditions may produce more subtle but permanent, neuropsychological deficits. Although further empirical studies are required to examine long-range deficits that persist even after children receive replacement of thyroid hormones, a gross neuropsychological screening may not be an effective approach to characterizing subtle deficits in these children. What may be required is better understanding of the specific role of thyroid hormones in promoting neural development.

One suggestion might be provided by the Whybrow and Prange (1981) hypothesis that thyroid hormones modulate beta-adrenergic norepinephrine receptors. It has been found that the release of norepinephrine seems to be a trigger for myelination of neural fibers. In vitro studies have shown that the synthesis of cyclic nucleotide phosphodieterase is increased when norepinephrine binds to a beta-adrenergic receptor (Prohaska & Smith, 1982). Depending on the specifics of this trigger mechanism, modulation of beta-adrenergic receptor sensitivity by thyroid hormones could alter the triggering of myelination. The increased latency of visual evoked potential is an important clinical sign of demyelinating disorders (Starr, Schmer, & Celesia, 1978).

Because thyroid hormones exert such pervasive effects on cellular metabolism, there are many other possible mechanisms of neurodevelopmental dysfunction (Eayrs, 1964). However, the hypothesis of a norepinephrine-mediated myelination deficit could lead to specific measures of electrophysiological and attentional function. Furthermore, this mechanism is a particularly interesting one because the noradrenergic pathway is responsive to environmental stimulation in development. Thus positive influences on the child's affect and level of arousal would normally augment myelination and thus natural efficiency. If congenital hypothyroidism disrupts this mechanism, it could lead the child's brain to be unresponsive to the beneficial effects of social and cognitive stimulations.

NEUROPSYCHOLOGICAL DYSFUNCTION IN ADULT THYROID DISORDERS

The material in this section was drawn from rather limited literature on cognitive function in thyroid disorders and the fairly extensive literature available on the role of the thyroid system in major affective disorder. Much of what is known about the role of thyroid hormones in mediating cognition and affect comes from clinical case studies. Many studies have used psychiatric referrals to obtain test cases rather than unselected cases of hypo- and hyperthyroidism. Too often, follow-up measures were not undertaken to establish the course and outcome after treatment. Follow-up is necessary in establishing the actions of thyroid hormone balance on cognition and affect as opposed to the acute toxic reaction of over- or underproduction of thyroid hormones. Furthermore, studies have used differing measures of thyroid function that are not comparable. There are numerous tests for assessing thyroid function (Ingbar & Woeber, 1981), each of which has inherent strengths and weaknesses. Future research needs to more carefully standardize the laboratory tests used to define thyroid disorders. The issue of appropriate control groups also needs attention. Studies have often used either no control group or have used only healthy volunteers to establish baseline comparisons for evaluation. Furthermore, it is important to use individuals with other endocrine disorders as additional control groups to establish the possible specificity of action of the thyroid system independently of general toxic states and acute disease.

Psychiatric diagnosis has changed considerably over the past decade to produce more reliable and objective diagnostic criteria (e.g., DSM-III). Additionally, the fields of neuropsychological testing (Lezak, 1983) and cognitive psychology (Reynolds & Flagg, 1977; Wingfield & Byrnes, 1981) have advanced beyond the methods used in most of the existing studies of the thyroid system and behavior. This leaves us with a body of data that are, at times, based upon unreliable, imprecise, and obsolete methodologies (such as DSM-II and mental status examinations) for assessing cognition and affect. The particular alterations produced by endocrine fluctuations are often subtle and specific (Beckwith & Sandman, 1982; Whelan, Schteingart, Starkman, & Smith, 1980). The actions of the thyroid system on cognition and affect are in need of study with the newer methodologies to establish more precisely the actions of thyroid hormones on specific cognitive and affective processes.

Cognitive Effects of Thyroid Hormones

Hyperthyroidism

An early attempt to apply systematic psychological assessment to the evaluation of hyperthyroidal patients was reported by Artunkal and Togrol (1964). Their patients showed slower reaction times than a matched group of normal control subjects, particularly on a more complex reaction time procedure requiring visual discrimination. Several other tasks examined aspects of motor performance, including tracing ability, steadiness, motility, and tapping. The hyperthyroidal patients were impaired on virtually all these measures, producing a performance pattern that Artunkal and Togrol described as appearing like that of fatigued normals. These authors emphasized that the brain dysfunction of hyperthyroidal patients appears especially to influence motor control. It should be noted that their measures included many motor tasks and only a few that would indicate higher cognitive processes. On one such task, the Rorschach Inkblot Test, the hyperthyroidal patients did show signs of altered cognition. They produced fewer responses and relied heavily on the form of the blot rather than other features such as color or shading; this would often be interpreted to reflect greater rigidity in the imaginative process. Further indication of a paucity in creative perception for the hyperthyroid patients in contrast to controls was a high incidence of whole responses and low rates of visualizing human movement.

Although earlier studies mentioned memory impairment and difficulty in concentration among hyperthyroidal patients (Hermann & Quarton, 1965), only three published studies were found that had gone beyond the clinical interview and mental status examination to the use of objective tests in assessing cognitive function in hyperthyroidism. In the first, Whybrow, Prange, and Treadway (1969) presented both hyper- and hypothyroidic patients with the Trail-Making and Porteus Maze Tests. Hyperthyroidic patients improved their performance after treatment and performed better on both tasks than did both treated and untreated hypothyroidic patients, but the authors did not use any control group to indicate how either healthy individuals or patients without thyroid disorders perform. Wybrow et al. (1969) also indicated that hyperthyroidal patients showed difficulty in concentration, impaired recent memory, and difficulty with simple arithmetic. In a more recent study, MacCrimmon et al. (1979) and Wallace et al. (1980) reported the results of a series of cognitive tasks performed by hyperthyroidal female patients and a matched group of healthy community volunteers. The tasks used were chosen to measure (a) concentration and memory: Stroop Color-Word Test, Paired Associate Learning, and the Spokes Test—Part B; and (b) motor and cognitive speed: Finger Tapping, the Spokes Test—Part A; the Competing Voice Message Test; and reading time on the Stroop Color-Word Test. Although there was no reliable difference between the patient and control groups with respect to mean or standard deviations of performance, serum T4 of the group of patients was correlated with impairment on tasks requiring concentration and memory. Moreover, cognitive performance 3 weeks after treatment was no longer correlated with serum T4. Finally, scores on the Paired Associate Learning task were still impaired for those patients who had shown initially high serum values of T4—especially those who were older. Alvarez, Gomez, Alavez, and Navarro (1983) compared the performance on the Tolouse-Pieron Concentration Attention Test of patients with hyperthyroidism to that of healthy control subjects. The patients performed consistently lower than control subjects throughout the period of assessment.

Another strategy for investigating central processes that may underlie cognition is the use of electrophysiological indexes of brain function. Although electrophysiological methods do reflect brain activity, provide continuous recordings from conscious subjects who can perform tasks or offer self-report, and remain completely noninvasive, they do have limitations that should be considered in their interpretation (Shagass, 1977). Among their limitations are: (a) surface recordings of the electroencephalogram (EEG) reflect a mix of events that take place in large numbers of neurons; (b) these events are recorded at a distance from their source, and the effect of distortion due to conduction through intervening tissues is not known; (c) recordings contain a mass of information that is quantifiable only by means of computer interfacing; and (d) statistical methods for quantifying and reducing data are still in the process of being developed. These caveats aside, several investigators have used EEG methodologies to investigate the effects of hyperthyroidism on the central nervous system.

In general, the results of EEG studies have indicated that hyperthyroidism is associated with increased slow rhythmic activity with paroxysmal features, increased alpha, and increased fast activity of large amplitude (Gibbs & Gibbs, 1941; Jackson & Reufrew, 1966; Olson et al., 1972; Skanse & Nyman, 1956; Wilson & Johnson, 1964). The EEG response to intermittent photic stimulation was augmented in hyperthyroidal patients who reported that this stimulation was very disagreeable (Wilson & Johnson, 1964). After treatment, there is a return to normal EEG patterns in nearly all patients (Olson et al., 1972; Wilson & Johnson, 1964). However, these EEG abnormalities appear not to be correlated with the severity of thyrotoxicosis (Olson et al. 1972; Skanse & Nyman, 1956). The incidence of EEG abnormalities has been reported to be greater in young females than in postmenopausal women or men of all ages (Wilson & Johnson, 1964). Also, hyperthyroidism has been associated with higher peak amplitude and negative area under the curve of slow brain potentials and increased reaction time compared to euthyroid controls (Lolas, De La Parra, & Gramegna, 1978). Finally, auditory brain stem responses in patients with hyperthyroidism were shortened with high amplitude, sharp peaks, and jittery contours (Himelfarb, Lakretz, Gold, & Shanon, 1981).

Another EEG strategy has been to administer thyroid hormones to healthy subjects and then to observe the resultant EEG alterations. Although these results cannot be directly equated with chronic or acute endogenous alterations of thyroid hormones, they do provide a pharmacological perspective on the actions of these hormones. Furthermore, convergent results obtained across divergent methodologies strengthen the external validity of the finding. The first to use this strategy were Wilson, Johnson, and Feist (1964) who administered T3 (300 µg/day orally) for 3 days to healthy volunteers. The EEG data showed decreased arousal in all subjects compared to their pretreatment baseline. About half of the subjects demonstrated increased responsiveness to photic stimulation, and a majority of subjects described distorted and intensified afterimages. In a follow-up study, Short, Wilson, and Gills (1968) showed that T3 facilitated visual evoked potentials (VEP) and increased latency and amplitude of secondary components of the VEP. There was no change in the primary components of the VEP. Subjects reported that light was more intense and more objectionable when treated with T3. Subjects also commonly reported having headaches after administration of T3. Although these results are interesting, they must be viewed with caution. These studies were neither done with a placebo control group nor done under double-blind control. Kopell, Wittner, Lunde, Warrick, and Edwards (1970) used a crossover, double-blinded placebo design to evaluate the effects of T3 (300 µg) on the VEP in healthy volunteer subjects. Their findings indicated that T3 induced shorter latencies of the VEP. Also, there was an increased amplitude of the VEP when the subjects were asked to attend to the absence of the flashes of light.

The tentative conclusions that may be drawn from these studies is that increased levels of thyroid hormones impair memory and concentration, alter EEG characteristics (especially alpha and slow wave characteristics) of those with hyperthyroidism, enhance VEPs in healthy volunteers given T3, and alter visual sensitivity of both patient and volunteer subjects. These studies have examined thyroid levels at extreme levels. An important possibility raised by the Whybrow and Prange (1981) hypothesis is that thyroid function may modulate brain activity and performance across a range of normal values. An initial examination of this issue was provided in research by Tucker, Penland, Beckwith, and Sandstead (1984). The thyroid function of normal university students was assessed with measures of T3, T4, and TSH. These data were related to measures of cognitive task performance and to spectral analysis of the EEG recorded as the tasks were performed. Higher plasma concentrations of T3 were correlated with increased delta in the left occipital region and a decreased delta in the right occipital region. Higher concentrations of T3 were also correlated with poorer performance on the digit span task and faster production of the correct responses given on a word fluency task. Although replication of these findings with an independent sample is required, they do provide support for the suggestion that brain activity and cognition are sensitive to thyroid function in the normal range.

Hypothyroidism

Early clinical impressions suggested that "intellectual impairment" was associated with hypothyroidism (Crown, 1949; Reitan, 1953). In the only study we could find using objective methods for assessing cognition in an unselected population with hypothyroidism, Whybrow *et al.* (1969) reported that hypothyroidism was associated with impaired recent memory, difficulty in concentration, and impairment with simple arithmetic. Also, hypothyroidal patients performance on the Trail-Making Test was far worse than that of hyperthyroidal patients and rated well within the Reitan norms for brain damage. This deficit on the Trail-Making Test persisted even after patients returned to the euthyroid state. Performance on the Porteus Maze did not differ from that of hyperthyroidal patients and did not improve after the patients returned to the euthyroidal state as was the case for patients with hyperthyroidism. Although interesting, these findings must, as indicated before, be considered with caution because there is no control group with which to compare performance.

EEG characteristics of hypothyroidal patients show slowing and reduction of amplitude of the dominant rhythms and reduced photic driving (Browning, Atkins, & Weiner, 1954; Lansing & Trunnell, 1963; Ross & Schwab 1939). Average latencies were longer, and average amplitudes were smaller for VEPs in hypothyroidal patients when compared to those of a control group matched for sex and age. Replacement therapy was followed by a return of normal VEPs in the patient group (Nishitani & Kooi, 1968). Levander and Rosenqvist (1979) compared performance of hypothyroidal patients on the Critical Flicker-Fusion and Vernier Visual Acuity Tests before and 7 wk and 1 yr after replacement therapy. Patients improved on both tasks after 7 wk but did not improve further at the 1-yr follow-up. This study did not include necessary control groups. Lolas *et al.* (1978) demonstrated that hypothyroidal patients demonstrated the lowest peak values and negative area under the curve of event-related slow potentials when compared to both euthyroid and hyperthyroid control groups. Himelfarb *et al.* (1981) showed that auditory brain stem responses of hypothyroidal patients were prolonged with diminished amplitude, flattened peaks, and poor synchronization. Although these results are opposite to those reported before for hyperthyroidal patients, they are congruent with descriptions of hearing impairment in hypothyroidism that is corrected with replacement therapy (Howarth & Loyd, 1956; Hilger, 1956). However, hearing impairment due to hypothyroidism may be restricted to younger patients (Parving, Parving, & Lyngsoe, 1983). Finally, sleep patterns of hypothyroidal patients are altered but return to normal with replacement therapy (Ruiz-Primo *et al.*, 1982). Adult hypothyroid patients (aged 20 yr and older) show lessened or absent slow wave sleep during the hormone deficit but younger patients (aged 14–18) had normal patterns of slow wave sleep. Latency for rapid eye movement sleep was initially depressed but increased to normal levels during replacement therapy for all patients.

As in the case for hyperthyroidism, hypothyroidal patients demonstrate cognitive changes as a result of hormonal imbalances. These alterations may be demonstrated in EEG as well as psychometric performance. In contrast to the results reported for hyperthyroidal patients, there may be some enduring cognitive deficits after return to the euthyroid state.

Emotional Effects of Thyroid Hormones

Hyperthyroidism

According to textbooks (see also Loosen & Prange, 1984 for a discussion of the thyroid and behavior) aimed at outlining the major psychiatric manifestations of medical illnesses, hyperthyroidism is accompanied by emotional instability, general hyperactivity, irritability, easy fatigability, heat intolerance, weight loss, diarrhea, amenorrhea (Walker, 1967), feelings of apprehension, restlessness, inability to concentrate, and emotional lability Popkin & Mackenzie, 1980). Hermann and Quarton (1965) compared the reported symptom and history items of hyperthyroid (n = 24) and euthyroid (n = 15) patients and found that several symptoms were significantly able to differentiate these groups: shakiness, intolerance of hot weather, palpitations, insomnia, difficulty in climbing stairs, impairment in memory, shortness of breath, change in menstrual flow, weight change, change in facial appearance, and change in hair. They also found marginal differences for change in skin, anxiety, irritability, and impaired concentration.

Whybrow *et al.* (1969) administered the Clyde Mood Scale, the Minnesota Multiphasic Personality Inventory (MMPI), and the Brief Psychiatric Rating Scale to hyperthyroidal (n = 7) and hypothyroidal (n = 10) patients. Hyperthyroidic patients demonstrated greater motor tension, less depressive mood, less motor retardation, and a lower total score on the Brief Psychiatric Rating Scale than did hypothyroidal patients. Mean ratings on the Clyde Mood Scale indicated that hyperthyroidal patients rated themselves as more "clear thinking" than did hypothyroidal patients. The MMPI profile of the hyperthyroidal patients was "somewhat elevated" with no mean scaled *t*-score greater than 70. Although these findings are interesting, they must be viewed with caution due to the lack of adequate comparison groups, failure to use a double-blind methodology, and the rather small sample size.

MacCrimmon *et al.* (1979) and Wallace *et al.* (1980) presented hyperthyroidal patients (n = 19) and healthy volunteers (n = 19) the Medical Facts Sheet, the MMPI, and the Psychiatric Status Schedule both before treatment and at follow-up periods up to 1 yr after beginning treatment. According to the Medical Facts Sheet, the hyperthyroidal patients scored higher on shakiness, weight loss, fatigability, palpitation of the heart, shortness of breath, intolerance of heat, muscular weakness, sweating, difficulty climbing stairs, change in menstrual flow, neck swelling, nervousness, jumpiness, restlessness, tension, irritability, and anxiety. The hyperthyroid patients' response to the Psychiatric Status Schedule indicated higher mean depression–anxiety scores and higher mean total symptom scores than the control group. But the authors concluded that the responses of the patient group on this scale were neither patterned after nor intense enough to suggest psychiatric illness. The MMPI data indicated a similar pattern to those of Whybrow *et al.* (1969) reported before in that no mean scaled *t*-score was greater than 70. When compared to the control group, hyperthyroidal patients demonstrated significant elevations on Scales 1 (Hypochondriasis), 2 (Depression),

3 (Hysteria), 7 (Psychasthenia), and 8 (Schizophrenia). All measures approached those of the control group upon return to euthyroidism.

In sum, there does appear to be an association between hyperthyroid state and "mental disturbance." Checkley (1978) evaluated 267 consecutively admitted patients with manic-depressive psychosis during the years 1950 and 1974. Only five of these patients had episodes (eight among the five patients) of well-documented thyrotoxicosis, and only three of the eight episodes coincided with an episode of affective illness. This and the fact that there are no reports of euphoria developing as part of the hyperthyroid state suggest that the relationship of affective disorders to hyperthyroidism is very weak. The psychiatric manifestation here may be more in line with increased anxietylike symptoms.

Hypothyroidism

Textbooks on psychiatric manifestations of medical illnesses indicate that hypothyroidal patients show symptoms of depression, emotional lability, mental sluggishness, indifference, self-accusatory ruminations, and suspiciousness Walker (1967). More recently, Popkin and Mackenzie (1980) advise that psychiatric presentations may be the first sign of thyroid failure and that signs may be easily missed unless "the physical signs are gross." They go on to suggest that, whereas affective and cognitive disturbances are common, psychoses are infrequent. Hermann and Quarton (1965) reported only one significantly differential feature (i.e., change in voice) for hypothyroidal patients ($n = 11$) and healthy controls ($n = 15$) based on data obtained through an interview. However, their sample was very small, and therefore statistically significant differences would be difficult to detect. They also report marginal differences for change in face, difficulty climbing stairs, change in hair, and impaired concentration.

As indicated before, Whybrow et al. (1969) reported differences between hyperthyroidal ($n = 7$) and hypothyroidal ($n = 10$) patients on the Brief Psychiatric Rating Scale, the Clyde Mood Scale, and the MMPI. The ratings from the Brief Psychiatric Rating Scale indicated that hypothyroidal patients scored higher on depressive mood and motor retardation and lower on motor tension than did hyperthyroidal patients. Hypothyroidal patients also produced higher total scores on the Brief Psychiatric Rating Scale than did hyperthyroidal patients. Hypothyroidal patients also rated themselves as less "clear thinking" than did hyperthyroidal patients on the Clyde Mood Scale. Finally, the MMPI scores indicated a clinically elevated profile (T-Scores above 70 on Scales 1 (Hypochondriasis), 2 (Depression), 3 (Hysteria), 7 (Psychasthenia), and 8 (Schizophrenia). It is interesting to note that these are the same scales that MacCrimmon et al. (1979) and Wallace et al. (1980) found elevated compared to healthy control subjects in hyperthyroidism. Furthermore, it is noteworthy that this MMPI pattern included an elevation in Scale 2 (Depression), which was the highest value on the mean profile, and a depressed Scale 9 (Hypomania), which was the lowest score on the profile. This is a classical MMPI profile for major affective disorders. Whybrow *et al.* (1969) indicated that, in general, their data support the conclusion that hypothyroidal patients are more grossly disturbed than are hyperthyroidal patients. Both the results from the MMPI and the Brief Psychiatric Rating Scale support this conclusion.

Based on these data, depression is a likely psychiatric manifestation of hypothyroidism. However, the data presented before are based upon identifying hypothyroidism at the level of alteration of peripheral T3 and T4. Recall from the earlier discussion of regulation of the thyroid axis that three levels of neuroendocrine control are complexly integrated: hypothalamic as represented by the control of TRH, pituitary as is represented by control of TSH, and thyroid gland as represented by control of thyroid hormones. Based on these regulatory mechanisms, three grades of hypothyroidism may be identified (Evered, Ormston, Smith, Hall, & Bird, 1973; Gold & Kronig, 1984). First, patients may have overt, or Grade 1, hypothyroidism, as represented by the cases we have been discussing. These patients show the classical signs of hypothyroidism with laboratory values showing decreased T4, increased TSH, and alteration of the TSH response to TRH (i.e., the TRH Stimulation Test). Mild, or Grade 2, hypothyroidism presents with few classical symptoms but numerous nonspecific complaints and normal T4, marginally elevated TSH, and an altered TRH Stimulation Test. Finally, subclinical, or Grade 3, hypothyroidism presents with few clinical symptoms and normal T4 and TSH with altered TRH Stimulation Test results. It is this latter group that has gained considerable attention in the psychiatric literature on depression. Several extensive reviews on empirical and clinical issues in using the TRH stimulation test are available (Extein, Pottash, & Gold, 1984; Gold & Kronig, 1984; Gold & Pearsall, 1983; Gold, Pottash, Extein, & Sweeney, 1981; Loosen & Prange, 1982; Prange & Loosen, 1980; Targum, 1983).

According to one suggested protocol (Gold & Kronig, 1984; Gold & Pearsall, 1983), the TRH Stimulation Test (TST) should be conducted on a patient who has not ingested anything by mouth since midnight the night before the test. The patient is placed in bed by 8:30 A.M., and an indwelling catheter is inserted for infusion of TRH and blood draws. Blood samples are obtained at 8:59 A.M. for determination of plasma concentration of T3, T4, and TSH. At 9:00 A.M., 500 micrograms of TRH (protirelin) are infused over a 30-second period. Blood samples are taken again at 15, 30, 60, and 90 min after the infusion of TRH to measure changes, relative to baseline, in plasma concentration of TSH. Side effects of infusion of TRH include desire to urinate, sensation of warmth, nausea, metallic taste, headache, dry mouth, tightness in the chest, and/or a pleasant genital sensation. These side effects are generally mild and transient. Of course, there has been considerable variation across studies of these parameters that may account for some of the inconsistent findings. Minimal variables that must be controlled to produce reliable results are nutritional state of patient; time of day; dose, route of administration, and rate of administration of TRH; and time of blood sampling (Loosen & Prange, 1982). The parameters selected before fit very nicely with the suggestions presented by Loosen and Prange (1982) who suggest, except in the case of anorexia nervosa, that the peak response for TSH is 30 min after administration of TRH and, therefore, that only a 39-min post-TRH sample is needed to evaluate the TST.

The other important consideration in conducting the TST is definition of blunting. Prange and his associates (Loosen & Prange, 1982) have defined a blunted response as the maximum change in TSH in response to TRH being 5.0 microunits per milliliter, whereas Gold and his associates (Gold & Kronig, 1984; Gold & Pearsall, 1983) used a change of 7 microunits per milliliter, and Karlberg and associates (Karlberg, Kjellman, & Kagedal, 1978) used a change of 2.5 microunits per milliliter. Obviously, the alteration in criterion has a dramatic effect on sensitivity and specificity of the test. Furthermore, the particular method for measuring TSH in the plasma influences the values recorded (Sternbach, Gwirstsman, Gerner, Pekary & Hershman, 1983). Several factors have been reported to reduce the TSH response to TRH in both healthy subjects and nonpsychiatric patients, including increasing age, being male, acute starvation, chronic renal failure, Klinefelter's syndrome, repetitive administration of TST, and administration of somatostatin, neurotensin, dopamine, thyroid hormones, and glucocorticoids (Loosen & Prange, 1982).

Despite these considerable complications in interpreting the TST, Loosen and Prange (1982) reported that up to the time of their review 41 studies, involving 917 depressed psychiatric patients of both sexes, reported a blunted response of TSH to TRH. On the other hand, 5 studies involving 36 patients have provided negative results, one of which used the 2.5 microunits per milligram standard. Furthermore, they reported that this blunted TST is specific to depression and closely related disorders. Blunting was characteristic of manic, anorexic, and alcoholic patients in some studies but not of schizophrenic patients. However, one study (Wolkin et al., 1984) has suggested that abnormal TSTs may also be characteristic of schizophrenic patients, whereas another (Roy-Byrne, Gwirtsman, Sternbach, & Gerner, 1984) suggested that abnormal TSTs are not a stress response to acute hospitalization. Blunted TSTs appear to be independent of increasing age, previous drugs, and severity of depression (Loosen & Prange, 1982). Loosen and Prange suggested that 25% of the depressed patients they had evaluated showed abnormal TSTs, whereas Gold et al. (1981) reported that 34% of their depressed patients showed an abnormal TST. Although results on the TST have not consistently predicted outcomes for specific treatments (Loosen & Prange, 1982), a persistent abnormal TST may provide a marker of early relapse for afflicted patients. Finally, it should be noted that recent studies (Gold, Pottash, & Extein, 1982; Nemeroff, Simon, Haggerty, & Evans, 1985) have shown the presence of antithyroid antibodies in depressed patients. This may yield yet another possible means of assessing the relationship between the thyroid system and depression.

What are we to conclude about the relationship between thyroid hormones and emotionality based on the literature reviewed? It appears that the thyroid system does have some relationship to affective disorders. Whereas excess of thyroid hormones contribute to a "tense dysphoria" (Whybrow & Prange, 1981), a reduction of thyroid function is related to depression. It is clear that lowered concentration of thyroid hormones is often associated with depression, may lower the threshold for depression (Whybrow & Prange, 1981), and that an abnormal TST is a concomitant of a large number of major affective disorders. These findings are consistent with the hypothesis of Whybrow and Prange (1981) suggesting that thyroid hormones alter mood by modulating the beta-adrenergic receptor sensitivity to catecholamines. Although, the precise clinical utility of thyroid assessment is still an open question (Baldessarini, 1983; Loosen & Prange, 1982), Loosen and Prange (1984) reviewed several studies showing the success of adjunctive treatment of depressed patients with thyroid hormones in addition to tricyclic antidepressants. Although this does not necessarily indicate a causal role of thyroid dysfunction in depression, it does indicate the possibility of considering thyroid physiology in clinical practice.

IMPLICATIONS FOR MEDICAL MANAGEMENT
AND REHABILITATION

Few concrete suggestions may be obtained from the limited data base available on neuropsychological findings to aid the clinician working toward medical management or rehabilitation. Of the data that do exist, two important conclusions are evident. First, there is an important relationship between thyroid hormones and brain development. The brain is uniquely susceptible to thyroid hormones during a limited period of development, a critical period, and if proper balance is not obtained by shortly after birth, the effects on intellect and motor function are irreversible. Even with appropriate treatment, subtle motor dysfunctions occur, and appropriate assessment has not been completed to see if cognitive function also suffers in afflicted individuals. Early screening for and careful follow-up of infants with hypothyroidism and hyperthyroidism is important. Neuropsychological assessment may offer important insights into intellectual and emotional development of individuals suffering from congenital hypothyroidism.

Second, the interaction of the thyroid system with adrenergic systems suggests that thyroid balance may be important in learning, memory, and affect. Few studies have been completed that assess the actions of thyroid hormones on learning and memory function in humans. This appears to offer a virtually uncharted area for future research. The evidence on thyroid regulation and affect is more extensive. It appears that hypothyroidism is accompanied by a relatively high incidence of depression. Also, thyroid hormones appear to act synergetically with antidepressants to enhance response to treatment. Furthermore, many individuals with major affective disorders show some dysregulation of the thyroid system—for example, an abnormal TST is found in at least 25% of these individuals. However, not all hypothyroidal patients present with major affective disorders, and not all depressed patients show evidence of thyroid dysregulation.

It is still not clear what these findings mean. Is an abnormal TST a biological marker for depression or an index of pervasive subclinical thyroid dysfunction? What is the potential of the TST alone and in combination with other endocrine assessment for diagnosing depression and predicting treatment and prognosis? What is the potential for assessing thyroid antibodies in assessing and predicting treatment and prognosis in depression? Many of these questions remain unanswered. What are the neuropsychological and cognitive ramifications of abnormal TSTs? Abnormal levels of thyroid antibodies? Much more research is necessary before the clinical utility of thyroid assessment is understood. This research should assess the differential effects of thyroid hormone balance in cases of mild, moderate, and severe thryroid disorder. It may be that in severe cases, particularly for hypothyroidism, the end result is a nonspecific organic brain syndrome, whereas in milder cases specific deficits may be detected.

To be able to characterize such specific deficits, improvements in cognitive and attentional assessment will be required. The typical approach to clinical neuropsychological assessment, based on a brain-damage model, may be inappropriate. The patient with a moderate variation in thyroid status may show more subtle alterations in attention and affect that require a focused and specific assessment. Designing the appropriate assessment procedures may be facilitated by more specific hypotheses about the neural systems that mediate the effects of thyroid hormones on brain function and behavior. In addition to greater specificity in cognitive assessment, this research requires greater standardization in the laboratory measures indicating thyroid function. Plasma levels of thyroid hormones may not characterize the individual's functioning as well as a dynamic challenge test. The use of brain electrophysiologic measures may prove helpful in indicating the state of brain activity that is thought to mediate between thyroid function and attention or mood. Finally, an important improvement in experimental design in research in this area is the inclusion of control groups with nonthyroid endocrinopathies (in addition to healthy control subjects) to control for the nonspecific aspects of the disease state. Given the increasing knowledge of the neurophysiological effects of thyroid hormones, it seems likely that neuropsychological research in this area can help characterize the role of an important physiological substrate of human mental and emotional functioning.

SUMMARY

The present review describes the synthesis, regulation, and actions of the thyroid hormones and the major disorders of the thyroid gland. Neuropsychological findings suggest that changes in thyroid hormone balance are associated with both cognitive and affective impairments. The major association appears to be between hypothyroidal states and depression. It is clear from the material presented that much cognitive and neuropsychological research is needed for us to understand and suggest the implications of thyroid control for the clinician.

REFERENCES

Alvarez, M. A., Gomez, A. Alavez, E., & Navarro, D. (1983). Attention disturbance in Grave's disease. *Psychoneuroendocrinology, 8,* 451–454.

Baldessarini, R. J. (1983). *Biomedical aspects of depression and its treatment.* Washington, DC: American Psychiatric Press.

Barchas, J. D., Akil, H., Elliot, G. R., Holman, R. B., & Watson, S. J. (1978). Behavioral neurochemistry: Neuroregulators and behavioral states. *Science, 200,* 964–973.

Beckwith, B. E., & Sandman, C. A. (1982). Central nervous system and peripheral effects of ACTH, MSH, and related peptides. *Peptides, 3,* 411–420.

Birrell, J., Frost, G. J., & Parkin, J. M. (1983). The development of children with congenital hypothyroidism. *Developmental Medicine and Child Neurology, 25,* 512–519.

Browning, T. B., Atkins, R. W., & Weiner, H. (1954). Cerebral metabolic disturbances in hypothyroidism: Clinical and electroencephalographic studies of the psychosis of myxedema and hypothyroidism. *Archives of Internal Medicine, 93,* 938–950.

Checkley, S. A. (1978). Thyrotoxicosis and the course of manic-depressive illness. *British Journal of Psychiatry, 133,* 219–223.

Crown, S. (1949). Notes on an experimental study of intellectual deterioration. *British Medical Journal, 2,* 684–685.

Davenport, J. W., Hagquist, W. W., & Hennies, R. S. (1975). Neonatal hyperthyroidism: Maturational acceleration and learning deficit in triiodothyronine-stimulated rats. *Physiological Psychology, 3,* 231–236.

DeGroot, L. J., Larsen, P. R., Refetoff, S., & Stanbury, J. B. (1984). *The thyroid and its diseases* (5th ed.). New York: Wiley.

Dratman, M. B., Futaesku, Y., Crutchfield, F. L., Berman, N., Payne, B., Sar, M., & Stumpf, W. E. (1982). Iodine-125-labeled triiodothyronine in rat brain: Evidence for localization in discrete neural systems. *Science, 215,* 309–312.

Eayrs, J. T. (1964). Effects of thyroid hormones on brain differentiation. In M. P. Cameron & M. O'Connor (Eds.), *Brain-thyroid relationships* (pp. 239–255). Boston: Little, Brown.

Evered, D. C., Ormston, B. J., Smith, P. A., Hall, R., & Bird, T. (1973). Grades of hypothyroidism. *British Medical Journal, 1,* 657–662.

Extein, I., Pottash, A. L. C., & Gold, M. S. (1984). The TRH test in affective disorders: Experience in a private clinical setting. *Psychosomatics, 25,* 379–389.

Gibbs, F. A., & Gibbs, E. L. (1941). *Atlas of electroencephalography* (Vol. 1). Cambridge: Addison-Wesley.

Gold, M. S., & Kronig, M. H. (1984). Comprehensive thyroid evaluation in psychiatric patients. In R. C. W. Hall & T. P. Beresford (Eds.), *Handbook of psychiatric diagnostic procedures* (Vol. 1, pp. 29–45). New York: SP Medical and Scientific Books.

Gold, M. S., & Pearsall, H. R. (1983). Hypothyroidism—or is it depression? *Psychosomatics, 24,* 646–656.

Gold, M. S., Pottash, A. L. C., Extein, I., & Sweeney, D. R. (1981). Diagnosis of depression in the 1980s. *Journal of the American Medical Association, 245,* 1562–1564.

Gold, M. S., Pottash, A. L. C., & Extein, I. (1982). "Symptomless" autoimmune thyroiditis in depression. *Psychiatry Research, 6,* 261–269.

Greenspan, F. S., & Rapoport, B. (1983). Thyroid gland. In F. S. Greenspan & P. H. Forsham (Eds.), *Basic and clinical endocrinology* (pp. 130–186). Los Altos: Lange Medical Publishers.

Ham, E. C., Alexander, F., & Carmichael, H. T. (1951). A psychosomatic theory of thyrotoxicosis. *Psychosomatic Medicine, 13,* 18–35.

Hermann, H. T., & Quarton, G. C. (1965). Psychological changes and pschogenesis in thyroid hormone disorders *Journal of Clinical Endocrinology, 25,* 327–338.

Hilger, J. A. (1956). Otolaryngologic aspects of hypometabolism. *Annals of Otolaryngology, 65,* 395–399.

Himelfarb, M. Z., Lakretz, T., Gold, S., & Shanon, E. (1981). Auditory brain stem responses in thyroid dysfunction. *The Journal of Laryngology and Otology, 95,* 679–686.

Howarth, A. E., & Lloyd, H. E. D. (1956). Perceptive deafness in hypothyroidism. *British Medical Journal, 1,* 431–438.

Hrbek, A., Fallstrom, S. P., Karlberg, P., & Olsson, T. (1982). Clinical application of evoked EEG responses in infants: III, Congenital hypothyroidism. *Developmental Medicine and Child Neurology, 24,* 164–172.

Ingbar, S. H., & Woeber, K. A. (1981). The thyroid gland. In R. H. Williams (Ed.), *Textbook of endocrinology* (pp. 117–247). Philadelphia: W. B. Sanders.

Jackson, I., & Reufrew, S. (1966). The diagnostic value of the EEG in thyrotoxicosis. *Acta Endocrinologica, 52,* 399–403.

Josephson, A. M., & MacKenzie, T. B. (1979). Appearance of manic psychosis following rapid normalization of hypothyroidism. *American Journal of Psychiatry, 136,* 846–847.

Kopell, B. S., Wittner, W. K., Lunde, D., Warrick, G., & Edwards, D. (1970). Influence of tri-iodothyronine on selective attention in man as measured by the visual averaged evoked potential. *Psychosomatic Medicine, 32,* 495–502.

Lansing, R. W., & Trunnell, J. B. (1963). Electroencephalographic changes accompanying thyroid deficiency in man. *Journal of Clinical Endocrinology, 23,* 470–480.

Leonard, J. L., Kaplan, M. M., Visser, T. J., Silva, J. E., & Larsen, P. R. (1981). Cerebral cortex responds rapidly to thyroid hormones. *Science, 214,* 571–573.

Leshner, A. I. (1978). *An introduction to behavioral endocrinology.* New York: Oxford University Press.

Levander, S., & Rosenqvist, U. (1979). Cerebral function in hypothyroid patients: A study of the vigilance level in patients with hypothyroidism before and during substitution therapy. *Neuropsychobiology, 5,* 274–281.

Levine, S., & Mullins, R. F. (1966). Hormonal influences on brain organization in infant rats. *Science, 152,* 1585–1592.

Lezak, M. D. (1983). *Neuropsychological assessment* (2nd ed.). New York: Oxford University Press.

Lolas, F., De La Parra, G., & Gramegna, G. (1978). Event-related slow potential (ERSP) correlates of thyroid gland function level. *Psychosomatic Medicine, 40,* 226–235.

Loosen, P. T., & Prange, A. J., Jr. (1982). Serum thyrotropin response to thyrotropin-releasing hormone in psychiatric patients: A review. *American Journal of Psychiatry, 139,* 405–416.

Loosen, P. T., & Prange, A. J., Jr. (1984). Hormones of the thyroid axis and behavior. In C. B. Nemeroff & A. J. Dunn (Eds.), *Peptides hormones and behavior* (pp. 533–577). New York: SP Medical and Scientific Books.

MacCrimmon, D. J., Wallace, J. E., Goldberg, W. M., & Streiner, D. L. (1979). Emotional disturbance and cognitive deficits in hyperthyroidism. *Psychosomatic Medicine, 41,* 331–340.

McGaugh, J. L. (1983). Preserving the presence of the past: Hormonal influences on memory storage. *American Psychologist, 38,* 161–174.

Nemeroff, C. B., Simon, J. S., Haggerty, J. J., Jr., & Evans, D. L. (1985). Antithyroid antibodies in depressed patients. *American Journal of Psychiatry, 142,* 840–843.

Nishitani, H., & Kooi, K. A. (1968). Cerebral evoked responses in hypothyroidism. *Electroencephalography and Clinical Neurophysiology, 24,* 554–560.

Olsen, P. Z., Stoier, M., Siersbaek-Nielsen, K., Hansen, J. M., & Kristensen, M. (1972). Electroencephalographic findings in hyperthyroidism. *Electroencephalography and Clinical Neu-rophysiology, 32,* 171–177.

Parving, A., Parving, H. H., & Lyngsoe, J. (1983). Hearing sensitivity in patients with myxedema before and after treatment with L-thyroxine. *Acta Oto-Laryngologica, 95,* 315–321.

Popkin, M. K., & Mackenzie, T. B. (1980). Psychiatric presentations of endocrine dysfunction. In R. C. W. Hall (Ed.), *Psychiatric presentations of medical illness* (pp. 139–156). New York: SP Medical and Scientific Books.

Prange, A. J., Jr., & Loosen, P. T. (1980). Some endocrine aspects of affective disorders. *Journal of Clinical Psychiatry, 41,* 29–34.

Prohaska, J., & Smith, T. (1982). Effect of dietary or genetic copper deficiency on brain cate-cholamines, trace metals, and enzymes in mice and rats. *Journal of Nutrition, 112,* 1706–1717.

Reitan, R. M. (1953). Intellectual functions in myxedema. *Archives of Neurology and Psychia-try, 69,* 436–449.

Reynolds, A. G., & Flagg, P. W. (1977). *Cognitive psychology.* Cambridge: Winthrop Publishers.

Ross, D. A., & Schwab, R. S. (1939). The cortical alpha rhythm in thyroid disorders. *Endo-crinology, 25,* 75–79.

Roy-Byrne, P., Gwirtsman, H., Sternbach, H., & Gerner, R. H. (1984). Effects of acute hospitaliza-tion on the dexamethasone suppression and TRH stimulation tests. *Biological Psychiatry, 19,* 607–612.

Ruiz-Primo, E., Jurado, J. L., Solis, H., Maisterrena, J. A., Fernandez-Guardiola, A. & Valverde-R, C. (1982). Polysomnographic effects of thyroid hormones in primary myxedema. *Electroen-cephalography and Clinical Neurophysiology, 53,* 559–564.

Schalock, R. L., Brown, W. J., & Smith, R. L. (1979). Long-term effects of propylthiouracil-induced neonatal hypothyroidism. *Developmental Psychobiology, 12,* 187–199.

Shagass, C. (1977). EEG and evoked potential approaches to the study of neuropeptides. In L. H. Miller, C. A. Sandman, & A. J. Kastin (Eds.), *Neuropeptide influences on the brain and behavior* (pp. 29–60). New York: Raven.

Short, M. J., Wilson, W. P., & Gills, J. P. Jr. (1968). Thyroid hormone and brain function: IV. Effects of triiodothyronine on visual evoked potentials and electroretinogram in man. *Elec-troencephalography and Clinical Neurophysiology, 25,* 123–127.

Skanse, B., & Nyman, G. (1956). Thyrotoxicosis as a cause of cerebral dysrhythmia and con-vulsive seizures. *Acta Endocrinologica, 22,* 246–263.

Sourkes, T. L. (1976). Psychopharmacology and biochemical theories of mental disorders. In D. J. Siegel, R. W. Alkers, R. Katzman, & B. W. Agranoff (Eds.), *Basic neurochemistry* (pp. 705–736). Boston: Little, Brown.

Starr, A., Sohmer, H., & Celesia, G. C. (1978). Some applications of evoked potentials to patients with neurological and sensory impairment. In E. Callaway, T. Tveting, & S. Koslow (Eds.), *Event-related potentials in man* (pp. 155–196). New York: Academic Press.

Sternbach, H. A., Gwirtsman, H. E., Gerner, R. H., Pekary, E., & Hershman, J. (1983). Meth-odological issues in the measurement of serum TSH—Implications for psychiatry. *Psycho-neuroendocrinology, 8,* 455–458.

Tucker, D. M., & Williamson, P. A. (1984). Asymmetric neural control systems in human self-regulation. *Psychological Reviews, 91,* 185–215.

Tucker, D. M., Penland, J. G., Beckwith, B. E., & Sandstead, H. H. (1984). Thyroid function in normals: Influences in the electroencephalogram and cognitive performance. *Psycho-physiology, 21,* 72–78.

Underwood, L. E., & van Wyk, J. J. (1981). Hormones in normal and aberrant growth. In R. H. Williams (Ed.), *Textbook of endocrinology* (pp. 1149–1191). Philadelphia: W. B. Saunders.

Walker, S., III. (1967). *Psychiatric signs and symptoms due to medical problems.* Springfield: Charles C Thomas.

Wallace, J. E., MacCrimmon, D. J., & Goldberg. W. M. (1980) Acute hyperthyroidism: Cognitive and emotional correlates. *Journal of Abnormal Psychology, 4,* 519–527.

Whelan, T. B., Schteingart, D. E., Starkman, M. N., & Smith, A. (1980). Neuropsychological deficits in Cushing's syndrome. *The Journal of Nervous and Mental Disease, 168,* 753–757.

Whybrow, P., & Ferrell, R. (1974). Thyroid state and human behavior: Contributions from a clinical perspective. In A. J. Prange, Jr. (Ed.), *The thyroid axis, drugs, and behavior* (pp. 5–28). New York: Raven.

Whybrow, P. C., & Prange, A. J., Jr. (1981). A hypothesis of thyroid-catecholamine-receptor interaction. *Archives of General Psychiatry, 38,* 106–113.

Whybrow, P. C., Prange, A. J., Jr., & Treadway, C. R. (1969). Mental changes accompanying thyroid gland dysfunction. *Archives of General Psychiatry, 20,* 48–63.

Wilson, W. P., & Johnson, J. E. (1964). Thyroid hormone and brain function: I. The EEG in hyperthyroidism with observations of the effect of age, sex, and reserpine in the production of abnormalities. *Electroencephalography and Clinical Neurophysiology, 16,* 321–328.

Wilson, W. P., Johnson, J. E., & Feist, F. W. (1964). Thyroid hormone and brain function: II. Changes in photically elicited EEG responses following the administration of triiodothyronine to normal subjects. *Electroencephalography and Clinical Neurophysiology, 16,* 329–331.

Wingfield, A., & Byrnes, D. L. (1981) *The psychology of human memory.* New York: Academic Press.

Wolkin, A., Peselow, E. D., Smith, M., Lautin, A., Kahn, I., & Rotrosen, J. (1984). TRH test abnormalities in psychiatric disorders. *Journal of Affective Disorders, 6,* 273–281.

9

Effects of Occupational Exposure to Chemicals on Neurobehavioral Functioning

BRENDA ESKENAZI and NEIL A. MAIZLISH

INTRODUCTION

Approximately 50,000 chemicals and 2 million mixtures are currently in use in the United States and more than 1,000 additional chemicals are developed each year (EPA, 1976). Large populations are unwittingly exposed to these agents when they either utilize commerical solvents or the agents are inadvertently released into the environment. Workers involved in chemical production or use frequently are exposed to much higher concentrations than those found in the environment (Landrigan, Kreiss, Xinteras, Feldman, & Heath, 1980). It is estimated that as many as 20 million workers are exposed to chemicals that have the potential to affect the nervous system (Tilson & Mitchell, 1984).

As part of the growing concern in the United States about chemical contamination in the workplace and in the environment, a series of Congressional acts (e.g., OSHA, TSCA, Clean Air, Clean Water) have been passed since 1970. Most of these acts mandate that research on the adverse effects of chemical exposure should examine, in addition to the more usual measure of toxicity, "motivational and behavioral factors" that might reflect toxic exposure. Some researchers (Silbergeld, 1983) have suggested that neurobehavioral evaluations are not only important in revealing the direct effects of chemicals on the central nervous system (CNS) but that they should form the primary basis for monitoring all toxic chemicals; they propose that the earliest signs of most intoxications involve changes in mood, affect, or mental processing even when the usual toxic effect is directed toward a nonneuronal tissue (e.g., porphyria, estrogenization) (Silbergeld, 1983). Rou-

BRENDA ESKENAZI • School of Public Health, University of California, Berkeley, California 94720.   NEIL A. MAIZLISH • California Occupational Health Program, California Department of Health Services, Berkeley, California 94704.

tine neurologic evaluations, however, are too gross to uncover subtle changes in function. Consequently, the use of neurobehavioral tools have been employed in recent years to evaluate workers for neurotoxic effects of chemical exposure. Some investigators have proposed specific batteries of tests sensitive to neurotoxic effects (Baker, Letz, & Fidler, 1985; Hänninen, Eskelinen, Husman, & Nurminen, 1976; Valciukas & Lilis, 1980).

The purpose of this chapter is to review the scientific evidence concerning the neurobehavioral effects of three of the most common chemical exposures in the workplace: lead, organic solvents, and organophosphate pesticides, and to present a plan for the clinical evaluation of individual workers.

INVESTIGATIONS OF NEUROTOXIC EFFECTS

With few exceptions, the studies to be described fall into two major categories: chamber or laboratory studies and cross-sectional epidemiologic studies. Although researchers performing chamber studies have more control over exposure dose, they typically only examine the acute effects of chemical exposure. Examining such short-term effects is important for planning accident procedures. In cross-sectional investigations, an exposed worker group is compared with either a group with lower exposure and/or a group with no exposure to the chemical in question. In the best case, the worker groups are similar in all other sociodemographic characteristics (e.g., age, education, race), and potential confounding factors, such as alcohol intake, are either controlled for or matched in the analysis. Moreover, if the time between exposure and outcome is sufficiently long, the study design allows the delayed or chronic effects of the exposure to be manifest.

In both chamber studies and cross-sectional field studies, the response measures should be reliable and valid, specific enough to measure the behaviors expected to be impaired (either by workers' complaint or by the scientific literature) and yet broad enough to measure the full range of potential effects (Melius & Schulte, 1981). If clinical judgments are to be made (i.e., what percentage of each group are within normal limits), then the tools should be standardized. In field studies, especially where large populations are to be evaluated, the tests should be simple, inexpensive, easy to score, and portable (Valciukas & Lilis, 1980).

LEAD

Lead is ubiquitous in the environment. Thus most individuals have a measureable body burden of lead. People are exposed to lead in food, beverages (e.g., contamination from cans, improperly glazed ceramics, and illicit "moonshine" whiskey), drinking water (e.g., from the leaching of lead in piping from soft water), and in air contaminated by automobile exhaust (lead is the antiknock agent present in gasoline) or lead smelter fumes. Young children can be exposed to lead through the ingestion of paint chips (pica). Over 1.25 million workers are exposed to lead in such industries as electric battery production, primary and secondary smelters, and the shipping industry.

Intoxication from exposure to inorganic lead has been recognized for over 2,000 years. Symptoms of lead intoxication include anemia, abdominal pain, vomiting, persistent headache, drowsiness, mood changes, depression, papillodema, ataxia, muscle weakness, paralysis, seizures, and even coma and death. Lead encephalopathy can result from a single severe exposure or a chronic exposure (Repko & Coram, 1979). The underlying pathologic changes associated with lead encephalopathy include brain edema, increased cerebrospinal fluid pressure, inflammation of the meninges, and proliferation and swelling of endothelial cells accompanied by the dilitation of capillaries and arterioles (Goyer & Rhyne, 1973).

Although lead encephalopathy is rarely seen in occupationally exposed adults, with most cases being reported in the United States having occurred in children, there is general agreement that chronic low levels of lead exposure can adversely affect nervous system functioning. In 1972, the National Research Council reported that no studies had examined for neurobehavioral change in workers exposed to concentrations below those that were known to produce overt symptoms of toxicity (Jason & Kellogg, 1980). Since that time, researchers in the United States, Italy, Sweden, Denmark, and Finland have demonstrated that occupational exposure to lead that results in blood lead levels considerably less than 80 μg/dl (a value previously thought to represent the upper limit of safety) produces not only symptoms of neurotoxicity but impairs performance on objective measures of neuropsychologic functioning. It is yet unclear what level of lead exposure is, in fact, safe for the nervous system.

Neurologic Signs and Symptoms

Workers exposed to lead, but not diagnosed as having lead encephalopathy, complain of nervousness, dizziness, headache, weakness of their extremities, fatigue, hyperirritability, somnolence and sleeplessness, a metallic sweet taste, nausea, loss of appetite, weight loss, abdominal cramping, and constipation (Fischbein et al., 1980). Most, but not all, studies have found a significant association between the number of symptoms reported and measures of lead body burden such as blood levels or zinc protoporphyrin (ZPP) levels (Baker et al., 1979; Zimmermann-Tansella, Campara, D'Andrea, Savonitto, & Tansello, 1983; Neri, Hewitt, & Johansen, 1983; Lilis, Valciukas, Malkin & Weber, 1985; Fischbein et al., 1980; Lilis et al., 1982). Not surprisingly, Neri, Hewitt, & Johansen (1983) found that blood lead levels correlated with lost workdays due to illness.

As many as 55% of secondary smelter workers whose lead levels never exceeded 80 μg/dl experience CNS symptoms (Lilis et al., 1977). In another study, a third of secondary smelter workers with a wider range of blood lead levels (21 to 117 μg/dl) reported hand tremor and 52% complained of fatigue (Winegar et al., 1977). Baker et al. (1979) have reported that 38% of workers in a small scrap smelter, all of whom had lead levels between 40 and 79 μg/dl, experienced wrist drop and/or gastroinestional symptoms. In contrast, only 13% ·of secondary smelter workers with a similar range of lead levels had these symptoms.

Two studies have compared symptom reports of lead workers to those of nonexposed controls. The first (Lilis et al., 1982) found that secondary smelter workers with moderate levels of blood lead (61.3 ± 12.8 μg/dl) employed for an average 11.3 yr (±9.2 yr) complained significantly more than did workers in the aluminum industry about personality changes, depression, sleepiness, dizziness, shaky handwriting, and weakness in the hands. The second study (Kirkby, Nielson, Nielson, & Gyntelberg, 1983) reported no difference in the number or frequency of subjective complaints of headache, tiredness, nervousness, or weight loss between smelter workers and a sample of workers drawn from the general population. Although the smelter workers in both studies had similar blood levels, those in the first study had been employed for a longer period of time (9 to 45 yr) than those in the second study.

Even workers with lead levels below 40 μg/dl may experience neurologic symptoms not experienced by unexposed controls (50 μg/dl is the current level that requires removal of the worker from the workplace.) For example, when workers in an electric battery plant, who had lead levels below 35 μg/dl ($M = 20.4 \pm 6.0$), were compared to workers with lead levels between 45 and 60 μg/dl (but never exceeding 60 μg/dl; $M = 52.5 \pm 5.1$) and to unexposed workers, both lead exposed groups had significantly more neurologic symptoms than did the controls (Zimmermann-Tansella et al., 1983).

Neurobehavioral Functioning in Exposed Workers

Table 1 reviews the major studies that examine neurobehavioral functioning of lead-exposed workers. The earliest studies reported by Repko, Morgan, and Nicholson (1975) found that battery workers with blood lead levels above 70 μg/dl were more likely to have hand tremor, poor eye–hand coordination, and higher hearing thresholds than were workers with lead levels below 70 μg/dl. Although some of the battery workers did have intellectual deficits, they did not find any systematic differences between groups on tests of intellectual functioning. They hypothesized that motivational factors may have influenced their test results (Repko, Corum, Jones, & Garcia, 1978). In a subsequent study (see Table 1) comparing nonexposed controls and battery workers with lower blood-lead levels than those studied in the previous study, Repko et al. (1978) did not find differences in hand tremor and eye–hand coordination between the two groups but did find differences in auditory acuity and in visual reaction time. Unfortunately, no tests of intellectual functioning were administered.

TABLE 1. Selected Studies of Psychologic Performance among Workers Exposed to Inorganic Lead

Authors	N	Job or industry	Length of employment (years)	Blood lead level (µg/dl)	Neuropsychological tests	Significant findings
Milburn, Mitnan, & Crockford (1976)	16	Pb-battery	M = 12 ± 9.5	M = 61 ± 12	1. Flicker Fusion (CFF)	No
	15	Plastics		M = 28 ± 10[a]	2. Reaction Time (RT)-Touch	No
					3. Grip strength	No
Grandjean, Arnvig, & Beckmann (1978)	42	Variety Pb (32/42 battery)	Median = 2 1 mo–25 yr	Median = 46.2 (12.6–88.2)	1. Visual Gestalts (learning & reproduction)	Reproduction only
	32	Edible oil and fatty acid processes		Median = 16.8 (10.5–27.3)	2. Word Pairs (learning & reproduction)	No
					3. Graphic Continuous Performance	Time only
					4. Finger Tapping	Nonpreferred hand only
					5. Sentence Repetition	No
					6. Story Recall	No
					7. Digit Learning	Yes
					8. WAIS	Info, comprehension arithmetic, similarities, vocabularly, digit symbol, block design, picture arrangement, and verbal, performance, full scale IQ

(continued)

TABLE 1 (Continued)

Authors	N	Job or industry	Length of employment (years)	Blood lead level (µg/dl)	Neuropsychological tests	Significant findings
Valciukas, Lilis, Fischbein, & Selikoff (1978); Valciukas et al. (1980)	90	Secondary smelter	—	M = 51.2 ± 12.0, 17% < 40, 61% 40–59, 21% ≧ 60	1. Block Design	Yes
					2. Digit Symbol	Yes
					3. Embedded Figures	Yes
					4. Santa Ana (dominant, both)	No
	25	Steelwork	—	94% < 40		
Repko, Corum, Jones, & Garcia (1978)	85	Storage battery	M = 8.7 ± 7.0	M = 46 ± 1.7	1. EMG-CV	Yes
	55	Light manufacture, service, unemployed	M = 4.8 ± 5.9	M = 18 ± 1.0	2. Muscle Strength Endurance, Recovery	No
					3. Tremor	No
					4. Michigan Eye–Hand Coordination	No
					5. Visual RT (Simple)	Yes
					6. Clinical Analysis Questionnaire	No
					7. Marlow-Crowe Scale	No
					8. Auditory Acuity (Threshold and Tone Decay)	Yes
Hänninen et al. (1978)	49	Storage battery, machine shop	—	M = 32.3 ± 10.6 (TWA = 37.9 ± 9.3)	1. Benton Visual Retention (time, errors)	No
	24	New battery work electronics	—	M = 11.9 ± 4.3	2. WAIS Similarities, Picture Comple-	No

Study	N	Group			Tests	Outcome
Hänninen et al. (1978)					tion, Block Design, Digit Span	
					3. Wechsler Memory Scale (WMS) (Visual Reproduction Logical Memory)	No
					4. Santa Ana (Right-hand, Left-hand coordination)	No
					5. Simple RT	No
					6. Choice RT	No
					7. Bourdon-Wiersma Vigilance Test (speed, errors)	No
					8. Eysenck Personality Inventory (Neuroticism, Impulsivity, Sociability, etc.)	No
Johnson, Burg, Xinteras, & Handke (1980)	164	Lead smelter[b]	$M = 12.4 \pm 10.0$	$M = 56. \pm 12.9$	1. Simple RT (visual)	No
					2. Choice RT (visual)	Yes
	194	Zinc plant	$M = 11.9 \pm 8.9$	$M = 39.3 \pm 16.8$	3. EMG-CV	Yes (peroneal)
	86	Residents < 2 miles from plant	—	$M = 22.3 \pm 8.9$	4. Michigan Eye–Hand Coordination	No
	108	Unexposed community	—	$M = 15.2 \pm 6.3$	5. Multiple Adjective Affect Checklist	Yes, depression hostility, anxiety
Mantere, Hänninen, & Hernberg (1982); Mantere, Hänninen, Hernberg, &	89	Prospective Study Storage battery	0	$M = 15.3 \pm 6.7$	1. WAIS (Similarities, Picture Completion, Block Design)	1, 2 yr Block Design
	24	1 yr exam	1	$M = 30.5 \pm 9.6$		
	16	2 yr exam	2	$M = 30.9 \pm 9.7$		
	11	4 yr exam	4	$M = 29.2 \pm 8.4$		

(continued)

TABLE 1 (*Continued*)

Authors	N	Job or industry	Length of employment (years)	Blood lead level (µg/dl)	Neuropsychological tests	Significant findings
Luukkonen (1984)	33	Cable manufacture & power plants			2. WMS Digit Span, Visual Reproduction, Logical Memory	2 yr digit span
		33 1 yr exam	0	$M = 10.5 \pm 3.7$		
		31 2 yr exam	1	$M = 10.3 \pm 4.0$	3. Santa Ana (Right-hand, left-hand coordination)	1,2,4 coordination
		10 4 yr exam	2	$M = 10.5 \pm 4.0$		
			4	$M = 6.9 \pm 2.5$	4. Bourdon-Wiersma	4 yr
					5. Eysenck Personality Inventory	
Hogstedt, Hane, Agnell, & Bodin (1983)	49	Mostly Secondary Pb. smelters & battery factory	18	48.3 TWA (27.3–65.1)	1. Benton Visual Retention (errors)	Yes
					2. Synonyms	No
	27	Steelwire, machinery, ammunition control	6	<21 TWA	3. Digit Symbols	No
					4. Simple RT (visual)	Yes
					5. Dots (speed, accuracy)	No
					6. Logical Function:	No

Study	N	Exposure		Blood lead	Test	H vs. L	H vs. C
					Unfolding, Block, VGA-III		No
					7. Psychomotor: Bolts test, pins, cylinders		Yes
					8. Clacson-Dahl-Learning		
Campara et al. (1984)	20	Electric battery (H) 45–60 µg/d1	—	$M = 52.2 \pm 5.1$	1. WAIS (Similarities, Digit Span, Vocabulary, Digit Symbol, Picture Completion, Block Design)	Yes except block design	Yes except block design
	20	Electric battery (L) <35	—	$M = 31.7 \pm 2.9$	2. Flicker fusion	No	No
					3. Simple RT (Auditory)	No	No
	20	Nurses (C)	—	$M = 20.4 \pm 6.0$	4. Card Sorting (time)	No	No
					5. Symbol Copying	Yes	No
					6. Finger Tapping	No	No
					7. Cancellation tasks	Yes	Yes
					8. Rey Figure	Yes	Yes
					9. Maudley Personality Inventory	Yes	Yes

[a]Eight had previously worked with lead but not for at least 5 yr prior to study.
[b]Female workers not included in table.

In a series of studies by Valciukas and colleagues (Valciukas, Lilis, Eisinger, Blumberg, Fischbein, & Selikoff, 1978; Valciukas, Lilis, Fischbein, & Selikoff, 1978; Valciukas & Lilis, 1980), secondary smelter workers, who had moderate blood-lead levels, were compared to various unexposed groups (steelworkers, Michigan residents) on three neuropsychological tasks that assessed visual-spatial and cognitive functioning (Block Design, Embedded Figures, and Digit Symbol), and a fourth task of manual dexterity and eye–hand coordination (Santa Ana). Significant differences between groups were found on the perceptual-cognitive tasks. Consistent with the findings of Repko *et al.*, both Valciukas, Lilis, Eisinger, Blumberg, Fischbein, and Selikoff (1978) and Johnson, Burg, Xinteras, & Handke (1980) demonstrated that smelter workers with lead levels in the moderate range did not manifest deficits in manual dexterity.

A Danish study (Grandjean, Arnuig, & Beckmann, 1978) and an Italian study both (Campara *et al.*, 1984) confirmed Valciukas's findings of cognitive impairment in battery workers; they found workers with moderate blood lead levels were impaired in cognitive functioning as measured on almost all subtests of the Wechsler Intelligence Scale when compared to nonexposed controls. All three groups of investigators found significant differences on the Digit Symbol subtest and two of the three reported differences in performance on the Block Design subtest as well.

The three investigations that examined visual memory in workers exposed to lead have demonstrated significant impairment in lead workers compared to controls (Grandjean *et al.*, 1978; Hogstedt, Hane, Agrell, & Bodin, 1983; Campara *et al.*, 1984). Three other studies have also found significantly prolonged visual reaction times in such workers compared to controls (Repko *et al.*, 1978; Hogstedt *et al.*, 1983; Johnson *et al.*, 1980).

Although workers exposed to lead in most cases perform within normal limits on standardized tests, their level of abnormal neuropsychological performance correlates with the various measures of lead exposure used to categorize them. For example, Baker *et al.* (1984) found that within a group of workers with blood lead levels ranging from 10 to 80 μg/dl, lead levels were negatively correlated with tests of verbal intelligence (Vocabulary and Similarities, WAIS), mental control (Wechsler Memory Scale), and reports of anger, depression, fatigue, and confusion (Profile of Moods Scale). Other authors have reported a negative correlation between blood lead levels and cognitive performance (Grandjean *et al.* 1978, Campara *et al.*, 1984). Although Valciukas, Lilis, Eisinger, Blumberg, Fischbein, and Selikoff (1978) observed some association between neurobehavioral performance and blood lead levels, the correlations with zinc protoporphyrin, a better measure of past exposure, were even stronger.

The previously mentioned studies suggest that functional impairments occur below the current U.S. occupational standards. Reports by Hanninen, Hernberg, Mantere, Vesanto, & Jalkanen (1978) and, more recently, by Mantere *et al.* (Mantere, Hanninen, & Hernberg, 1982; Mantere, Hanninen, Hernberg, & Luukkonen, 1984) demonstrated that workers exposed to substantially lower levels (averaging around 30 μ/dl) than those mentioned in the studies previously cited are impaired compared to unexposed groups and to their own preexposure functioning. Hanninen et al. found that the time weighted average (TWA) of lead exposure in workers whose lead levels had never exceeded 70 μg/dl (average below 40 μg/dl) correlated negatively with performance on tests of spatial relations (Block Design), visual memory, and manual dexterity (Santa Ana). However, they found no statistical differences between exposed and nonexposed workers. Mantere et al. (1984) examined the performance of battery workers and cable manufacturers 1, 2, and 4 yr after the start of employment. They observed that within the first year of employment the lead levels of the group had doubled and that with an average blood-lead level at 30 μg/dl battery workers demonstrated deficits relative to controls in tests of spatial relations and coordination. Although average lead levels were increased above legal standards by the second year of employment, lead-exposed workers were more impaired in terms of their immediate recall memory for digits in the second year than they were in the first year of their employment.

Reductions in nerve conduction velocities and fibrillations in electromyographic recordings have been demonstrated in many studies of workers with blood-lead levels below 70 μg/dl (Seppalainen & Hernberg, 1972; Seppalainen, Tola, Hernberg, & Kock, 1975; Repko et al., 1978; Johnson et al., 1980). Decreased conduction velocities have been reported for the ulnar (Seppalainen & Hernberg, 1972; Seppalainen et al., 1975; Repko et al., 1978), median (Seppalainen & Hernberg, 1972; Seppalainen et al., 1975), and fibular (Rosen, Wildt, Gullberg, & Berlin, 1983) motor nerves and for the median and sural sensory nerves (Singer, Valciukas, & Lilis, 1983). In contrast, other investigators have not been able to demonstrate slowing in the ulnar and peroneal motor nerves (Baloh et al., 1979; Seppalainen, Hernberg, & Koch, 1979) nor in the median and sural nerves (Jeyaratham, Devathasan, Ong, Phoon, & Wong, 1985). In relation to blood-lead levels, Singer et al. (1983) found that ZPP levels correlated with medial and peroneal motor conduction slowing. Importantly, Araki, Honma, Yanagihara, and Ushio (1980) reported that improvements in median conduction velocity following chelation therapy correlated with changes in blood lead levels.

Workers with moderate levels of lead burden (an average of about 60 μg/dl) demonstrate a decrease in saccade accuracy and a nonsignificant decrease in velocity as compared to controls (Baloh et al., 1979; Baloh, Langhofer, Brown, & Spivey, 1980; Spivey et al., 1980; Glickman, Valciukas, Lilis, & Weissman, 1984). Specchio et al. (1981) reported that lead workers have jerky, irregular, pursuit eye movements.

ORGANIC SOLVENTS

His walk is uncoordinated and wavering and he is looking for support on the walls; loud voices, music or car horns scare him. If he reads a newspaper, he already forgot the first line before he starts the second; traffic signs, faces, names, and even his own vital statistics seem constantly to escape his memory. His dragging incoherent speech and glazed eyes seem to indicate an alcoholic. However, Ben Johnson, forty years old and an experienced painter from Copenhagen is not a drinker.

—translated from Der STERN
February 23, 1984

There is little debate over the acute intoxication resulting from high exposure to most organic solvents. In fact, the euphoric intoxicating effects of solvents have led to their abuse. Sniffing of solvent-containing substances such as lacquer thinner, spot remover, glues, and even marker pens and their resulting CNS effects have been reported widely in the literature (see Cohen, 1975; Oliver & Watson, 1977; Press & Done, 1967; Watson, 1980). There is, however, great controversy over the existence of a so-called "organic solvent syndrome," a syndrome that supposedly results from *chronic* exposure to relatively low levels of organic solvents. Support for this syndrome emanates from CAT-scan reports of house painters that described cerebral atrophy in almost 80% of those with measured intellectual impairment (Arlien-Soborg, Bruhn, Gyldensted, & Melgaard, 1979), pneumoencephalographic findings of cortical atrophy in 64% of workers referred because of suspected organic solvent intoxication (Juntunen, Hupli, Hernberg, & Luisto, 1980), and slightly but significantly reduced cerebral blood flow in house painters (Arlien-Soborg, Henriksen, Gade, Gyldensted, & Paulson, 1982) and paint manufacturers (Risberg & Hagstadius, 1983). Solvent exposure has been implicated also in the etiology of such diseases as multiple sclerosis (Amaducci, Arfaioli, Inzitari, & Marchi, 1982) and Parkinson's disease (Ohlson & Hogstedt, 1981). The Scandinavian literature on the chronic neurotoxicity of solvents is extensive; however, a number of editorials particularly in British journals (Cavanaugh, 1985) have questioned the long-term sequelae of organic solvents.

Another issue that researchers have tried to address is the hazard of low-level, *acute* exposure to organic solvents. Johnson and Anger (1983) have proposed that such exposures may be a common cause of accidents in the workplace.

The evidence for and against the notion that low levels of solvent exposure adversely affect human behavior originates from epidemiologic investigations of neuropsychiatric morbidity in solvent-exposed workers, cross-sectional investigations of exposed and nonexposed populations, case reports, and chamber studies. In many of the occupational studies, workers have been exposed to more than one solvent and, although levels of individual solvents may be within safe levels, interactions between solvents may have enhanced their toxicities. Similarly, ethanol probably operates synergistically with most solvent exposures.

The effects of exposure to organic solvents in the workplace have been reviewed recently (Axelson, Hane, & Hogstedt, 1980; Baker, Smith, & Landrigan, 1985; Seppalainen, 1981; Grasso, Sharratt, Davies, & Irvine, 1984; Johnson & Anger, 1983).

Investigations of Exposures to Single Solvents

Styrene

As is the case for exposure to most solvents, workers acutely exposed to styrene report symptoms of fatigue, difficulties with concentration, nausea, dizziness, and a drunken feeling (Harkonen, 1977; Lorimer et al. 1978).

Scandinavian reports demonstrate that workers in the boat-building industry, who were chronically exposed to styrene (average of 5 years of employment) are more likely to have an abnormal electroencephalograms (EEG) (Harkonen, 1977) and impaired visual motor and psychomotor performance (Lindstrom, Harkonen, & Hernberg, 1976) than controls. These abnormalities were found 20 hr after their last work shift and especially in those whose estimated exposure was at least 25 ppm. A British study by Cherry and co-workers (Cherry, Waldron, Wells, Wilkinson, & Wilson, 1980; Cherry, Rodgers, Venables, Waldron, & Wells, 1981) evaluated boat builders about 48 hr after work who were exposed on average to 93 ppm of styrene. They found that the workers' reaction times were slower than that of an unexposed referent group but did not correlate with years of solvent exposure. However, reaction times did correlate with urinary levels of mandelic acid, a metabolite of styrene. Slowing of reaction times has been found to persist for 4 days with complete recovery occurring after 35 days of no further exposure (Kjellberg, Wigaeus, & Engstrom, 1979). No slowing of reaction times was observed in a very small study of workers exposed to 25 ppm of styrene 8-hr TWA (time weighted average) (Edling & Ekberg, 1985).

Toluene

A recent chamber study of volunteers exposed for 4 hours to 100 ppm of toluene has demonstrated a small but significant impairment in vigilance (Dick et al., 1984). Winneke, Kastka, and Fodor (1974), however, did not find such an effect of the same dose of toluene (for 3 1/2 hr) on the measures of vigilance they utilized. Another chamber study in which volunteers were exposed to 100, 300, 500, and 700 ppm for 20 min each, simple reaction time was found to increase at 300 ppm; complex reaction time increased at 500 ppm, whereas perceptual speed did not increase until 700 ppm was achieved (Gamberale & Hultengren, 1972).

The neurobehavioral effects of chronic exposure to toluene are not well documented. Iregren (1982) reported on a group of 34 rotogravure printers who were exposed almost exclusively to toluene (an average of 16 years) (Elofsson et al., 1980). Measurements obtained in the 5 years immediately preceding the study indicated that the exposure to toluene had decreased from about 150 ppm to 50 ppm during that time period. The investigators compared performance by these printers to a group of painters exposed to a mixture of solvents and to an unexposed control group. They found that, 60 hr after work, the printers performed at least comparably to the nonexposed group on visual spatial skills (Block Design), vocabulary, and perceptual speed (Digit Symbol), and better than the painters with one exception: in a test of simple reaction time the printers were slower than the two other groups. Another study found that the printers compared to the same groups demonstrated a decrease in the amplitude of their nerve action potentials obtained for the sural nerve. These findings are in agreement with those of Cherry, Hutchins, Pace, and Waldron (1985) who failed to detect significant differences between rubber shed workers exposed to greater than 100 ppm toluene and in-plant controls on tests of abstraction (Trail-Making), visual-spatial intelligence (Block Design), perceptual speed (Digit Symbol), manual dexterity (Pegboard), or simple reaction time. Earlier, Finnish (Hanninen & Lindstrom, 1979, cited by Lindstrom, 1982) and German studies (Schneider & Seeber, 1979, cited by Lindstrom, 1982), however, have reported finding minor decrements in short-term memory in such workers.

Carbon Disulfide (CS$_2$)

Carbon disulfide is primarily used in the viscose rayon industry and as a grain fumigant. Hanninen (1971) compared 50 CS$_2$-poisoned workers, 50 CS$_2$-exposed workers, who were not poisoned but had been exposed for at least 5 yr, and 50 nonexposed controls on a battery of psychological tests measuring intelligence (WAIS Digit Span, Similarities, Block Design, Picture Completion, and Digit symbol), vigilance (Bourdon-Wiersma), manual dexterity (Santa Ana), personality (Rorschach), visual memory (Benton), and psychomotor behavior (Mira, Symmetry Drawing). In the 10 yr prior to evaluation, the CS$_2$ levels in the factory ranged from 30 to 130 mg/m3 (10–30 ppm). The authors reported a 15 to 25% poorer performance in the poisoned groups when compared to the nonexposed group in measures of speed, vigilance, dexterity, and intelligence (Picture Completion, Digit Symbol). The exposed group, who was not poisoned, also showed impairments but the changes were less severe (5 to 15% decrements). The manifestations of latent and overt CS$_2$ poisoning differed not only in terms of intensity but also in quality. The latent cases were characterized by a depressed mood, slight motor disturbances, and mild intellectual changes.

Subsequent reports (Hanninen, Hurminen, Tolonen, & Mastelin, 1978; Tolonen & Hanninen, 1978) on a larger sample of viscose rayon workers, confirmed the findings of differences in neurobehavioral functioning between exposed and nonexposed workers. These differences were somewhat less pronounced, however, because of lower levels of exposure in later studies. A discriminant analysis revealed that psychomotor performance and psychological factors (introversion, fatigue) were the best predictors of observed CS$_2$ toxicity. Tuttle, Wood, and Grether (1976) found that after adjusting for age, estimates of CS$_2$ exposure correlated with reaction time, dexterity, visual-spatial skills (block design), and visual search.

Workers exposed to CS$_2$ often demonstrate decreased motor nerve conduction velocities. Ten yr after termination of exposure to CS$_2$, 95% of workers, who had been exposed to high levels of CS_2, but only 23% of those with discontinuous exposure histories had evidence of residual peripheral neuropathy (Corsi, Maestrelli, Picotti, Manzoni, & Negrin, 1983). Case reports of workers, who were exposed to fumigants that contained in excess of 20 ppm of CS_2 as well as other chemicals, suggest that most of these workers have extrapyramidal signs and symptoms (Peters, Levine, Matthews, Sauter, & Rankin, 1982).

Methyl Chloride

The neurotoxicity of methyl chloride has been reviewed by Repko and colleagues (Repko & Lashley, 1979; Repko, 1981). Methyl chloride was used as an anesthetic and as a refrigerant. Its present use is as a methylating agent in the production of silicones, butyl rubber, and organic lead compounds, and as a blowing agent for polystyrene foams.

Cases of methyl chloride poisoning present with encephalopathic symptoms including headache, drowsiness, giddiness, and ataxia. A report of 15 workers 13 yr after an accidental exposure to methyl chloride from a leaky refrigeration unit found that 5 had died, and, of the survivors, only 5 were free of neurologic signs (Gudmundsson, 1977).

Chamber studies have revealed no behavioral effects of exposure to 100 ppm of methyl chloride for 7.5 hr (Stewart et al., 1977) or to 200 ppm of methyl chloride for 3.5 hr (Putz-Anderson, Setzer, & Croxton, 1981) as measured by tests of attention, vigilance, compensatory tracking, or time discrimination.

Long-term sequelae of prior methyl chloride exposure include depression, irritability, insomnia, and visual changes (Repko, 1981). Neurological examination of 122 workers exposed to approximately 34 ppm of methyl chloride and 49 nonexposed workers did not detect differences in EEGs, but the exposed group exhibited increased finger tremor and impaired performance on cognitive time-sharing tasks (Repko et al., 1976).

Trichloroethylene (TCE)

Trichloroethylene has been used in the dry cleaning industry (now replaced by perchloroethylene), for degreasing of metal parts, as an adhesive in the shoe and boot industry, and as an ingredient in painting ink, lacquers, and varnishes. TCE acts directly on the CNS as a depressant and has analgesic effects at concentrations of 5,000 ppm. Feldman (1979) has written the most recent review on the neurotoxicity of TCE. Most of the effects reported have resulted from high levels of acute exposure.

Chalupa, Synkova, and Sevcik (1960) observed five cases of acute TCE intoxication; four cases had abnormal EEGs, and three had memory disturbance. Feldman, Mayer, and Taub (1970) reported a case of a worker exposed to TCE vapor from a malfunctioning degreasing machine that resulted in visual field constriction; anesthesia of the face, mouth, and tongue due to trigeminal involvement; and difficulty in chewing and facial and jaw weakness presumably due to cranial nerve VII neuropathy. After 18 mon of no further exposure, some return of sensation was noted, but even after 12 yr, the patient continued to have patches of reduced sensitivity over the periphery of his face.

Chamber studies comprised of a small number of participants have tried to identify the safe level of TCE exposure. Participants exposed to 1,000 ppm of TCE for 2 hr have shown a lowering in the fusion limit of optokinetic nystagmus (Kylin, Axell, Samuel, & Lindborg, 1967). Stopps and McLaughlin (1967) evaluated one participant on tests of manual dexterity (Crawford), mental reversals (Necker cube), card sorting, complex reaction time, and vigilance while exposed to either 100, 200, 300, or 500 ppm for 2 1/2 hr. They found that performance deteriorated as the concentration of TCE increased. At 500 ppm, the participant complained of drowsiness, and there was a pronounced decrease in performance of reversals on the Necker cube test. Another study found that performance on texts of spatial perception (Howard-Dolman), steadiness, and fine motor coordination (Purdue pegboard) were affected at a concentration of 1,000 ppm (Vernon & Ferguson, 1969).

Salvini, Binaschi, and Riva (1971a,b) have observed that volunteers exposed to 110 ppm of TCE for two 4-hr exposure periods were impaired in immediate memory (WMS), complex reaction time, manual dexterity, and on a tachistoscopic perception test. Stewart et al. (1974) were unable to replicate these findings. In contrast, they found that volunteers exposed to 0, 50, and 110 ppm TCE for 7 hr per day for 5 consecutive days showed no difference across exposures on the same tests employed by Salvini et al. (1971a,b). They did, however, find a statistical difference with increasing TCE exposure on a test of manual coordination (Flanagan) (Stewart, Dodd, Gay, & Erley, 1970). In a later study, Stewart and co-workers (1974) found that 100 ppm exposure for a 7 1/2-hr day was sufficient to produce alterations in visual evoked potentials and 200 ppm increased amount of slow waves recorded by EEG.

As early as 1955, Grandjean and co-workers (Grandjean et al., 1955) noted that workers (n = 50) chronically exposed to an average of 25 ppm TCE for 3 to 4 yr frequently complained of fatigue, inability to tolerate alcohol, dizziness, and of autonomic symptoms such as excessive perspiration, tremor, palpitations, and the like. They diagnosed 34% of these workers as having a "psychoorganic syndrome." The number of workers observed with neurologic and autonomic complaints was directly related to their estimated exposure. It is unclear, however, whether the symptoms reported were the result of acute or chronic intoxication. Moreover, it should be noted that a field study of printers exposed to an average of 50 ppm TCE demonstrated no differences in perceptual speed (letter search), verbal intelligence (vocabulary), and immediate memory before and after a weekend or a vacation (Triebig, Schaller, Erzigkeit, & Valentin, 1977).

Tetrachloroethylene (Perchloroethylene)

Perchloroethylene (PCE) is currently the most widely used solvent in the dry cleaning industry. Two studies, a chamber study and a field study, have examined the neurotoxic effects of PCE. Because of the relatively long half-life of PCE, both of these studies examined the acute effects of exposure. Tuttle, Wood, and Grether (1977) compared 18 dry cleaners and 9 nonexposed workers before and after a workday. The dry cleaners, whose exposures ranged between 11 and 32 ppm with peaks of 215 ppm of PCE, were slightly but not significantly more likely to show neurologic deficits; the deficits were related to prior use of Stoddard's solvent, not to their use of PCE. The cleaners showed significant impairment after a workday in perceptual and psychomotor skills, but the decrement correlated with ratings of fatigue. A chamber study by Stewart et al. (1977) found that at exposures of 100 ppm PCE for 7 1/2 hr (substantially higher than most workplace exposures), most of the 12 participants had early signs of narcosis as measured by the EEG. Some of the exposed participants were impaired in terms of coordination as measured by the Flanagan but on neither the Michigan Eye–Hand Coordination test nor on a rotary pursuit test.

Trichloroethane (Methyl Chloroform)

Trichloroethane is primarily used in cold cleaning and metal degreasing. Most chamber studies have failed to find decrements in performance following exposure to levels of methylchloroform as high as 500 ppm. Stewart, Gay, Schaffer, Duncan, and Rowe (1969) found no differences on manual dexterity and coordination in 11 participants exposed to 500 ppm for approximately 7 hr for 5 days; Salvini et al. (1971a,b) observed no decrement in manual dexterity, complex reaction time, memory (WMS), or perception (tachistoscopic presentation) in 6 volunteers exposed to 450 ppm twice for 4 hr, and Savolainen, Riihimaki, Laine, and Kekoni (1981) failed to observe a difference in body sway, visual reaction time, finger tapping, nystagmus, or fusion frequency in participants exposed to a single 4-hr dose of 200 and 400 ppm. However, Gamberale and Hultengren (1977) reported significant decrements at 350 ppm for a perceptual search task (identical number) and at 450 ppm for simple and choice reaction time, manual dexterity, and a perceptual speed task (Trails).

Effects of Exposure to Solvent Mixtures

Solvent Poisoning

A number of Finnish studies have examined workers who had been clinically diagnosed as "solvent poisoned" following exposure to high doses of various solvents for an average of 8 to 10 yr (Lindstrom, 1973, 1980; Juntunen et al., 1980; Seppalainen, Lindstrum, & Martelin, 1980; Seppalainen & Antiti-Poika, 1983). The diagnosis of solvent poisoning in these studies was made between 1971 and 1973 and was based on the worker's history of past solvent exposure and on medical examinations. These studies found that "solvent-poisoned" workers, when compared to unexposed construction workers, performed significantly more poorly in tests of verbal memory (Digit Span), perceptual speed (Digit Symbol), manual dexterity (Santa Ana), and several other tests of psychomotor functioning (Mira Test, Symmetry Drawing) (Lindstrom, 1973, 1980). In another study (Seppalainen et al., 1980) of a larger sample of "solvent poisoned" workers, a number of the WAIS subtest scores were significantly below that for the Finnish standardization sample. Although in the smaller study (Lindstrom, 1980), neuropsychological deficits did not correlate with length of exposure, manual dexterity was found to be related to length of exposure in the larger investigation (Seppalainen et al., 1980).

Sixty-five percent of the poisoned workers had abnormal EEGs that were characterized by increased slow wave activity. More than half of the workers had excessive beta activity on their EEG, and 62% had at least one abnormally slow nerve conduction velocity determination. None of the individuals considered to have low exposures had abnormal EEGs. A follow-up study (Seppalainen & Antti-Poika, 1983) of some of these workers, 3 to 9 yr later, found that the prevalence of abnormal slow wave abnormalities on EEG decreased but a larger percentage had paroxysmal abnormalities. Overall, 47% showed improvements in EEGs. However, more of the patients now showed evidence of neuropathy.

The clearest improvement on psychologic functioning in the follow-up studies was found for a measure of verbal intelligence (Similarities) (Lindstrom, Antti-Poika, Tola, & Hyytiainen, 1982). Short-term memory changed little. Repeated clinical evaluations of some of the solvent-poisoned individuals indicate progressive deterioration even though they had been removed from continued exposure, whereas others have recovered completely. The factors that influence individual differences in recovery from "solvent poisoning" are as yet unknown; age, sex, duration and level of exposure, the termination of exposure after diagnosis, other diseases, and the use of alcohol did not correlate with prognosis in one study (Antti-Poika, 1982), but in another study (Lindstrom et al., 1982), overall psychological prognosis was better with younger age and a longer duration of follow-up, and a poorer prognosis was found for those who used medicines or had other neurological effects.

Painters and Lacquerers

Gregerson and co-workers (Gregerson et al., 1978) noted that following the acute symptoms of solvent intoxication, many painters develop an organic cerebral syndrome characterized by "intellectual and emotional symptoms of a dementia state leading toward a social decline." Table 2 reviews some of the cross-sectional studies that have investigated the effects of chronic exposure to relatively low levels of solvent mixtures.

Finnish investigators have compared age-matched nonexposed referents to 102 car painters who had worked an average of 15 yr (Husman, 1980). The workers had been exposed to solvent concentrations at approximately one third of the recommended occupational standard in Finland. They were exposed to a wide variety of organic solvents including toluene, sylene, white spirit, acetone, methylisobutylketone, isopropanol, and ethanol (Husman, 1980). Toluene at 300 ppm was the major component of the solvent mixture. Painters reported a higher prevalence of fatigue, concentration difficulties, and disturbance of vigilance than did the controls (Husman, 1980). Their acute symptoms during the workshift included irritation and "prenarcotic symptoms" such as itching, nausea, drunkenness, dizziness, and absentmindedness. Polish investigators also have reported symptoms of anorexia, irritability, headaches, malaise, diminished libido, and dyssomnia in shipyard painters (Forycki, 1979).

Clinical neurologic exams revealed that the Finnish car painters when compared to railway workers were more likely to have decrements in light touch, pain and vibration sensation, particularly in the lower extremities (Husman & Karli, 1980). More of the painters were judged to have a "psycho-organic syndrome" as characterized by impaired judgment, comprehension, memory, attention, speed of response, and the ability to provide relevant answers to simple questions. The Finnish car painters performed significantly worse on tests of verbal intelligence (WAIS similarities), visual-spatial intelligence (WAIS Block Design), verbal memory (Digit Span and WMS Logical Memory and Paired Associate Memory), visual memory (Benton test of Visual Retention), and psychomotor function (Santa Ana Dexterity Finger Tapping, and Mira tests) (Hänninen et al., 1976). Simple reaction time, though longer in the exposed workers, was not elevated significantly. (Most studies have found that simple reaction time is a sensitive measure of exposure; see later discussion.) No differences were found for car painters or house painters in frequency of abnormal EEGs or in sensory or motor nerve conduction velocities (Seppalainen, Husman, & Murtenson, 1978; Seppalainen & Lindstrom, 1982).

A Swedish investigation compared car and industrial spray painters with two referent populations of electronics workers (Elofsson et al., 1980). The painters were exposed to an assortment of 20 different aromatic, halogenated hydrocarbons, ketones, alcohols, and acetates at a cumulated dose of about 20% of the recommended occupational standard. Swedish car, industrial, and house painters complained of having many of the same symptoms the Finnish painters and the Danish lacquerers who were exposed to toluene and xylene had (Sabroe & Olson, 1979). Compared to printers, who were exposed mostly to toluene, painters show more symptoms such as fatigue, nervousness, and lack of manual dexterity, a syndrome designated by the authors as the "neuroasthenic syndrome" (Struwe & Wennberg, 1983). The painter group performed less well on many of the same psychological measures as did the Finnish painters including visual-spatial intelligence (WAIS Block Design), perceptual speed (WAIS Digit Symbol, Bourdon-Wiersma

TABLE 2. Selected Cross-Sectional Studies of Psychologic Performance among Workers with Long-Term Exposures to Mixtures of Organic Solvents[a]

Authors	Populations[b]		Major solvents in mixture[c]		Average years of exposure	Significant findings[d]	
	Exposed	Nonexposed	Solvent(s)	Concentration (ppm)[e]		Impaired abilities	Psychological tests[f]
Hänninen, Eskelinen, Husman, & Nur-minen (1976)	Car painters (N = 100)	Railway engineers (N = 101)	Toluene	30		Verbal intelligence	BD
			Xylene	6		Visual intelligence	Benton
			Butyl acetate	7	15	Memory	Mira
						Manual dexterity	SA
							Others
Knave et al. (1978)	Fuel handlers (N = 30)	In-plant controls (N = 30)	Hydrocarbon mixture	43–141	17	Perceptual speed	BW
						Mental arithmetic	
Hane et al. (1977)	House painters (N = 52)	Industrial workers (N = 52)	Hydrocarbon mixture	>100	14	Visual intelligence	FC
Elofsson et al. (1980)	Car, industrial painters (N = 80)	Electronics assemblers (N = 80)	Toluene	13		Visual memory	BW
			Met-Cl	7		RT	Benton
			White spirit	18	18	Manual dexterity	Others
						RT	
Olson (1982)	Paint makers (N = 47)	Warehousers, machine ops. (N = 47)	Toluene	23		Perceptual accuracy	BW
			Met-Cl	199		Visual memory	Benton
			Isopropanol	53	20		
Iregren (1982)	Printers (N = 34)	Painters (N = 34) Electricians (N = 34)	Toluene	50–150	16	Perceptual speed	DS
						Visual memory	Benton
						RT	

Study	Exposed group	Comparison group	Solvents[c]	Exposure	Duration (yr)	Effects[d]	Tests[f]
Maizlish et al. (1985)	Industrial spray painters, printers (N = 124)	Assemblers, material handlers (N = 116)	Isopropanol, Naphtha, Hexane, Xylene, Toluene	68, 10, 8, 4, 3	7	Verbal memory, concentration (not dose dependent)	Digit Span
Cherry, Hutchins, Pace, & Waldron (1985)	Shipyard painters (N = 44)	Joiners (N = 44)	White spirit, Methylene Cl, TCE, Butanol	30–145, 60, —, —	12	Visual intelligence manual dexterity memory, RT	BD, Pegboard
	Rubbershed workers (N = 52)	In-plant (N = 52)	Toluene	>100	>5, N = 38	None	
Valciukas, Lilis, Singer, & Glickman (1985)	Shipyard painters (N = 55)	Other shipyard workers (N = 55)	MiBK, xylene, perchloroethylene, ethylene glycol, mineral spirits		~25	Visual intelligence visuospatial perception	BD, Embedded Figures

[a] Exposed and controls matched on age, sex, and other variables.

[b] All subjects tested at least 15 hr after last work exposure.

[c] Airborne solvent levels expressed as a time-weighted average. White spirit assumed to have the same composition as VM & P naphtha; hydrocarbon mixture in Knave et al. (1977) assumed to be same as gasoline; Met-CL = methylene chloride.

[d] $p < .05$ in t-tests of mean performance.

[e] Solvent exposure of nonexposed was not documented but assumed to be 0.

[f] BD = Block Design (Wechsler Adult Intelligence Scale, WAIS); DS = digit symbol (WAIS); Benton-Benton tests of visual memory (retention or reproduction); Mira = Mira psychomotor test; SA = Santa Anna Test of manual dexterity; BW = Bourdon-Wiersma Dots (visual search); RT = simple reaction time; FC = Figure classification.

dots letter cancellation), visual memory (reproduction), and finger dexterity. Unlike the results of the Finnish study, the Swedes found a significant reduction of reaction time among painters. In general, industrial painters performed less well than did car painters.

A study of Swedish house painters working for at least 5 yr found decreased intellectual capacity, psychomotor coordination, visual memory, and choice reaction time than expected based on premorbid testing (Hane et al., 1977). As in the Finnish study, no differences were found in the frequency of abnormal EEGs, but abnormalities were found in motor (peroneal) and sensory (sural) nerve conduction velocities.

Studies from Great Britain and the United States do not support the Scandinavian findings of an organic solvent syndrome. A recent British study of shipyard painters (Cherry et al., 1985) who had worked an average of 12 yr found significant differences in the number of symptoms reported from in-plant controls. The two groups also were significantly different in reading, visual search, trailmaking, visual spatial abilities (Block Design), manual dexterity (Grooved Pegboard), reaction time, and verbal memory (Bushcke). These differences persisted after all of the scores were corrected for premorbid functioning as predicted by reading scores but were diminished when painters were compared to another referent group who were more similar to the painters in reading abilities. Maizlish and co-workers (Maizlish et al., 1985) in the United States found a small, but significant, increase in the number of self-reported symptoms and a decrease in digit span in workers exposed to a low level of solvents for an average of 7 yr. However, their findings did not correlate with solvent levels measured in the breathing zone. Valciukas and associates (Valciukas, Lilis, Singer, & Glickman, 1985) in the United States compared shipyard painters exposed to a variety of solvents (in most cases for at least 20 yr) with age, sex, race, and education matched controls. They found that painters experienced more symptoms and performed significantly more poorly on Block Design and on Embedded Figures tests than did the controls.

Aircraft Factory Workers

Jet fuels contain raw gasoline and kerosene as their principal components (approximately 90%) as well as a variety of aromatics such as benzene, toluene, xylene, and trimethylbenzene. The 30 most heavily exposed workers (who had been exposed for an average of 17 yr with a TWA of 300 mg/m^3) at a jet-engine assembly plant were significantly more likely to complain of fatigue, apathy, dizziness, tightness in chest, sleep disturbances, and memory impairment than were nonexposed workers (Knave et al., 1978; Knave, Persson, Goldberg, & Westerholm, 1976). Impairments of the exposed workers in perceptual speed (Bourdon-Wiersma) and mental arithmetic were the only differences observed in test performance. No differences were found in the number of workers with abnormal EEGs. Sural nerve amplitudes and ulnar nerve condition velocities were significantly lower in the exposed group. Vibratory thresholds were higher but not significantly in the exposed group. A previous study by the same investigators reported that as many as 85% of the highly exposed group had symptoms of a polyneuropathy (Knave et al., 1976).

Case-Referent Studies

A number of different research groups have examined pension or disability records and found that workers who retire with neuropsychiatric illness are more likely to have been exposed to solvents than are those without neuropsychiatric problems. Alcohol use (Olsen & Sabroe, 1980) was controlled for, or workers with diagnoses of alcoholism were excluded from these studies (Axelson, Hane, & Hogstedt, 1976; Lindstrom, Riihmaki, & Hanninen, 1984). Axelson and co-workers (1976) in Sweden were the first to find an elevated risk of exposure to solvents in workers who received disability pension for neuropsychiatric disease than those who received disability pensions but were free of any kind of mental disorder. Almost twice as many workers with neuropsychiatric illness were painters, varnishers, or carpet layers, all of whom had been exposed to solvents. Danish cabinet-makers, especially those with high exposure to lacquers and glues, were more than twice as likely to receive disability or early pension for neuro-psychiatric illness (including neuroses, psychoses, dementia, and other diseases of the nervous system and sense organs) than were carpenters (Olsen & Sabroe, 1980). A Finnish study of construction workers who had been granted a disability pension for neuropsychiatric illness (including dementia, psychosis, neurosis, psychosomatic disease, cerebral atrophy, vertigo or encephalopathy, or nervositas) were compared to those who had received disability for other diagnoses (Lindstrom et al., 1984). Those with neuroses were 5.5 times more likely and those with any neuropsychiatric illness were 1.6 times as likely to have been either painters or carpet layers (two professions in which solvent exposure is common) than were those without such diagnoses.

Another case-referent study compared males who were admitted to a geriatric unit with dementia or any other kind of encephalopathy and those admitted for other reasons (e.g., heart and respiratory disease) (Rasmussen, Olsen, & Lauritsen, 1985). Each individual was classified as never, rarely, often, or always exposed to organic solvents on the job he had held for the longest time. Those with dementia and psychotic disease as well as those with cerebrovascular disease were more likely, although not significantly, to have been exposed to solvents.

ORGANOPHOSPHATE PESTICIDES (OP)

Estimates of the incidence of pesticide-related health problems are uncertain. The annual worldwide estimates of pesticide poisonings is between 500,000 (WHO, 1973) and 2.9 million (Jeyaratnam, 1985) with a case fatality rate of approximately 1%. In the United States, the number of pesticide-related illnesses may be between 150,000 and 300,000 per yr (Coye, 1985). In developed countries, the percentage of cases with long-standing neuro-psychologic sequelae following acute poisonings ranges from 4 to 9% in large case series (Holmes & Gaon, 1956; Tabershaw & Cooper, 1966; Hirshberg & Lerman, 1984). These estimates, which do not include potential effects of lower level chronic exposure, suggest that neuropsychologic problems of considerable magnitude may be associated with pesticide use. The following is a review of the neuropsychologic and behavioral effects of pesticides in humans.

Short-Term CNS Effects of Acute Exposure

Short-term CNS effects of acute exposure have been observed in pesticide poisonings and in laboratory studies. Single large exposures to OP pesticides cause substantial impairments of the peripheral and central nervous systems. The action of OP pesticides is mediated by irreversible inhibition of cholinesterase in nervous tissue and the subsequent ill effects of persistent high levels of acetylcholine at nerve synapses in effector organs. (Carbamate pesticides have a similar mode of action but are reversible inhibitors of cholinesterase.) The metabolism and mechanisms of action of OP pesticides have been extensively reviewed by others (Gilman, Goodman, & Gilman, 1980; Hayes, 1982; Murphy, 1975).

In acute poisoning, initial symptoms generally correlate with the degree of inhibition of the serum cholinesterase activity: 20 to 50% inhibition in mild poisoning, 80 to 90% inhibition in moderate poisoning, and greater than 90% inhibition in severe poisoning (Grob & Harvey, 1953; Namba, Nolte, Jackel, & Grob, 1971).

The signs and symptoms following OP poisoning have been categorized by the class of receptors affected: muscarinic, nicotinic, and CNS (see Table 3). CNS effects may occur in the absence of peripheral effects (Bowers et al., 1964). In a review of 236 OP poisonings (Hirshberg & Lerman, 1984), muscarinic, nicotinic, and CNS effects were observed in 92%, 44%, and 40% of cases, respectively. Concurrent involvement of all three classes of receptors was less common (17%).

The onset and duration of symptoms in acute poisonings depends on the inherent toxicity of the OP, the dose, the route of exposure, and host factors (e.g., underlying poor health or dermatitis) that increase individual susceptibility. The signs and symptoms of OP poisoning are summarized in Table 3. Symptoms can develop during exposure but usually occur within 4 hr (Morgan, 1982). Mild systemic symptoms may persist for a few hours. Moderate severe symptoms may not peak until 4 to 8 hr after onset and can persist from 1 to 6 days. Recovery may take even longer, for example, in a moderately severe poisoning of fieldworkers exposed to foliar residues of mevinphos (Phosdrin) and phosphamidon (Dimecron), anxiety and other symptoms were still being reported 70 days after exposure (Whorton & Obrinsky, 1983; Mitling, et al., 1985).

TABLE 3. Signs and Symptoms of Acute Organophosphate Poisoning[a]

Site of action	Signs and symptoms
	Following local exposure
1. Muscarinic manifestations	
Pupils	Miosis, occasionally unequal
Cilary body	Frontal headache, blurring of vision
Nasal mucous membranes	Rhinorrhea, hyperemia
Bronchial tree	Tightness in chest, wheezing suggestive of broncho-constriction, dyspnea, increased bronchial secretion, cough, pulmonary edema, cyanosis[b]
	Following systemic absorption
Gastrointestinal system	Anorexia, nausea, vomiting, abdominal tightness and cramps, diarrhea, tenesmus, involuntary defecation
Sweat glands	Increased sweating
Salivary glands	Increased salivation
Lacrimal glands	Increased lacrimation
Heart	Slight bradycardia
Bronchial tree	Same as local effects above
Pupils	Miosis, occasionally unequal
Cilary body	Blurring of vision
Bladder	Frequency, involuntary micturation
2. Nicotinic manifestations	
Striated muscle	Easy fatigue, mild weakness, muscular twitching, fasciculations, cramps, generalized weakness including muscles of respiration[b]
Sympathetic ganglia	Pallor, tachycardia, elevation in blood pressure[b]
3. Central nervous system	Giddiness, tension, anxiety, restlessness, emotional lability, excessive dreaming, insomnia, nightmare, headache, apathy, withdrawal and depression, drowsiness, difficulty in concentrating, slowness of recall, confusion, slurred speech, ataxia, generalized weakness, coma with absence of reflexes, convulsion, depression of respiratory centers, death[b]

[a]Adapted from Grob and Harvey, 1953; Namba, Nolte, Jockrel, & Grob, 1971.
[b]Gastrointestinal, pulmonary, nicotinic, and central nervous system symptoms listed in approximate order of appearance.

In mild to moderate poisonings, early CNS effects include (in order of appearance), tension, anxiety, jitteriness, restlessness, emotional lability and giddiness, which may be followed by insomnia with excessive dreaming and nightmares. With higher levels of acute exposure, headache, tremor, drowsiness, difficulty in concentrating, slowness in recall, and mental confusion may develop. In massive doses that result in near fatal and fatal poisonings, ataxia, slurring or repetitive speech, coma, convulsions, and depression of the respiratory center may occur (Grob & Harvey, 1953; Namba et al., 1971).

Table 4 reviews the laboratory studies on acute neurobehavioral effects of exposure to OPs. Acute dermal doses of a sarin analog sufficient to cause a

TABLE 4. Selected Case Reports of Neurobehavioral Function and Chronic, Persistent, or Latent Neuropsychiatric Conditions Associated with Organophosphate Pesticide Exposures in Workers

Authors	Total cases	Occupation(s)	Mean age (years)	Pesticide(s)	Length; type of exposure	Findings
Holmes & Gaon (1956), USA	600	Factory workers	NA[a]	Various OP pesticides	Acute; accidental	Irritability, confusion, forgetfulness in 25 (4%)
Gershon & Shaw (1964), Australia	16	Greenhouse techs, farmers, agr inspectors	NA	Parathion, malathion carbophenthion, azinphos-methyl	1.5–10 yr; chronic	Schizoid and depressive reaction; memory and concentration impairments; recovery in 6 mon–1 yr
Dille & Smith (1961), USA	2	Cropduster pilots	36	Various OPs and OCs[b]	10 yr; chronic	Psychotic depression, acute anxiety, pesticide intolerance
Durham, Wolfe, & Quimby (1965), Washington state	187	NA	NA	Parathion, TEPP mevinphos, demeton	Acute	11 cases tested showed improvement on vigilance and choice reaction time tests during convalescence

Reference	N	Occupation	OP[b]		Exposure	Effects
Tabershaw & Cooper (1966), California	114	Mixer, loader applicator, fieldwkrs, pilots	Parathion, mevinphos, phorate, demeton	34	NA; acute & chronic	Nervousness, irritability, tremors insomnia persisted > 6 months in 9% of cases interviewed 3 yr after acute poisoning; pesticide intolerance in 18% of cases
Hayes (1982), USA	NA	NA	Parathion, fenthion, trichlorfon, dichlorvos, dimethoate	NA	NA	Delirium, combativeness, depression hallucinations, psychosis
Whorton & Obrinsky (1983), California	19	Agr fieldworkers	Mevinphos, phosphamidon	26	Acute	Anxiety persisted 4 months after mild to mod. severe acute poisoning
Hirshberg & Lerman (1984), Israel	236	Occupational (58%), accidental (31%), suicide (11%)	Parathion, malathion	24	NA	Depression, confusion, agitation, insomnia, motor weakness in 4% of cases

[a]NA = not available or stated.
[b]OC = organochlorine pesticides.

60 to 90% depression in cholinesterase activity were associated with anxiety, psychomotor depression, unusual dreaming, and intellectual impairment (Bowers et al., 1964). Dichlorvos at 0.1–0.3 g/l inhaled for 16 hours per
week over 13 weeks significantly decreased plasma cholinesterase activity
but failed to affect choice visual reaction time, flicker fusion, visual acuity,
visual fields, and stereoscopic vision or color vision (Rasmussen et al.,
1963). One or 2 mg of ethyl parathion or 4 mg methyl parathion ingested on 5
consecutive days over an 8-week period failed to alter two subjects' preexposure performance on tests of Verbal Memory, Benton Visual Memory,
Choice Reaction Time, Language, Vigilance (EX test), Proprioception, or the
Taylor Manifest Anxiety Scale (Rodnitzky, Levin, & Morgan, 1978).

Subchronic Effects of Intermediate Exposure

Daily doses of OPs that are insufficient to cause signs and symptoms of
acute poisoning may produce an influenza-type illness characterized by
weakness, anorexia, and malaise (Morgan, 1982). In this chronic, lower level
exposure, depression of cholinesterase activity may be cumulative, and
there is no predictable correlation between the severity of symptoms and the
degree of erythrocyte or plasma cholinesterase inhibition. Individuals with
cumulative and severely inhibited cholinesterase activity may be asymptomatic. These individuals are susceptible to ill effects, however, if additional
exposure occurs (Grob & Harvey, 1953).

Long-Term CNS Effects

The existence and nature of long-term neurobehavioral effects of OP
exposure is both controversial and unresolved. The evidence supporting the
existence of delayed, persistent, or latent neuropsychologic effects of OPs in
humans includes case reports and large case series and cross-sectional epidemiologic field studies of agricultural workers.

Case Reports

Numerous case reports and four studies have reviewed over 1,100 cases
of acute poisonings of mostly agricultural workers (see Table 5). These reports indicate that between 4 to 9% of acutely poisoned individuals experience neurobehavioral sequelae such as depression, confusion, agitation,
weakness (Hirshberg & Lerman, 1984), nervousness, irritability, insomnia
(Tabershaw & Cooper, 1966), forgetfulness, confusion (Holmes & Gaon,
1956), and schizoid and depressive reactions (Gershon & Shaw, 1961).

In particular, Gershon and Shaw (1961) reported schizoid and depressive reactions and impaired memory and concentration in 16 Australian
male agricultural workers referred by local physicians. This group was exposed to a variety of OP pesticides for 1 1/2 to 10 yr (see Table 5), and
complete recovery was reported within 1 year. However, in an ecologic
study of the same catchment area, Stoller, Krupinski, Christophers, and

TABLE 5. Toxicologic Studies of Neurobehavioral Function and Chronic, Persistent, or Latent Neuropsychiatric Conditions Associated with Organophosphate Pesticide Exposures in Workers

Authors	Exposed (N)	Controls (N)	Mean age (years)	Pesticide(s)	Dose/route of exposure	Findings
Rasmussen, Jensen, Stein, & Hayes (1963)	30	30	30 exposed; 37 controls	Dichlorvos	Inhalation 0.1–0.3 μg/1, 16 hr/wk for 13 weeks	No significant differences between exposure groups on reaction time or flicker fusion; plasma ChE significantly depressed in exposed
Bowers, Goodman, & Sim (1964)	93	0	NA[a]	Sarin analog	Single dermal	Anxiety, psychomotor depression, intellectual function, impaired attention at 60–90% CHE inhibition
Rodnitzky, Levin, & Morgan (1978)	2	2[b]	62,53	Ethyl and methyl parathion	Ingested 1–4 mg/day for 5 days	No differences, pre-/postexposure on Verbal Recall, Benton Visual Memory, Choice Reaction Time, Language, EX, Proprioception or Taylor Manifest Anxiety Scale

[a]NA = not available or stated.
[b]Exposed served as their own controls during preexposure period.

Blanks (1965) were not able to find a significant correlation between pesticide sales and the incidence of new admissions to mental institutions. Both studies included highly selected study groups; this has been a source of criticism.

Acquired intolerance to pesticides or solvent odors was reported in 18% of 114 workers examined 3 yr after an acute poisoning (Tabershaw & Cooper, 1966). In a case report of a cropduster who had an anxiety and psychotic depressive reaction following exposure to OPs, subsequent exposure to low levels has triggered the same symptoms (Dille & Smith, 1964).

Occupations most frequently mentioned in case reports involve workers with direct contact with OP pesticides: mixers, loaders, applicators, pilots, flaggers, nursery and greenhouse workers, pesticide manufacturing workers, and agricultural and pest control inspectors. Harvest workers exposed primarily to pesticide residues on plant foliage have been reported less often. Parathion, mevinphos (Phosdrin), and malathion were the most frequently cited pesticides. Hayes (1982) attributed persistent mental disturbances (e.g., delirium, combativeness, hallucinations, or psychoses) to the small proportion of cases of pesticide poisonings that involve parathion, trichlorphon, dichlorvos, fenthion, and dimethoate. Approximately 15% of cases with long-standing neurobehavioral sequelae have had repeated or multiple exposures (Tabershaw & Cooper, 1966).

Cross-Sectional Epidemiologic Studies

Standardized neuropsychologic assessments have been carried out on approximately 500 human subjects in a limited number of cross-sectional epidemiologic field studies. Table 6 reviews some of these studies. Workers have been assessed on simple and choice visual reaction times, letter-scanning vigilance tests (Gersoni U, EX), abstraction (Halstead-Reitan Trail-Making), intellectual functioning (Digit Span, Block Design, Vocabulary), visual memory (Benton Visual Retention), verbal memory (Story Recall, Trigram Recall), language (Armed Forces Qualifying Test, Multilingual Aphasic Tests), proprioception and affective behavior and mood (MMPI, Taylor Manifest Anxiety Scale). Many studies, however, were limited in the range of functions evaluated. Only a few studies have employed the same measures, which impairs comparison between studies.

In general, the subjects of these studies have tended to be young, mostly male, and employed in agricultural occupations for unspecified time periods. In field studies, quantitative exposure data were generally lacking, although significant acute exposures were likely in studies of workers with physician-diagnosed poisonings (Savage et al., 1982; Durham, Wolfe, & Quinby, 1965). The exposed groups included asymptomatic farmers (Korsak & Sato, 1977), pest control workers (Maizlish et al., 1987), industrial workers with accidental exposure (Metcalf & Holmes, (1968), and a wide variety of agricultural workers tested a number of years after a physician diagnosed acute poisoning (Savage et al., 1982).

TABLE 6. Cross-Sectional Epidemiologic Studies of Neurobehavioral Function and Chronic, Persistent, or Latent Neuropsychiatric Conditions Associated with Organophosphate Pesticide Exposures in Workers

Authors	Exposed (N)	Controls (N)	Mean age (years)	Exposed occupations	Battery or tests	Significant findings in exposed group
Durham, Wolfe, & Quimby (1965)	53–68	25	NA[a]	Mixer, loader, pilot, flagger, applicator, warehousemen	Gersoni U, EX test (vigilance tests); Choice Reaction Time	Fewer lines attempted on Gersoni U; no differences in errors of omission or comission or mean reaction time
Metcalf & Holmes (1969)	70	NA	NA	Factory workers	WAIS (Block Design, Digit Span, Similarities); Benton Vis Retent, Story Recall	Disturbed memory, difficulty in maintaining alertness or focusing attention
Rodnitzky, Levin, & Mick (1975) Levin, Rodnitzky, & Mick (1976)	24	24	39	Farmers, pest control workers	Verbal memory, Benton Vis Retent, Choice Reaction Time, Language Proprioception, Taylor MAS	Increased Taylor MAS anxiety score among pest control workers but not farmers; plasma ChE significantly depressed in pest control wkrs
Korsak and Sato (1977)	16	16	34 Exposed 41 Controls	Farmers	Halstead-Reitan, Bender Visual Gestalt	Poorer on Part B of Trail-Making and Bender
Savage et al. (1982)	100	100	NA	Mixer, loader, flagger pilots, mixing plant workers greenhouse, farmworkers	Halstead-Reitan, MMPI	Poorer on 4 of 5 summary scores and 18 of 34 subtests; Exposed group was tested on average 9 years after a physician-diagnosed, severe acute poisoning, usually due to ethyl or methyl parathion

[a]NA = not available or stated.

Researchers using subtests of the Halstead-Reitan battery found significantly poorer performance among the exposed on Trailmaking Part B (Korsak & Sato, 1977), poorer summary scores and poorer performance on a majority of subtests involving intellectual functioning, academic skills, abstraction, flexibility of thought, and motor skills (Savage et al., 1982). Using subtests of the WAIS, Metcalf and Holmes (1968) reported memory disturbances, inability to maintain alertness and focused attention, slower perceptual ability, and poorer verbal skills among exposed workers. Using a computer-assisted neurobehavioral battery (Baker et al., 1985), Maizlish Schenker, Weisskopf, Seiber, and Samuels (1987), investigated neurobehavioral function among 46 diazinon applicators and 56 nonapplicators with an average employment duration of 39 days before testing. Although symbol–digit pairing speed was slower among applicators as a group, performance on this task, eye–hand coordination, pattern recognition, finger tapping, and choice reaction time were not correlated with levels of urinary metabolites of diazinon. Median diethylphosphate (DETP) levels among applicators were 23 ppb and 8 ppb among nonapplicators. Levin, Rodnitsky, and Mick (1976) found increased anxiety scores among pest control operators as measured on the Taylor Manifest Anxiety Scale, and Savage et al. (1982), using the MMPI, found increased rates of emotional problems. Victims of recent pesticide poisonings were found to improve on vigilance tests during convalescence (Durham et al., 1965). Other studies (Durham et al., 1965; Rodnitzky, Levin, & Mick, 1975) have failed to associate poorer neurobehavioral function in asymptomatic workers with presumed pesticide exposure or measureable but minor depression of plasma cholinesterase activity (Rodnitzky et al., 1975).

Neuropsychiatric Disease Mortality and Accidents

Analyses of causes of death and occupation reported on death certificates (Standardized Proportional Mortality) suggest that agricultural workers are at elevated risk of mortality from neuropsychiatric disease and accidents. Milham (1983) observed approximately twice the expected mortality from neuropsychiatric disorders in white male farm workers and orchard laborers from the state of Washington. Stubbs, Harris, and Spear (1984) reported similar findings for California farm workers but not for farm owners.

Both the California and Washington studies as well as one from British Columbia (Gallagher, Threlfall, Spinelli, & Band, 1984) suggest that excess deaths from major vehicle accidents occur in farm workers. The role of pesticides in the mortality patterns is unknown. Poor quality of medical care or alcoholism have been postulated, but excess mortality due to cirrhosis of the liver with or without alcoholism has not been observed in either farm laborers or orchard laborers. Based on worker reports of feeling "fuzzy" at the end of the workday, Tabershaw and Cooper (1966) speculated that farm workers' exposure to pesticides has impaired judgment and coordination that may contribute to an increased rate of motor vehicle accidents. There are numerous case reports of near misses and fatal workplace accidents involving farm machinery and crop dusting aircraft in which behavioral effects of pesticides have been implicated (Durham et al., 1965; Hayes, 1982; Redhead, 1968; Reich & Berner, 1968; Smith, Stavinoha, & Ryan, 1968; Wood, Brown, Watson, & Benson, 1971).

CLINICAL EVALUATION

Most workers who are referred for neurotoxicity evaluations have been exposed to lead, solvents, or pesticides. Certainly, other toxins that affect the nervous system are known, but exposures to these materials are rarer (e.g., mercury). Exposures will depend upon which industries are nearby (e.g., workers referred for pesticide exposure will be more common in agricultural states). Referrals to evaluate neurotoxicity may emanate not only from neurology or psychiatry but also from occupational medicine. The reasons for referral are similar to that for other types of neuropsychologic evaluation: confirming complaints with test findings, differentiating between psychogenic and organic etiology, determining whether symptoms result from toxic exposure or some other disease process, providing baseline data prior to intervention (e.g., removal from the workplace, chelation therapy), suggesting vocational guidance such as whether the worker is capable of returning to work, and proposing appropriate rehabilitation programs. Most workers who are referred, however, are involved in lawsuits, either worker's compensation cases or liability cases. Clinicians should be concerned about whether secondary gain plays a role in the clinical picture. However, it is important not to dismiss the individual's symptoms without a thorough and thoughtful evaluation.

In most cases, the worker presents with primarily subjective complaints. The neuropsychologist must determine with reasonable certainty whether these complaints are due to toxic exposure. This requires knowledge of the potential effects of a particular exposure and to set up an evaluation program most likely to reveal the deficits. It is also important to include in the evaluation tests of function that are likely to remain intact. Not only does this help to separate out malingering, but it also helps to determine premorbid functioning. A history of substance abuse as well as prior occupations should be taken because multiple chemical exposures may have synergistic effects.

Very often, workers who are referred show signs of depression on mood or personality scales. It is difficult to determine whether their depression is organic or is a secondary reaction to loss in function or to loss of a job or of property (in an environmental disaster). Moreover, their depression may affect their motivation to perform.

Workers should be evaluated on reliable and valid standardized tests. Ideally, these tests would be standardized for worker populations; because of self-selection, workers may be better or worse at some skills than most others in the general population.

Of particular concern is the recent use of computerized versions of some of the standardized tests. These tests should not be used in clinical evaluations until they have been properly standardized. They do, however, provide a more economical way to evaluate large populations of workers in a research setting, provided adequate control groups are employed.

CONCLUSIONS

Neuropsychologic impairment from short-term high-level exposure to neurotoxins including lead, organic solvents, and pesticides has been established. In an increasing number of epidemiologic reports on workers, subtle behavioral changes detected by neuropsychologic evaluations have been associated with chronic low-level exposures. The characteristics of these subtle impairments may not be distinguishable from those of a nonoccupational etiology. Sufficient quantitative data on exposure levels or duration have not been available to elucidate dose-response relationships, but studies of workers with long-term employment have been consistent in demonstrating functional changes. Few studies have examined workers prospectively to assess the duration and reversibility of effects, nor have factors influencing individual susceptibility been researched adequately. Preexisting neuropsychiatric disease may be exacerbated by exposure to neurotoxins, for example, organophosphate pesticides (Rowntree, Nevin, & Wilson, 1950). Further clarification is needed on the role of age, sex, medication, and ethanol use as well as other personal factors that may modify or act synergistically with neurotoxins.

REFERENCES

Amaducci, L., Arfaioli, C., Inzitari, D., & Marchi, M. (1982). Multiple sclerosis among shoe and leather workers: An epidemiological survey in Florence. *Acta Neurologica Scandinavica, 65,* 94–103.

Antti-Poika, M. (1982). Prognosis of symptoms in patients with diagnosed chronic organic solvent intoxication. *International Archives of Occupational and Environmental Health, 51,* 81–89.

Araki, S., Honma, T., Yanagihara, S., & Ushio, K. (1980). Recovery of slowed nerve conduction velocity in lead-exposed workers. *International Archives of Occupational Environmental Health, 46,* 151–157.

Arlien-Soborg, P., Bruhn, P., Gyldensted, C., & Melgaard, B. (1979). Chronic painter's syndrome. *Acta Neurologica Scandinavica, 60,* 149–156.

Arlien-Soborg, P., Henriksen, L., Gade, A., Gyldensted, C., & Paulson, O. B. (1982). Cerebral blood flow in chronic toxic encephalopathy in house painters exposed to organic solvents. *Acta Neurologica Scandinavica, 66,* 34–41.

Axelson, O., Hane, M., & Hogstedt, C. (1976). A case-referent study on neuropsychiatric disorders among workers exposed to solvents. *Scandinavian Journal of Work, Environment, & Health, 2,* 14–20.

Axelson, O., Hane, M., & Hogstedt, C. (1980). Current aspects of solvent-related disorders. In C. Zenz (Ed.), *Developments in occupational medicine* (pp. 237–258). Chicago: Yearbook Medical Publishers.

Baker, E. L., Landrigan, P. J., Barbour, A. G., Cox, D. H., Folland, P. S., Ligo, R. N., & Throckmorton, J. (1979). Occupational lead poisoning in the United States: Clinical and biochemical findings related to blood lead levels. *British Journal of Industrial Medicine, 36*, 314–322.

Baker, E. L., Feldman, R. G., White, R. A., Harley, J. P., Niles, C. A., Dinse, G. E., & Berkey, C. S. (1984). Occupational lead neurotoxicity: A behavioral and electrophysiological evaluation. Study design and year one results. *British Journal of Industrial Medicine, 41*, 352–361.

Baker, E. L., Smith, T. J., & Landrigan, P. J. (1985). The neurotoxicity of industrial solvents: A review of the literature. *American Journal of Industrial Medicine, 8*, 207–217.

Baker, E. L., Letz, R., & Fidler, A. (1985). A computer-administered neurobehavioral evaluation system for occupational and environmental epidemiology. *Journal of Occupational Medicine, 27*, 206–212.

Baloh, R. W., Spivey, G. H., Brown, C. P., Morgan, D., Campion, D. S., Browdy, B. L., Valentine, J. L., Gonick, H. C., Massey, F. J., & Culver, B. P. (1979). Subclinical effects of chronic increased lead absorption—A prospective study. Results of baseline neurologic testing. *Journal of Occupational Medicine, 21*, 490–496.

Baloh, R. W., Langhofer, L., Brown, C. P., & Spivey, G. H. (1980). Quantitative eye tracking tests in lead workers. *American Journal of Industrial Medicine, 1*, 109–113.

Bowers, M. B., Goodman, E., & Sim, V. M. (1964). Some behavioral changes in man following anticholinesterase administration. *Journal of Nervous and Mental Disease, 138*, 383–389.

Campara, P., D'Andrea, F., Micciolo, R., Saronitto, C., Tansella, M., & Zimmermann-Tansella, C. (1984). Psychological performance of workers with blood-lead concentration below the current threshold limit value. *International Archives of Occupational and Environmental Health, 53*, 233–246.

Cavanaugh, J. B. (1985). Solvent neurotoxicity. *British Journal of Industrial Medicine, 42*, 433–434.

Chalupa, B., Synkova, J., & Sevcik, M. (1960). The assessment of electroencephalographic changes and memory disturbances in acute intoxications with industrial poisons. *British Journal of Industrial Medicine, 17*, 238–241.

Cherry, N., Waldron, H. A., Wells, G. G., Wilkinson, R. T., & Wilson, H. K. (1980). An investigation of the acute behavioral effects of styrene on factory workers. *British Journal of Industrial Medicine, 37*, 234–240.

Cherry, N., Rodgers, B., Venables, H., Waldron, H. A., & Wells, G. G. (1981). Acute behavioral effects of styrene exposure: A further analysis. *British Journal of Industrial Medicine, 38*, 346–350.

Cherry, N., Hutchins, H., Pace, T., & Waldron, H. A. (1985). Neurobehavioral effects of repeated occupational exposure to toluene and paint solvents. *British Journal of Industrial Medicine, 42*, 291–300.

Cohen, S. (1975). Glue sniffing. *Journal of the American Medical Association, 231*, 653–654.

Corsi, G., Maestrelli, R., Picotti, G., Manzoni, S., & Negrin, P. (1983). Chronic peripheral neuropathy in workers with previous exposure in carbon disulphide. *British Journal of Industrial Medicine, 40*, 209–211.

Coye, M. J. (1985). The health effects of agricultural productions: I. The health of agricultural workers. *Journal of Public Health Policy, 6*, 349–370.

Dick, R., Setzer, J. V., Wait, R., Hayden, M. B., Taylor, B. J., Tolos, B., & Putz-Anderson, V. (1984). Effects of acute exposure of toluene and methyl ethyl ketone on psychomotor performance. *International Archives of Occupational and Environmental Health, 54*, 91–109.

Dille, J. R., & Smith, P. W. (1964). Central nervous system affects of chronic exposure to organophosphate insecticides. *Aerospace Medicine, 35*, 475–478.

Durham, W. F., Wolfe, H. R., & Quinby, G. E. (1965). Organophosphorus insectides and mental alertness. *Archives of Environmental Health, 10*, 55–66.

Edling, C., & Ekberg, K. (1985). No acute behavioral effects of exposure to styrene: A safe level of exposure? *British Journal of Industrial Medicine, 42*, 301–304.

Eloffson, S. A., Gamberale, F., Hindmarsh, T., Iregren, A., Isaksson, A., Johnsson, I., Knave, B., Lydahl, E., Mindus, P., Persson, H. E., Philipson, B., Steby, M., Struwe, G., Soderman, E., Wennberg, A., & Widen, L. (1980). Exposure to organic solvents. A cross-sectional epidemiologic investigation on occupationally exposed car and industrial spray painters with special reference to the nervous system. *Scandinavian Journal of Work, Environment, & Health, 6*, 239–273.

Environmental Protection Agency, Office of Toxic Substances. (1976). Core activities of the Office of Toxic Substances. Report no. 560/4-76-005. Washington, DC: Author.

Feldman, R. G. (1979). Trichloroethylene. In P. J. Vinken & G. W. Bruyn (Eds.), *Intoxications of the nervous system* (pp. 457–464). Amsterdam: North-Holland Publishing Company.

Feldman, R. G., Mayer, R. M., & Taub, A. (1970). Evidence for peripheral neurotoxic effect of trichloroethylene. *Neurology, 20*, 599–606.

Fischbein, A., Thornton, J. C., Lilis, R., Valciukas, J. A., Bernstein, J., & Selikoff, I. J. (1980). Zinc protoporphyrin, blood lead and clinical symptoms in two occupational groups with low-level exposure to lead. *American Journal of Industrial Medicine, 1*, 391–399.

Forycki, Z. (1979). State of health of shipyard painters as index of exposure to the action of organic solvents. *Instytat Medyeyny Moiskiei i Tonpikalnei w Gdyni Bulletin, 30*, 259–268.

Gallagher, R. P., Threlfall, W. J., Spinelli, J. J., & Band, P. R. (1984). Occupational mortality patterns and British Columbia farm workers. *Journal of Occupational Medicine, 26*, 906–908.

Gamberale, F., & Hultengren, M. (1972). Toluene exposure. II. Psychophysiological functions. *Scandinavian Journal of Work, Environment, & Health, 9*, 131–139.

Gamberale, F. & Hultengren, M. (1973). Methylchloroform exposure II. Psychophysiological functions. *Scandinavian Journal of Work, Environment, & Health, 10*, 82–92.

Gershon, S., & Shaw, F. H. (1961). Psychiatric sequelae of chronic exposure to organophosphorus insecticides. *Lancet, 1*, 1371–1374.

Gilman, A. G., Goodman, L. S., & Gilman, A. (1980). *The pharmacological basis of therapeutics* (6th ed.). New York: Macmillan.

Glickman, L., Valciukas, J. A., Lilis, R., & Weissman, I. (1984). Occupational lead exposure. Effects of saccadic eye movements. *International Archives of Occupational and Environmental Health, 34*, 115–125.

Goyer, R. A., & Rhyne, B. C. (1973). Pathological effects of lead. In G. W. Richter, & M. A. Epstein (Eds.), *International review of experimental pathology* (pp. 1–77). New York: Academic Press.

Grandjean, E., Munchinger, R., Turrian, V., Haas, P. A., Knoepfel, H. K., & Rosenmund, H. (1955). Investigations into the effects of exposure to trichlorethylene in mechanical engineering. *British Journal of Industrial Medicine, 12*, 131–142.

Grandjean, P., Arnvig, E., & Beckmann, J. (1978). Psychological dysfunctions in lead-exposed workers. Relation to biological parameters of exposure. *Scandinavian Journal of Work, Environment, & Health, 4*, 295–303.

Grasso, P., Sharratt, M., Davies, D. M., & Irvine, D. (1984). Neurophysiological and psychological disorders and occupational exposure to organic solvents. *Food and Chemical Toxicology, 22*, 819–852.

Gregersen, P., Mikkelsen, S., Klausen, H., Dossing, M., Nielsen, H., & Thygesen, P. (1978). A chronic cerebral syndrome in painters. Dementia due to inhalation or of cryptogenic origin. *Ugeskrift for Laeger, 140*, 1638–1644.

Grob, D., & Harvey, A. M. (1953). The effects and treatment of nerve gas poisoning. *American Journal of Medicine, 14*, 52–63.

Gudmundsson, G. (1977). Methyl chloride poisoning 13 years later. *Archives of Environmental Health, 32*, 236–237.

Hane, M., Axelson, O., Blume, J., Hogstedt, C., Sundell, L., & Ydreburg, B. (1977). Psychological function changes among house painters. *Scandinavian Journal of Work, Environment, & Health, 3*, 91–99.

Hänninen, H. (1971). Psychological picture of manifest and latent carbon disulphide poisoning. *British Journal of Industrial Medicine, 28*, 374–381.

Hänninen, H., Eskelinen, L., Husman, K., & Nurminen, M. (1976). Behavioral effects of long-term exposure to a mixture of solvents. *Scandinavian Journal of Work, Environment, & Health, 4*, 240–256.

Hänninen, H., Hernberg, S., Mantere, P., Vesanto, R., & Jalkanen, M. (1978). Psychological performance of subjects with low exposure to lead. *Journal of Occupational Medicine, 20*, 683–689.

Hänninen, H., Nurminen, M., Tolonen, M., & Martelin, T. (1978). Psychological tests as indicators of excessive exposure to carbon disulfide. *Scandinavian Journal of Psychology, 19*, 163–174.

Harkonen, H. (1977). Relationship of symptoms to occupational styrene exposure and to the findings of electroencephalographic psychological examinations. *International Archives of Occupational and Environmental Health, 40*, 1–19.

Hayes, W. J. (1982). *Pesticides studied in man.* Baltimore: Williams & Wilkins.

Hirshberg, A., & Lerman, Y. (1984). Clinical problems in organophosphorus insecticide poisoning: The use of a computerized information system. *Fundamentals of Applied Toxicology, 4*, 5209–5214.

Hogstedt, C., Hane, M., Agrell, A., & Bodin, L. (1983). Neuropsychological tests results and symptoms among workers with well-defined long-term exposure to lead. *British Journal of Industrial Medicine, 40*, 99–105.

Holmes, J. H., & Gaon, M. D. (1956). Observations on acute and multiple exposures to anticholinesterase agents. *Transactions of the American Clinical Climatology Association, 68*, 86–101.

Husman, K. (1980). Symptoms of car painters with long-term exposure to a mixture of organic solvents. *Scandinavian Journal of Work, Environment, & Health, 6*, 19–32.

Husman, K., & Karli, P. (1980). Clinical neurological findings among car painters exposed to a mixture of organic solvents. *Scandinavian Journal of Work, Environment & Health, 6*, 33–39.

Iregren, A. (1982). Effects on psychological test performance of workers exposed to a single solvent (toluene)—A comparison with effects of exposure to a mixture of organic solvents. *Neurobehavioral Toxicology and Teratology, 4*, 695–701.

Jason, K. M., & Kellogg, C. K. (1980). Behavioral neurotoxicity of lead. In R. C. Singhal & J. A. Thomas (Eds.), *Lead toxicity* (pp. 241–271). Baltimore: Urban & Schwarzenberg.

Jeyaratnam, J. (1985). Health problems of pesticide usage in the Third World. *British Journal of Industrial Medicine, 42*, 505–506.

Jeyaratnam, J., Devathasan, G., Ong, C. N., Phoon, W. O., & Wong, P. K. (1985). Neurophysiological studies on workers exposed to lead. *British Journal of Industrial Medicine, 42*, 173–177.

Johnson, B. L., & Anger, W. K. (1983). Behavioral toxicology. In W. N. Rom (Ed.), *Environmental and occupational medicine* (pp. 329–350). Boston: Little, Brown.

Johnson, B. L., Burg, J. R., Xinteras, C., & Handke, J. L. (1980). A neurobehavioral examination of workers from a primary nonferrous smelter. *Neurotoxicology, 1*, 561–581.

Juntunen, J., Hupli, V., Hernberg, S., & Luisto, M. (1980). Neurological picture of organic solvent poisoning in industry. *International Archives of Occupational and Environmental Health, 46*, 219–231.

Kirkby, H., Nielsen, C. J., Nielsen, V. K., & Gyntelberg, F. (1983). Subjective symptoms after long term lead exposure in secondary lead smelting workers. *British Journal of Industrial Medicine, 40*, 314–317.

Kjellberg, A., Wigaeus, E., & Engstrom, J. (1979). Long-term effects of exposure to styrene in a polyester plant. *Arbete och Halse, 18*. Stockholm: Arbetskyddsverket.

Knave, B., Persson, H. E., Goldberg, J. M., & Westerholm, P. (1976). Long-term exposure to jet fuel. An investigation on occupationally exposed workers with special reference to the nervous system. *Scandinavian Journal of Work, Environment, & Health, 3*, 152–164.

Knave, B., Olson, B. A., Elofsson, S., Gamberale, F., Isaksson, A., Mindus, P., Persson, H. E., Struwe, G., Wennberg, A., & Westerholm, P. (1978). Long term exposure to jet fuel. II. A cross-sectional epidemiologic investigation on occupationally exposed industrial workers with special reference to the nervous system. *Scandinavian Journal of Work, Environment, & Health, 4*, 19–45.

Korsak, R. J., & Sato, M. M. (1977). Effects of chronic organophosphate pesticide exposure on the central nervous system. *Clinical Toxicology, 11*, 83–95.

Kylin, B., Axell, K., Samuel, H. E., & Lindborg, A. (1967). Effect of inhaled trichloroethylene on the CNS. *Archives of Environmental Health*, 15, 48–52.

Landrigan, P. J., Kreiss, K., Xinteras, C., Feldman, R. G., & Heath, Jr., C. W. (1980). Clinical epidemiology of occupational neurotoxic disease. *Neurobehavioral toxicology*, 2, 43–48.

Levin, H. S., Rodnitsky, R. L., & Mick, D. L. (1976). Anxiety associated with exposure to organophosphate components. *Archives of General Psychiatry*, 33, 325–328.

Lilis, R., Fischbein, A., Eisinger, J., Blumberg, W. E., Diamond, S., Anderson, H. A., Rom, W., Rice, C., Sarkozi, L., Kon, S., & Selikoff, I. J. (1977). Prevalence of lead disease among secondary lead smelter workers and biological indicators of lead exposure. *Environmental Research*, 14, 255–285.

Lilis, R., Valciukas, J. A., Kon, S., Sarkosi, L., Campbell, C., & Selikoff, I. J. (1982). Assessment of lead health hazards in a body shop of an automobile assembly plant. *American Journal of Industrial Medicine*, 3, 33–51.

Lilis, R., Valciukas, J. A., Malkin, J., & Weber, J. P. (1985). Effects of low-level lead and arsenic exposure on copper smelter workers. *Archives of Environmental Health*, 40, 38–47.

Lindstrom, K. (1973). Psychological performance on workers exposed to various solvents. *Scandinavian Journal of Work, Environment, & Health*, 10, 151–155.

Lindstrom, K. (1980). Changes in psychological performances of solvent-poisoned and solvent-exposed workers. *American Journal of Industrial Medicine*, 1, 69–84.

Lindstrom, K. (1982). Behavioral effects of long-term exposure to organic solvents. *Acta Neurologica Scandinavica* 66 (Suppl. 92) 131–141.

Lindstrom, K., Antti-Poika, M., Tola, S., & Hyytiainen, A. (1982). Psychological prognosis of diagnosed chronic organic solvent intoxication. *Neurobehavioral Toxicology and Teratology*, 4, 581–588.

Lindstrom, K., Harkonen, H., & Hernberg, S. (1976). Disturbances in psychologic function of occupational workers exposed to styrene. *Scandinavian Journal of Work, Environment, & Health*, 3, 129–139.

Lindstrom, K., Riihimaki, H., & Hanninen, K. (1984). Occupational solvent exposure and neuropsychiatric disorders. *Scandinavian Journal of Work, Environment, & Health*, 10, 321–323.

Lorimer, W. V., Lilis, R., Fischbein, A., Daum, S., Anderson, H., Wolff, M. S., & Selikoff, I. J. (1978). Health status of styrene-polystyrene polymerization workers. *Scandinavian Journal of Work, Environment, & Health*, 4, 220–226.

Maizlish, N. A., Langolf, G. D., Whitehead, L. W., Fine, L. J., Albers, J. W., Goldberg, J., & Smith, P. (1985). Behavioral evaluation of workers exposed to mixtures of organic solvents. *British Journal of Industrial Medicine*, 42, 579–590.

Maizlish, N. A., Schenker, M., Weisskopf, C., Seiber, J., & Samuels, S. (1987). A behavioral evaluation of pest control workers with short-term, low-level exposure to the organophosphate diazinon. *American Journal of Industrial Medicine*, 12, 153–172.

Mantere, P., Hanninen, H., & Hernberg, S. (1982). Subclinical neurotoxic lead effects: Two-year follow-up studies with psychological test methods. *Neurobehavioral Toxicology and Teratology*, 4, 725–727.

Mantere, P., Hanninen, H., Hernberg, S., & Luukkonen, R. (1984). A prospective follow-up study on psychological effects in workers exposed to low levels of lead. *Scandinavian Journal of Work, Environment, & Health*, 10, 43–50.

Melius, J. M., & Schulte, P. A. (1981). Epidemiologic design for field studies. Occupational neurotoxicity. *Scandinavian Journal of Work, Environment, & Health*, 7, 34–39.

Metcalf, D. R., & Holmes, J. H. (1969). EEG, psychological and neurological alterations in humans with organophosphate exposure. *Annals of the New York Academy of Sciences*, 160, 357–365.

Milburn, H., Mitran, E., & Crockford, G. W. (1976). An investigation of lead workers for subclinical studies of lead using three performance tests. *Annals of Occupational Hygiene*, 19, 239–249.

Milham, S. (1983). *Occupational mortality in Washington State, 1950–1979*. US DHH (NIOSH) Contract No. 210-80-0088. Washington, DC: U.S. Government Printing Office.

Mitling, J. E., Barnet, P. G., Coye, M. J., Velasco, A. R., Romero, P., Clements, C. L., O'Malley, M., Tobin, M. W., Rose, T. G., & Monosson, I. H. (1985). Clinical management of field worker organophosphate poisoning. Western Journal of Medicine, 142, 514–518.

Morgan, D. P. (1982). Recognition and management of pesticide poisoning (3rd ed.). Washington, DC: U.S. Government Printing Office.

Murphy, S. (1975). Pesticides. In L. J. Cassaret & J. Doull (Eds.), Toxicology (pp. 408–453). New York: Macmillan.

Namba, T., Nolte, C. T., Jackrel, J., & Grob, D. (1971). Poisoning due to organophosphate insecticides: Acute and chronic manifestations. American Journal of Medicine, 50, 475–492.

Neri, L. C., Hewitt, D., & Johansen, H. (1983). Health effects of low level occupational exposures to lead: The Trail, British Columbia Study. Archives of Environmental Health, 38, 180–189.

Ohlson, C. G., & Hogstedt, C. (1981). Parkinson's disease and occupational exposure to organic solvents, agricultural chemicals and mercury-A case-referent study. Scandinavian Journal of Work, Environment, & Health, 7, 252–256.

Oliver, J. S., & Watson, J. M. (1977). Abuse of solvent for "kicks." Lancet, 1, 84–86.

Olsen, J., & Sabroe, S. (1980). A case-reference study of neuropsychiatric disorders among workers exposed to solvents in the Danish wood and furniture industry. Scandinavian Journal of Social Medicine Supplement, 16, 44–49.

Olson, B. A. (1982). Effects of organic solvents on behavioral performance of workers in the paint industry. Neurobehavioral Toxicology and Teratology, 4, 703–708.

Peters, H. A., Levine, R. L., Matthews, C. G., Sauter, S. L., & Rankin, J. H. (1982). Carbon disulfide-induced neuropsychiatric changes in grain storage workers. American Journal of Industrial Medicine, 3, 373–391.

Press, E., & Done, A. K. (1967). Solvent sniffing. Physiologic effects and community control measures for intoxication from the intentional inhalation of organic solvents. I. Pediatrics, 39, 451–461.

Putz-Anderson, V., Setzer, J. A., & Croxton, J. S. (1981). Effects of alcohol, caffeine, and methyl chloride on man. Psychological Reports, 48, 715–725.

Rasmussen, H., Olsen, J., & Lauritsen, J. (1985). Risk of encephalopathia among retired solvent-exposed workers. Journal of Occupational Medicine, 27, 561–566.

Rasmussen, W. A., Jensen, J. A., Stein, W. J., & Hayes, W. J. (1963). Toxicological studies of DDVP for disinfection of aircraft. Aerospace Medicine, 34, 593–600.

Redhead, I. H. (1968). Poisoning on the farm. Lancet, 1, 686–688.

Reich, G. A., & Berner, W. H. (1968). Aerial application accidents 1963–1965. Archives of Environmental Health, 17, 776–784.

Repko, J. D. (1981). Neurotoxicity of methyl chloride. Neurobehavioral Toxicology and Teratology, 3, 425–429.

Repko, J. D., & Corum, C. R. (1979). Critical review and evaluation of the neurological and behavioral sequelae of inorganic lead absorption. CRC Critical Reviews in Toxicology, 6, 1–187.

Repko, J. D., & Lashley, S. M. (1979). Behavioral, neurological, and toxic effects of methyl chloride: A review of the literature. CRC Critical Reviews in Toxicology, 6, 283–302.

Repko, J. D., Morgan, Jr., B. B., & Nicholson, J. (1975). Behavioral effects of occupational exposure to lead. NIOSH 75-184. Washington, DC: U.S. Government Printing Office.

Repko, J. D., Jones, P. D., Garcia, L. S., Schneider, E. J., Roseman, E., & Corum, C. E. (1976). Behavioral and neurological effects of methyl chloride: NIOSH CDC 99-74-20. Washington, DC: U.S. Government Printing Office.

Repko, J. D., Corum, C. R., Jones, P. D., & Garcia, L. S. (1978). The effects of inorganic lead on behavioral and neurologic function. Washington, DC: U.S. Government Printing Office.

Risberg, J., & Hagstadius, S. (1983). Effects on the regional cerebral blood flow of long-term exposure to organic solvents. Acta Psychiatrica Scandinavica, 67(Suppl.303), 92–99.

Rodnitzky, R. L., Levin, H. S., & Mick, D. L. (1975). Occupational exposure to organophospate pesticides: A neurobehavioral study. Archives of Environmental Health, 30, 98–103.

Rodnitzky, R. L., Levin, H. S., & Morgan, D. P. (1978). Effects of ingested parathion on neurobehavioral function. Clinical Toxicology, 13, 347–359.

Rosen, I., Wildt, K., Gullberg, B., & Berlin, M. (1983). Neurophysiological effects of lead exposure. *Scandinavian Journal of Work, Environment, & Health, 9,* 431–441.

Rowntree, D. W., Nevin, S., & Wilson, A. (1950). The effects of diisopropylfluoro phosphate in schizophrenia and manic depressive psychoses. *Journal of Neurology, Neurosurgery, and Psychiatry, 13,* 47–62.

Sabroe, S., & Olson, J. (1979). Health complaints and work conditions among laquerers in the Danish furniture industry. *Scandinavian Journal of Social Medicine, 7,* 97–104.

Salvini, M., Binaschi, S., & Riva, M. (1971a). Evaluation of the psychophysiological functions in humans exposed to trichloroethylene. *British Journal of Industrial Medicine, 28,* 293–295.

Salvini, M., Binaschi, S., & Riva, M. (1971b). Evaluation of the psychophysiological functions in humans exposed to the "Threshold Limit Value" of 1,1,1-trichloroethane. *British Journal of Industrial Medicine, 28,* 286–292.

Savage, E. P., Keefe, T. J., Mounce, L. M., Lewis, J. A., Heaton, R. K., & Parks, L. H. (1982). *Chronic neurological sequelae of acute organophosphate pesticide poisoning: An epidemiologic study.* Fort Collins: Colorado Epidemiologic Pesticide Studies Center.

Savolainen, K., Riihimaki, V., Laine, A., & Kekoni, J. (1981). Short-term exposure of human subjects to m-xylene and 1,1,1-trichloroethane. *International Archives of Occupational and Environmental Health, 49,* 89–98.

Seppalainen, A. M. (1981). Neurophysiological findings among workers exposed to organic solvents. *Scandinavian Journal of Work, Environment, & Health, 7,* 29–33.

Seppalainen, A. M., & Antti-Poika, M. (1983). Time course of electrophysiological findings for patients with solvent poisoning. *Scandinavian Journal of Work, Environment, & Health, 9,* 15–24.

Seppalainen, A. M., & Hernberg, S. (1972). Sensitive technique for detecting subclinical lead neuropathy. *British Journal of Industrial Medicine, 29,* 443–449.

Seppalainen, A. M., & Lindstrom, K. (1982). Neurophysiological findings among house painters exposed to solvents. *Scandinavian Journal of Work, Environment, & Health, 8,* 131–135.

Seppalainen, A. M., Lindstrom, K., & Martelin, T. (1980). Neurophysiological and psychological picture of solvent poisoning. *American Journal of Industrial Medicine, 1,* 31–42.

Seppalainen, A. M., Husman, K., & Murtenson, C. (1978). Neurophysiologic effects of long-term solvent exposure to a mixture of organic solvents. *Scandinavian Journal of Work, Environment, & Health, 4,* 304–314.

Seppalainen, A. M., Hernberg, S., & Koch, B. (1979). Relationship between blood lead levels and nerve conduction velocities. *Neurotoxicology, 1,* 313–332.

Seppalainen, A. M., Tola, S., Hernberg, S., & Kock, B. (1975). Subclinical neuropathy at "safe" levels of lead exposure. *Archives of Environmental Health, 30,* 180–183.

Silbergeld, E. K. (1983). Indirectly acting neurotoxins. *Acta Psychiatrica Scandinavica, 67* (Suppl. 303), 16–25.

Singer, R., Valciukas, J. A., & Lilis, R. (1983). Lead exposure and nerve conduction velocity: The differential time course of sensory and motor nerve effects. *Neurotoxicology, 4,* 193–202.

Smith, P. W., Stavinoha, W. B., & Ryan, L. C. (1968). Cholinesterase inhibition in relation to fitness to fly. *Aerospace Medicine, 39,* 754–758.

Specchio, L. M., Bellomo, R., Pozio, G., Dicuonzo, F., Assennato, G., Federici, A., Misciagna, G., & Puca, F. M. (1981). Smooth pursuit eye movements among storage battery workers. *Clinical Toxicology, 18,* 1269–1276.

Spivey, G. H., Baloh, R. W., Brown, C. P., Browdy, B. L., Campion, D. S., Valentine, J. L., Morgan, E. E., & Culver, B. D. (1980). Subclinical effects of chronic increased lead absorption—A prospective study. III. Neurologic findings at follow-up examination. *Journal of Occupational Medicine, 22,* 607–612.

Stewart, R. D., Gay, H. H., Schaffer, A. W., Duncan, S. E., & Rowe, V. R. (1969). Experimental human exposure to methyl chloroform vapor. *Archives of Environmental Health, 19,* 467–472.

Stewart, R. D., Dodd, H. C., Gay, H. H., & Erley, D. S. (1970). Experimental human exposure to trichloroethylene. *Archives of Environmental Health, 20,* 64–71.

Stewart, R. D., Hake, C. L., Lebran, A. J., Kalbfleisch, J. H., Newton, P. E., Peterson, J. E., Cohen,

H. H., Strable, R., & Bush, K. A. (1974). Effects of trichloroethylene on behavioral performance capabilities. In C. Xintaras, B. L. Johnson, & I. de Groot (Eds.), *Behavioral toxicology: Early detection of occupation hazards.* Washington, DC: U.S. Government Printing Office.

Stewart, R. D., Hake, C. L., Wu, A., Kalbfleisch, J., Newton, P. E., Marlow, S. E., & Vucicevic-Salama, M. (1977). Effects of perchloroethylene/drug interaction on behavior and neurological function. Washington, DC: U.S. Government Printing Office.

Stoller, A., Krupinski, J., Christophers, A. J., & Blanks, G. K. (1965). Organophosphorus pesticides and major mental illness: An epidemiological investigation. *Lancet, 1,* 1387–1388.

Stopps, G. J., & McLaughlin, M. (1967). Psychophysiological testing of human subjects exposed to solvent vapors. *American Industrial Hygiene Association Journal, 28,* 43–50.

Struwe, G., & Wennberg, A. (1983). Psychiatric and neurological symptoms in workers occupationally exposed to organic solvents—Results of a differential epidemiological study. *Acta Psychiatrica Scandinavica, 67,*(Suppl. 303), 68–80.

Stubbs, H. A., Harris, J., & Spear, R. C. (1984). A proportionate mortality of California agricultural workers. *American Journal of Industrial Medicine, 6,* 305–320.

Tabershaw, I. R., & Cooper, W. C. (1966). Sequelae of acute organic phosphate poisoning. *Journal of Occupational Medicine, 8,* 5–20.

Tilson, H. A., & Mitchell, C. L. (1984). Neurobehavioral techniques to assess the effects of chemicals on the nervous system. *Annual Review of Pharmacology and Toxicology, 24,* 425–450.

Tolonen, M., & Hänninen, H. (1978). Psychological tests specific to individual carbon disulfide exposure. *Scandinavian Journal of Psychology, 19,* 241–245.

Triebig, G., Schaller, K. H., Erzigkeit, H., & Valentin, H. (1977). Biochemical and psychological studies of workers chronically exposed to trichloroethylene considering an exposure-free interval. *International Archives of Occupational and Environmental Health, 38,* 149–162.

Tuttle, T. C., Wood, G. D., & Grether, C. B. (1976). *Behavioral and neurological evaluation of workers exposed to carbon disulfide (CS2).* Washington, DC: U.S. Government Printing Office.

Tuttle, T. C., Wood, G. D., & Grether, C. B. (1977). *A behavioral and neurological evaluation of dry cleaners exposed to perchloroethylene.* Washington, DC: U.S. Government Printing Office.

Valciukas, J. A., & Lillis, R. (1980). Psychometric techniques in environmental research. *Environmental Research, 21,* 275–297.

Valciukas, J. A., Lilis, R., Eisinger, J., Blumberg, W. E., Fischbein, A., & Selikoff, I. J. (1978). Behavioral indicators of lead neurotoxicity: Results of a clinical field survey. *International Archives of Occupational and Environmental Health, 41,* 217–236.

Valciukas, J. A., Lilis, R., Fischbein, A., & Selikoff, I. (1978). Central nervous system dysfunction due to lead exposure. *Science, 201,* 465–467.

Valciukas, J. A., Lilis, R., Singer, R., Fischbein, A., Anderson, H. A., & Glickman, L. (1980). Lead exposure and behavioral changes: Comparisons of four occupational groups with different levels of lead absorption. *American Journal of Industrial Medicine, 1,* 421–426.

Valciukas, J. A., Lilis, R., Singer, R. M., & Glickman, L. (1985). Neurobehavioral changes among shipyard painters exposed to solvents. *Archives of Environmental Health, 40,* 47–52.

Vernon, R. J., & Ferguson, R. K. (1969). Effects of tricholorethylene on visual-motor performance. *Archives of Environmental Health, 18,* 894–900.

Watson, J. M. (1980). Solvent abuse by children and young adults: A review. *British Journal of Addiction, 75,* 27–36.

Whorton, M. D., & Obrinsky, D. L. (1983). Persistence of symptoms after mild to moderate acute organophosphate poisoning among 19 farm field workers. *Journal of Toxicology and Environmental Health, 11,* 347–354.

Winegar, D. A., Levy, B. S., Andrews, J. S., Landrigan, P. J., Scruton, W. H., & Krause, M. J. (1977). Chronic occupational exposure to lead: An evaluation of the health of smelter workers. *Journal of Occupational Medicine, 19,* 603–606.

Winneke, G., Kastka, J., & Fodor, G. G. (1974, October). *Psychophysiological effects of low-level exposure to trichloroethylene.* Paper presented at the Second Industrial and Environmental Neurology Congress, October 22–26, 1974, Prague.

Wood, W. W., Brown, H. W., Watson, M., & Benson, W. W. (1971). Implication of organophosphate pesticide poisoning in the plane crash of a duster pilot. *Aerospace Medicine, 42,* 1111–1113.

World Health Organization. (1973). Safe use of pesticides. Geneva: Technical Report Series No. 9.

Zimmermann-Tansella, C., Campara, P., D'Andrea, F., Saronitto, C., & Tansella, M. (1983). Psychological and physical complaints of subjects with low exposure to lead. *Human Toxicology, 2,* 615–623.

10

Cancer

RICHARD A. BERG

INTRODUCTION

Treatment for cancer has increasingly become more effective as indicated by the progressively longer survival of afflicted individuals. Consequently, comprehensive clinical management must address not only the medical status of the patient but, additionally, caretakers must be concerned with the person's psychological condition and overall social adjustment. The patient's emotional reactions, subjective feelings, functional behavioral capacity, interpersonal relationships, and psychosocial adjustment are encompassed by the multidimensional construct *quality of life*.

One important factor influencing quality of life is cognitive capacity. Cancer, and its treatment, can cause a variety of cognitive impairments that range from mild to severe (Oxman & Silberfarb, 1980). Determination of the cognitive capacities of the cancer patient is especially important because cognitive dysfunction in such patients is often indicative of a poor medical prognosis (Folstein, Fetting, Lobo, Niaz, & Capozzoli, 1984). Moreover, a cognitive impairment can profoundly impact on the individual in any and all facets of daily life to the point where independent functioning is compromised. Where there is significant cognitive impairment, the patient's abilities to be a competent informant, relate relevant historical information, and comply with a treatment regimen are also potentially impaired. For these latter reasons, valuable information from the neuropsychological evaluation can be obtained that can practically maximize the efficacy of medical management.

This chapter reviews the neuropsychological effects of cancer in children and adults. Each of these two different populations presents unique problems. Not only are the types of cancer different, but also the cognitive sequelae and the impact of the disease on life quality are different.

RICHARD A. BERG • Department of Behavioral Medicine and Psychiatry, West Virginia University Medical Center, Charleston, West Virginia 25326.

INCIDENCE AND PREVALENCE

There are numerous forms of cancers in humans. To specifically address each type would require far more space than can be devoted to a single chapter. For this reason, only a comparatively few forms of cancers and their effects will be discussed. The types of cancers considered in this chapter are the ones most likely to be encountered by neuropsychologists in the course of clinical practice.

Adults

The most prevalent form of cancer in adults is carcinoma. Carcinoma refers to cancer of epithelial tissue, that is, tissue that lines the various body organs. The most frequent organs involved are the lungs, liver, stomach, and breast. Leukemias are the next most prevalent forms of cancers; the most common types are the chronic and acute nonlymphocytic varieties. Acute lymphocytic leukemia is comparatively rare in adults. Cancer of the lymph system (lymphoma) is another common variety. Malignancies in the central nervous system are the last type of cancer encountered in adults that will be considered here. Epidemiological data for the various types of cancers in adults and children are presented in Table 1. The mortality rate from the various cancers is summarized in Table 2. It can be seen that the prognosis varies according to the type of cancer. For adults with carcinoma, such as lung and breast cancers, the prognosis is poor despite advances that have been made since the mid-1960s in prolonging survival. The same is generally true for the adult leukemias and for some types of CNS tumors.

Children

In contrast to adults, leukemia is the most common form of cancer in children. Although there are several different varieties of leukemias, as a

TABLE 1. Cancer Incidence by Site for Adults and Children[a]

Site	Percentage		Per 100,000	
	Adult	Child	Adult	Child
All Sites	100.0	100.0	325.4	36.9
Carcinoma	88.4	5.7	281.0	2.1
Brain	1.4	19.8	5.2	7.2
Leukemia	2.7	31.0	9.6	11.8
Bone	0.2	4.8	0.8	1.6
Lymphoma	1.8	12.5	11.9	4.3
Other sites (combined)	5.4	26.1	16.9	70.3

[a]Adapted from Young et al. (1982), Cancer Incidence and Mortality in the United States, 1973–1977.

TABLE 2. Cancer Mortality by Site for Adults and Children[a]

Site	Per 100,000	
	Adult	Child
All sites	140.3	12.6
Carcinoma	124.5	3.0
Brain	2.2	3.3
Leukemia	4.6	4.4
Bone	0.7	0.4
Lymphoma	3.3	1.6
Other sites (combined)	12.9	0.1

[a]Adapted from Young et al. (1982), Cancer Incidence and Mortality in the United States, 1973–1977.

group, the leukemias account for over 30% of all types of cancers. The next most prevalent forms of cancers found in children are neoplasms of the brain and other regions of the central nervous system; these cancers account for about 20% of cases.

The prognosis for childhood cancer has markedly improved during the past 20 years. Childhood leukemia, particularly the acute lymphocytic variety, has a survival rate of about 50% at 5 yr from the time of initial diagnosis (Mauer, 1980). Certain other tumors in children have a 5-yr survival rate of over 70%.

ANATOMY AND PHYSIOLOGY

Carcinomas

The etiology of the carcinomas is still uncertain. It is quite likely that multiple factors are involved. A number of speculations deserve consideration, however. It is possible that the presence of a tumor leads to the production of autoimmune antibodies in a number of tissues, including nervous system tissue (Wilkinson, 1964). It is hypothesized that these antibodies are able to penetrate the blood–brain barrier or attach themselves to peripheral nerve or muscle tissue. If this is indeed what occurs, pathologic changes may arise in the affected tissues that would not be incompatible with some of the changes described later. The theory of antibody formation has received some support from the description of antibrain antibodies in "carcinomatous neuromyopathy" and antibodies against neurons in sensory carcinomatous neuropathy (Wilkinson & Zeromski, 1965).

There is also the likelihood that some changes in structure are the result of a chronic viral infection (Gilroy & Meyer, 1975). This notion is supported by the description of intraneuronal inclusion bodies in some cases of progressive multifocal leukoencephalopathy. Infection by a neurotropic virus could conceivably occur following reduction in body defenses secondary to the development of a carcinoma or any other form of neoplasia (Gilroy & Meyer, 1975).

Finally, some of the abnormalities occurring in association with malignancies may be the result of concomitant endocrine or metabolic disturbances. Some carcinomas are known to produce endocrinelike substances that may have the effect of the true hormone (Gilroy & Meyer, 1975). Although each condition is described here as a distinct entity, it should be realized that it is common to find a number of conditions in any one patient. The term carcinomatous neuromyopathy has been used to cover disorders affecting the central and peripheral nervous systems and muscles in a single patient (Morton, Itaboshi, & Grimes, 1966).

Carcinoma in children is relatively rare (Young et al., 1982) and, therefore, will not be discussed at length here. In those instances where a childhood carcinoma does occur, the neoplasm acts much the same in children as it does in adults.

Leukemia

The neoplastic proliferation of white blood cells or their precursors may be followed by diffuse infiltration of many organs including the nervous system (Wells & Silver, 1957). It has been estimated that the nervous system is affected in roughly 25% of cases in both the chronic and acute types (Freireich, Thomas, Frei, Fritz, & Folkner, 1960). Perhaps the most common complication of leukemia in adults is intracerebral hemorrhage that occurs predominantly in the white matter (Freireich et al., 1960). It appears that leukemic cells block the penetrating vessels in the brain and infiltrate the vessel walls to form a leukemic nodule from which there is a hemorrhage into the white matter.

Leukemic patients are highly susceptible to infections of the nervous system, particularly when receiving treatment with cytotoxic agents (Currie & Henson, 1971). As a result, the incidence of herpes zoster neuritis, encephalitis, acute and subacute meningitis, and brain abscesses is increased during the course of the disease.

Childhood Leukemia

Of childhood leukemias, 98% are of the acute variety in which primitive blast cells predominate and proliferate in the bone marrow at the expense of normal blood-making tissues (Bowman, 1981). In the acute forms of the disease, roughly 80% are lymphocytic, and the remaining 20% consist of acute myelogeneous leukemia or one of its variants (Bowman, 1981). Nervous system effects are generally thought to be the result of blood-borne seeding of leukemic cells in the meninges of the brain prior to the initiation of treatment. The central nervous system is thought to be a "pharmacologic sanctuary" where leukemic cells are protected and continue to proliferate because chemotherapy cannot cross the blood–brain barrier (Evans, Gilbert,

& Sandstra, 1970; Sullivan, 1957). The unhindered leukemic cells, then, destroy unprotected brain tissue and eventually recede back in the bone marrow (Mauer, 1980). The exact manner in which the leukemic cells destroy nervous tissue is, as yet, unknown.

Hodgkin's Disease

Hodgkin's disease is a neoplastic condition of lymphoid tissue that originates in lymphatic or reticuloendothelial cells (Geller & Lacher, 1966). The cells exhibit local invasiveness as well as the ability to spread to other parts of the body. Any organ system may become involved. The condition is common in males with the highest incidence between 20 and 40 yr. Approximately 10% of patients with the disease demonstrate evidence of direct involvement of the nervous system. Neurologic involvement, especially direct invasion of the nervous tissue, occurs largely in those categories of the disease in which there is mixed cellularity and lymphocytic depletion (Sohn, Valensi, & Miller, 1967).

Direct invasion of the brain or spinal cord is quite rare and may present as a solitary lesion of Hodgkin's sarcoma (Gaelen & Levitan, 1967; Kaufman, 1965). Gilroy and Meyer (1975) report a tendency toward invasion of the hypothalamus and optic chiasm with the production of diabetes insipidus and visual field defects or invasion of the temporal lobes and focal seizure activity. These authors also note that the floor of the skull and the meninges may be affected with subarachnoid hemorrhages being a potential complication.

Non-Hodgkin's Lymphoma

Non-Hodgkin's lymphomas (NHL) are a heterogenous group of lymphoid cancers that are characterized by a natural history that ranges from indolent to aggressive. Although the specific etiology of NHL is not yet known, there appears to be a link to congenital immunodeficiencies and suppressed immune systems (Ultmann & Jacobs, 1985). Neurologic complications may result either directly from the neoplasms or from some aspect of their treatment and may mimic the symptoms associated with an intracranial space-occupying lesion (Hoppe, Kushlan, & Kaplan, 1981; Portlock, 1980).

Other lymphomas (e.g., follicular lymphoma, reticulum-cell sarcoma, lymphosarcoma) may also give rise to neurologic complications (see Walton, 1977, for a complete description). These lymphomas are beyond the scope of this chapter and so will not be discussed here.

CEREBRAL TUMORS

Etiology

The etiologic factors underlying the development of cerebral tumors are poorly understood. A number of factors are assumed to underlie the development of cerebral tumors. These include the following:

Heredity

The familial occurrence of brain tumors is rare except for the development of meningiomas, astrocytomas, and the neurofibromas associated with von Recklinghausen's disease (Joynt & Perret, 1965).

Trauma

There have been occasional reports of brain tumors, particularly meningiomas, arising at the site of cranial cerebral injury. The evidence for such an etiologic association is, however, extremely tenuous. Generally, trauma is not considered to be related to the subsequent development of tumors of the central nervous system (Walton, 1977).

Radiation

The central nervous system is sensitive to radiation. Exposure can cause degenerative changes (Kramer & Lee, 1974). There is currently no evidence, however, that brain irradiation will induce the development of a glioma (Young et al., 1982), although there are reports that meningiomas (Young et al., 1982) and nonspecific tumor development may follow irradiation (McCormick, Menezes & Gin, 1972).

Viruses

Although there are some reports implicating an association between certain viral infections and subsequent development of neoplasia (e.g., lymphoma), no firm relationship has yet been established (Gilroy & Meyer, 1975; Young et al., 1982). Of note, however, is an increased incidence of tuberculous infection in a series of patients who developed cerebral gliomas (Ward, Mattison, & Fian, 1973); however, there have been no recent follow-ups of these preliminary findings.

Classification

Tumors are classified into two major groupings. The first type is infiltrative tumors; these tumors take over and destroy nerve tissue. The second type is noninfiltrative tumors. These tumors cause dysfunction by compression and displacement of tissue. These two major groups are further subdivided into the following specific types of tumor.

Glioblastoma. The glioblastoma multiforme is the most common infiltrative tumor. Glioblastomas are neoplastic proliferations of glial cells. This type of tumor typically arises in middle age and is usually found in the cerebral hemispheres. The rapid growth rate of the tumor results in pronounced neurologic symptoms early in the course of the disease (Golden, Moses, Coffman, Miller, & Strider, 1983).

Astrocytomas. Astrocytomas are infiltrative tumors of astrocytes, a star-shaped glial cell. These tumors are generally more slow growing than glioblastomas; however, the tissue destruction and behavioral manifestations resulting from astrocytomas are quite similar to glioblastomas. Because astrocytomas are slower growing than glioblastomas, they allow for greater cerebral compensation of psychologic functioning.

Meningioma. The most common extrinsic noninfiltrative tumor is the meningioma, accounting for about 15% of all cases of cerebral tumors (Robbins, 1974). Extrinsic noninfiltrative tumors arising in the membranes surrounding the brain are usually less serious than infiltrative tumors; however, severe behavioral symptoms nonetheless may be manifest. Meningiomas, arising in the arachnoid layers of the meninges, create an irregular growth that presses upon the brain. Because their effects are produced by pressure rather than tissue destruction, the neurological and psychological consequences of meningiomas and other noninfiltrative tumors tend to be somewhat less precise than those of infiltrative tumors. It is quite possible for a meningioma to displace brain tissue to such an extent that the foci of the behavioral manifestations are essentially unrelated to the location of the tumor. Alternatively, if the brain is not compressed substantially by the tumor, there may be no behavioral symptoms (Golden *et al.*, 1983).

Metastatic Tumors. These are infiltrative tumors that migrate to the brain from carcinomas that occur initially elsewhere in the body, most commonly in the lungs, breasts, adrenal system, and lymphatic system (Earle, 1955). They are generally fast-growing tumors. The clinical presentation can be similar to other tumors; however, because these tumors are multiple in nature, the overall behavioral and cognitive effects can be much more severe than the symptoms resulting from a single tumor.

PSYCHOLOGICAL DEFICIT ASSOCIATED WITH SPECIFIC TUMOR LOCATIONS

Frontal Lobe Tumors

Cognitive Sequelae

Typically, striking neurologic signs are absent in frontal tumors; however, mental distrubancess are frequently observed (Golden *et al.*, 1983). Tumors of the left and right frontal regions are commonly also associated with cognitive impairments that are most pronounced when both lobes are involved (Strauss & Keschner, 1935). Lesions of the dominant hemisphere are most likely to disrupt the person's capacity to plan and organize goal-directed behavior—an impairment attributable to the brain's incapacity to exercise the so-called "executive" functions (Luria, 1966).

Although dementia is probably the most frequent diagnosis in patients with frontal lobe tumors (Golden et al., 1983), memory disturbances have also been reported. Hecaen and Ajuriaguerra (1956) found that "amnesie de fixation" was prominent in 10 of 80 cases. However, because the failure of memory frequently occurs in conjunction with profound apathy, it is difficult to determine whether a patient is either actually impaired cognitively or is not motivated.

Cognitive distrubances resulting from frontal lobe tumors usually also include a loss of spontaneity, inertia, and a generalized slowing of mental efficiency (Luria, 1966). Speech may be slow and labored even in the absence of dysphasia or dominant frontal lobe involvement. Akinetic states, in which the patient is mute and immobile yet when roused shows normal orientation, have also been reported (Golden et al., 1983).

Certain specific cognitive disturbances are associated with frontal lobe tumors but only in the absence of a massive or an acute lesion. In diffuse lesions, the ability to organize behavior is reduced or even lost, especially when the dominant frontal lobe is involved (Luria, 1966). Deficits in this regard are seen on complex tasks in which the patient must utilize internal language to mediate behavior and flexibly respond to the task demands (Luria, 1966). Consequently, response perseveration is commonly seen on problem-solving tests such as the Halstead Category Test (Halstead, 1947) and the Wisconsin Card Sorting Test (Milner, 1963). Moreover, deficits can be readily elicited on tests such as the Stroop Color-Word Test (Perrett, 1974). This task requires the person to be fluent verbally as well as to suppress the effects of a distracting stimulus on performance.

Right frontal lobe deficits on cognitive tests are generally less well defined than those of the left frontal lobe. As a result, they are less likely to be noticed during clinical evaluation. Impairments, where manifest, may be seen in speech-related processes; however, subtle deficits may also be present on other aspects of cognition such as musical expression (Botez & Wertheim, 1959), behavior sequencing ability, and in performing complex spatial tasks (Corkin, 1965; Milner, 1971; Teuber, 1964).

Emotional Sequelae

Affective symptoms that are characteristic of a frontal lobe tumor include irritability, depression, euphoria, and apathy. Direkze, Bayliss, and Cutting (1971) described several patients initially admitted to psychiatric facilities for treatment of depression who upon reevaluation were found to have frontal lobe tumors. This study illustrates the difficulty of diagnosis based solely on behavioral signs and symptoms. Tumors of the frontal lobe should thus be suspected where there are behavioral changes in the absence of neurologic signs and intellectual deficits. In about 25% of patients, personality changes occur prior to any cognitive deficits (Strauss & Keschner, 1935). These changes are featured by irresponsibility, childishness, disinhibition, a lack of reserve, lack of insight, an indifference to the current situation, and a denial of illness.

Temporal Lobe Tumors

Cognitive Sequelae

Tumors occurring in the front temporal region produce the highest frequency of mental disorder (Golden et al., 1983). This is due, in part, to symptoms associated with temporal lobe epilepsy, although numerous cognitive deficits are present even when there is no seizure disturbance (Keschner, Bender, & Strauss, 1936). Approximately 50% of individuals with temporal lobe tumors experience seizures (Strobos, 1953). Apart from symptoms associated with temporal lobe epilepsy, no specific mental disturbance is manifest where the tumor is in the left frontotemporal region. Although some investigators have reported that an early onset and rapidly progressive dementia may be characteristic of frontotemporal tumors (Keschner et al., 1936), this may instead be the result of a dysphasia (Hecaen & Ajuriaguerra, 1956). Neoplasms of the nondominant frontotemporal region may remain clinically silent until they are very advanced and of large size.

In a report of a large series of patients, Bingley (1958) concluded that tumors in the dominant hemisphere produce substantially greater intellectual impairments, involving both verbal and nonverbal capacities, than nondominant hemisphere tumors. Slowing and reduced speech spontaneity also have often been reported in patients with temporal lobe tumors. In one study of temporal lobe neoplasms, 63% of patients demonstrated dullness, apathy, and impaired spontaneous speech (Keschner et al., 1936). When these patients were roused, speech was deliberate but without dysphasic features. Indifference to the environment as well as impaired memory also was noted in patients with temporal lobe tumors.

Tumors located in the middle to posterior region of the dominant temporal lobe are most notably featured by disturbances in language comprehension, whereas tumors in the nondominant middle to posterior temporal regions typically result in a more subtle symptom presentation. The most common disturbances are in visual and auditory pattern analysis (Kimura, 1963; Meier & French, 1965).

Emotional Sequelae

Changes in affect are relatively common. Euphoria may be present as frequently with temporal tumors as in frontal tumors (Schlesinger, 1950). Anger outbursts, anxiety, depression, and irritability have all been reported to be sequelae of temporal lobe tumors. Bingley (1958) found that temporal lobe tumors in the dominant hemisphere generally lead to more emotional changes, especially flattening of affect, than nondominant tumors. Depression appears to be more common in nondominant lesions. Neoplasms in the frontal and temporal regions have twice the frequency of affective changes than tumors in other cerebral regions (Hecaen & Ajuriaguerra, 1956).

Specific personality changes do not seem to be associated with temporal lobe tumors. Facetiousness and childish behavior similar to that seen with frontal lesions may, however, appear. More frequently, psychopathic and paranoid tendencies emerge that are accompanied by irritability and hypo- chondriasis.

Occasionally, schizophreniform psychoses are observed in patients with temporal lobe tumors. Davison and Bagley (1969), reviewing a group of 77 cases of this comparatively rare condition, found a significantly higher proportion of temporal and pituitary tumors in the schizophreniform group compared to other tumor locations. In the schizophreniform disorders, com- plex hallucinations may also be present. In one study, Keschner *et al.* (1936) noted that 15 of 110 patients demonstrated hallucinations in the absence of seizures. Unlike the "functional" psychoses, once the patient recognizes the physical basis of the hallucinations, insight into their nature is gained, a distinction that separates temporal lobe lesions from schizophrenia (Lish- man, 1978).

Parietal Lobe Tumors

Cognitive Sequelae

Complex cognitive disorders are commonly associated with parietal lobe tumors. A dysphasia or ideational dyspraxia may occur in patients if the lesion is in the dominant hemisphere (Brown, 1974). The Gerstmann syn- drome consisting of finger agnosia, dyscalculia, dysgraphia and right–left confusion may also be seen as a circumscribed disorder or as part of a global cognitive disruption. Nondominant parietal tumors are more likely to be associated with visual-spatial disorientation, dressing dyspraxia, and topo- graphical disturbances (Brown, 1974). Nondominant parietal neoplasms are additionally associated with disorders of body image and awareness. These disturbances can include denial of the existence of a limb paralyzed by the neurologic lesion as well as attribution of the affected limb to another person.

Parietal lobe tumors are almost invariably marked by signs of tactile, kinesthetic, and proprioceptive disorders. These disturbances can include the loss or inability to analyze sensation, locate body parts, recognize objects by touch, and recognize the location of sensation on the body (Chusid, 1973; Golden, 1981; Roland, 1976). A large lesion in either parietal lobe may result in a bilateral disorder, particularly in cases of a fast-growing tumor and where the dominant hemisphere is involved (Corkin, Milner, & Taylor, 1973).

Emotional Sequelae

Psychiatric changes appear to be less likely with tumors in the parietal areas of the brain than other brain regions. Depression has, however, been noted (Hecaen & Ajuriaguerra, 1956). In contrast, personality changes are rare (Golden *et al.*, 1983).

Occipital Tumors

Cognitive Sequelae

The dominant symptom associated with occipital tumors is a visual half-field impairment. Small tumors may result in a scotoma. Tumors located in the dominant occipital lobe commonly produce a loss of verbal-visual skills and a visual agnosia (Brown, 1974).

Emotional Sequelae

Detailed comparisons of tumors located in various parts of the brain have not revealed a disproportionate frequency of emotional disorders in occipital tumors (Lishman, 1978).

Corpus Callosum Tumors

There is a high prevalence of intellectual disturbance associated with corpus callosum tumors. Schlesinger (1950) found mental changes in 92% of patients with rostral tumors, 57% with midcallosal tumors, and 89% with tumors of the splenium. The frequency of mental symptoms due to anterior and posterior callosal tumors, when compared with those of the middle sections of the corpus callosum, has been subsequently confirmed by Selecki (1964). Anterior callosal neoplasms notably result in rapid mental deterioration. A personality change or a florid psychosis may ensue. The reasons for the prominent mental changes are not entirely clear but may result from involvement of the tumor with adjacent brain structures. For example, anterior callosal tumors may invade the frontal regions, whereas those of the genu invade the thalamus and midbrain posteriorly. Most tumors of the corpus callosum also invade the third ventricle and diencephalon at some point in the course of the illness, culminating ultimately in somnolence, akinesia, and stupor (Selecki, 1964). A lesion of the callosum may also result in disturbance of interhemispheric integration as well as disrupt association areas lying adjacent to the cingulate gyrus (Schlesinger, 1950).

Thalamic and Hypothalamic Tumors

Diencephalic tumors are relatively uncommon. Where present, however, these tumors have striking effects (Walton, 1977).

A severe memory problem is a typical sequel of tumors located near the third ventricle (Delay, Brion, & Derouesne, 1964). Impairments in learning and short-term memory are present; however, remote memory as well as other cognitive processes may remain largely unaffected (Lishman, 1978). Confabulation, as seen in Korsakoff psychosis, may also be present (Scoville & Milner, 1957).

A steady and progressive dementia may occur as the result of cortical atrophy following chronic obstruction of cerebrospinal fluid circulation.

Craniopharyngiomas may present with clinical syndromes that are dominated by a failure of intellect and memory in the absence of obvious neurologic signs (Russell & Pennybacker, 1961). Symptoms of hypothalamic disturbance, such as somnolence, may provide the distinguishing clue for implicating the presence of a tumor in the diencephalon.

Pituitary Tumors

The range of cognitive sequelae of pituitary tumors has not been researched. The most common impairment, observed upon clinical evaluation, is a visual disturbance. Elevated CSF pressure and endocrine changes in pituitary tumors may underlie the cognitive and psychiatric disturbances (Golden et al., 1983).

Infratentorial Tumors

This region includes the cerebellum, cerebellopontine angle, and brain stem. Cognitive, affective, and personality disorders are comparatively infrequent with tumors in these areas. Keschner, Bender, and Strauss (1938a) found that the symptoms that did emerge were typically mild, rarely persistent, and occurred in the later stages of the illness.

When cognitive dysfunction occurs, it appears to be closely associated with increased intracranial pressure. In these cases, the cognitive impairment tends to be generalized, develops insidiously, and parallels the development of hydrocephalus. Profound ventricular enlargement may occur with slow-growing infratentorial tumors before an accompanying dementia becomes apparent (Keschner, Bender, & Strauss, 1938b).

Cerebral Tumors in Children

Several important factors have relevance for the study of the neuropsychological effects in childhood tumors, including age at the time of diagnosis and treatment, and the location, extent, and permanence of the lesion (Boll & Barth, 1981). The presence of hydrocephalus, the aggressiveness of surgery, irradiation, and chemotherapy treatment also may have a substantial impact on functional cognitive capacities. The assessment of children surviving brain tumors has traditionally been restricted to a global clinical evaluation of neurological status at various intervals following treatment without reference to these latter factors.

It has been estimated that between 70 to 80% of surviving children function at or near their premorbid level (Abramson, Raben, & Cavanaugh, 1974; Bloom, Wallace, & Henk, 1969; Gjerris, 1976; Harisiadis & Chang, 1977). In-depth evaluations have, on the other hand, found a greater prevalence (approximately 40%) of functional impairment after treatment (Bamford et al., 1976; Danoff, Cowchock, Marquette, Mulgrew, & Kramer, 1982; Kun, Mulhern, & Crisco, 1983; Spunberg, Chang, Goldman, Auricchio, & Bell, 1981).

Age-at-Diagnosis

The importance of the developmental status of the central nervous system at the time of injury is still a cause for debate in neuropsychology. Evidence in support of, as well as opposition to, the contention that the immature brain is more "plastic" with respect to cognitive recovery and future development of psychological functioning has been extensively documented (Chelune & Edwards, 1981; Satz & Fletcher, 1981; St. James-Roberts, 1979). A review of the literature on childhood brain lesions suggests that age at the time of injury and type of lesion (focal versus diffuse) may interact to determine the level of cognitive functioning. Young children with diffuse injuries display less recovery than older children. In contrast, young children with focal injuries demonstrate better recovery of cognitive function than older children (Chelune & Edwards, 1981).

The research on the outcome of brain neoplasms in childhood has not systematically addressed the issue of age at the time of diagnosis (Mulhern, Crisco, & Kun, 1983). In one of the few studies investigating age effects, Kun et al. (1983) were unable to find a relationship between age at diagnosis and subsequent neuropsychological functioning; however, clinically apparent deficiencies in attention and concentration were more frequently observed in younger children. Marked changes have been noted in children posttreatment for tumors at age 2 or younger (Spunberg et al., 1981). In this latter study, 77% of the children seen at follow-up were functioning below normal on standard intelligence tests.

Tumor Location

In comparison to adults, the relationship between location of a cerebral neoplasm and cognitive functioning in children has not been investigated extensively. Among those studies that classified children by tumor location, the investigations were confined primarily to patients with infratentorial tumors (Berry, Jenkin, Keen, Nair, & Simpson, 1981; Raimondi & Tomita, 1979; Silverman et al., 1982; Tamaroff, Salwen, Allen, Murphy, & Nir, 1982). The prevalence of neurologic disturbance in children with these types of lesions is quite variable. This is due, in part, to the diversity of treatment strategies such as the differential use of cranial rather than local or no irradiation and the use of chemotherapy for advanced or especially malignant tumors. Infratentorial tumors treated by surgery result in a 27%–59% incidence of neuropsychological deficits and behavioral disturbances (Hirsch, Reneir, Czernichow, Benveniste, & Pierre-Kahn, 1979).

Gjerris (1976) found two to three times the prevalence of neurological disturbance in children with supratentorial tumors compared to children with infratentorial tumors. Kun et al. (1983) reported approximately twice the incidence of disability in supratentorial as compared to infratentorial brain tumors. The deficits observed in the children in these studies are quite varied and include visuospatial, attentional, and auditory-processing impairments (Mulhern et al., 1983). A large discrepancy between Verbal and

Performance IQ scores has also been noted; however, this finding is not consistent across studies (Mulhern et al., 1983).

Childhood Leukemia

The most widely investigated cancer, at least with respect to its neuro-psychological sequelae, is childhood leukemia. The treatment of children with leukemia has improved significantly in the past decade; however, the extent to which there are adverse effects on the central nervous system has not been extensively researched.

A number of reports have indicated that CNS prophylaxis produces long-term cognitive deficits, particularly when radiation is combined with chemotherapy (Eiser & Lansdown, 1977; Eiser, 1980; Moss, Nannis & Poplack, 1981). A past study found that children with leukemia who received CNS irradiation obtained lower scores on tasks measuring visual-motor ability, spatial memory, and arithmetic had lower IQ scores than nonirradiated children (Copeland et al., 1985). Goff, Anderson, and Cooper (1980) reported a distinct pattern of attention and concentration deficits in long-term leukemia survivors. Additionally, it has been reported that the cognitive deficits occur within 1 yr from the time of diagnosis and initial treatment (Stehbens, Kisker, & Wilson, 1983). Language-related abilities have also been reported to decline in children treated for leukemia (Moehle, Berg, Ch'ien, & Lancaster, 1983).

A number of other investigations have not found evidence for a cognitive impairment in individuals treated for leukemia (e.g., Ivnik, Colligan, Obetz, & Smithson, 1981; Obetz et al., 1979). One long-term study, assessing cognitive functioning in a group of children treated for leukemia at least 6 years previously, observed no significant deficits (Berg et al., 1983; Berg, Tuseth, Ochs, & Cummins, 1984). In none of these studies was the age at the time of diagnosis found to be a significant factor. From the foregoing discussion, it can be concluded that the effects of leukemia and its treatment on neuropsychological status are still not well understood and in need of further research.

The emotional impact of having cancer has not been widely studied. However, of the research that has been conducted, some surprising results have been obtained. Children who are not informed of their diagnosis reported a sense of impending death with younger children expressing more concern about separation, pain, and disfigurement (Binger et al., 1969). These authors also report that older children tend to become protective of their parents. A general regression to more immature behaviors such as bed wetting and soiling has also been noted. It has also been found that there is an exacerbation of undesirable behaviors accompanied by generalized fearfulness (D'Angio, 1980). D'Angio (1980), citing two separate studies of children treated for cancer, noted some confusion and inconsistencies in the literature. In one study, all survivors were found to be well adjusted, whereas a second study found that almost 50% of the sample exhibited some form of psychological disturbance that ranged from mild to severe. The most common symptoms were depression and anxiety.

CARCINOMA AND OTHER FORMS OF CANCER

When carcinomas and other cancers metastasize, one of the most probable sites for seeding is the brain. This leads to the development of cerebral tumors that produce effects that are the same as those discussed earlier.

Nonmetastatic Involvement of the Brain Resulting from Carcinoma

Dementia

Dementia may occur as a remote manifestation of a carcinoma alone or in association with other degenerative conditions including cerebellar degeneration and encephalomyelopathy (Gilroy & Meyer, 1975). The dementia is moderately rapid and progressive with associated impairments in judgment, insight, and memory (Kaplan & Itabashi, 1974).

Progressive Multifocal Leukoencephalopathy

This condition is characterized by a number of foci of demyelination of the white matter in the brain and spinal cord. The sizes of the affected areas range widely from being just visible with the naked eye to large confluent areas. Typically, the myelin sheath disappears with preservation of the neuron (Martin & Banker, 1969).

Progressive multifocal leukoencephalopathy is a comparatively rare disorder. It usually occurs as a terminal event in patients with disorders of the blood (e.g., leukemias) but will occasionally also occur in the carcinomas (Davies, Hughes, & Oppenheimer, 1973). The disorder is generally fatal from within 3 to 6 mon from onset. However, remission and 5-yr survival have been reported. Hemiplegia, quadraplegia, aphasia, dysarthria, ataxia, and visual field defects or blindness are common manifestations of progressive multifocal leukoencephalopathy (Hedley-White, Smith, Tyler, & Peterson, 1966).

Encephalomyelopathy

This disorder is usually associated with the oat cell type of bronchial carcinoma and may occasionally occur with carcinoma of the breast or uterus (Henson, Hoffman, & Urich, 1965). There is perivascular cuffing, some neuronal loss, and microglial proliferation in the hippocampal formation, amygdala, cingulate gyrus, and orbital cortex (Gilroy & Meyer, 1975). Similar changes occur throughout the brain stem, with a variable loss of neurons in the motor nuclei. There is also generally some loss of anterior horn cells accompanied by demyelination of the posterior columns. Peripheral nerve tissue also may demyelinate (Henson *et al.*, 1965).

Encephalomyelopathy results in a progressive dementia with intellectual impairment, fluctuating levels of awareness, and alternating periods of consciousness and somnolence. Bulbar involvement results in external ophthalmoplegia, nystagmus, ataxia, dysarthria, and dysphagia (Gilroy & Meyer, 1975).

Hodgkin's Disease and Other Lymphomas

The neuropsychologic sequelae of Hodgkin's disease have not been studied. On rare occasion, Hodgkin's disease directly invades the brain and spinal cord (Gaelen & Levitan, 1967; Kaufman, 1965). When this occurs, there appears to be a tendency toward invasion of the hypothalamus and optic chiasm. The temporal lobes can also be invaded, leading to seizure disorders.

IMPLICATIONS FOR MEDICAL MANAGEMENT AND REHABILITATION

The assessment of the presence and magnitude of brain dysfunction is only a first step, although an important one, in providing comprehensive care for the individual with brain damage. Information obtained from the neuropsychological evaluation is important because of the relationship between cognitive capacity and psychosocial adjustment, or quality of life.

It is not the primary task of the neuropsychologist to localize lesions in the cerebrum because this information can be more readily obtained using neuroradiologic techniques. Rather, the neuropsychological evaluation is most appropriately utilized for describing cognitive strengths and deficits that can then assist in either vocational rehabilitation or for monitoring the effects of treatment.

Assessment of the patient's emotional status is additionally important. Patients with cancer frequently suffer from what Koocher (1973) first described as the "Damocles syndrome," that is, living under the constant threat that the "cured" disease will recur or that a second malignancy will develop. Emotional status can significantly impact on the efficiency of the rehabilitation program (Golden, 1981). In some cases, emotional difficulties may be so severe as to preclude a successful treatment program. In many cases, therefore, treatment of the emotional disorder is necessary either as a prelude to rehabilitation or as an integral part of the rehabilitation process. Individuals with cancer face an extraordinary number of problems over and above those typically encountered by patients who have suffered brain damage from some other cause. Seeking gainful employment is extremely difficult as most employers are reluctant to hire a person who has had cancer because of the possibility of a recurrence of the disease and the costs to the employer. Thus, for this and other reasons, people will often not willingly associate with those who have received treatment for cancer, thus further leading to emotional and social isolation of the patient.

The treatment for cancer often involves procedures that ultimately result in some form of physical disfigurement such as the loss of a limb due to amputation, loss of a breast due to mastectomy, and loss of hair that may be either temporary or permanent resulting from chemo- and/or radiation therapy. The cancer patient, therefore, may additionally have to learn to reconcile a significant change in body image with any attendant cognitive and emotional difficulties.

CASE STUDIES

Case No. 1—CD

CD was a 6-year-old white male when he had his first neuropsychological evaluation. He had been diagnosed as having acute lymphocytic leukemia (ALL) at 2 1/2 years of age. He received the standard treatment available at that time that consisted of combination chemotherapy including intravenous and intrathecal (injected into the spinal canal) methotrexate as well as 2,400 rads of Co60 craniospinal irradiation for CNS prophylaxis. In all, CD was evaluated three times over a 3-year period. Each evaluation consisted of a modified version of the Reitan-Indiana or Halstead-Reitan Neuropsychological Test Battery for Children, Wechsler Intelligence Scale for Children—Revised, Wide Range Achievement Test, and Bender Visual-Motor Gestalt Test.

CD was in complete and continuous remission from initial treatment through the second evaluation. CD's hearing had been evaluated in his school as part of a normal screening program. Although his hearing acuity was found to be normal, the audiologist conducting the screening suspected a difficulty in auditory discrimination that was later confirmed through a complete audiological evaluation. During the course of the first two neuropsychological evaluations, CD was somewhat distractible but easily recalled to the task at hand with minimal prompting. Additionally, instructions and questions had to be repeated frequently.

Shortly after the second evaluation, a CNS relapse was discovered, and CD underwent a second complete round of treatment, including a second course of cranial irradiation. He was in remission again at the time of the third evaluation. During this testing session, CD was recalled to the task at hand only with a good deal of prompting. Of interest is the fact that he noted recalling many of the tasks but did not know how he was able to do them before because "they were so hard now." Approximately 6 months after the third evaluation, CD contracted a viral infection and eventually died.

The results of the three evaluations are presented in Table 3. As can be seen, a gradual decline in cognitive abilities occurred across the first two evaluations. What is quite remarkable about this case is the dramatic decrease in functioning seen at the third evaluation, at which time there

TABLE 3. D's Neuropsychological Performance Over 3 Years

Tests	Evaluation 1 (Age 6)	Evaluation 2 (Age 7)	Evaluation 3 (Age 8)
WISC–R			
Information	9	9	5
Similarities	15	13	2
Arithmetic	9	10	4
Vocabulary	8	7	9
Comprehension	11	10	6
Digit Span	12	10	5
Picture Completion	9	9	4
Picture Arrangement	8	8	6
Block Design	10	9	1
Object Assembly	9	8	6
Coding	8	7	4
WRAT Standard Scores			
Reading	98	94	47
Spelling	112	103	68
Arithmetic	111	101	33
Selected Reitain-Indiana Battery tests[a]			
Tapping (Dominant)	56	48	32
Tapping (Nondominant)	55	44	27
TPT (dominant)	49	45	30
TPT (nondominant)	51	50	36
Trail-Making A	57	54	45
Trail-Making B	52	49	28
Categories	65	58	32

[a]Unless otherwise stated, test scores for the Reitan-Indiana/Halstead-Reitan Battery are reported in t-scores ($M = 50$; $SD = 10$) based on normative data (Knights, 1980) and are scaled such that a higher score represents better performance.

was a drop in IQ of over 25 points as well as decreases in almost all cognitive areas. Particularly noteworthy was the deterioration in visual-motor skills as evidenced in CD's reproduction of the Bender figures (Figure 1). Not shown here is the fact that the first two administrations of the Bender figures yielded reproductions that were normal.

This case illustrates that cancer and its treatment can result in both a subtle decline in ability, as demonstrated in the slight changes between the first two evaluations, as well as marked and severe deterioration, as revealed by the performance decrements manifest on the third evaluation.

Case No. 2 — RH

RH was a 33-year-old white female who was referred for evaluation because of a sudden onset of unusual behavior. She had been employed in an administrative capacity in a governmental agency where she supervised several employees and was responsible for the department budget.

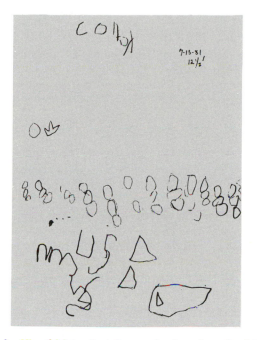

FIGURE 1. CD's Bender Visual-Motor Gestalt reproductions from the third evaluation. Performance from evaluations 1 and 2 was average or better.

At work one day, she reportedly displayed a number of emotional outbursts for no apparent reason and then became stuporous for approximately 5 minutes. After this episode, she continued with her work. The next day, she misplaced a large amount of cash that was to have been deposited and reported "hearing strange voices and sounds" as well as "seeing stars and firebursts." She was brought to the emergency room by a co-worker where a neurological exam was conducted. The co-worker reported that RH had said things over the past several days that did not make sense and seemed to have some trouble in understanding what was said to her. Upon neurological examination, bilateral signs and a developing hemiparesis were noted. RH was admitted for further tests, and a CAT scan revealed a "soft-ball sized" mass in the left frontal quadrant of the brain as well as a shift of the midline to the right. Prior to surgery, a neuropsychological evaluation was requested to obtain a baseline from which recovery could be gauged. The results of the evaluation are presented in Figure 2. As can clearly be seen, the neuropsychological tests revealed a severe impairment.

Neurosurgery revealed a large meningioma in the left frontal region that was excised with no complications. RH was then reevaluated approximately 6 weeks postsurgery. A summary of the results of this evaluation are presented in Figure 3. The results revealed a dramatic improvement in cognitive functioning, although deficits still clearly exist. It is not clear, however, whether RH will be able to return to her premorbid level of functioning.

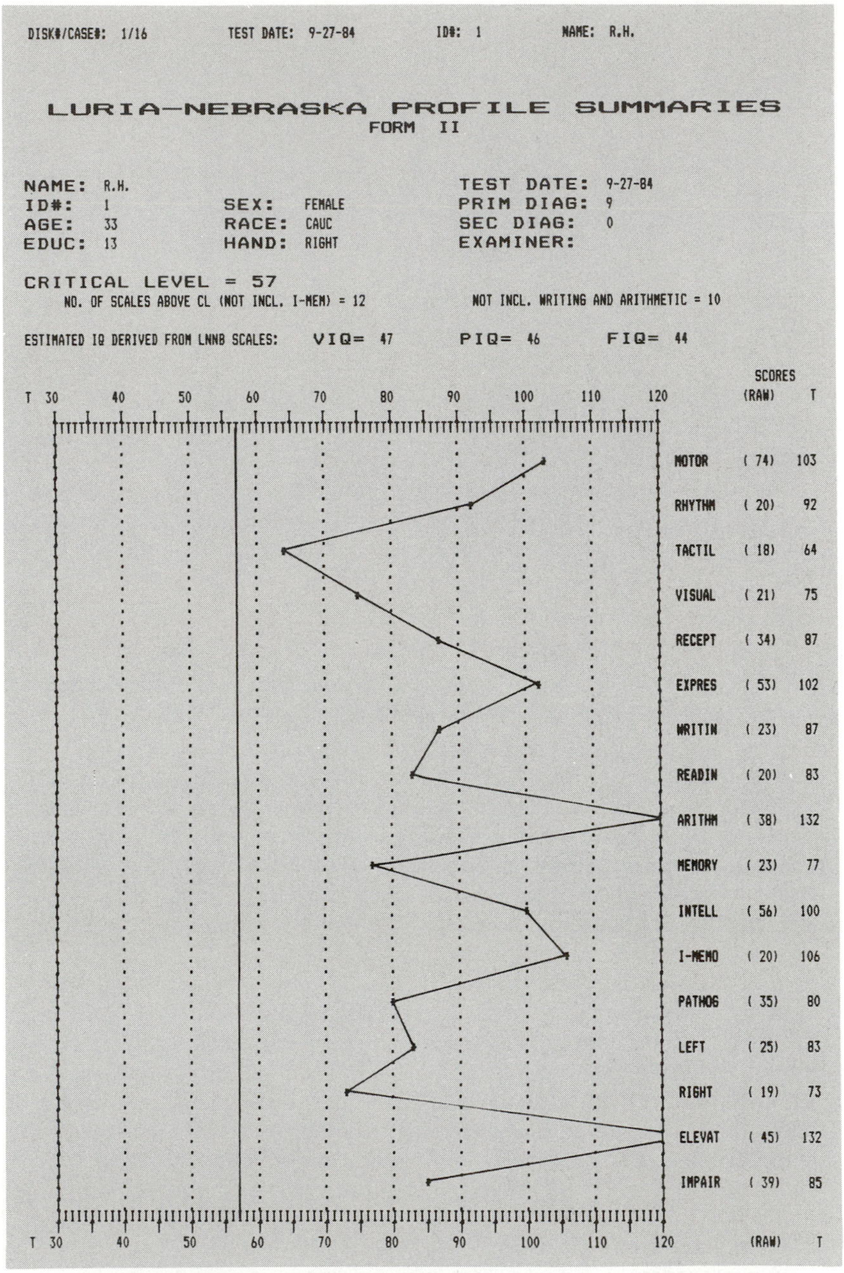

FIGURE 2. Results of evaluation one for RH (presurgical). Higher scores indicate poorer performance. Any score greater than the Critical Level as indicated by the solid vertical line is
indicative of impaired performance on that scale.

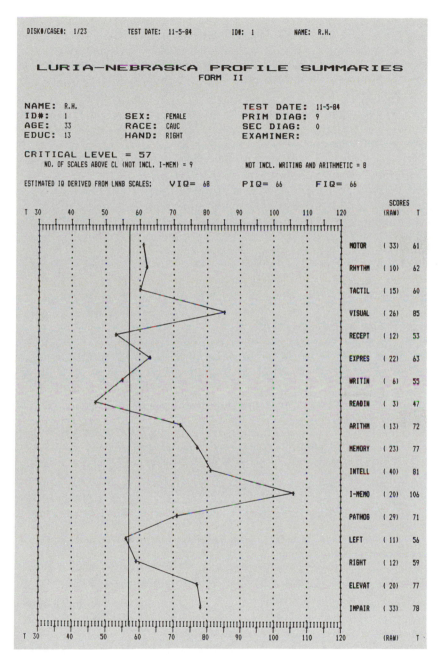

FIGURE 3. Neuropsychological evaluation results for RH 6 weeks postsurgically.

SUMMARY

The neuropsychological manifestations of cancer are many and varied. The type of cancer, its natural history, location, and the patient's age and form of treatment all interact to determine both the magnitude and type of cognitive and emotional impairment. Thus, the clinician, in evaluating cancer patients, must be cognizant of the numerous factors that may affect the neuropsychologic expression of the disease.

This chapter has attempted to delineate the multiple disease processes involved and how specific aspects of cognitive disorder may be related to the particular type of cancer. Such information, in the clinical context, can provide important information for both monitoring the course of the disease and its treatment, and for maximizing the social adjustment or life quality of the affected person.

REFERENCES

Abramson, N., Raben, M., & Cavanaugh, P. J. (1974). Brain tumors in children: Analysis of 136 cases. *Radiology, 112,* 669–672.

Bamford, F. N., Jones, P. M., Pearson, D., Ribeiro, G. G., Shalet, S. M., & Beardwell, C. G. (1976). Residual disabilities in children treated for intracranial space-occupying lesions. *Cancer, 37,* 1149–1151.

Berg, R. A., Ch'ien, L. T., Bowman, W. P., Ochs, J., Lancaster, W., Goff, J. R., & Anderson, H. R., Jr. (1983). The neuropsychological effects of acute lymphocytic leukemia and its treatment—A three year report: Intellectual functioning and academic achievement. *Clinical Neuropsychology, 5,* 9–13.

Berg, R. A., Tuseth, S., Ochs, J., & Cummins, J. (1984, August). *Neuropsychological sequelae of acute lymphocytic leukemia and its treatment—A longitudinal study.* Paper presented at the 92nd Annual Meeting of the American Psychological Association, Toronto, Canada.

Berry, M. P., Jenkin, D. T., Keen, G. W., Nair, B. D., & Simpson, W. J. (1981). Radiation for medulloblastoma. *Journal of Neurosurgery, 55,* 43–51.

Binger, C. M., Ablin, A. R., Feuerstein, R. C., Kushner, J. H., Zoger, S., & Mikkelsen, C. (1969). Childhood leukemia: Emotional impact on patient and family. *The New England Journal of Medicine, 280,* 414–418.

Bingley, T. (1958). Mental symptoms in temporal lobe epilepsy and temporal lobe glioma. *Acta Psychiatrica et Neurologica Scandinavia, 120,* 1–151.

Bloom, H. J. G., Wallace, E. N. K., & Henk, J. M. (1969). The treatment and prognosis of medulloblastoma in children. *American Journal of Roentgenology, 105,* 43–62.

Boll, T. J., & Barth, J. T. (1981). Neuropsychology of brain damage in children. In S. B. Filskov & T. J. Boll (Eds.), *Handbook of clinical neuropsychology* (pp. 418–452). New York: Wiley.

Botez, M. I., & Wertheim, N. (1959). Expressive aphasia and amnesia following right frontal lesion in a right-handed man. *Brain, 82,* 186–202.

Bowman, W. P. (1981). Childhood acute lymphocytic leukemia: Progress and problems in treatment. *CMA Journal, 124,* 129–142.

Brown, J. W. (1974). *Aphasia, apraxia and agnosia: Clinical and theoretical aspects.* Springfield, IL: Charles C Thomas.

Chelune, G. J., & Edwards, P. (1981). Early brain lesions: Ontogenetic-environmental considerations. *Journal of Consulting and Clinical Psychology, 49,* 777–790.

Chusid, J. G. (1973). *Correlative neuroanatomy and functional neurology* (15th ed.). Los Altos, CA: Lange Medical Publications.

Copeland, D. R., Fletcher, J. M., Pffefferbaum-Levine, B., Jaffe, N., Ried. H., & Maor, M. (1985). Long-term survivors of childhood cancer: Effects of CNS treatment. *Pediatrics, 75,* 745–753.

Corkin, S. (1965). Tactually guided maze learning in man. Effects of unilateral cortical excisions and bilateral hippocampal lesions. *Neuropsychologia, 3,* 339–351.

Corkin, S., Milner, B., & Taylor, L. (1973). Bilateral sensory loss after unilateral cerebral lesion in man. *Transactions of the American Neurological Association, 98,* 118.

Currie, S., & Henson, R. A. (1971). Neurological syndromes in the reticuloses. *Brain, 94,* 307–310.

D'Angio, G. J. (1980, November). Late sequelae after cure of childhood cancer. *Hospital Practice,* 109–121.

Danoff, B., Cowchock, F., Marquette, C., Mulgrew, L., & Kramer, S. (1982). Assessment of long-term effects of primary radiation therapy for brain tumors in children. *Cancer, 49,* 1580–1586.

Davies, J. A., Hughes, J. T., & Oppenheimer, D. R. (1973). Richardson's disease (progressive multifocal leukoencephalopathy). *Quarterly Journal of Medicine, 42,* 481–489.

Davison, K., & Bagley, C. R. (1969). Schizophrenia-like psychoses associated with organic disorders of the central nervous system: A review of the literature. In R. N. Herrington (Ed.), *Current problems in neuropsychiatry* (pp. 125–147). Ashford Kent: Headley Brothers.

Delay, J., Brion, S., & Derouesne, C. (1964). Syndrome de Korsakoff et etiologie tumorale. *Revue Neurologique, 111,* 97–133.

Direkze, M., Bayliss, S. G., & Cutting, J. C. (1971). Primary tumors of the frontal lobe. *British Journal of Clinical Practice, 25,* 207–213.

Earle, K. M. (1955). Metastatic brain tumors. *Diseases of the Nervous System, 16,* 86–93.

Eiser, C. (1980). Effects of chronic illness on intellectual development. *Archives of Disease in Children, 55,* 766–770.

Eiser, C., & Lansdown, R. (1977). Retrospective study of intellectual development in children treated for acute lymphoblastic leukemia. *Archives of Disease in Children, 52,* 525–529.

Evans, A. E., Gilbert, E. S., & Sandstra, R. (1970). The incidence of central nervous system leukemia in children. *Cancer, 26,* 404–410.

Folstein, M. F., Fetting, J. H., Lobo, A., Niaz, U., & Capozzolli, K. D. (1984). Cognitive assessment of cancer patients. *Cancer, 31,* 2250–2257.

Gaelen, L. H., & Levitan, S. (1967). Solitary intracranial metastasis by Hodgkin's disease. *Archives of Internal Medicine, 120,* 740–745.

Geller, W., & Lacher, M. J. (1966). Hodgkin's disease. *Medical Clinics of North America, 50,* 819–832.

Gilroy, J., & Meyer, J. S. (1975). *Medical neurology* (2nd ed.). New York: Macmillan.

Gjerris, F. (1976). Clinical aspects and long-term prognosis of intracranial tumors in infancy and childhood. *Developmental Medicine and Child Neurology, 18,* 145–159.

Goff, J. R., Anderson, H. R., Jr., & Cooper, P. F. (1980). Distractibility and memory deficit in long-term survivors of acute lymphoblastic leukemia. *Journal of Developmental and Behavioral Pediatrics, 1,* 158–161.

Golden, C. J. (1981). *Diagnosis and rehabilitation in clinical neuropsychology* (2nd ed.). Springfield, IL: Charles C Thomas.

Golden, C. J., Moses, J. A., Jr., Coffman, J. A., Miller, W. R., & Strider, F. D. (1983). *Clinical neuropsychology: Interface with neurologic and psychiatric disorders.* New York: Grune & Stratton.

Halstead, W. C. (1947). *Brain and intelligence.* Chicago: University of Chicago Press.

Harisiadis, L., & Chang, C. H. (1977). Medulloblastoma in children: A correlation between staging and results of treatment. *International Journal of Radiation Oncology and Biological Physics, 2,* 833–841.

Hecaen, H., & Ajuriaguerra, J. (1956). *De troubles mentaux au cours des tumeus intracraniennes.* Paris: Masson.

Hedley-White, E. T., Smith, B. P., Tyler, H. R., & Peterson, W. P. (1966). Multifocal leukoencephalopathy with remission and five year survival. *Journal of Neuropathology and Experimental Neurology, 25,* 107–112.

Henson, R. A., Hoffman, H. L., & Urich, H. (1965). Encephalomyelitis with carcinoma. *Brain, 88,* 449–464.

Hirsch, J. F., Reneir, D., Czernichow, R., Benveniste, L., & Pierre-Kahn, A. (1979). Medullablastoma in childhood. Survival and functional results. *Acta Neurochirurgica, 48,* 1–15.

Hoppe, R. T., Kushlan, P., & Kaplan, H. S. (1981). The treatment of non-Hodgkin's lymphoma: A preliminary report of a randomized trial comparing single agent chemotherapy, combination chemotherapy, and whole body irradiation. *Blood, 58,* 592–598.

Ivnik, R. H., Colligan, R. C., Obetz, S. W., & Smithson, W. A. (1981). Neuropsychologic performance among children in remissions from acute lymphocytic leukemia. *Journal of Developmental and Behavioral Pediatrics, 2,* 29–34.

Joynt, R. J., & Perret, C. E. (1965). Familial meningiomas. *Journal of Neurology, Neurosurgery, and Psychiatry, 28,* 163–164.

Kaplan, A. M., & Itabashi, H. H. (1974). Encephalitis associated with carcinoma. *Journal of Neurology, Neurosurgery, and Psychiatry, 37,* 1166–1172.

Kaufman, G. (1965). Hodgkin's disease involving the central nervous system. *Archives of Neurology, 13,* 555–558.

Keschner, M., Bender, M. B., & Strauss, I. (1936). Mental symptoms in cases of tumor of the temporal lobe. *Archives of Neurology and Psychiatry, 110,* 572–596.

Keschner, M., Bender, M. B., & Strauss, I. (1938a). Mental symptoms in cases of subtentorial tumor. *Archives of Neurology and Psychiatry, 37,* 1–15.

Keschner, M., Bender, M. B., & Strauss, I. (1938b). Mental symptoms associated with brain tumor: A study of 530 verified cases. *Journal of the American Medical Association, 110,* 714–718.

Kimura, D. (1967). Right temporal lobe damage: Perception of unfamiliar stimuli after damage. *Archives of Neurology, 8,* 264–271.

Knights, R. M. (1980). *Revised smoothed normative data on the neuropsychological test battery for children.* Unpublished manuscript.

Koocher, G. P. (1973). Childhood, death, and cognitive development. *Developmental Psychology, 9,* 369–375.

Kramer, S., & Lee, K. F. (1974). Complications of radiation therapy: The central nervous system. *Seminars of Roentgentology, 9,* 75–83.

Kun, L. E., Mulhern, R. K., & Crisco, J. J. (1983). Quality of life in children treated for brain tumors: Intellectual, emotional and academic function. *Journal of Neurosurgery, 58,* 1–6.

Lishman, W. (1978). *Organic psychiatry: The psychological consequences of cerebral disorder.* Oxford: Blackwell.

Luria, A. R. (1966). *Higher cortical functions in man.* New York: Basic Books.

Martin, J. B., & Banker, B. Q. (1969). Subacute multifocal leukoencephalopathy with widespread intranuclear inclusions. *Archives of Neurology, 21,* 590–595.

Mauer, A. E. (1980). Therapy of acute lymphocytic leukemia in childhood. *Blood, 56,* 1–10.

McCormick, W. F., Menezes, A. H., & Gin, O. I. (1972). Meningioma occurring in a patient treated for medulloblastoma. *Journal of the Iowa Medical Society, 62,* 67–71.

Meier, M. J., & French, L. A. (1965). Lateralized deficits in complex visual discrimination and bilateral transfer of reminiscence following unilateral temporal lobotomy. *Neuropsychologia, 3,* 261–272.

Milner, B. (1963). Effects of different brain lesions on card sorting. *Archives of Neurology, 9,* 90.

Milner, B. (1971). Interhemispheric differences in the localization of psychological processes in man. *British Medical Bulletin, 27,* 272.

Moehle, K. A., Berg, R. A., Ch'ien, L. T., & Lancaster, W. (1983). Language-related skills in children with acute lymphocytic leukemia. *Journal of Developmental and Behavioral Pediatrics, 4,* 257–261.

Morton, D. L., Itaboshi, H. H., & Grimes, O. F. (1966). Nonmetastatic neurologic complications of bronchogenic carcinoma: The carcinomatous neuromyopathies. *Journal of Thoracic and Cardiovascular Surgery, 51,* 14–29.

Moss, H. A., Nannis, E. D., & Poplack, D. G. (1981). The effects of prophylactic treatment of the central nervous system on the intellectual functioning of children with acute lymphocytic leukemia. *American Journal of Medicine, 71,* 47–52.

Mulhern, R. K., Crisco, J. J., & Kun, L. E. (1983). Neuropsychological sequelae of childhood brain tumors: A review. *Journal of Clinical Child Psychology, 12,* 66–73.

Obetz, S. W., Ivnik, R. J., Smithson, W. A., Colligan, R. C., Groover, R. V., Gilchrist, G. J., Houser, D. W., Burgert, F. O., & Klass, D. W. (1979). Neuropsychological follow-up study of children with acute lymphocytic leukemia: A preliminary report. *American Journal of Pediatric Hematology/Oncology, 1,* 207–213.

Oxman, T. E., & Silberfarb, P. M. (1980). Serial cognitive testing in cancer patients receiving chemotherapy. *American Journal of Psychiatry, 137,* 1263–1265.

Perret, E. (1974). The left frontal lobe of man and the suppression of habitual responses in verbal categorical behavior. *Neuropsychologia, 12,* 323–330.

Portlock, C. S. (1980). Management of the indolent non-Hodgkins' lymphomas. *Seminars in Hematology, 7,* 292–301.

Raimondi, A. J., & Tomita, T. (1979). Advantages of total resection of medullablastoma and disadvantages of full head post-operative radiation therapy. *Child's Brain, 5,* 550–551.

Robbins, S. L. (1974). *Pathologic basis of disease.* Philadelphia: Saunders.

Roland, P. E. (1976). Astereognosis. *Archives of Neurology, 33,* 543–550.

Russell, R. W. R., & Pennybacker, J. B. (1961). Craniopharyngioma in the elderly. *Journal of Neurology, Neurosurgery, and Psychiatry, 24,* 1–13.

St. James-Roberts, I. (1979). Neurological plasticity, recovery from brain insult and child development. In H. W. Reese (Ed.), *Advances in child development and behavior* (Vol. 14, pp. 113–133). New York: Academic Press.

Satz, P., & Fletcher, J. M. (1981). Emergent trends in neuropsychology: An overview. *Journal of Consulting and Clinical Psychology, 49,* 851–865.

Schlesinger, B. (1950). Mental changes in intracranial tumors and related problems. *Confina Neurologia, 10,* 225–263.

Scoville, W. B., & Milner, B. (1957). Loss of recent memory after bilateral hippocampal lesions. *Journal of Neurology, Neurosurgery, and Psychiatry, 20,* 21–22.

Selecki, B. R. (1964). Cerebral mid-line tumors involving the corpus callosum among mental hospital patients. *Medical Journal of Australia, 2,* 954–960.

Silverman, C. L., Thomas, P. R., Palkes, H., Kovnar, E., Talent, B., & Bedwinek, J. M. (1982). Late psychological and intellectual effects on patients and their families following definitive radiotherapy for childhood medullablastoma. *American Society of Clinical Oncology Abstracts, 23,* 49.

Sohn, D., Valensi, Q., & Miller, S. P. (1967). Neurologic manifestations of Hodgkin's disease. *Archives of Neurology, 17,* 429–436.

Spunberg, J. J., Chang, C. H., Goldman, M., Auricchio, E., & Bell, J. (1981). Quality of long-term survival following irradiation for intracranial tumors in children under the age of two. *International Journal of Radiation Oncology and Biological Physics, 7,* 727–736.

Stehbens, J. A., Kisker, C. T., & Wilson, B. K. (1983). Achievement and intelligence test-retest performance in pediatric cancer patients at diagnosis and one year later. *Journal of Pediatric Psychology, 8,* 47–56.

Strauss, I., & Keschner, M. (1935). Mental symptoms in cases of tumor in the frontal lobe. *Archives of Neurology and Psychiatry, 33,* 986–1007.

Strobos, R. R. J. (1953). Tumors of the temporal lobe. *Neurology, 3,* 752–760.

Sullivan, M. P. (1957). Intracranial complications of leukemia in children. *Pediatrics, 20,* 757–785.

Tamaroff, M., Salwen, R., Allen, J., Murphy, M., & Nir, Y. (1982). Neuropsychological test performance in children treated for malignant tumors of the posterior fossa. *American Society of Clinical Oncology Abstracts, 23,* 50.

Teuber, H. L. (1964). The riddle of frontal lobe function in man. In J. M. Warren & K. Akert (Eds.), *The frontal granular cortex and behavior* (pp. 75–97). New York: McGraw-Hill.

Ultmann, J. E., & Jacobs, R. H. (1985). The non-Hodgkin's lymphomas. *Ca-A Cancer Journal for Clinicians, 35,* 66–87.

Walton, J. N. (Ed.). (1977). *Brain's diseases of the nervous system* (8th ed.). New York: Oxford University Press.

Ward, D. W., Mattison, M. C., & Fian, R. (1973). Association between previous tuberculous infection and cerebral glioma. *British Medical Journal, 1,* 83–84.

Wells, C. E., & Silver, R. T. (1967). Neurologic manifestations of the acute leukemias: Clinical study. *Annals of Internal Medicine, 46,* 439–449.

Wilkinson, P. C. (1964). Serological findings in carcinomatous neuromyopathy. *Lancet, 1,* 1301–1303.

Wilkinson, P. C., & Zeromski, J. (1965). Immunofluorescent detection of antibodies against neurons in sensory carcinomatous neuropathy. *Brain, 88,* 529–538.

Young, J. L., Percy, C. L., Asire, A. J., Berg, J. W., Cusano, M. M., Gloecker, L. A., Horm, J. W., Lourie, W. I., Pollack, E. S., & Shambaugh, E. M. (1982). *Cancer incidence and mortality in the United States, 1973–1977* (Monograph No. 57). Washington, DC: National Cancer Institute.

Nutrition and Childhood Neuropsychological Disorders

MICHAEL L. LESTER and DIANA H. FISHBEIN

INTRODUCTION

Nutrition is the relationship of foods to health. Adequate nutrition is essential for normal organ development and functioning; for normal reproduction, growth, and maintenance; for optimum activity level and working efficiency; for resistance to infection and disease; and for the ability to repair bodily damage or injury (Kirschmann, 1981). Malnutrition, on the other hand, is not solely undernutrition but includes all forms of nutritional deficits; it exists whenever inadequate amounts of essential nutrients are supplied to tissues and organ systems. From infancy to maturity, the brain and body experience tremendous growth and development. Heredity and environment jointly affect the development and functional effectivities of organ systems that, in total, determine each child's developmental potential. However, too seldom considered within this scheme is the fact that nutrition is of primary importance for the expression of psychological as well as physical capabilities.

From a systems point of view (Weiss, 1969), a major distinction between a young animal and a mature one with regard to nutrition is the relative utilization of nutrients by each for (a) ongoing functions, such as mobility or the propagation of action potentials in the nervous system, (b) overhead functions, such as repair and maintenance of tissue, and (c) investment functions, such as growth and development of new tissue and storage of nutrients for later use. Throughout life, nutrients are sequestered into each of these functional areas; however, over the life span, the emphasis for nutrient utilization in each of these domains changes dramatically. For the fetus and infant, nutrient use for investment functions predominates; whereas, by adulthood, nutrient utilization for ongoing and overhead functions is pri-

MICHAEL L. LESTER • Children's Medical Center, Department of Pediatrics, Tulsa, Oklahoma 74135.   DIANA H. FISHBEIN • Addiction Research Center, National Institute on Drug Abuse, and the University of Baltimore, Baltimore, Maryland 21224.

mary. In the absence of severe disease, injury, or forced labor, the demands of the adult system for nutrients are relatively stable. In comparison, the developing organism's general nutrient needs are increased compared to the adult's, and the demand for specific nutrients for the development of particular structures and functions over time exhibit much fluctuation.

At one time, scientists thought the brain was relatively impervious to nutritional inadequacies after birth, particularly with respect to brain size and chemical composition. Moreover, deficits incurred from most forms of malnutrition after birth were believed to be completely reversible with appropriate rehabilitative regimens (Levine & Wiener, 1976). Recent studies not only challenge these assumptions but suggest that the developing brain in infancy and childhood is particularly susceptible to deleterious effects of nutritional improprieties such that if they occur during certain developmental stages and the nutritional deprivation is severe, the adverse effects on the brain may be permanent. Moreover, the nature of the deficit may reflect the period of growth during which the child was nutritionally deprived and may also be specific to the form of dietary disadvantage (Booyens, Luitingh, & Van Rensburg, 1977; Dasen, Lavallee, & Retschitzki, 1977; De Licardie & Cravioto, 1974; McKay, Sinisterra, McKay, Gomez, & Lloreda, 1978; Monckeberg, 1968; Sky & Barnes, 1973).

Cavioto and Arrieta (1983) reviewed the "critical" or "sensitive period" hypothesis of brain development and nutritional effects. During embryonic and early postnatal development, periods of accelerated growth of brain structures occur (Dobbing, 1976; Dodge, Prensky, & Feigin, 1975). According to the hypothesis, the timing of exposure to exogenous and endogenous factors that play important roles in the elicitation and maximization of a growth stage may be more critical than the duration or intensity of exposure. Disruptions of the growth process, even when mild, may produce irreparable anatomical and functional disturbances, whereas interferences of equal intensity prior to or following this period may be relatively ineffectual.

Malnutrition may directly affect maturation of the brain, particularly during a period of maximum growth, or it may indirectly affect neuropsychological development by depressing the energy level of the child (Dobbing, 1976). For example, malnutrition may reduce activity levels and limit the ability to utilize and respond to the environment, a condition that in itself will impair cognitive development. In addition, however, an informationally deprived social environment may exacerbate the effects of malnutrition. The level of environmental enrichment, as estimated by socioeconomic status and similar variables, appears to contribute synergistically with nutritional variables in determining a child's mental development.

These general principles of nutrition and neuropsychological development are presented as a backdrop for consideration of studies reviewed in this chapter. Regardless of the particular set of nutrient and behavior variables examined in a study, basic factors such as quality, quantity, and duration of nutrient deprivation, developmental stage of subjects, concurrent level of environmental enrichment, and history of past nutrient and environmental deprivations, also should be considered to be influential.

CARBOHYDRATE INTAKE, GLUCOSE TOLERANCE, AND BEHAVIOR

Over the past two decades, a number of clinical reports have suggested that diets high in refined carbohydrates can contribute to or aggravate behavioral and learning disorders of children (Fishbein, 1982; Kronick, 1975; Powers, 1974; Von Hilsheimer, 1974). These case histories indicated that behavioral abnormalities, such as irritability, hyperactivity, and short attention span, normalized following dietary improvements involving reduced refined carbohydrate intake. The underlying mechanisms for these relationships between diet and behavior disorders are, however, unclear. Powers (1974), and Powers & Presley (1978) have reported that many learning-disabled children show an abnormal glucose tolerance response and that this deviant blood glucose response and abnormal behaviors may be related to a history of refined sugar consumption.

A quasi-experimental evaluation of the hypothesized relationship between diet, glucose tolerance test (GTT) response, and behavior was reported by Langseth and Dowd (1978). In their study, blood and urine chemistry and GTT responses were examined in 261 hyperactive children between the ages of 7 and 9. Based on a GTT response criterion of abnormality as a 20-point deviation below or above the GTT median value for normal subjects, blood glucose values were abnormal for 88% of the hyperactive children when measured 1 hr after oral glucose administration. When categorized with respect to GTT response curve abnormality of form, 74% of the children's GTT responses were classified as being abnormal.

Figure 1 shows the prototypal GTT response curve used in the Langseth

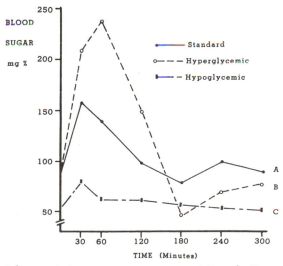

FIGURE 1. Glucose tolerance test response curves representative of a "normal reference" (1A) and of two classes of abnormal response that might be termed hyperglycemic (1B) and hypoglycemic (1C). Response curves are similar to those given in Langseth and Dowd (1978) and Powers (1974).

and Dowd study (1978) and similar studies as a normative reference (Powers, 1974). Also schematized are the major deviant GTT response patterns observed for children with behavioral and learning disorders. In the Langseth and Dowd (1978) study, 45% of the children exhibited hypoglycemic (low blood sugar) GTT responses similar to 1B; for 19% of the children, a hyperglycemic GTT (high blood sugar) response similar to 1C was observed. A hyperglycemic GTT response is elicited from diabetic children and interestingly, two other conditions common in diabetes—glucose in the urine and elevated cholesterol levels—were found in roughly 20% of the children with the 1C form of abnormal GTT response. Another 11% of the children had abnormal GTT responses that were different from these basic patterns, and for 26% of the children the GTT appeared "normal".

Langseth and Dowd (1978) claimed that their results indicate that one "causative" factor of hyperactive behavior for certain children is the consumption of diets high in refined carbohydrates and the resultant abnormal glucose blood levels that develop from this pattern of dietary consumption. However, in view of the methodological shortcomings of their study, a more guarded conclusion that the results are "suggestive only" seems warranted. For instance, objective criteria for classification of the children as hyperactive were not given; GTT response classifications were done retrospectively, apparently with knowledge of other response measures for subjects; a close documentation of dietary consumption patterns was not reported; and, a comparison control group was not used. The latter is of particular importance considering the degree of variance in GTT responses observed in "normal" children (Knopf, Cresto, Dujovne, Ramos, & de Majo, 1977).

In a similar, but methodologically improved study (Prinz, Roberts, & Hantman, 1980), 28 hyperactive children were compared with a "normal" control group of children matched for age, sex, and socioeconomic class. In this study, the dietary consumption of sugar and refined carbohydrate products was used as the independent predictor variable, and destructive-aggressive and motor activity behaviors were the dependent measures. Diets were assessed using 7-day dietary records, and behaviors were evaluated using records of carefully defined categories of behavior observed under controlled conditions. Raters scored diet and behavior without knowledge of whether the children belonged to the "normal" or "hyperactive" group. The two groups did not differ in the amount of sugar or refined carbohydrate in their diets or the ratio of these products to "more nutritional" foods in their diets; nevertheless, there was a significant interaction between the diet variables, subject group membership, and behavior. For the "hyperactive children", significantly positive correlations between refined carbohydrate variables and destructive-aggressive behaviors were found. The strongest correlation was $r = .54$ for "the ratio of sugar to nutritional foods" and destructive-aggressive behavior. Correlations between diet variables and destructive-aggressive behaviors were not significant for the "normal" children. However, general activity of a non-aggressive-destructive nature was significantly correlated with sugar for the "normal" children ($r = .59$) but not for the "hyperactive" children (r = −.06). Thus, this study indicates that both total sugar and refined carbohydrate content of the diets can be associated significantly with increased motor activity for both "hyperactive" and "normal children," but, more importantly, this increased motor behavior is expressed in qualitatively different ways in the two groups of children.

Refined Carbohydrates—Just a Matter of Taste?

In a strongly worded statement on diet and behavior, a panel of distinguished professionals from the mainstream of the medical research community has discounted, on the basis of conceptual and methodological flaws, studies that have suggested a link between sugar and/or refined carbohydrates and abnormal behavior (Lipton & Wender, 1984). The expert panel consisted of scientists who attended a research conference in November of 1983 to organize the symposium, "Diet and Behavior: A Multi-Disciplinary Evaluation." Among other things, the panel claimed that "there exists a large body of scientifically sound information establishing sugar as a nutrient that is safe within the wide range of amounts ordinarily consumed in U.S. diets" (p. 200). The panel concluded its statement by defining the few hypotheses concerning the relationship between diet and behavior that, in their opinion, warranted further study.

Three assumptions were implicit in the statement and position adopted by the panel: (a) the degree of articulation of a mechanism of association between a predisposing factor and a health status variable should be the predominant criterion for evaluating the importance of a phenomenon for allocation of future research resources; (b) the amount of sugar currently consumed in U.S. diets is known with a reasonable degree of accuracy; and, (c) from what is known about sucrose consumption, a general statement about its safety can be supported. Each of these assumptions is false.

Concerning the first assumption, the history of medicine offers numerous examples of the discovery of clinically important relationships between an antecedent substance, condition, or procedure and resultant health disorder occurring in the complete absence of any knowledge of a specific mechanism of action for such a relationship. Semmelweis's discovery of the vitally important relationship between antiseptic examination procedures and the incidence of "childbirth fever" in postpartum women is one such example (Thompson, 1949). Another is the discovery by Takaki, director general of the Japanese Naval Medical Service, roughly 25 yr before the concept of vitamins, that protein foods added to the diet of sailors on long voyages would prevent the occurrence of the thiamine deficiency disease—beriberi (Sandstead, 1980).

The second false assumption is that precise, conclusive information about the current rate of sugar consumption and its range of effects (short- and long-term) is available. According to U.S. Department of Agriculture statistics, the pattern of dietary intake of carbohydrates by Americans has changed dramatically in a relatively short time (U.S. Senate, 1977). From the early 1900s to 1976, the percentage of total carbohydrate intake from starch food sources had decreased from 68% to 47%, whereas the intake from sugars (mostly sucrose) had increased from 32% to 53% (Figure 2). This change to a highly sugar-based diet in a two and one-half generation time span is a significant departure from the complex carbohydrate diet that has been the nutritional base during human beings' evolution and is still the primary source of calories for most people living in the nonindustrial nations of the world (Drash, Becker, Kenien, & Steranchak, 1981; Gaulin & Konner, 1977).

Two interrelated phenomenon—(a) the prevalence of obesity and (b) the trends in the incidence of diabetes in American society—undermine the sugar-intake-at-current-levels-is-safe assumption. The total caloric intake by children in the United States is excessive as evidenced by the extraordinarily high prevalence of obesity in American children compared to other populations. Roughly 5 to 10% of schoolchildren and 10 to 15% of adolescent children are clinically overweight (Knittle et al., 1981). An estimated 10 million people in the United States are diabetics; approximately 90% of diabetics (mostly over age 20) are obese (Friedman, 1980). Two percent of the diabetic population are children under 16 years of age, making it the most frequent serious chronic disease of childhood (Drash et al., 1981). Of greatest concern, however, is that the National Commission on Diabetes has reported that between 1967 and 1973 the incidence of diabetes increased by 50% (Friedman, 1980).

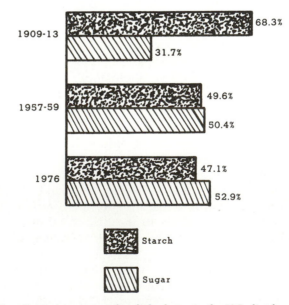

FIGURE 2. Relative change in sources of carbohydrates in the U.S. diet from the period 1909–1913 to 1976 (U.S. Senate, 1977). Data are based on U.S. Department of Agriculture statistics on total food product consumption in the United States.

ABNORMAL CARBOHYDRATE METABOLISM, BRAIN FUNCTION, AND BEHAVIOR

Hypoglycemia and Behavior

Available research suggests several mechanisms that might account for the observed relations between diet-intake patterns, abnormal blood glucose responses, CNS dysfunction, and concomitant behavioral disorders. First, however, a review of the unique relationship between blood glucose and cerebral energy metabolism of children is necessary. Under usual circumstances (early infancy and states of extreme starvation excepted), glucose is the only substrate normally available to the blood that is capable of providing the brain with enough energy to maintain normal function (Sokoloff, Fitzgerald, & Kaufman, 1977). Furthermore, based on quantitative data on cerebral circulation and oxygen consumption in man, Kennedy and Sokoloff (1957) have determined that a child 5 to 6 years of age has a cerebral metabolic rate that is roughly 50% greater than that of a young adult. The authors speculated that this extaordinarily high cerebral metabolic rate in children is related to the extra energy requirements for processes associated with growth and development of the brain. Because children utilize glucose at a much higher rate than do adults for normal cerebral energy metabolism, a greater sensitivity of cerebral function to a lowering of the blood glucose from baseline levels might be expected in children as compared to adults.

Hypoglycemia is a condition characterized by recurrent low blood glucose. Based on the factors that precipitate its onset, hypoglycemia is categorized as (a) fasting, or (b) reactive. Fasting or spontaneous hypoglycemia (e.g., glycogen storage disease) occurs after a few hours without food and results from abnormal regulatory responses that act to maintain a stable blood glucose level by retrieving supplies of stored glucose. Reactive or postprandial hypoglycemia is a far more prevalent form of the condition. Reactive hypoglycemia occurs typically within 90 to 250 min following a meal and is thought to be related to delayed and/or excessive insulin secretion (hyperinsulinism) in response to food intake (Hofeldt, Lufkin, & Hagler, 1974; Maclaren, 1981). This condition is elicited in susceptible persons by a diet high in simple carbohydrate and is treated with a diet low in simple carbohydrate, adequate in complex carbohydrate, and high in protein.

Most research on hypoglycemic GTT responses and behavior has been performed with adult subjects. A number of these studies have suggested that emotional disturbances are common in individuals exhibiting hypoglycemic responses (Hudspeth, Peterson, Soli, & Trimble, 1981; Yaryura-Tobias, 1973). Johnson, Dorr, Swenson, and Service (1980) found that hypoglycemic patients had significantly elevated scores on the Hysteria, Depression and Hypochondriasis scales of the Minnesota Multiphasic Personality Inventory (MMPI) when compared to general medical patients. However, neither plasma glucose nadir (lowest blood glucose measurement) nor the rate of the descent of the glucose level during GTT monitoring correlated

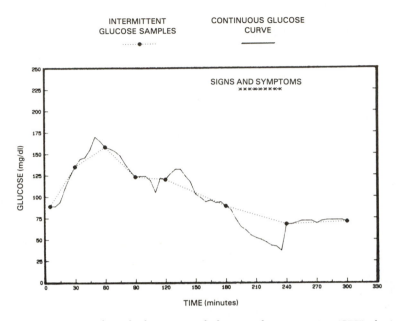

FIGURE 3. A comparison of results between oral glucose tolerance testing (GTT) obtained by continuous glucose monitoring and the standard intermittent glucose sampling. Signs refer to objective evidence of hypoglycemia perceived by an observer, for example, sweating, pallor, tremor, elevated pulse rate or blood pressure. Symptoms refer to subjective reports by the subject of his or her condition such as fatigue, headache, change in mentation, warmth, etc. The timing and level of the true glucose nadir is accurately identified only by continuous glucose monitoring. (The figure is previously unpublished but is from the data of Chalew et al., 1984. Reproduced with permission.)

significantly with the onset of the emotional disturbance as reported by their patients. This fact led the authors to conclude that the oral GTT was not reliable for the diagnosis of reactive hypoglycemia and that the previously observed relationships between the GTT response and emotional disorders may have been spurious.

The weak correlations between GTT parameters and reported psychological condition are not surprising given the degree of imprecision inherent in each of these measures. In fact, the standard method of blood sampling at 60-min fixed intervals has been shown to be incapable in principle of accurately characterizing the GTT nadir that occurs at unpredictable times following glucose ingestion (Chalew et al., 1984). Figure 3 is a comparison of continuous glucose monitoring and the results of the more standard periodic glucose sampling.

EEG and Behavioral Abnormalities in Hypoglycemia

A more objective and reliable measure of neuropsychological state than subjective reports by patients of mood, anxiety level, and arousal would be desirable. The electroencephalogram (EEG) is an objective measure of brain electrophysiological function. In addition, fluctuations in EEG parameters can be precisely time referenced for direct comparison with observed changes in GTT parameters over time. Studies performed more than 40 yr ago demonstrated that the EEG can be used to cross-validate a suspected relation between carbohydrate intolerance and neuropsychiatric disorder (Engel & Margolin, 1941; Hoagland, Rubin, & Cameron, 1937). Specifically, Engel and Margolin (1941) found that patients with hypoglycemia exhibited one or more neuropsychiatric symptoms such as psychopathic behavior, excessive or inappropriate mood swings, impairment of insight and judgment, choreiform dyskinesias, convulsions, syncope, neuritic disorders, and scotomas. Symptoms elicited during the GTT revealed personality changes, uncooperative behavior, abusiveness, apprehension, and dysarthria. The simultaneously recorded EEG revealed abnormalities that paralleled both the monitored glucose changes and observed behavioral or emotional disturbances.

More recent studies have demonstrated a similar relationship between EEG abnormalities and hypoglycemia (Deutsch, Sohmer, Weidenfeld, Zelig, & Chowers, 1983; Feise, Kogure, Busto, Scheinberg, & Reinmuth, 1976; Marks & Rose, 1981). A consistent finding in each of these studies was that increased slow wave activity occurs near or during the glucose nadir. In addition, as generalized slow wave activity increases, bursts of slow frequency, high amplitude EEG are observed along with occasional electrical spikes. Based on the observation that these EEG irregularities were most noticeable over the temporal lobes, Marks and Rose (1981) have suggested that the temporal region may be more sensitive to hypoglycemia then other brain areas, perhaps due to an increased demand for glucose.

Cerebral Energy Utilization

Studies of cerebral blood flow and rates of glucose utilization in brain tissue of rats indicate that a threefold difference in glucose demand is observed in gray matter, depending on the particular brain structure examined (Sokoloff et al., 1977). Generally, greater glucose utilization is observed for cortical as compared to subcortical structures. The latter is consistent with recent electrophysiological research that indicates that brain stem activity does not appear to be disrupted by induced hypoglycemia (Deutsch et al., 1983). Recent advances in the use of radioactively labeled deoxyglucose in positron emission tomography (PET) studies of the human brain have led to a more precise knowledge about the energy dynamics of the CNS in normal and dysfunctional states (Phelps & Mazziotta, 1985). In the PET-scan studies, a direct correlation between sites of dramatically increased glucose utilization and EEG spiking in individuals with abnormal behavior has been demonstrated. In addition, these studies have shown that during interictal (EEG nonspike) periods, the electrically pathogenic tissue is reliably identified as being a distinctly hypometabolic zone of cerebral tissue.

The close correspondence that exists between various quantitative EEG parameters and several measures of brain metabolism presumably exists because of the brain's exquisite sensitivity to ambient blood glucose concentration. The inability of neurons to extract glucose from the circulation in the presence of a weak concentration gradient emphasizes the crucial importance of maintaining a plasma glucose concentration within physiological bounds that allows a transfer of glucose from the blood to the brain (Cryer, 1981). However, GTT-associated responses appear to be inadequate indicators of the severity of the central nervous system dysfunction that occurs in hypoglycemia or in association with carbohydrate intolerance (Ferrendelli & Chang, 1973). Reports of symptom inducement, both physiological and psychological, in the absence of abnormal GTT responses are quite common. In addition, the continuous blood-monitoring research of Chalew et al. (1984) suggests that hormones such as epinephrine and cortisol (which tend to co-vary with blood glucose), correlate with patients' postprandial dysfunction better than do the glucose nadir following GTT.

Temporal Concordance of Brain, Behavior, and Glucose Fluctuations

Although behavioral symptoms and standard GTT blood glucose response parameters are not highly correlated (Hofeldt et al., 1974; Johnson et al., 1980), relationships between symptoms and EEG abnormalities are much stronger. Past studies (Hudspeth et al., 1981; Marks & Rose, 1981) indicate that EEG measures co-vary with plasma glucose and insulin levels and provide a sensitive objective index of the neuropsychological events that accompany the subjective, symptomatic phase of the GTT. Continuous monitoring of blood glucose and hormones may improve the degree to which the three variable sets—carbohydrate metabolites, EEG parameters, and behavior—can be related and usefully utilized for diagnostic and therapeutic purposes.

Metabolites that co-vary with the GTT response may also affect the availability to the brain of various neurotransmitter precursors. That this is the case is suggested by the findings in animal research that have demonstrated a direct relationship between the protein and carbohydrate composition of various diets, brain function, and behavior (Chiel & Wurtman, 1981; Cohen & Wurtman, 1979; Platt, Pampiglione, & Stewart, 1965). The mechanism by which the dietary carbohydrate consumption affects serotonin synthesis will be reviewed in the section on the modulation of neurotransmitter precursor availability by dietary constituents.

An Ecological Approach to Nutritional Effects on Brain and Behavior

The line of reasoning that seems to have dominated the study of mammalian energy physiology is that because glucose is the principal substrate for cellular energy metabolism, glucose is the appropriate orally administered food substance to use as a standard for evaluation of the system's mechanisms of blood glucose control. However, foods with a high glucose concentration have always been a minor source of the dietary carbohydrates ingested by mammals, in general, and only recently have they been a major ingredient in man's diet. Crapo, Reaven, and Olefsky (1976) have evaluated the GTT responses of normal subjects ($N = 19$) to orally administered 50-g equivalent samples of glucose, sucrose, or starch in solid and liquid forms. The major findings from this study can be summarized as follows: (a) starch ingestion results in a 44% lower blood glucose level and a 35–65% lower insulin response than does either glucose or sucrose ingestion; (b) the plasma glucose response is similar for glucose and sucrose within the 3-hr monitoring period; however, sucrose elicited a 20% greater plasma insulin response than did glucose from 30 min to 2 hr postingestion; and (c) The plasma glucose response to carbohydrate given in solid form is 40 to 60% lower than when the same amount and type of carbohydrate is given as a drink.

Figure 4 illustrates the plasma glucose and insulin responses observed

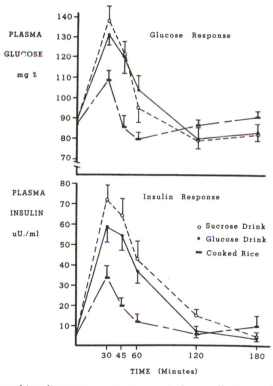

FIGURE 4. Glucose and insulin responses to 50-g equivalent orally ingested loads of (a) sucrose drink, (b) glucose drink, and (c) cooked rice. Sucrose and glucose drink responses based on 19 normal young adults; cooked rice responses based on 13 normal young adults. Mean responses and one standard deviation points indicated. Figure based on data given in Table 2 of Crapo, Reaven, & Olefsky (1976). (Reproduced with permission from the American Diabetes Association.)

over a 3-hr period after ingestion of equivalent 50-g loads of glucose and sucrose drinks and for a starch meal of cooked rice. Of the three, the cooked rice meal is the most representative food stable to which the human system may be said to be best attuned. A sucrose drink appears to place the greatest demands on the system's regulatory response to maintain normal blood glucose levels.

Unfortunately, standard GTT response measures do not reliably depict the points of highest or of lowest blood glucose that occur after a test load (Chalew et al., 1984). Even though the glucose levels at nadir are systematically overestimated by the standard GTT, a regular symmetry of the response has been observed such that responses that evidence the largest blood glucose increase early in the test also show the lowest blood glucose levels at the nadir (Maclaren, 1981). A relatively brief (undetected) period of unusually low blood glucose could account for the seemingly paradoxical hypoglycemic symptoms exhibited by diabetics in response to insulin-mediated normalization of elevated glucose concentrations. Another possible mechanism for the diabetic "hypoglycemic response," however, is repression of the blood–brain glucose transfer conditioned by chronic hyperglycemia (elevated blood glucose levels). Such a phenomenon has been demonstrated in rats maintained in a state of hyperglycemia with blood glucose levels at two and one-half times normal (Gjedde & Crone, 1981). In such animals, the maximum glucose transport capacity of the blood–brain barrier decreased by 25%. When plasma glucose was lowered to normal value, glucose transport into the brain in these animals was found to be 20% below that observed for control animals.

Regardless of whether blood glucose levels prove to be meaningfully related to the various behavioral disorders of children or not, it is reasonable to suspect that there are limits to the sugar load that the system of regulatory mechanisms can adequately accommodate to maintain a normal glucose level. If such is the case, the exponential rise illustrated in Figure 5 for sucrose-rich soft drink consumption in the United States may be cause for concern.

For the clinical and experimental studies that have been reviewed, special populations of children with behavioral problems were studied to evaluate the degree of relationship that could be shown to exist between behavior, diet, and GTT-response variables. However, if nutritional status is a significant ecological factor that affects neuropsychological function generally, then, in any fairly large sampling of children in which gradations of dietary imbalance occur, a relationship between the quality of the diet and intellectual performance should be evident. To test this hypothesis, Lester, Thatcher and Monroe-Lord (1982) selected for study, without regard to academic or deviant behavior status, 200 children from a nonindustrial, rural region of Maryland. EEG and evoked potential data, 24-hr and long-term dietary assessments, hair mineral and trace metal concentrations, and intelligence as well as academic achievement measures were collected on these children for analysis. For 184 of the children, complete records were available for all

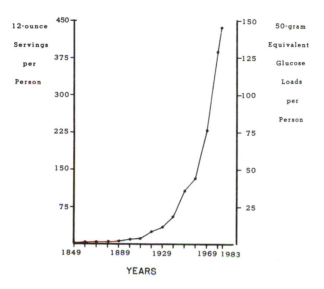

FIGURE 5. Average per person per year growth in soft drink consumption in the United States given at 10-year intervals from 1849 to 1983. Left-hand y-axis is 12-ounce servings per person as estimated by the National Softdrink Association. Right-hand y-axis is the estimated number of 50-g equivalent glucose loads per person per year and is based on the formula: 50-g Equivalent Glucose Loads = ([(S) × (.89) × (37.5 g)]/100], where S is the number of 12-ounce servings per person in the year and .89 is a correction factor taking into account that 11% of soft drinks consumed were diet drinks (in 1976); 37.5 is the estimated amount of sucrose per soft drink (Pennington & Church (1980)), and 100-g sucrose equals 50 g of glucose; thus the division by 100 rather than 50. (Adapted with permission from Brewster & Jacobson, 1983.)

measures except the hair data; hair data were available for only 149. For the entire sample of 184 children, an average of 34% of the calories in the diet were derived from refined sucrose and snack foods (range 0 to 88%). Examples of refined sucrose and snack foods were given as carbonated sodas and sweetened beverages, candy, sugar, pies, cookies, cake, ice cream, and high sugar cereals. Regression analysis indicated that the higher the proportion of refined carbohydrate in the diet, the lower the IQ score for the children studied (Lester *et al.*, 1982). Although this inverse relationship between the amount of dietary refined carbohydrates and IQ was small ($r = -.24$), the relationship proved to be significant even after adjusting for the effects of potentially confounding variables such as socioeconomic status (SES), race, sex, age, and hair heavy metal content (lead and cadmium).

With respect to the various measures of neurophysiological and cognitive functions, the EEG delta (slow wave) and interhemispheric fronto-temporal coherence (a measure of wave-form similarity) in delta recorded in the EEG were shown to be predictive of reading ability in the children studied (Thatcher, McAlaster, Lester, & Cantor, 1985). Children with higher amplitude delta activity in the left temporal region and with more left frontal-temporal delta coherence were more likely to have reading problems.

Correspondingly, the children with reading problems and abnormalities in temporal delta EEG activity were more likely to have an increased proportion of refined carbohydrates in their diet (Thatcher *et al.*, 1985). These findings suggest that, for at least a subset of children with learning problems, a history of refined carbohydrate intake may affect brain function and the ability to learn.

ZINC, CADMIUM, AND CARBOHYDRATE INTOLERANCE

Although the diet may influence neuropsychological function, a determination of the specific nutritional factors and the metabolic mechanisms involved is desirable to devise effective preventive and rehabilitative programs. In this respect, it is well known that the trace metals—zinc and cadmium—affect both glucose metabolism and brain function.

Whether the object of study is the external geological or internal biological ecology, the metals cadmium and zinc cannot be considered independently of each other. Cadmium and zinc are found together in the same ore bodies, and they have quite similar chemical properties (Venugopal & Luckey, 1980). However, whereas zinc is an essential trace element that is a critical co-factor in the activation of over 160 metalloenzymes involved in nucleic acid, protein, carbohydrate, and lipid metabolism (Vallee & Falchuk, 1983); cadmium is a heavy metal poison that, because of its extensive use in the plastic, paint, and metal-plating industries, has become a common environmental pollutant (Nriagu, 1981). Interestingly, many of the symptoms of cadmium toxicity have been demonstrated to be characteristic of zinc deficiency (Powell, Miller, Morton, & Clifton, 1964). In addition, cadmium toxicity effects such as testicular necrosis, anemia, and weight loss can be prevented or corrected with zinc supplementation (Neathery, 1981).

Diet and Cadmium Body Burden

Dietary intake is directly related to the cadmium body burden inasmuch as foods are the primary medium by which cadmium is introduced into the body (Friberg, Piscater, & Nordberg, 1971). Cadmium is readily incorporated into the stem and leaves of plants during growth. Thus, cadmium enters humans' food chain via stock animals raised for meat that have ingested cadmium contaminated feed or more directly from grain-based foods grown on cadmium-contaminated soil (Sharma, 1981). Animals (including humans) have inefficient mechanisms for excreting cadmium; thus, the metal tends to accumulate in the soft tissues of the body, particularly the kidney and liver (Fox, 1976; Gross, Yeager, & Middendorf, 1976; Nordberg & Nishiyama, 1972; Oleru, 1976). In recognition of the insidious nature by which cadmium stores slowly accumulate to a dangerous level with age, the World Health Organization established a provisionary recommended maximum limit of 57 to 71 μg cadmium per day intake from the food supply

(Cheftel *et al.*, 1972). With this figure in mind, it is of interest to note that the current estimated average cadmium intake for U.S. adults is 50 µg per day (Duggan & Corneliussen, 1972).

An additional consideration concerning the relationship between food intake and the body burden of cadmium is that zinc has been shown to be biologically antagonistic to cadmium such that generous supplies of zinc in the diet prevent a toxic accumulation of this heavy metal (Buell, 1975). Thus the zinc to cadmium ratio present in food is critical for determining the dietary contribution to the cadmium body burden. Refined grains have been shown to have a much lower zinc to cadmium ratio than do whole grains or whole grain products (Schroeder 1973). Zinc is more concentrated in the germ and bran of grains that is removed as a result of the milling process to produce white flour or rice, whereas cadmium that is more concentrated in the endosperm of the grain is not removed. Thus whole-wheat flour has a zinc to cadmium ratio of over 100, whereas, white flour has a ratio of only 17. Because there is more cadmium than zinc in refined sugar, the zinc to cadmium ratio of this common food substance is less than 1. It must be evident from these data that food processing contributes importantly to the cadmium intake from foods. Moreover, Schroeder (1974) reported that certain carbonated colas contained higher concentrations of cadmium than the allowable limit set by the U.S. Public Health Service for drinking water. Correspondingly, Lester *et al.* (1982) found that children whose diets contained large proportions of refined sucrose and snack foods tended to have greater body burdens of cadmium as measured by hair cadmium content.

Zinc and Carbohydrate Metabolism

Insulin plays a significant role in carbohydrate metabolism by stimulating the transport of glucose into muscle and adipose tissue and by stimulating the formation of glycogen, the major form of storage carbohydrate. The net effect of these various functions of insulin is to metabolize for immediate use the required amount of glucose and to store for later use the surfeit of blood glucose related to a recent feeding. Insulin is synthesized in the beta cells of the islets of Langerhans within the pancreas. Biochemical and electron microscopic studies indicate that this is a zinc-intensive process. Zinc forms an insoluble zinc–insulin complex that is stored in the secretory granules of the pancreatic beta cells (Vallee & Hoch, 1959). Upon insulin release, zinc ions identify the place and constitute the visible form of insulin within the beta cells (Yoshinaga & Ogawa, 1975).

Roth and Kirchgessner (1981) induced zinc deficiency in rats using a zinc-restricted diet and then compared them to pair-fed controls with respect to response parameters over time following a glucose load. The zinc-deficient animals were found to have a 58% reduction in their pancreatic zinc content prior to glucose injection. However, the concentration of zinc in the plasma of these animals was approximately 50% that of the controls, and neither zinc nor insulin plasma concentrations increased over a 30-min time after administration of a glucose load; whereas, the control rats' plasma zinc increased 30%, and plasma insulin levels increased 190% over this same time period in response to tbe same glucose load. The glucose tolerance curves for the zinc-deficient animals were hyperglycemic and similar in form to those of humans with diabetes.

Cadmium and Carbohydrate Metabolism

On the other hand, Merali and Singhal (1981) have demonstrated that cadmium interferes with carbohydrate metabolism, by disrupting pancreatic insulin production. The exact mechanism of this disruption is uncertain; however, evidence suggests that cadmium stimulates both hepatic gluconeo-genic enzymes and the adrenal secretion of epinephrine that, in turn, further inhibits pancreatic insulin synthesis and enhances the production of glucose by gluconeogenesis and glycogenolysis. Cadmium also disrupts the normal physiology of the pancreatic beta cells by inhibiting their uptake of calcium, which along with zinc, has been shown to be an integral part of the insulin molecule (Sudmeier, Bell, Storm, & Dunn, 1981). Furthermore, zinc admin-istered simultaneously with cadmium appears to ameliorate the adverse effects of cadmium such that the glucose and insulin responses to a glucose load of the cadmium-plus-zinc-treated animals were not significantly differ-ent from those of normal control animals (Merali & Singhal, 1981).

ZINC, CADMIUM, AND NEUROPSYCHOLOGICAL FUNCTION

The Role of Zinc in the Development and Function of the Hippocampus

Although the major influence of zinc on neuropsychological function may occur indirectly via metabolic processes that regulate energy supplies to the brain, recent neuroscience research suggests a more direct relationship between zinc levels and the functional integrity of the hippocampus. Specif-ically, zinc is much more concentrated in the hippocampus than in any other structure within the mammalian brain (Crawford, 1983). Furthermore, a clearly defined developmental sequence for zinc in the hippocampus has been described (Crawford & Connor, 1971). In the rat, zinc concentrations in the hippocampus become significantly different from those of whole brain after the fourteenth postnatal day but not before. Adult zinc hippocampus levels are reached by the twenty-second day in pups provided normal sup-plies of nutrient zinc. Trace element studies of the human brain indicate that the major increases in hippocampus zinc occur during the first 5 yr (Volkl, Berlet, & Ule, 1974) with a fairly uniform distribution of zinc observed for the infant brain except for its considerably greater concentration within the hippocampus. The hippocampal zinc of young adults is about twice the prepubescent level.

A number of studies have associated zinc levels with structural and functional properties of the mossy fiber boutons of the hippocampus. Haug (1967), using a modified silver-staining technique and electron microscopy, showed that punctate metallic zinc deposits were associated with the cytoplasm and vesicles of the mossy fiber boutons. In an associated anterograde degeneration study (Haug, Blackstad, Zimmer, & Simonsen, 1971), mossy fiber changes in structure and reactivity to staining for zinc were evaluated over time after experimental lesions were produced in the granule cell layer. The fact that reactivity for zinc staining diminished rapidly after production of the lesions, whereas morphological modifications in the boutons were not evident until much later, was interpreted as indicating that zinc (or a substance containing zinc) plays a metabolically labile functional role rather than a structural role within the hippocampus.

Electrophysiological data comparing zinc-deficient adult rats and controls supports the concept that mossy fiber zinc plays a functional role in the hippocampus (Hesse, 1979). In normal animals, the evoked potential (EP) response amplitude of cells within the CA3 layer of the hippocampus (the mossy fiber terminal field) does not decline with increased frequency of stimulation via the mossy fiber tracts; however, the EP response amplitude observed in zinc-deficient rats is attenuated by 50% when the rate of stimulation is increased from 1 to 20 Hz. However, when the CA3 layer is stimulated via the commissural tract, no difference in EP responses between control and zinc-deficient animals is observed, indicating that the decrement response observed in the mossy fiber stimulation studies is not due to a generalized effect of zinc deficiency on the nervous system's response properties.

The specific neurotransmitter mediating the transmission of signals from the mossy fibers to the pyramidal cells of the hippocampus is unknown. However, research addressing this issue suggests that glutamic acid is likely to play a dominant role in this process (Crawford, 1983). Interestingly, the glutamic acid content of rat brain has been found to double between 14 and 21 days (Agrawal, Davis, & Himwich, 1966), the exact time period in which zinc levels dramatically increase in the hippocampus.

The limbic structures of the CNS form a highly integrated functional system. As a central component of this system, the hippocampus has been implicated in many of the complex processes that appear to be dependent upon limbic system operation such as emotion, affect, memory, and attention. Human and animal research on behavioral effects of zinc deficiency suggest that deficits exist in each of these areas in zinc-deficient animals. Henkin and associates (Henkin, Patten, Re, & Bronzert, 1975) have described the psychological manifestations of severe acute zinc deficiency in humans. In these studies, acute zinc deficiency was induced by a large dose of histidine that produces a rapid, massive hyperzincuria. Plasma zinc in the subjects so treated ranged from 40 to 60 µg/dl as compared to pretreatment plasma zinc levels of 60 to 105 µg/dl. The neuropsychological signs observed in these volunteers included dysarthria, poor visual acuity, lethargy, memory loss, impairments of speech and directed thought, depression, irritability, visual agnosia, and receptive aphasia. Prior to these psychological effects, each subject experienced a loss of appetite and a diminution in the senses of taste and smell.

Behavioral manifestations of zinc deficiency in children have been described as follows: moodiness, depression, irritability, photophobia (Moynahan, 1976), antagonism, temper tantrums, and learning problems (Kronick, 1975). Zinc-deficient rats have been described as being hyperresponsive to mild stress and novelty situations that may account for their poor performance in open-field, conditioned avoidance and Lashley water maze tests (Hesse, Hesse, & Catalanotto, 1979). In experimental studies in which lesions of the hippocampus have been produced or in which zinc-chelating agents have been introduced into the hippocampus, learning and memory of animals has been impaired severely (Crawford, 1983). Furthermore, hypnogenic responses induced by hippocampus stimulation has suggested a functional involvement for this structure in arousal mechanisms (Green, 1964). In light of these empirical findings, Pribram and McGuinness (1975) have accorded to the hippocampus the major function of directing or focusing cognitive effort in their model of attention.

However, despite these intriguing aspects of the interrelationships of zinc sufficiency and hippocampal function, no direct correlation between hippocampal zinc, plasma zinc, and any neurological disorder related to hippocampal dysfunction has been demonstrated. However, in a very interesting set of experiments, Sarrat (1980) has demonstrated a relationship between pancreatic islet beta-cell function and granule cell functioning of the hippocampus, whereby lesions within either tissue appeared to disrupt the functioning of the other. This finding, in conjunction with the study of Hesse (1979) that demonstrated a functional deficit in the hippocampal EP response to trains of stimulation in zinc-deficient rats and the studies of Roth and Kirchgessner (1981) that demonstrated a significant reduction in plasma zinc in zinc-deficient animals, suggests a close association between plasma zinc, hippocampal zinc, and hippocampal function.

Cadmium, Zinc, and Neuropsychological Disorders

Children, perhaps because of heightened metabolic requirements due to growth, are at greater risk than adults for neurological impairment from heavy metal environmental pollutants (Rutter, 1983). Not only do children absorb heavy metals more readily than adults, but the systemic damage resulting from a given level of intake appears to be greater for children. Although research has focused almost exclusively on the effects of lead, recent studies have suggested that low body-burden levels of cadmium may be related to childhood learning disabilities (Lester et al., 1982; Pihl & Parkes, 1977; Thatcher & Lester, 1985; Thatcher, Lester, McAlaster, & Horst, 1982; Thatcher, McAlaster, & Lester 1984).

Laboratory animal research suggests that superior nutrition can protect against the harmful effects of heavy metal toxins and promote general development (Bremner & Campbell, 1980; Cerklewski & Forbes, 1976; Fox, 1974; Jones & Fowler, 1980; Kimura, 1981; Mahaffey, 1981; Neathery, 1981; Petering, 1978). This research has demonstrated further that functional toxicity cannot be described by a simple dose response relationship; instead, tolerance for a given dose of poison was found to depend on the animals' status for specific nutrients, such as calcium, copper, iron, phosphorus, and zinc, with which the poisons interact metabolically.

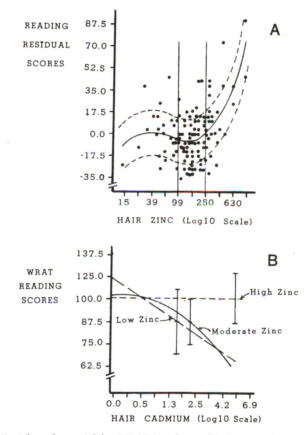

FIGURE 6. (A) Best-fit polynomial for WRAT Reading subtest residual scores as a function of log10 hair zinc in ppm after significant effects due to SES, age, sex and log10 hair cadmium were statistically removed. The cubic regression curve is given by the function $Y = 61X^3 - 335X^2 + 591X - 339$; where Y is the predicted reading residual score and X is the log10 transformed value of hair zinc in ppm. The dashed lines indicate the plus and minus one standard error of estimate region about the regression line. (B) Best-fit polynomials for WRAT reading scores as a function of log10 hair cadmium for Low, Moderate, and High Zinc subjects. The lines perpendicular to the x-axis shown in plot A designate the cut points along the hair zinc continuum for defining the zinc groups. The respective regressions for the groups are: Low Zinc, $Y = -56X + 125$; Moderate Zinc, $Y = -76X^2 + 9.5X + 114.5$; and High Zinc, $Y = 113.3$; where Y is the predicted WRAT reading score and X is the log10 transformed value of hair cadmium in ppm. For each regression, plus and minus one standard error of estimate bars are indicated. (Reprinted, with permission, from Lester, Horst & Thatcher, 1987.)

Recent research with school-age children suggests a protective action for zinc against the detrimental effects on cognitive function of cadmium body burden (Lester, Horst, & Thatcher, 1986). In this study, academic achievement in reading for children between the ages of 5 and 16 was assessed with the Reading subtest of the Wide Range Achievement Test (Jastak & Jastak, 1978). In addition, measures of socioeconomic status (SES), hair cadmium, and hair zinc were determined for each child. Figure 6A shows the best-fit polynomial function for the relationship of zinc to Reading performance after variance related significantly to SES, age, sex and hair cadmium has been removed. Figure 6B is the same relationship but displayed in interaction form showing the effect of cadmium on Reading performance for subjects grouped by zinc status, defined by ranges of hair zinc concentration. The particular levels of hair zinc selected as cut points were High Zinc (Zn > 250 ppm, N = 30); Moderate Zinc (100 ppm < Zn < 250 ppm, N = 81); and Low Zinc (Zn < 100 ppm, N = 30). As indicated in Figure 6, increased hair cadmium was associated with a steep decline in Reading performance for the children with Low Zinc status; whereas, no significant decrement in the performance of children with High Zinc hair concentrations was seen, and intermediate decrements were noted in children with increased cadmium body burdens and moderate levels of hair zinc.

In the study described, only 13% of the total sample was found to have a zinc status (hair zinc in excess of 250 ppm) that was adequate to offer protection against the adverse effects of an above-average cadmium body burden, whereas, 20% of the sample was found to have a marginal zinc status (hair zinc less than 100 ppm) that offered no protection against even the slightest body burden of cadmium.

Populations At Risk for Zinc Insufficiency

Animals require a regular intake of zinc for maintenance of normal function, especially during periods of growth and of tissue repair. Although this is true for all essential nutrients, the chronic dependency of the body for a regular exogenous supply of zinc appears to be greater than for most other micronutrients. There are two reasons for this: (a) the body does not have a special storage form of zinc (Sandstead, 1981); and (b) except for plasma zinc, the zinc in the body is not readily mobilized for use as are iron and other essential body metals (Li & Vallee, 1980).

Sandstead (1973) suggested more than a decade ago that zinc nutriture might be inadequate for large numbers of individuals in the United States. Groups that were indicated to be at particular risk for zinc deficiency were pregnant and lactating women, infants, teenagers, institutionalized individuals, and those living on low incomes. Points of particular importance in consideration of the optimal level of zinc intake for promoting brain development and function are the following: (a) during the last 20 weeks of pregnancy, the mother's zinc requirement is three to four times that of a nonpregnant woman; (b) during the first 6 mon of life, zinc requirements are one and one-half to two times those required in later infancy; (c) from age 11 to 17, the zinc requirement for males is two to four times that required either pre- or postpuberty; and (d) from approximately age 10 to 12, females require two to three times as much zinc as is required either before or after these ages.

From all indications, the recommended daily allowance (RDA) for zinc as established by the Food and Nutrition Board (1974) is adequate to meet the physiological needs of the overwhelming majority of the population, even those who are within special phases of growth or development in which zinc requirements are increased. However, the consumption of a diet that acutally contains the RDA for zinc is apparently rare.

None of the diets reviewed by Sandstead (1973) were adequate when referenced to the RDA standard. In addition, when Holden, Wolf, and Mertz (1979) evaluated the zinc content for self-selected diets of educated, middle-class adult volunteers ($N = 22$) over a 2-week period, the average zinc intake was 8.6 mg/day that was 57% of the RDA for this group. Moreover, the average consumption of zinc for 68% of the study population was less than two thirds of the RDA. More importantly, no subject in the study actually consumed a diet that was adequate when referenced to the RDA standard for zinc.

Based on hair zinc concentrations (hair zinc less than 70 ppm), 50% of the children between 3 mon and 4 yr from middle- and upper-income families in the Denver area of Colorado were evaluated to have insufficient zinc nutriture (Hambidge, Hambidge, Jacobs, & Baum, 1972). Furthermore, studies have shown that children from low-income families are at even higher risk for insufficient zinc intake with a correspondingly higher risk for delayed growth and development than are children in the general population.

In several studies of zinc nutriture and growth (Butrimovitz & Purdy, 1978; Hambidge et al., 1976), biochemical indexes of zinc nutriture have been lower in children from low-income families than for comparable aged children from middle-income families. In addition, zinc status was highly correlated with growth within the low-income group of children. In one study (Hambidge et al., 1976), over 65% of the children entering a Head-Start preschool program were indicated to have inadequate zinc nutrition. In a subgroup of these children, zinc nutriture improved dramatically over a 3-mon period of time in the program. Poor zinc nutriture and income may be related by the fact that zinc-rich food sources, such as meats and nuts, tend to be higher priced and may be relatively less abundant in the meals available to low-income households.

DIET, NEUROTRANSMITTER SYNTHESIS, AND NEUROPSYCHOLOGICAL FUNCTION

A rudimentary knowledge of several major neurotransmitters, of the functional systems in which they play an integral role, and of the factors that limit their synthesis and utilization is critical for appreciating the dynamic relationship between nutrition and neuropsychological function (Growden, 1979; Wurtman & Fernstrom, 1974). Four major neurotransmitters, their functional significance, and the research on the dietary and metabolic factors that influence their precursor availability will be discussed. The implications that these relationships suggest for the clinical diagnosis and management of neuropsychological dysfunction also will be explored.

Neurotransmitters are chemical substances within the central nervous system that mediate electrochemical communication between neurons. The four neurotransmitters that will be discussed are serotonin (5-hydroxytryptamine or 5-HT), the catecholamines dopamine (DA) and norepinephrine (NE), and acetylcholine (ACh). These neurotransmitters are intricately involved in the regulation of behavior, emotion, and mood; subtle imbalances in one or more of these neurotransmitters can produce profound disruptions in each of these functional areas (Wurtman & Wurtman, 1979).

Appropriate precursors for the synthesis of the aforementioned neurotransmitters must be supplied to the brain from exogenous sources. Thus, the levels of brain serotonin, acetylcholine, and the catecholamines are in part a function of the dietary availability of the precursors of tryptophan, choline, and tyrosine, respectively, and the level of these precursors in the blood. Consequently, levels of these precursors available to the brain for transmitter synthesis can be manipulated at least in part by controlling the content of a meal (Wurtman & Wurtman, 1979). Insomuch as particular classes of behaviors are associated with distinct neurotransmitter systems (Barchas, Akil, Elliott, Holman, & Watson, 1978), physiological mechanisms exist whereby behavior can be influenced directly via alterations in the diet. The clinical implications are that useful therapeutic approaches to the remediation of cognitive or psychiatric disorders can be based on neurotransmitter precursor manipulation of the diet. Such therapeutic effects in fact may prove to be safe alternatives to current drug and psychotherapeutic regimens.

Foods can potentially affect brain function with respect to neurotransmitter synthesis via two fundamental mechanisms: (a) directly, by providing the biochemical precursors from which neurons synthesize neurotransmitters; and (b) indirectly, via dietary constituents that either affect the concentration of a precursor in the blood and/or its competition for transport systems across the blood–brain barrier and thus its availability to the brain (Lieberman, Corkin, Spring, Growden, & Wurtman, 1984).

Serotonin Synthesis and Clinical Applications

One year after the discovery of serotonin, or 5-hydroxytryptamine (5-HT), in the mammalian brain, Woolley and Shaw (1954) observed that lysergic acid diethylamide produced profound cognitive and visual disturbances and was structurally similar to 5-HT; subsequently, they proposed that 5-HT may operate as a neurotransmitter in the brain and may play an important role in the etiology of some mental disorders. Since the early 1960s considerable evidence has accumulated to support this idea.

Subsequent research has shown that the brain depends on an exogenous source, namely the amino-acid precursor, L-tryptophan, for serotonin synthesis (Fernstrom & Wurtman, 1971; Lieberman, Corkin, Spring, Growden & Wurtman, 1984; Wurtman & Wurtman, 1979). Tryptophan is transported across the blood–brain barrier, as are other large neutral amino acids (LNAAs), such as valine, leucine, isoleucine, tyrosine, methionine and phenylalanine, by a carrier mechanism. Competition among these amino acids for the limited number of specific transport carrier sites serves as the rate limiting step in brain availability of these amino acids. Thus, the availability of tryptophan to the brain depends upon the ratio of the molar concentration of tryptophan to that of the various competing LNAAs. When pure tryptophan is consumed, the ratio of tryptophan to other LNAAs increases; it also rises following a carbohydrate meal or pure glucose ingestion. Although tryptophan is present only in protein, a diet high in carbohydrate has been shown to increase the availability of tryptophan to the brain for the synthesis of serotonin (Wurtman, 1980; Zeisel, Mauron, Watkins & Wurtman, 1981). Conversely, the consumption of a high-protein diet has either no effect and possibly even an adverse effect on brain concentrations of serotonin because it reduces the concentration of tryptophan relative to the other LNAAs (Cohen & Wurtman, 1979).

This rate-limiting mechanism controlling the transport and subsequent synthesis of serotonin in the brain is modulated by the unique property of tryptophan to bind to plasma albumin (Green, 1978). Because nonesterified fatty acids (NEFA) compete with tryptophan for binding sites on albumin, treatments that alter the levels of NEFA effectively alter plasma tryptophan binding to albumin. Thus, following the administration of either insulin or the consumption of a carbohydrate-rich meal (which elicits an insulin response), serum NEFA levels decline, thereby allowing more tryptophan to bind to albumin, and less tryptophan is thereby available for transport into the brain. In addition, insulin release promotes the influx of competing LNAAs into skeletal muscle from plasma. The net result of both of these insulin-mediated actions is to increase plasma tryptophan levels relative to that of other LNAAs that in turn promotes tryptophan transport into the brain. Diets that enhance tryptophan availability to the brain could potentially influence cognitive and psychiatric conditions associated with tryptophan and serotonin irregularities.

For neuropsychological dysfunctions in which serotonin deficiency is implicated, a corrective regimen might include the administration of tryptophan supplements. The daily recommended intake of tryptophan is 11 mg/kg/day, whereas therapeutic dosages of tryptophan are an order of magnitude greater and range from 2 to 10 g/day (Kirschmann, 1981; Wurtman & Wurtman, 1979). A correspondent decrease in catecholamine synthesis by the brain may be expected to occur as a result of supplementation because tyrosine and phenylalanine (both catecholamine precursors) and tryptophan compete for a common transport system into the brain. If the symptoms for which treatment is sought are mania or certain types of hyperactivity for which evidence exists for excessive catecholamine production by the brain, a reduction in brain catecholamine content may be the desired effect and might be achieved by the use of a tryptophan-rich diet. Another means of effectively increasing brain tryptophan and serotonin relative to the catecholamines is to increase the dietary intake of carbohydrate or to administer insulin. On the other hand, some conditions may require restriction of tryptophan-containing foods in an effort to reduce the serotonin content of the brain relative to that of catecholamines.

Because serotonergic neurons contribute to the inducement of slow wave sleep and may elicit REM sleep, both tryptophan and serotonin have been used as hypnotic agents. In this regard, tryptophan administration has been shown to increase subjective drowsiness and fatigue without impairing sensorimotor performance or the anxiety level (Greenwood, Lader, Kantameni, & Curzon, 1975; Hartmann, 1977; Moja, Mendelson, Stoff, Gillin, & Wyatt, 1979; Yuwiler, Brammer, Morley, Raleigh, Flannery, & Geller, 1981). Yogman, Zeisel, and Roberts (1984) found that infants fed formula high in tryptophan content spent relatively more time in active sleep and less time being alert, as well as, entered quiet and active sleep sooner than did infants fed valine-rich formula. The "sedative" effect of tryptophan-induced serotonin synthesis may explain why several studies have found that a high carbohydrate consumption, rather than being associated with hyperactivity and aggressivity as expected, seems to be correlated instead with lethargy and fatigue in children. These behavioral symptoms would be expected from the effect that a carbohydrate-rich diet has on brain tryptophan levels relative to the brain content of other LNAAs.

Serotonin deficiency and tryptophan metabolic disturbances have been related causally to the onset of depression, and treatments with tryptophan have improved depressive symptoms in some cases (Coppen, 1967; Green & Costain, 1979; Kline & Shah, 1973; Lehmann, 1971, 1973; Shopsin, 1978). Tryptophan can be shown to have a dose-dependent pharmacologic effect of an antidepressant (Young & Sourkes, 1977). Moller, Kirk, and Fremming (1976) measured the tryptophan/ LNAA ratio in depressed patients and found that in those with decreased tryptophan levels relative to the other LNAA, improvement could be demonstrated as a result of tryptophan administration, whereas those patients with normal ratios of tryptophan/LNAA were not improved with tryptophan administration. This finding suggests that the classification of depression syndromes according to particular biochemical markers may have important diagnostic and clinical-therapeutic utility. Specifically, an individual suffering from depression that has a biochemical profile indicative of a serotonin neurotransmitter deficiency may respond to dietary intervention procedures that enhance tryptophan availability to the brain.

Studies disagree as to whether serotonin excesses or deficiencies are associated with schizophrenia, and the therapeutic efficacy of tryptophan supplementation for the alteration of brain serotonin levels in schizophrenia is controversial (Gilmour, Manowitz, Frosch, & Shopsin, 1973; Manowitz, Gilmour, & Racevskis, 1973; Pollin, Cardon, & Kety, 1961; Price, Brown. &

Peters, 1959; Wurtman & Wurtman, 1979; Yaryura-Tobias, 1973). However, these inconsistent results may be due to numerous methodological short-comings, such as ineffective modes of tryptophan administration; inadequate dietary history information; no consideration of the plasma concentrations of other relevant amino acids (LNAAs); inadequate methods for measuring brain serotonin and tryptophan levels; and inability to ascertain whether the postulated biochemical imbalance contributes to, or results from, the psychiatric disturbance. In summary, too little research has been done in this area to determine whether or not a major abnormality of the serotonin system is a contributing factor in schizophrenia (Joseph, Baker, Crow, Riley, & Risby, 1979). However, most psychotic and schizophrenic syndromes do not have a known etiology; for certain of individuals with these syndromes, a serotonin disorder may be present and be related pathogentically to the neuropsychological disorder. Thus, individual biochemical assessments, when available, are recommended.

In addition to depression and sleeping disorders, abnormal plasma serotonin levels, recognized metabolic disorders in tryptophan metabolism, and manipulation of the dietary content of tryptophan have been shown to be associated with alterations of intellectual function (Johnson & Chernik, 1982; Weingartner, Rudorfer, Buchsbaum, & Linnoila, 1983; Wurtman, Hefti, & Melamed, 1981), pain sensitivity (Hosobuchi, Lamb, & Bascomb, 1980; Messing & Lytle, 1977; Seltzer, Stoch, Marcus, & Jackson, 1982), locomotor activity (Hornykiewicz, 1973; Lhermitte, Peterfalvi, Marteau, Gazengel, & Serdaru, 1971; Van Woert, Jutkowitz, Rosembaum, & Bauers, 1976; Van Woert, Rosembaum, Howieson, & Bauers, 1977), and aggression (Mizuno & Yugari, 1974; Nyhan, 1976).

Catecholamine Metabolism and Clinical Applications

Brain levels of norepinephrine (NE) and epinephrine as well as their metabolic precursor, dopamine (DA), co-vary as a function of the dietary content of the amino acid tyrosine (Gibson & Wurtman, 1977, 1978). The transport mechanism for tyrosine into the brain is identical to that described previously for tryptophan. After tyrosine enters the brain, it is converted to DOPA by the action of tyrosine hydroxylase, an enzyme found within catecholaminergic neurons. Subsequently, DOPA is converted to dopamine by the enzyme aromatic L-amino acid decarboxylase. Brain neurons synthesize norepinephrine and then epinephrine from dopamine. As with tryptophan, increasing neuronal concentrations of the catecholamine precursors accelerate the conversion process. However, unlike the effects of tryptophan on serotonin levels, tyrosine levels do not directly influence brain catecholamine synthesis. For example, the administration of tyrosine does not elevate brain NE or epinephrine but does increase brain DOPA concentration. This indicates that either tyrosine hydroxylase exerts a rate limiting function or that a supply–demand negative feedback mechanism may be in operation. The latter is indicated by the fact that as the dopaminergic neurons become more active, tyrosine hydroxylase accelerates the synthesis of DOPA to cate-cholamines (Green & Costain, 1981; Wurtman & Wurtman, 1979).

Tyrosine, which is found primarily in high-protein foods, must be avail-able along with various other food constituents such as pyridoxine (vitamin B6) in order for the brain to synthesize adequate amounts of dopamine, norepinephrine, and epinephrine. The amino acid phenylalanine (the pri-mary component of aspartame) is converted to tyrosine in the liver by the action of phenylalanine hydroxylase (Green & Costain, 1981). As was the case with tryptophan, the availability of tyrosine to the brain depends upon the molar ratio of the other LNAAs to tyrosine found in the diet as they all compete for the same transport carrier. Thus a restriction in the amount of protein-containing foods in the diet during tyrosine administration may en-hance brain levels of catecholamines by enhancing tyrosine entry into the brain.

Imbalances in both the dopamine and norepinephrine systems are known to contribute to a variety of behavioral and emotional disorders (Bell-ak, 1978; Hornykiewicz, 1978; Mefford, Baker, & Boehme, 1983; Pijnenburg, Honig, & Van Der Heyden, 1976; Schildkraut, 1965; Stein & Wise, 1971; Van Kammen et al., 1983). The fact that the primary effect of neuroleptics is to increase the brain level of dopamine metabolites along with evidence of a concomitant acceleration in dopaminergic firing rates suggests that tyro-sine's clinical utility relates to changes in the brain content of these cate-cholamine neurotransmitters (Carlsson & Lindquist, 1963). In addition, as the behavioral effects of amphetamines resemble certain psychoses and worsen schizophrenic symptoms presumably by altering the effects of dopamine, it has been suggested that dopamine is involved in the abnormal brain function that characterizes schizophrenics (Snyder, 1980).

A subpopulation of depressive individuals have an abnormally low uri-nary level of 3-methoxy-4-hydroxylphenylglycol (MHPG), a catabolite of norepinephrine. This finding has been interpreted to indicate that some depressive individuals suffer from a deficiency of NE (Snyder, 1980). In addition, antidepressant drugs appear to enhance the effects of NE.

Dopamine and norepinephrine are catabolized, in part, by monoamine oxidase (MAO). Consequently, one method of treatment for depression has been to manipulate the levels of MAO by the administration of MAO inhib-itors that block the degradation of norepinephrine. However, there are few studies that document a therapeutic psychological effect of tyrosine supple-mentation in such individuals despite the fact that experimental manipula-tion of tyrosine has been demonstrated to affect the neuronal synthesis of dopamine and, particularly, that of norepinephrine (Gibson & Wurtman, 1977, 1978). Depression is associated frequently with a reduction in dopa-minergic activity in the brain (Muscettola, Wehr, & Goodwin, 1977; Schildkraut, 1965; Snyder, 1980; Wurtman & Wurtman, 1979). Thus, clinical trials in which tyrosine supplements are used in conjunction with a reduc-tion in the amount of other LNAAs should be instituted to augment the brain's content of DA and NE to test the efficacy of dietary intervention in the treatment of depression. However, a potential problem for any dietary manipulation of tyrosine in the CNS is that the release of NE and epinephrine from the autonomic nervous system will be increased as well (Alonso, Agharanya, & Wurtman, 1978).

The daily requirement for tyrosine intake has been estimated to be 11 mg/kg/day (Kirschmann, 1981). This intake level has been increased several orders of magnitude to induce a therapeutic effect for depressive disorders. Gelenberg, Gibson, and Wojcik, (1982) in a double-blind intervention trial, administered 100 mg/kg/day of tyrosine to six depressed outpatients and a placebo to eight. They reported that the 24-hr urinary MHPG excretion increased 24% in the tyrosine-treated group, suggesting an effect on NE turnover. Tyrosine plasma levels also increased 27%. What is most important is that improvements in the depression rating scale were noted for the treatment group that suggested that a decrease in the degree of depression may have occurred in response to an increase in the NE turnover rate induced by tyrosine administration.

Acetylcholine Synthesis and Clinical Applications

With the discovery of the first neurotransmitter, ACh, the idea that nerves communicate with each other by releasing chemicals was established (Snyder, 1980). Acetylcholine is also the neurotransmitter that activates the contraction of voluntary muscles and is the neurochemical involved in many of the involuntary (autonomic) nervous system synapses in the body. In addition, it plays a major role in mediating neural activation in memory, learning, and motor coordination (Davis, Mohs, & Trinklenberg, 1979; Green & Costain, 1981; Peters & Levine, 1977; Snyder, 1980). Diminished brain levels of ACh are characteristic of the aged who exhibit varying degrees of senile dementia and in some cases of Alzheimer's disease (Bartus, Dean, Beer, & Lippa, 1982; Growden, Hirsch, Wurtman, & Weiner, 1977; Marsh, Flynn, & Potter, 1985; Perry & Perry, 1980).

Acetylcholine is synthesized in neurons from choline, a common nutrient generally associated with the vitamin B complex. Fish, poultry, and eggs are said to be "brain foods" due to their high concentration of choline. Phosphatidylcholine, one of the lecithin compounds, when given either orally or parenterally, increases the brain's content of ACh (Cohen & Wurtman, 1975; Haubrich, Wang, Clody, & Wedeking, 1975). The phosphatidylcholine content present in most diets, transiently, doubles the blood choline concentration postprandially. This increment can be raised five to sixfold by a single large dose of lecithin (Wurtman, Hirsch, & Growden, 1977). Lecithin is more effective than choline in increasing plasma choline levels after oral administration because choline, but not lecithin, is largely destroyed in the intestinal tract by bacterial fermentation.

Chronic phosphatidylcholine intake does not produce adverse pharmacological side effects for either the central or peripheral cholinergic systems (Ulus, Hirsh, & Wurtman, 1977). Under normal conditions, cholinergic neurons require no more than minimal amounts of choline; however, when cortical activity increases due to some pathology or toxicosis, an elevated choline requirement may be needed to prevent neuronal damage. Evidence in support of such an assumption is the finding that cognitive improvement in some patients can be incurred with pharmacologic inhibition of acetylcholinesterase, an ACh hydrolyzer (Davis *et al.*, 1979; Peters & Levine, 1977).

Studies examining the effects of dietary phosphatidylcholine administration suggested a role for such therapy in the treatment of children with Down's syndrome (DS). Nerve cell pathology is known to occur in DS children by 8 to 9 mon of age (Scott, Becker, & Petit, 1983). In particular, significant alterations in the dendritic spine structure of neurons present in the hippocampus have been reported in DS children (Marin-Padilla, 1976; Purpura, 1977). The hippocampal region is rich in cholinergic neurons (Wurtman, Magil, & Reinstein, 1981). Moreover, as DS patients increase in age, they develop a slowly progressive dementia and a variety of new neurological abnormalities. Clinical and pathological studies of autopsy material obtained from individuals with DS suggest a marked reduction in the function of cholinergic neurons (Burger & Vogel, 1973; Ellis, McCullough, & Corley. 1974; Yates, Simpson, Maloney, Gordon, & Reid, 1980).

An exploratory study that utilized dietary ACh precursor supplementation with a DS child in conjunction with assessment of the computerized EEG features has been reported recently (Cantor, Thatcher, Ozand, Kumin, & Rothschild, 1986). In this study, the EEG features were referenced to normative life-span EEG measures (John, Ahn, Prichep, Trepetin, Brown, &

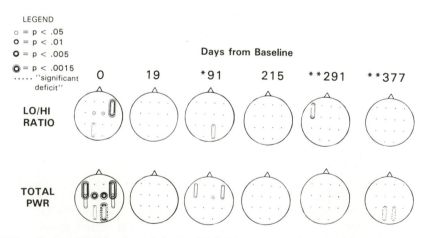

FIGURE 7. Z-scored bipolar data of the low/high (slow wave to fast wave) ratio EEG measure and for total power (amplitude) for the time course indicated. Increasing thickness of lines encircling regions indicates increasing probability of abnormal ($p < .05$ to $p < .001$) when compared to developmental norms. Solid lines indicate excesses and dotted lines indicate deficits. *Recordings after 10-day abstinence from choline prior to test; **placebo began following test Day 215. (Reprinted with permission from Cantor, Thatcher, Ozand, Kumin, & Rothschild, 1986.)

Kaye, 1980) for indications of deviance from normal and to determine the direction and extent of change in brain function, if any, measured over the course of the dietary supplementation period. Preliminary results indicated a trend toward normalcy in various EEG measures of asymmetry, coherence, relative power, and total power in the DS child receiving supplementation. The results were interpreted by the author to indicate that some improvement in the brain functioning of the child had occurred (see Figure 7).

Development of Neurotransmitter Synthesis in the Brain

The amount of any particular neurotransmitter in the brain is determined by (a) the number of neurons that utilize the neurotransmitter, (b) the number of synaptic boutons on each neuron's axonal branchings and (c) the number of neurotransmitter molecules present in each bouton. During early development, these parameters change dramatically. Consequently, the demand for a neurotransmitter precursor should follow the maturational pattern for the particular neurotransmitter system within the CNS. In addition, CNS development might be limited or enhanced by the availability of neurotransmitter precursors during periods of rapid maturation. However, there are relatively few studies that address this issue. Those that do seem to support the general rule that there is a correlation between the functional maturation and the CNS content of the particular neurotransmitter. For example, levels of NE and 5-HT within the brain of newborn rats are, respectively, 20% and 50% of adult levels. Adult levels are reached at 4 to 7 weeks of age (Dodge et al., 1975). With respect to NE, Coyle and Axelrod (1971) have suggested that the functional development of the noradrenergic neuronal systems present in the rat can be assessed by measures that quantitate the active uptake of NE within the brain. In their studies, an active uptake of NE cannot be demonstrated prior to 14 days of age; thereafter NE uptake is rapid and achieves adult levels by 28 days of age. Similarly, the levels of ACh within the brain and the activity of the enzymes responsible for its synthesis and degradation have been observed to increase rapidly in the caudate nucleus following phases of increased dendritic growth and synaptic proliferation in these areas (McCaman & Aprison, 1964).

FOOD SENSITIVITIES

Reports that some children become irritable, anxious, and sleepless following ingestion of certain foods have occurred in the medical literature since 1908 (Alvarez, 1946; Shofield, 1908). More serious reactions, for example, headache (Ghose & Carroll, 1984; Randolph, 1944), myalgia (Randolph, 1951), arthralgia and arthritis (Randolph, 1959; Rinkel, Randolph, & Zeller, 1951), fatigue (Crook, 1980; Randolph, 1947; Speer, 1970), and even schizophrenic reactions (Dohan, 1978; Philpott, 1977; Singh & Kay, 1976) to certain foods, have been noted in susceptible individuals but have been considered to be indiosyncratic and quite rare.

However, other studies provide evidence that certain neuropsychological disorders can be provoked by foods or food constituents more commonly than has been believed previously (Crook, 1975; Egger, Carter, Graham, Gumley, & Soothill, 1985; Feingold, 1975; Rapp, 1981; Speer, 1975). The mechanisms responsible for such food–brain-behavior connections are, as yet, unknown. There are suggestions, however, that the components of certain foods have pharmacologically active properties that interfere with normal neurochemical activities and are responsible for these phenomena (Augustine & Levitan, 1980; Ghose & Carroll, 1984; Swanson & Kinsbourne, 1980).

Synthetic Food Additives and Childhood Hyperactivity

Benjamin Feingold's (1975, 1976, 1980) work on food sensitivity and hyperactivity is perhaps the best known and most controversial on this subject. Feingold has stated that 30% to 60% of childhood hyperactivity cases are *primarily* due to CNS reactions to artificial food coloring, artificial flavors, or natural salicylates. Based on a number of controlled, double-blind challenge experiments in which neither experimenter nor patient knew whether an active substance or placebo had been administered, the Feingold hypothesis has been repudiated (Connors, Goyette, Southwick, Lees, & Andrulonis, 1976; Lipton, Nemeroff, & Mailman, 1979; Sobotka, 1978; Wender, 1977). However, a few recent studies have supported the Feingold hypothesis (Egger *et al.*, 1985; Swanson & Kinsbourne, 1980; Weiss *et al.*, 1980). Certain methodological differences that exist between these more recent positive experiments and earlier negative studies provide reasons for the conflicting experimental results.

The Swanson and Kinsbourne (1980) study, for example, differed in three fundamental respects from previously performed controlled double-blind, crossover challenge experiments that had tested the relationship between hyperactivity and food dye ingestion. First, either a 100-mg or 150-mg dose of food dye was used as the challenge. Previous studies had used challenge doses of 1 to 26 mg. Swanson and Kinsbourne thought that such small doses might be below the threshold level because the average daily intake of synthetic food dyes by children between the ages of 5 and 12 yr is 76.5 mg (Sobotka, 1976). Second, behavioral rating scales were the behavioral assessment instrument of choice in most previous experiments, whereas, Swanson, and Kinsbourne used a paired associate learning task that they maintain is more sensitive to food-induced effects because attentional-learning deficits are a central attribute of the syndrome (Rosenthal & Allen, 1978). Third, Swanson and Kinsbourne categorized their hyperactive subjects into two physiologically homogeneous groups for the comparison of food dye effects on cognitive function. Specifically, 20 children identified as hyperactives who responded positively to amphetamine treatment and another 20 children who either demonstrated an adverse or no positive behavioral effects in response to the drug were studied. In the dye challenge experiments,

85% of the positive drug responders experienced an adverse effect after ingestion of food dye, whereas only 15% of the drug nonresponders experienced such a reaction.

This observation is particularly pertinent to the evaluation of previous experiments that based their conclusions of "no dye effect" on small samples of hyperactive children. According to the Feingold hypothesis, only a proportion of hyperactive children would be expected to respond adversely to a synthetic dye challenge. The implications of this *sensitive subpopulation* aspect of the hypothesis for its statistical evaluation have been described (Weiss, 1983). To expect a statistically significant effect from a small sample in which only 30% of a heterogeneous group of hyperactive children would be expected to respond is inappropriate.

> A population containing 30% responders would require a sample of 265 subjects to be certain of finding a statistically significant difference 90% of the time, even if the susceptible members of the group, on the whole, responded as much as 1 standard deviation . . . beyond the control mean. (Weiss, 1983, p. 35)

The Egger *et al.* (1985) study is of major interest because of the difference in experimental approach taken by the investigators. Their study demonstrates the complexity of the task of attempting to identify the specific provoking food constituents in particular children. The study involved several phases. The first consisted of a 4-week baseline standard nonreactive agent phase. The second phase consisted of a provocative food introduction and test phase. Finally, a controlled double-blind, crossover active agent, placebo trial phase was completed for a subgroup of subjects that evidenced a food sensitivity reaction in Phase 2. Because the group of children had been originally referred for a suspected food-based behavior problem, the fact that 81.5% of them demonstrated one or more food reactions in phase 2 is probably less impressive than it would otherwise appear. The controlled trial phase of the experiment consisted of a study of 28 subjects. All cognitive and behavioral rating scale results for these 28 children showed statistically superior performance scores during the placebo as compared to the active agent trials. However, a wide variety of over 40 foods or food constituents were found to evoke neuropsychological reactions in these children. Significantly, neither dyes nor preservatives alone were offensive but in combination with each other (as they often are in the food supply), 79% of the children experienced an adverse behavioral reaction.

Therefore, the introduction of a synthetic food dye, flavor, or preservative may not, in isolation, produce psychopharmacological changes. However, the entire food complement may produce a reaction due to the combined synergistic toxic effect of a number of the contained artificial food additives. In addition, foods high in additives are usually processed, highly refined items that have large amounts of sugar and reduced quantities of essential nutrients and fiber that may enhance the risk of experiencing a deleterious neuropsychological effect. Food toxicology research indicates that diets low in fiber appear to amplify the toxicity of synthetic food additives in laboratory animals (Ershoff, 1976).

Several aspects of the research in the area of synthetic food additives and behavioral toxicity deserve further comment. First, the fact that relatively low doses of food dye (less than 30 mg) were used in trial challenges for children prior to 1980 appears to be because the mean daily intake of food colors was estimated to be 27 mg in 1968 (Weiss, 1983). However, for children 5 to 12 years of age in 1976, the artificial food color intake was estimated to be 76.5 mg per day (Sobotka, 1976). Although a direct comparison of a total population average with an average based on a restricted childhood age range is not appropriate; these data, in conjunction with Figure 5 on U.S. soft drink consumption, indicate a dramatic increase in synthetic food additive intake experienced by children in recent years. In addition, most experiments have concentrated on synthetic food dyes of which there are only eight; however, there are approximately 1500 artificial flavors and many preservatives that have received little or no attention (Weiss, 1983).

Food Allergy and Neuropsychological Disorder

One mechanism by which food may affect neuropsychological function is that foods, like pollens and other allergens, can produce immunological reactions that bring into play reaginic (IgE)- and/or nonreaginic (nonIgE)-mediated immune responses (Crook, 1975; Speer, 1970) that lead to vascular, endocrine, and/or neurotransmitter alterations. Classic allergies are reactions incited by an antigen or allergen that are IgE mediated. A food sensitivity can be of an allergic type but need not necessarily be so; moreover, any organ system can be the target of a food sensitivity. Foods commonly identified as "allergens" by U.S. clinicians are often abundant in the Western diet. These foods include milk, chocolate, cola, corn, eggs, peanuts, citrus fruits, tomatoes, wheat and small grains, and artificial food colors (Feingold, 1975; Lockey, 1972, 1976; Rapp, 1981; Speer, 1975).

Sensitivities to various food constituents such as lactose, phenylethalmine (as in chocolate), tyramine (in aged cheese and Chianti), sodium nitrate, monosodium glutamate, xanthines, or asparatame are recognized. However, the precise nature of most food sensitivities, the physiological mechanisms and the neurochemical responses that account for their central nervous system symptoms, remain elusive.

Several clinical reports have suggested that food sensitivities and allergies may influence neurotransmitter and endocrine systems (Buckley, 1972; Ghose & Carroll, 1984; Rapp, 1981; Weiss & Kaufman, 1971; Williams & Kalita, 1977). There are indications that serotonergic activity, measured as circulating blood levels of serotonin and its metabolites, is reduced in person's experiencing allergy-type reactions to food. These observations have not been verified by systematic monitoring of blood in controlled experiments, however. In some food-sensitive persons, histamine, a neurotransmitter naturally released during classic allergic reactions, increases in the blood upon challenge by the offending constituent as do unique Ig (immunoglobulin) subclasses. Prostaglandin (PG) levels also become elevated and cause swelling, irritability, agitation, general discomfort, and other symptoms. The behavioral and cognitive effects would appear to be related more to cerebral vascular effects than anything else, however. Blood glucose levels may fall, thereby producing the signs and symptoms of hypoglycemia. However, no systematic studies have documented these effects that are based primarily on anecdotal clinical reports.

Clinicians report the following symptoms as being indicative of possible food sensitivity: nasal symptoms, intestinal discomfort, muscle or leg aches, headache, sleep disturbance, excessive perspiration, fatigue, mental dullness, hyperactivity, and behaviors that are out of character for the individual. The cognitive and perceptual deficits appear to be secondary to the physical complaints.

The detection of food sensitivities and the identification of the food or constituent responsible are difficult and tedious tasks. Questions pertaining to those foods that are eaten or craved most often, the time of day symptoms appear, and when and where meals are ingested immediately preceding onset of symptoms are sometimes revealing. Before measures such as an "elimination diet" are employed in attempts to isolate a food allergen, tests should be performed to exclude the possibility of endocrine or other systemic disorders.

CONCLUSIONS

In the preceding pages we have reviewed clinical and experimental studies on the putative relation between nutrition and childhood neuropsychological disorders. Nutritional variables have been implicated in disorders of mood, arousal, attention, learning, memory, and academic performance. Although the mechanisms that mediate these effects are a matter of considerable dispute, the fact that foods affect brain function and behavior appears to be established.

Heretofore, the principal paradigm for studying nutrition and neuropsychological effects in humans has been to examine brain and behavior sequelae of severe protein-calorie malnutrition experienced during different periods of development. However, the focus of this chapter has been nutrition in relation to neuropsychological disorders of children who have never experienced malnutrition as typified by protein-calorie deprivation. Instead, the malnutrition discussed has been related to selective micronutrient insufficiency (e.g., zinc) or abnormalities (e.g., abnormal glucose tolerance), interactions with environmental pollutants (e.g., cadmium), nutrient imbalances (e.g., neurotransmitter precursor availability), or to chemical exposures experienced through the food supply (e.g., chemical additives to enhance food appearance or shelf life). The fact that certain food consumption patterns or food constituents provoke explicit neuropsychological symptoms in some children raises the possibility that similar, but less detectable effects, are produced in a much larger fraction of the population.

The history of the human race has been one of alternating episodes of feast and famine. Large portions of the world still contend with such conditions. Generally, people residing in the industrial nations claim a priviledged nutritional status. Food is both plentiful and is present in a seemingly endless variety. At the same time, the nature of the food supply in the industrial nations is quite different from that of the nonindustrial nations and differs from that of any diet in the prior experience of humans. A high proportion of the consumed foods in technologically advanced nations are processed and packaged days, weeks, or months prior to their consumption. Whereas evolution has prepared humans to tolerate brief periods of malnutrition due to protein-calorie insufficiency, in modern societies the dominant type of malnutrition may be characterized by (a) chronic insufficiency or marginal availability of certain essential nutrients required to function normally, or (b) unusual and metabolically disadvantageous proportions of one nutrient relative to another, or (c) experience with substances (some intentionally, some inadvertently) added to foods that produce reactions in a significant number of individuals within the population.

Developmental nutrition and neuropsychology, as a field of study, is emerging from separate scientific disciplines that are, themselves, multidisciplinary and complex. Years of basic research will be necessary to adequately address the multitude of important conceptual and methodological issues present in this field. One area in which basic research is particularly needed is establishment of a common set of valid, reliable, developmentally referenced normative measures for human nutrition and neuropsychological assessment. For example, hair analysis is a potentially useful method for the assessment of environmental heavy metal pollutant exposure (e.g., for lead, cadmium) and for essential element nutriture (e.g. for zinc); however, a set of developmental reference norms for hair data, based on a large sample of healthy children representative of the U.S. population, has not yet been established (Hambidge, 1982). Similarly, for GTT parameters (even from continuous monitoring) to be evaluated with confidence, developmental reference norms are a necessity. Without such reference data, the range of variation to be expected due to normal biochemical individuality (Williams, 1956) is unknown; consequently, the justifiability for labeling a particular GTT response as *abnormal* is uncertain. For EEG measures, developmentally referenced normative data currently exist (John *et al.*, 1980; Karmel, Kaye, & John, 1978), and have been used (a) to relate hypoglycemic behavioral symptoms and GTT response abnormalities to aberrant neurophysiological brain features (Hudspeth *et al.*, 1981); (b) to correlate the quality of nutrition with reading performance and EEG normality (Thatcher *et al.*, 1985); and (c) to monitor the effects of neurotransmitter precursor therapy in a child with Down's syndrome (Cantor, Thatcher, Ozand, Kumin, & Rothschild, 1986). However, whether electrophysiological parameters other than those referenced by these particular studies are more sensitive as indexes of CNS function is open to debate and future investigation.

Regardless of the strides made in accumulating new knowledge, the significance of any accomplishment will depend upon the progress in the application of the information. The need for improved nutritional education applies to the general population as well as to the medical profession (Connor, 1979; Olson, 1978). Supplementation of bread and cereals with vitamins and minerals has improved the general micronutrient status of the population (Brin, 1976). However, in view of the increasing amounts of cadmium present in the food supply and the pattern of consumption of refined foods that have been depleted of zinc, the adequacy of current levels of zinc supplementation of foods needs to be reevaluated. Finally, if improved neuropsychological development of children is to be achieved in general, public action is needed to improve the nutritional status of persons living on low incomes (Citizens' Commission on Hunger in New England, 1984) and of pregnant women within the low-income category (Sanders, 1984).

ACKNOWLEDGMENTS

Preparation of this manuscript as well as research cited from the work of the Applied Neuroscience Research Institute, University of Maryland Eastern Shore, was supported by grants from the United States Department of Agriculture SEA/CSRS HRD0200 and NUT-0402, R. W. Thatcher, principal investigator, and from NIH Grant 1-F32ES05251, to Diana H. Fishbein. Appreciation is extended to the staff of Applied Neuroscience Research for help in the preparation of the manuscript and to Ms. Elsa Satchell for assistance in securing reference material.

REFERENCES

Agrawal, H. C., Davis, J. M., & Himwich, W. A. (1966). Postnatal changes in free amino acid pool of rat brain. *Journal of Neurochemistry, 13,* 607.

Alonso, R., Agharanya, J., & Wurtman, R. J. (1978). *Effects of carbidopa or precursor (tyrosine) loading on urinary catecholamine levels in rats.* Abstract presented at the Society for Neuroscience.

Alvarez, W. C. (1946). Puzzling "nervous storms" due to food allergy. *Gastroenterology, 7,* 241.

Augustine, G., & Levitan, H. (1980). Neurotransmitter release from vertebrate neuromuscular synapse affected by a food dye. *Science, 207,* 1489–1490.

Barchas, J. D., Akil, H., Elliott, G. R., Holman, R. B., & Watson, S. J. (1978). Behavioral neurochemistry: Neuroregulators and behavioral states. *Science, 200,* 964–973.

Bartus, R. T., Dean, R. L., Beer, B., & Lippa, A. S. (1982). The cholinergic hypothesis of geriatric memory dysfunction. *Science, 217,* 408–417.

Bellak, P. (1978). *Disorders of the schizophrenic syndrome* (pp. 45–135). New York: Basic Books.

Booyens, J., Luitingh, M. L., & Van Rensburg, C. F. (1977). The relationship between scholastic progress and nutritional status. Part II. A one-year follow-up study. *South African Medical Journal, 52,* 650–652.

Bremner, I., & Campbell, J. K. (1980). The influence of dietary copper intake on the toxicity of cadmium. In O. A. Levander & L. Cheng (Eds.), *Micronutrient interactions: Vitamins, minerals and hazardous elements* (Vol. 355, pp. 319–331). New York: Annals of New York Academy of Sciences.

Brewster, L., & Jacobson, M. (1983). *The changing American diet: A chronicle of American eating habits from 1910–1980.* Washington, DC: Center for Science in the Public Interest.

Brin, M. (1976). Nutrient intervention to improve nutritional status. In A. M. Altschul (Ed.), *New protein foods, Vol. 2, Technology*, (Part B, pp. 222–238). New York: Academic Press.

Buckley, R. E. (1972). A neurophysiologic proposal for the amphetamine response in hyperkinetic children. *Psychosomatics, 13*, 93.

Buell, G. (1975). Some biological aspects of cadmium toxicology. *Journal of Occupational Medicine, 17*, 193.

Burger, P. C., & Vogel, F. S. (1973). The development of pathologic changes of Alzheimer's disease and senile dementia in patients with Down's syndrome. *American Journal of Pathology, 73*, 157–476.

Butrimovitz, G. P., & Purdy, W. C. (1978). Zinc nutrition and growth in a childhood population. *American Journal of Clinical Nutrition, 31*, 1409–1412.

Cantor, D. S., Thatcher, R. W., Ozand, P., Kumin, L., & Rothschild, J. (1986). A report on phosphatidylcholine therapy in a Down's syndrome child. *Psychological Reports, 58*, 207–217.

Carlsson, A., & Lindquist, M. (1963). Effect of chorpromazine and haloperidol on formation of 3-methantyramine and norepenephrine in mouse brain. *Acta Pharmacologica Toxicologica, 20*, 140–144.

Cavioto, J., & Arrieta, R. (1983). Malnutrition in childhood. In M. Rutter (Ed.), *Developmental neuropsychiatry* (pp. 32–51). New York: Guilford.

Cerklewski, F. L., & Forbes, R. M. (1976). Influence of dietary zinc on lead toxicity in the rat. *Journal of Nutrition, 106*, 689–696.

Chalew, S., McLaughlin, J., Mersey, J., Adams, A. J., Cornblath, M., & Kowarski, A. (1984). The use of the plasma epinephrine response in the diagnosis of idiopathic postprandial syndrome. *Journal of the American Medical Association, 251*, 612–615.

Cheftel, H., Cotta-Ramusino, F., Egan, H., Kojima, K., Mietinen, J. K., Smith, D. M., Bergland, F., Blumenthal, H., Goldberg, L., Kazantzis, G., Piscator, M., Truhaut, R., Tsaubaki, T., & Najcev, A. N. (1972). Evaluation of certain food additives and the contaminants mercury, lead, and cadmium. *World Health Organization Technical Report Series, 505*, 20–24.

Chiel, H. J., & Wurtman, R. J. (1981). Short term variations in diet composition change the pattern of spontaneous motor activity in rats. *Science, 213*, 676–677.

Citizens' Commission on Hunger in New England. (1984). *American hunger crisis: Poverty and health in New England*. Boston: Harvard School of Public Health.

Cohen, E. L., & Wurtman, R. J. (1975). Brain acetylcholine: Increase after systemic choline administration. *Life Sciences, 16*, 1095–1102.

Cohen, E. L., & Wurtman, R. J. (1979). Nutrition and brain neurotransmitters. In M. Winick (Ed.), *Human nutrition: Pre and postnatal development* (Vol. 1, pp. 103–132). New York: Plenum Press.

Connors, C. K., Goyette, C. H., & Southwick, D. A., Lees, & Andrulonis (1976). Food additives and hyperkinesis: A controlled double-blind experiment. *Pediatrics, 58*, 154–166.

Connor, W. E. (1979). Too Little or too much: The case for preventive nutrition. *The American Journal of Clinical Nutrition, 32*, 1975–1978.

Coppen, A. (1967). The biochemistry of affective disorders. *British Journal of Psychiatry, 113*, 1237–1264.

Coyle, J. T., & Axelrod, J. (1971). Development of the uptake and storage of L-(3-H)norepinephrine in the rat brain. *Journal of Neurochemistry, 18*, 2061.

Crapo, P. A., Reaven, G., & Olefsky, J. (1976). Plasma glucose and insulin responses to orally administered simple and complex carbohydrates. *Daibetes, 25*, 741–747.

Crawford, I. L. (1983). Zinc and the hippocampus: Histology, nerochemistry, pharmacology, and putative functional relevance. In I. E. Dreosti & R. M. Smith (Eds.), *Neurobiology of the trace Elements. Vol. 1, Trace element neurobiology and deficiencies* (pp. 163–211). Clifton, NJ: Humana Press.

Crawford, I. L., & Connor, J. D. (1971). Zinc distribution in developing rat brain. *Pharmacologist, 13*, 275.

Crook, W. G. (1975). *Can your child read? Is he hyperactive?* Jackson, TN: Pedicenter Press.

Crook, W. G. (1980). Can what a child eats make him dull, stupid or hyperactive? *Journal of Learning Disabilities, 13,* 281–286.

Cryer, P. E. (1981). Glucose counterregulation in man. *Diabetes, 30,* 261–264.

Dasen, P. R., Lavallee, M., & Retschitzki, J. (1977). Early moderate malnutrition and the development of sensorimotor intelligence. *Environmental Child Health, 1,* 146–145.

Davis, K. L., Mohs, R. C., & Trinklenberg, J. R. (1979). Enhancement of memory by physotigmine. *New England Journal of Medicine, 301,* 94.

De Licardie, E. R., & Cravioto, J. (1974). Behavioral responsiveness of survivors of clinical severe malnutrition to cognitive demands. In J. Cravioto, L. Hambraeus, & B. Valhquist (Eds.), *Early Malnutrition and Mental Development.* Uppsala: Almquist & Wilsells.

Deutsch, E., Sohmer, H., Weidenfeld, J., Zelig, S., & Chowers, I. (1983). Auditory nerve-brainstem evoked potentials and EEG during severe hypoglycemia. *Electroencephalography and Clinical Neurophysiology, 55,* 714–716.

Dobbing, J. (1976). Vulnerable period in brain growth and somatic growth. In D. F. Roberts & A. M. Thomson (Eds.), *The biology of human fetal growth,* London: Taylor & Francis.

Dodge, P. R., Prensky, A. L., & Feigin, R. D. (1975). *Nutrition and the developing nervous system.* St. Louis: C. V. Mosby.

Dohan, F. C. (1978). Schizophrenia: Are some food-derived polypeptides pathogenic? In G. Hemmings & W. A. Hemmings (Eds.), *The biological basis of schizophrenia* (pp. 167–178). Lancaster: MTP Press Limited.

Drash, A. L., Becker, D. J., Kenien, A. G., & Steranchak, L. (1981). Nutritional considerations in the treatment of the child with diabetes mellitus. In R. M. Suskind (Ed.), *Textbook of pediatric nutrition* (pp. 449–457). New York: Raven Press.

Duggan, R. E., & Corneliussen, P. E. (1972). Dietary intake of pesticide chemicals in the United States (III), June 1968–April 1970. *Pesticide Monitoring Journal, 5,* 331–341.

Egger, J., Carter, C. M., Graham, P. J., Gumley, D., & Soothill, J. F. (1985). Controlled trial of oligoantigenic treatment in the hyperkinetic syndrome. *Lancet, 14,* 540–545.

Ellis, W. G., McCullough, J. R., & Corley, C. L. (1974). Presenile dementia in Down's syndrome: Ultrastructural identity with Alzheimer's disease. *Neurology, 24,* 101–106.

Engel, G. L., & Margolin, S. G. (1941). Clinical correlation of the EEG with carbohydrate metabolism. *Archives of Neurological Psychiatry, 45,* 890.

Ershoff, B. H. (1976). Synergistic toxicity of food additives in rats fed a diet low in dietary fiber. *Journal of Food Science, 41,* 949–951.

Feingold, B. F. (1975). *Why your child is hyperactive?* Westminster, MD: Random House.

Feingold, B. F. (1976). Hyperkinesis and learning disabilities linked to the ingestion of artificial food colors and flavors. *Journal of Learning Disabilities, 9,* 551–569.

Feingold, B. F. (1980). Hyperkinesis and learning difficulties. In: *Nutrition and mental health. Hearing before the Select Committee on Nutrition and Human Needs of the United States Senate, 95th Congress. June, 1980 Update* (pp. 80–90). Washington, DC: U.S. Government Printing Office.

Feise, G., Kogure, K., Busto, R., Scheinberg, P., & Reinmuth, O. M. (1976). Effect of insulin hypoglycemia upon cerebral energy metabolism and EEG activity in the rat. *Brain Research, 126,* 263.

Fernstrom, J. D., & Wurtman, R. J. (1971). Brain serotonin content: Physiological dependence on plasma tryptophan levels. *Science, 173,* 149–152.

Ferrendelli, J. A., & Chang, M. M. (1973). Brain metabolism during hypoglycemia. *Archives of Neurology, 28,* 173–177.

Fishbein, D. H. (1982). The contribution of refined carbohydrate consumption to maladaptive behavior. *Journal of Orthomolecular Psychiatry, 11,* 1.

Food and Nutrition Board. (1974). *Recommended dietary allowances* (8th ed.). Washington, DC: National Academy of Sciences National Resource Council.

Fox, M. R. (1974). Effect of essential minerals on cadmium toxicity: A Review. *Journal of Food Science, 37,* 321–324.

Fox, M. R. (1976). Cadmium metabolism—A review of aspects pertinent to evaluating dietary cadmium intake by man. In A. S. Prasad (Ed.), *Trace elements in human health and disease, Vol. II, Essential and toxic elements* (pp. 401–416). New York: Academic Press.

Friberg, L., Piscator, M., & Nordberg, G. F. (1971). *Cadmium in the environment.* Cleveland: Chemical Rubber Company Press.

Friedman, G. J. (1980). Diet in treatment of diabetes mellitus. In R. S. Goodhart & M. E. Shils (Eds.), *Modern nutrition in health and disease* (6th ed., pp. 977–997). Philadelphia: Lea & Febiger.

Gaulin, S. J. C., & Konner, M. (1977). On the natural diet of primates, including humans. In R. J. Wurtman & J. J. Wurtman (Eds.), *Nutrition and the brain, Vol. 1, Determinants of the availability of nutrients to the brain* (pp. 2–69). New York: Raven Press.

Gelenberg, A. J., Gibson, C. J., & Wojcik, J. D. (1982). Neurotransmitter precursors for the treatment of depression. *Psychopharmocology Bulletin, 18,* 7–18.

Ghose, K., & Carroll, J. D. (1984). Mechanism of tyramine-induced migraine: Similarity with dopamine and interactions with disulfiram and propranolol in migraine patients. *Neuropsychobiology, 12,* 122–126.

Gibson, C. J., & Wurtman, R. J. (1977). Physiological control of brain catecholamine synthesis by brain tyrosine concentration. *Biochemical Parmacology, 26,* 1137–1142.

Gibson, C. J., & Wurtman, R. J. (1978). Physiological control of brain norepinephrine synthesis by brain tyrosine concentration. *Life Sciences, 22,* 1399–1406.

Gilmour, D. G., Manowitz, P., Frosch, W. A., & Shopson, B. (1973). Association of plasma tryptophan levels with clinical change in female schizophrenic patients. *Biological Psychiatry, 6,* 119–128.

Gjedde, A., & Crone, C. (1981). Blood brain glucose transfer: Repression in chronic hyperglycemia. *Science, 214,* 456–457.

Green, A. R. (1978). The effects of dietary tryptophan and its peripheral metabolism on brain 5-hydroxytryptamine synthesis and funcfion. *Essays in Neurochemistry and Neuropharmachology* (Vol. 3). Chichester: Wiley.

Green, A. R., & Costain, D. W. (1979). The biochemistry of depression. In E. S. Paykel & A. Coppen (Eds.), *Psychopharmacology of affective disorders.* Oxford: Oxford University Press.

Green, A. R., & Costain, D. W. (1981). *Pharmacology and biochemistry of psychiatric disorders.* Toronto: Wiley.

Green, J. D. (1964). The hippocampus. *Physiological Review, 44,* 561–607.

Greenwood, M. H., Lader, M. H., Kantameni, B. D., & Curzon, G. (1975). The acute effects of oral L-tryptophan in human subjects. *British Journal of Clinical Psychiatry, 2,* 145–172.

Gross, S. B., Yeager, D. W., & Middendorf, M. S. (1976). Cadmium in liver, kidney and hair of humans, fetal through old age. *Journal of Toxicology and Environmental Health, 2,* 153–167.

Growden, J. H. (1979). Neurotransmitters in the diet: Their use in the treatment of brain diseases. In R. J. Wurtman & J. J. Wurtman (Eds.), *Nutrition and the brain, Vol. 3, Disorders of eating, and nutrients in treatment of brain Diseases* (pp. 117–181). New York: Raven Press.

Growden, J. H., Hirsch, M. J., Wurtman, R. J., & Weiner, W. (1977). Oral choline administration to patients with tardive dyskinesia. *New England Journal of Medicine, 297,* 524–527.

Hambidge, M. K. (1982). Hair analysis: Worthless for vitamins, limited for minerals. *The American Journal of Clinical Nutrition, 36,* 943–949.

Hambidge, M. K., Hambidge, C., Jacobs, M., & Baum, J. D. (1972). Low levels of zinc in hair, anorexia, poor growth, and hypogeusia in children. *Pediatric Research, 6,* 868–874.

Hambidge, M. K., Walravens, P. A., Brown, R. M., Webster, J., White, S., Anthony, M., & Roth, M. (1976). *The American Journal of Clinical Nutrition, 29,* 734–738.

Hartmann, E. (1977). L-tryptophan: A rational hypnotic with clinical potential. *American Journal of Psychiatry, 134,* 366–370.

Haubrich, H. G., Wang, P. F. L., Clody, D. E., & Wedeking, P. W. (1975). Increase in rat brain acetylcholine induced by choline or deanol. *Life Sciences, 17,* 975–980.

Haug, F. M. S. (1967). Electron microscopical localization of zinc in hippocampal mossy fibre synapses by a modified sulfide silver procedure. *Histochemistry, 8,* 355–368.

Haug, F. M. S., Blackstad, T. W., Zimmer, J., & Simonsen, A. H. (1971). Timm's sulfide silver reaction for zinc during experimental anterograde degeneration of hippocampal mossy fibers. *Journal of Comparative Neurology, 142,* 23–32.

Henkin, R. I., Patten, B. M., Re, P. K., & Bronzert, D. A. (1975). A syndrome of acute zinc loss. *Archives of Neurology, 32,* 745–751.

Hesse, G. W. (1979). Chronic zinc deficiency alters neuronal function of hippocampal mossy fibers. *Science, 205,* 1005–1007.

Hesse, G. W., Hesse, K. A., & Catalanotto, F. A. (1979). Behavioral characteristics of rats experiencing chronic zinc deficiency. *Physiology and Behavior, 22,* 211–215.

Hoagland, H., Rubin, M. A., & Cameron, D. E. (1937). The EEG of schizophrenics during insulin hypoglycemia recovery. *American Journal of Physiology, 120,* 59.

Hofeldt, F. D., Lufkin, E. G., & Hagler, L. (1974). Are abnormalities in insulin secretion responsible for reactive hypoglycemia? *Diabetes, 23,* 589–596.

Holden, J. M., Wolf, W. R., & Mertz, W. (1979). Zinc and copper in self-selected diets. *Journal of the American Dietetic Association, 75,* 23–28.

Hornykiewicz, O. (1973). Psychopharmacological implications of dopamine and dopamine antagonists: A critical evaluation of current evidence. *Neuroscience, 3,* 773–783.

Hosobuchi, V., Lamb, S., & Bascomb, D. (1980). Tryptophan loading may reverse tolerance to opiate analgesics in humans: A preliminary report. *Pain, 9,* 161–169.

Hudspeth, W. J., Peterson, L. W., Soli, D. E., & Trimble, B. A. (1981). Neurobiology of the hypoglycemia syndrome. *Journal of Holistic Medicine, 3,* 60–71.

Jastak, J. F., & Jastak, S. (1978). *Wide Range Achievement Test Manual.* Wilmington, DE: Jastak Association Incorporated.

John, E. R., Ahn, H., Prichep, L., Trepetin, M., & Kaye, H. (1980). Developmental equations for the electroencephalogram. *Science, 210,* 1255–1258.

Johnson, L. C., & Chernik, D. A. (1982). Sedative-hypnotics and human performance. *Psychopharmacology, 76,* 101–113.

Johnson, D. D., Dorr, K. E., Swenson, W. M., & Service, J. (1980). Reactive hypoglycemia. *Journal of the American Medical Association, 243,* 11.

Jones, H. S., & Fowler, B. A. (1980). Biological interactions of cadmium with calcium. In O. A. Levander & L. Cheng (Eds.), *Micronutrient interactions: Vitamins, minerals and hazardous elements,* (Vol. 355, pp. 309–317). New York: Annals of the New York Academy of Sciences.

Joseph, M. H., Baker, H. F., Crow, T. J., Riley, G. J., & Risby, D. (1979). Brain tryptophan metabolism in schizophrenia: A post mortem study of metabolites on the serotonin and kynurenine pathways in schizophrenics and control subjects. *Psychopharmacology, 62,* 279.

Karmel, B. Z., Kaye, H., & John, E. R. (1978). Developmental neurometrics: The use of quantitative analysis of brain electrical activity to probe mental function throughout the lifespan. In A. Collins (Ed.), *Minnesota Symposium on Child Psychology* (pp. 141–198). Hillsdale, NJ: Lawrence Erlbaum.

Kennedy, C., & Sokoloff, L. (1957). An adaptation of the nitrous oxide method to the study of the cerebral circulation in children: Normal values for cerebral blood flow and cerebral metabolic rate in childhood. *Journal of Clinical Investigation, 36,* 1130–1137.

Kimura, M. (1981). Effects of cadmium on growth and bone metabolism. In J. O. Nriagu (Ed.), *Cadmium in the environment, Part II. Health effects* (pp. 757–781). New York: Wiley.

Kirschmann, J. D. (1981). *Nutrition almanac.* New York: McGraw-Hill.

Kline, N. S., & Shah, B. K. (1973). Comparable therapeutic efficacy of tryptophan and imipramine: Average therapeutic ratings versus "true equivalence." An important difference. *Current Therapy Research, 15,* 484–487.

Knittle, J. L., Merritt, R. J., Dixon-Shanies, D., Ginsberg-Fellner, Timmers, K. I., & Katz, D. P. (1981). Childhood obesity. In R. M. Suskind, (Ed.), *Textbook of pediatric nutrition* (pp. 415–434). New York: Raven.

Knopf, C. F., Cresto, J. C., Dujovne, I. L., Ramos, O., & de Majo, S. F. (1977). Oral glucose tolerance test in 100 normal children. *Acta Diabetologica Latina, 14,* 95–103.

Kronick, D. A. (1975). A case history: Sugar, fried oysters, and zinc. *Academic Therapy, 11,* 119.

Langseth, L., & Dowd, J. (1978). Glucose tolerance and hyperkinesis. *Food, Cosmetics and Toxicology, 16,* 129–133.

Lehmann, J. (1971). Levodopa and depression in Parkinsonism. *Lancet, 1,* 140.

Lehmann, J. (1973). Tryptophan nonabsorption in levodopa-treated Parkinsonian patients. Effect of tryptophan on mental disturbances. *Acta Medica Scandinavica, 194,* 181–189.

Lester, M. L., Thatcher, R. W., & Monroe-Lord, L. (1982). Refined carbohydrate intake, hair cadmium levels and cognitive functioning in children. *Nutrition and Behavior, 1,* 1–14.

Lester, M. L., Horst, R., & Thatcher, R. W. (1987). Protective effects of calcium and zinc against heavy metal impairment of cognitive function. *Nutrition and Behavior, 3,* 145–161.

Levine, S., & Wiener, S. (1976). A critical analysis of data on malnutrition and behavioral deficits. *Advances in Pediatrics, 22,* 113–136.

Lhermitte, F., Peterfalvi, M., Marteau, R., Gazengel, J. V., & Serdaru, M. (1971). Pharmacological analysis of a case of postanoxic intention and action myoclonus. *Review of Neurology, 124,* 21–31.

Li, P. K., & Vallee, B. L. (1980). The biochemical and nutritional roles of other trace elements. In R. S. Goodhart & M. E. Shils (Eds.), *Modern nutrition in health and disease* (6th ed.; pp. 408–441). Philadelphia: Lea & Febiger.

Lieberman, H. R., Corkin, S., Spring, B. J., Growden, J. H., & Wurtman, R. J. (1987). Effects of food constituents on human mood and performance. In H. R. Lieberman, & R. J. Wurtman (Eds.), *Research Strategies for Assessing the Behavioral Effects of Foods and Nutrients* (pp. 69–93). New York: Pergamon.

Lipton, L. A., & Wender, E. H. (1984). Statement of the resource conference on diet and behavior. *Nutrition Review, 42,* 200–201.

Lipton, M. A., Nemeroff, C. B., & Mailman, R. B. (1979). Hyperkinesis and food additives. In R. J. Wurtman & J. J. Wurtman (Eds.), *Nutrition and the brain, Vol. 4, Toxic effects of food Constituents on the brain* (pp. 1–27). New York: Raven.

Lockey, S. D. (1972). Sensitizing properties of food additives and other commercial products. *Annals of Allergy, 30,* 638–641.

Lockey, S. D. (1976). Sensitivity to FD & C dyes in drugs, foods and beverages. In L. D. Dickey (Ed.), *Clinical ecology.* Springfield, IL: Charles C Thomas.

Maclaren, N. K. (1981). Nutritional considerations in the etiology and treatment of hypoglycemia. In M. Suskind, (Ed.), *Textbook of pediatric nutrition,* (pp. 459–464). New York: Raven Press.

McCaman, R. E., & Aprison, M. H. (1964). The synthetic and catabolic enzyme systems for acetylcholine and serotonin in several discrete areas of the developing rabbit brain. *Progress in Brain Research, 9,* 220.

McKay, H., Sinisterra, L. McKay, A., Gomez, H., & Lloreda, P. (1978). Improving cognitive ability in chronically deprived children. *Science, 200,* 270–278.

Mahaffey, K. R. (1981). Nutritional factors in lead poisoning. *Nutrition Reviews, 39,* 353–362.

Manowitz, P., Gilmour, D. G., & Racevskis, J. (1973). Low plasma tryptophan levels in recently hospitalized schizophrenics. *Biological Psychiatry, 6,* 102–118.

Marin-Padilla, M. (1976). Pyramidal cell abnormalities in the motor cortex of a child with Down's syndrome: A Golgi study. *Journal of Comparative Neurology, 167,* 63–82.

Marks, V., & Rose, F. C. (1981). *Hypoglycaemia* (2nd ed., pp. 464–473). Oxford: Blackwell Scientific Publications.

Marsh, D. C., Flynn, D. D., & Potter, L. T. (1985). Loss of M2 muscarine receptors in the cerebral cortex in Alzheimer's disease and experimental cholinergic denervation. *Science, 228,* 1115–1117.

Mefford, I. N., Baker, T. L., Boehme, R., Foutes, A. S., Ciaranello, R. D., Barchas, J. D., & Dement, N. C. (1983). Narcolepsy: Biogenic amine deficits in an animal model. *Science, 220,* 629–632.

Merali, Z., & Singhal, R. L. (1981). Biochemistry of cadmium in mammalian systems: Pancreotoxic and hepatotoxic manifestations. In J. O. Nriagu (Ed.), *Cadmium in the environment, Part II, Health effects* (pp. 617–637). New York: Wiley.

Messing, R. B., & Lytle, L. D. (1977). Serotonin-containing neurons: Their possible role in pain and analgesia. *Pain, 4*, 1–21.

Mizuno, T. I., & Yugari, Y. (1974). Self mutilation in the Lesch-Nyhan syndrome. *Lancet, 1*, 761.

Moja, E. A., Mendelson, W. B., Stoff, D. M., Gillin, J. C., & Wyatt, R. J. (1979). Reduction of REM sleep by a tryptophan-free amino acid diet. *Life Sciences, 24*, 1467–1470.

Moller, S. E., Kirk, L., & Fremming, K. H. (1976). Plasma amino acids as an index for subgroups in manic depressive psychosis: Correlation to effect of tryptophan. *Psychopharmacology, 49*, 205–213.

Monckeberg, F. (1968). Mental retardation from malnutrition: "Irreversible." *Journal of the American Medical Association, 201*, 30–31.

Moynahan, E. J. (1976). Zinc deficiency and disturbances of mood and visual behaviors. *Lancet, 1*, 91.

Muscettola, G., Wehr, T., & Goodwin, F. K. (1977). Effect of diet on urinary MHPG excretion in depressed patients and normal control subjects. *American Journal of Psychiatry, 134*, 914–916.

Neathery, M. W. (1981). Metabolism and toxicity of cadmium in animals. In J. O. Nriagu (Ed.), *Cadmium in the environment, Part II, Health effects* (pp. 553–581). New York: Wiley.

Nordberg, G. F., & Nishiyama, K. (1972). Whole body and hair retention of cadmium in mice. *Archives of Environmental Health, 24*, 209–214.

Nriagu, J. O. (1981). Production, uses, and properties of cadmium. In J. O. Nriagu (Ed.), *Cadmium in the environment, Part II, Health effects* (pp. 36–39). New York: Wiley.

Nyhan, W. L. (1976). Behavior in the Lesch-Nyhan syndrome. *Journal of Autism and Child Schizophrenia, 6*, 235–252.

Oleru, G. (1976). Kidney, liver, hair and lungs as indicators of cadmium absorption. *American Industrial Hygiene Association Journal, 37*, 617–621.

Olson, R. E. (1978). Clinical nutrition: An interface between human ecology and internal medicine. *Nutrition Reviews, 36*, 161–178.

Pennington, J. A. T., & Church, H. N. (1980). *Bowes and Church's food Values of portions commonly used* (13th ed.). New York: Harper & Row.

Perry, E. K., & Perry, R. H. (1980). The cholinergic system in Alzheimer's disease. In P. J. Roberts (Ed.), *Biochemistry of dementia*. Chichester: Wiley.

Petering, H. G. (1978). Some observation on the interaction of zinc, copper and iron metabolism in lead and cadmium toxicity. *Environmental Health Perspectives, 25*, 141–145.

Peters, B. H., & Levine, H. S. (1977). Memory enhancement after physostigmine in the amnesic syndrome. *Archives of Neurology, 34*, 215–219.

Phelps, M. E., & Mazziotta, J. C. (1985). Positron emission tomography: Human brain function and biochemistry. *Science, 228*, 799–809.

Philpott, W. (1977). Ecologic and biochemical observations in the schizophrenic syndrome. *Journal of Orthomolecular Psychiatry, 6*, 277–282.

Pihl, R. O., & Parkes, M. (1977). Hair element content in learning disabled children. *Science, 198*, 204–206.

Pijnenburg, A. J. J., Honig, W. M. M., & Van Der Heyden, J. A. M. (1976). Effects of chemical stimulating of the mesolimbic dopamine system upon locomotor activity. *European Journal of Pharmacology, 35*, 45–58.

Platt, B. S., Pampiglione, G., & Stewart, R. J. C. (1965). Experimental protein-calorie deficiency: Clinical, electroencephalographic, and neuropathological changes in pigs. *Developmental Medicine and Child Neurology, 7*, 9–26.

Pollin, W., Cardon, P. V., & Kety, S. S. (1961). Effects of amino acid feedings in schizophrenic patients treated with Iproniazid. *Science, 133*, 104–105.

Powell, G. W., Miller, W. J., Morton, J. D., & Clifton, C. M. (1964). Influence of dietary cadmium level and supplemental zinc and cadmium toxicity in the bovine. *Journal of Nutrition, 84*, 205–214.

Powers, H. W. S. (1974). Dietary measures to improve behavior and achievement. *Academic Therapy, 9*, 203–214.

Powers, H., & Presley, J. (1978). *Nutrition and your child's behavior.* New York: St. Martin's Press.

Pribram, K. H., & McGuinness, D. (1975). Arousal, activation, and effort in the control of attention. *Psychological Review, 82,* 116–149.

Price, J. M., Brown, R. R., & Peters, H. A. (1959). Tryptophan metabolism in porphyria schizophrenia and a variety of neurologic and psychiatric diseases. *Neurology, 9,* 456–468.

Prinz, R. J., Roberts, W. A., & Hantman, E. (1980). Dietary correlates of hyperactive behavior in children. *Journal of Consulting and Clinical Psychology, 48,* 760–769.

Purpura, D. P. (1977). Dendritic differential in human cerebral cortex: Normal and aberrant developmental patterns. In G. W. Kretzberg (Ed.), *Advances in Neurology* (Vol. 12, pp. 91–116). New York: Raven Press.

Randolph, T. G. (1944). Allergic headache: An unusual case of milk sensitivity. *Journal of the American Medical Association, 126,* 430–432.

Randolph, T. G. (1947). Allergy as a causative of fatigue, irritability and behavior problems in children. *Journal of Pediatrics, 31,* 560–572.

Randolph, T. G. (1951). Allergic myalgia. *Journal of the Michigan State Medical Society, 50,* 487–494.

Randolph, T. G. (1959). Musculoskeletal allergy in children. *International Archives of Allergy and Applied Immunology, 14,* 84–96.

Rapp, W. (1981). *Allergies and the hyperactive Child.* New York: Simon & Schuster.

Rinkel, H. J., Randolph, T. G., & Zeller, M. (1951). *Food Allergy.* Springfield, IL: Charles C Thomas.

Rosenthal, R. H., & Allen, T. W. (1978). An examination of attention, arousal, and learning dysfunctions of hyperkinetic children. *Psychological Bulletin, 85,* 689–715.

Roth, H. P., & Kirchgessner, M. (1981). Zinc and insulin metabolism. *Biological Trace Element Research, 3,* 13–32.

Rutter, M. (1983). Low level lead exposure: Sources, effects and implications. In M. Rutter & R. R. Jones (Eds.), *Lead versus health: Sources and effects of low level lead exposure* (pp. 333–370). New York: Wiley.

Sanders, A. (1984). *The widening gap: The incidence and distribution of infant mortality and low birth weight in the United States, 1978–1982.* Washington DC: Food Research and Action Center.

Sandstead, H. H. (1973). Zinc nutrition in the United States. *The American Journal of Clinical Nutrition, 26,* 1251–1260.

Sandstead, H. H. (1981). Clinical manifestations of certain classical deficiency diseases. In R. S. Goodhart & M. E. Shils (Eds.), *Modern nutrition in health and disease* (6th ed.; pp. 685–696). Philadelphia: Lea & Febiger.

Sandstead, H. H. (1980). Zinc in human nutrition. In F. Bronner & J. W. Coburn (Eds.), *Disorders of mineral metabolism, Vol. 1, Trace minerals* (pp. 93–157). New York: Academic Press.

Sarrat, R. (1980). Morphological and functional relations between pancreatic islets and allocortex. *Zentralblatt of Veterinary Medicine: Comparative Anatomy, Histology and Embryology, 9,* 52–64.

Schildkraut, J. J. (1965). The catecholamine hypothesis of affective disorders: A review of supporting evidence. *American Journal of Psychiatry, 122,* 509–522.

Schroeder, H. A. (1973). *The trace elements and man* (pp. 1–21). Old Greenwich, CT: Delvin-Adair.

Schroeder, H. A. (1974). *The poisons around us* (pp. 6–58). Bloomington, IN: University Press.

Scott, B. S., Becker, L. E., & Petit, T. L. (1983). Neurobiology of Down's syndrome. *Progress in Neurobiology, 21,* 199–237.

Seltzer, S., Stoch, R., & Marcus (1982). Alteration of human pain thresholds by nutritional manipulation and L-tryptophan supplementation. *Pain,* 385–393.

Schofield, A. T. (1908). A case of egg poisoning. *Lancet, 1,* 716.

Sharma, R. P. (1981). Soil-plant-animal distribution of cadmium in the environment. In J. O. Nriagu (Ed.), *Cadmium in the environment: Part II, Health effects* (pp. 588–605). Burlington, Ontario: Wiley.

Shopsin, B. (1978). Enhancement of the antidepressant response to L-tryptophan by a liver pyrrolase inhibitor: A rational treatment approach. *Neuropsychobiology*, 4, 188–192.

Singh, M. V., & Kay, S. R. (1976). Wheat gluten as a pathogenic factor in schizophrenia. *Science, 191*, 401–402.

Sky, D. A., & Barnes, R. H. (1973). Malnutrition and animal behavior. In D. J. Kallen (Ed.), *Nutrition, development and social behavior* (pp. 242). DHEW Publication No. NIH 73. Washington DC: U.S. Government Printing Office.

Snyder, S. H. (1980). *Biological aspects of mental disorder.* New York: Oxford University Press.

Sobotka, T. J. (1976). Estimates of average, 90th percentile and maximum daily intakes of FD & C artificial colors in one day's diets among two age groups of children. *Food and Drug Administration Biochemical Toxicology Branch Report.* Washington, DC: U.S. Government Printing Office.

Sobotka, T. (1978). Hyperkinesis and food additives: A review of experimental work. *FDA By-Lines,* 4, 165–176.

Sokoloff, L., Fitzgerald, G. G., & Kaufman, E. E. (1977). Cerebral nutrition and energy metabolism. In R. J. Wurtman & J. J. Wurtman (Eds.) *Nutrition and the brain, Vol. 1, Determinants of the availability of nutrients to the brain* (pp. 87–139). New York: Raven Press.

Speer, F. (1970). *Allergy of the nervous system.* Springfield, IL: Charles C Thomas.

Speer, F. (1975). Multiple food allergy, *Annals of Allergy, 34,* 71–76.

Stein, L., & Wise, C. D. (1971). Possible etiology of schizophrenia: Progressive damage to the noradrenergic reward system by 6-hydroxydopamine, *Science, 171,* 1032–1036.

Strauss, H., & Wechsler, I. S. (1945). Clinical and EEG studies of changes of cerebral function associated with variations in the blood. *American Journal of Psychiatry, 102,* 34.

Sudmeier, J. L., & Bell, S. J. (1981). Cadmium-113 nuclear magnetic resonance studies of bovine insulin: Two-zinc insulin hexamer specifically binds calcium. *Science, 212,* 560–562.

Swanson, J., & Kinsbourne, M. (1980). Food dyes impair performance of hyperactive children on a laboratory learning test. *Science, 207,* 1485–1487.

Thatcher, R. W., & Lester, M. L. (1985). Nutrition, environmental toxins and computerized EEG: A mini-max approach to learning disabilities. *Journal of Learning Disabilities, 18,* 287–297.

Thatcher, R. W., Lester, M. L., McAlaster, R., & Horst, R. (1982). Effects of low levels of cadmium and lead on cognitive functioning in children. *Archives of Environmental Health, 37,* 159–166.

Thatcher, R. W., McAlaster, R., & Lester, M. L. (1984). Evoked potentials related to hair cadmium and lead. In R. Karrer, D. Cohen, & P. Tueting (Eds.), *Brain and Information: Event related potentials* (Vol. 425, pp. 421–423). New York: New York Academy of Sciences.

Thatcher, R. W., McAlaster, R., Lester, M. L., & Cantor, D. S. (1985). Comparisons among nutrition, EEG and trace elements in predicting reading ability in children. In S. J. White & V. Tellar (Eds.), *Discourses in reading and linguistics* (Vol. 433, pp. 87–96). New York: New York Academy of Sciences.

Thompson, M. (1949). *The cry and the covenant.* Garden City, NY: Doubleday & Company.

Ulus, I., Hirsch, M. J., & Wurtman, R. J. (1977). Transsynaptic induction of adrenomedullary tyrosine hydroxylase activity by choline: Evidence that choline administration increases cholinergic transmission. *Proceedings of the National Academy of Sciences, 74,* 798–800.

U.S. Senate Commission on Nutrition and Human Needs. (1977). *Dietary goals for the United States.* Washington, DC: U.S. Government Printing Office.

Vallee, B. L., & Falchuk, K. H. (1983). Gene Expression and zinc. In B. Sarkar (Ed.), *Biological aspects of metals and metal-related diseases* (pp. 1–14). New York: Raven.

Vallee, B. L., & Hoch, F. L. (1959). Trace elements in cellular functions, *International Review of Cytology, 8,* 345–386.

Van Kammen, D. P., Mann, L. S., Sternberg, D. E., Scheinin, M., Ninan, P. T., Marder, S. R., Van Kammen, W. B., Rieder, R. O., & Linnoila, M. (1983). Dopamine-B-hydroxylase activity and homovanollic acid in spinal fluid of schizophrenics with brain atrophy. *Science, 220,* 974–976.

Van Woert, M. H., Jutkowitz, R., Rosembaum, D., & Bauers, M. B. (1976). Serotonin and myoclonus. *Monograms in the Neurological Sciences, 3,* 71–80.

Van Woert, M. H., Rosembaum, D., Howieson, J., & Bauers, M. B. (1977). Long-term therapy of myoclonus and other neurologic disorders with L-5-hydroxytryptophan and carbidopa. *New England Journal of Medicine, 296,* 70–75.

Venugopal, B., & Luckey, T. D. (1980). *Metal toxicity in mammals* (Vol. 2, pp. 76–86). New York: Plenum Press.

Volkl, A., Berlet, H., & Ule, G. (1974). Trace elements (Cu, Fe, Mg, Zn) of the brain during childhood. *Neuropediatrics, 5,* 236–242.

Von Hilsheimer, G. (1974). *Allergy, toxins and the learning disabled child.* San Rafael, CA: Academic Therapy Publications.

Weingartner, H., Rudorfer, M. V., Buchsbaum, M. S., & Linnoila, M. (1983). Effects of serotonin on memory impairments produced by ethanol. *Science, 221,* 472–473.

Weiss, B. (1983). Behavioral toxicity of Food Additives. In J. Weininger & G. M. Briggs (Eds.), *Nutrition update* (Vol. 1, pp. 22–38). New York: Wiley.

Weiss, B., Williams, J., Margen, S., Abrams, B., Caan, B., Citron, L., Cox, C., McKibben, J., Ogar, D., & Schultz, S. (1980). Behavioral responses to artificial food colors. *Science, 270,* 1487–1489.

Weiss, J. M., & Kaufman, H. S. (1971). A subtle organic component in some cases of mental illness, *Archives of General Psychiatry, 25,* 74.

Weiss, P. A. (1969). The living system: Determinism stratified. In A. Koestler & J. R. Smythies (Eds.), *Beyond reductionism: New perspectives in the life sciences* (pp. 3–55). London: Hutchinson.

Wender, E. (1977). Food additives and hyperkinesis. *American Journal of the Diseases of Children, 131,* 1204.

Williams, R. J. (1956). *Biochemical individuality.* Austin: University of Texas Press.

Williams, R. J., & Kalita, D. K. (1977). *A physician's handbook on orthhomolecular medicine.* Elmsford, NY: Pergamon Press.

Woolley, D. W., & Shaw, E. (1954). A biological and pharmacological suggestion about certain mental disorders. *Proceedings of the National Academy of Sciences, 40,* 228.

Wurtman, R. J. (1980). Nutritional control of brain tryptophan and serotonin. In O. Hayaiski, Y. Ishimura, & R. Kido (Eds.), *Biochemical and medical aspects of tryptophan metabolism.* Elsevier: North-Holland Biomedical Press.

Wurtman, R. J., & Fernstrom, J. D. (1974). Effects of diet on brain neurotransmitters. *Nutrition Review, 23,* 193–208.

Wurtman, R. J., & Wurtman, J. J. (1979). *Nutrition and the brain, Vol. 3, Disorders of eating and nutrients in treatment of brain diseases.* New York: Raven Press.

Wurtman, R. J., Hirsch, M. J., & Growden, J. H. (1977). Lecithin consumption raises serum free choline levels. *Lancet, 2,* 68–69.

Wurtman, R. J., Hefti, F., & Melamed, E. (1981). Precursor control of neurotransmitter synthesis. *Pharmacological Reviews, 32,* 315–335.

Wurtman, R. J., Magil, S. G., & Reinstein, D. K. (1981). Piracetam diminishes hippocampal acetylcholine level in rats. *Life Sciences, 28,* 1091–1093.

Yaryura-Tobias, J. A. (1973). The behavioral-gluco-dysrhythmic triad. *American Journal of Psychiatry, 130.*

Yates, C. M., Simpson, J., Maloney, A., Gordon, A., & Reid, A. H. (1980). Alzheimer-like cholinergic deficiency in Down's syndrome. *Lancet, 8,* 979–981.

Yogman, M. W., Zeisel, S. H., & Roberts, C. (1987). Dietary precursors of serotonin and newborn behavior. In R. J. Wurtman (Ed.), *Research Strategies for Assessing the Effects of Foods and Nutrients* (pp. 44–68). New York: Pergamon.

Yoshinaga, T., & Ogawa, S. (1975). Electron microscopic study of zinc in beta-cells of pancreatic islets of rat under conditions stimulating the excretion of insulin. *Acta Histochemistry, 53,* 161–174.

Young, S. N., & Sourkes, T. L. (1977). Tryptophan in the central nervous system: Regulation and significance. *Advances in Neurochemistry, 2,* 133.

Yuwiler, A., Brammer, G. L., Morley, J. E., Raleigh, M. J., Flannery, J. W., & Geller, E. (1981). Short-term and repetitive administration of oral tryptophan in normal men. *Archives of General Psychiatry, 38,* 619–626.

Zeisel, S. H., Mauron, C., Watkins, C. J., & Wurtman, R. J. (1981). Developmental changes in brain indoles, serum tryptophan and other serum neutral acids in the rat. *Developmental Brain Research, 1,* 551–564.

Index